Y0-AVA-669

Canadian Publishers & Canadian Publishing

CANADIAN PUBLISHERS & CANADIAN PUBLISHING

Royal Commission on Book Publishing

THE QUEEN'S PRINTER FOR ONTARIO

MINISTRY OF EDUCATION, ONTARIO
COMMUNICATION SERVICES BRANCH
13TH FLOOR, MOWAT BLOCK
TORONTO, ONTARIO M7A 1L3

ONTARIO

ROYAL COMMISSION ON BOOK PUBLISHING

To His Honour,
The Lieutenant Governor of Ontario.

May It Please Your Honour,

We the Commissioners, appointed as a Royal Commission by Orders-in-Council OC–3991/70 and OC–3534/71 pursuant to the provisions of The Public Inquiries Act, R.S.O. 1960, c. 323, and approved by Your Honour on the 23rd day of December, A.D. 1970, and on the 18th day of November, A.D. 1971, to report upon matters relating to the publishing industry in Ontario:
beg to submit to Your Honour the following Final Report of the Commission:

Richard Rohmer, Q.C., *Commissioner (Chairman)*

Dalton Camp, *Commissioner*

December 1st, 1972

Marsh Jeanneret, *Commissioner*

ORDERS-IN-COUNCIL

OC–3991/70

Certified to be a true copy of an Order-in-Council approved by His Honour the Lieutenant Governor, dated the 23rd day of December, A.D. 1970.

Upon the recommendation of the Honourable the Prime Minister, the Committee of Council advise that pursuant to the provisions of The Public Inquiries Act, R.S.O. 1960, Chapter 323, a Commission be issued appointing

Richard Heath Rohmer, Q.C.,
Dalton Kingsley Camp, and
Marsh Jeanneret,

and naming the said Richard Heath Rohmer as Chairman thereof, to conduct an examination of and report upon:

(a) the publishing industry in Ontario and throughout Canada with respect to its position within the business community;

(b) the functions of the publishing industry in terms of its contribution to the cultural life and education of the people of the Province of Ontario and Canada;

(c) the economic, cultural, social or other consequences for the people of Ontario and of Canada of the substantial ownership or control of publishing firms by foreign or foreign-owned or foreign-controlled corporations or by non-Canadians.

The Committee further advise that pursuant to The Public Inquiries Act, R.S.O. 1960, Chapter 323, the Commissioners shall have the power of summoning any person and requiring him or her to give evidence on oath and to produce such documents and things as the Commissioners deem requisite to the full examination of the matters into which they are appointed to examine.

And the Committee further advise that all Governmental departments, boards, agencies and committees shall assist the Commissioners to the fullest extent possible in order to assist them to carry out their duty and functions, and that the Commissioners shall have the authority to obtain such counsel, staff, technical advisers and clerical staff as they deem proper and the rate of remuneration and reimbursement to be approved by Treasury Board.

Certified,

J. J. Young
Clerk, Executive Council

OC–3534/71

Certified to be a true copy of an Order-in-Council approved by His Honour the Lieutenant Governor, dated the 18th day of November, A.D. 1971.

Upon the recommendation of the Honourable the Prime Minister, the Committee of Council advise that Order-in-Council dated the 23rd day of December, A.D. 1970, and numbered OC–3991/70, be amended by adding clause (d) after clause (c) as follows:

(d) the contracts or proposed contracts between any geographical wholesaler of mass market paperback books and periodicals and any retailer of such goods that creates or tends to create an obligation on the retailer to purchase all merchandise supplied by the wholesaler from that wholesaler to the exclusion of other sources of supply and, without limiting the generality of the foregoing, to inquire into the merchandising of paperback books, periodicals, and other merchandise normally carried by geographical wholesalers and sold by their retailers.

The Committee further advise that the Commission issued to Messrs. Richard Heath Rohmer, Q.C., Dalton Kingsley Camp and Marsh Jeanneret, under the provisions of the said Order-in-Council numbered OC–3991/70, be amended accordingly.

Certified,

J. J. Young
Clerk, Executive Council

Published by the
Ministry of the Attorney General.
Printed by the
Queen's Printer for Ontario.
Province of Ontario
Toronto, Canada

©1973 Government of Ontario

Paper Edition: ISBN 0–7743–0003–5
Cloth Edition: ISBN 0–7743–0002–7

Contents

1 *Book Publishing in Canada Today* 1

The Publishing Function 10
Three Kinds of Publishing 13
The Departments of Book Publishing 17
Trade Books 17
Educational, Reference, and Scholarly Books 19
Government Publishing 21
Development of Canadian Schoolbook Publishing 26
A Crisis in Educational Publishing 32
Organization of the Canadian Book Industry 33
Publishers and Authors 45
International Standards 49

2 *The Question of Ownership* 51

Canadian and Non-Canadian Publishers 51
The Subsidiary as Publisher and as Agent 58
Creative Criticism in Publishing Houses 63
Repatriation of Canadian Publishing 64
The College and University Level 67
Importance of Residual Canadian Ownership 68
Parallel Situations Abroad 69
Does Ownership Matter? 72

3 *Copyright and Book Publishing* 79

The Question of Jurisdiction 80
The Nature of Copyright 80
Agency Publishing and Co-publishing 82

Format Copyright *87*
Unauthorized Copying *88*
The Public Lending Right *97*
The United States Manufacturing Provisions *102*
Other Desirable Statutory Revisions *105*
International Copyright *112*
The Competition Act (Bill C–256) *114*
The Need for Research *119*

4 *Book Markets and Book Marketing* *122*

The Economics of Canadian Publishing *125*
Children's Books *128*
The University and College Market *130*
The Paperback Myth *132*
Quality Paperbacks and Mass-Market Paperbacks *133*
Mass-Market Paperbacks *134*
Book Publishers and Booksellers *136*
The Promotion of Trade Books *139*
Coordination of Marketing *143*
A Canadian Book Centre in Ontario *146*
The Small Publisher *151*
International Standard Book Numbers *155*
Publishers and Libraries *156*
Readers' Club of Canada Survey *162*

5 *Educational Publishing* *168*

The Vanishing Textbook *168*
Implications for Canadian Publishers *170*

Textbook Stimulation Grants Policy   *171*
Discontinuation of Book Stimulation Grants   *173*
Establishment of County School Districts   *175*
Circular 14   *181*
Annual Revision of Circulars 14 and 15   *185*
A Changing Kind of Education   *188*
Canadian Preference in Circular 14   *189*
Canadian Preference and Canadian Culture   *192*
Limitations on Canadian Preference   *197*
Some Implications of Canadian Preference   *198*
Canadian Preference Outside Ontario   *200*
Interprovincial Coordination of Curriculum   *201*
Publishing for Franco-Ontarians   *202*
Comparative Cost of Textbooks   *204*
Book Expenditure Levels   *210*
Changing Significance of Circular 14   *212*

6   *Nurturing a Canadian Identity*   *219*

Book Publishing and the Book Industry   *219*
Negative Censorship   *220*
Misconceptions Regarding Book Imports   *222*
Publishing—A Creative Act   *223*
Publishing Needs of Canadian Native Peoples   *224*
Canadian Studies in Canadian Schools   *225*
The Canada Studies Foundation   *226*
Canadian Scholarly Publishing   *228*
Reviews and Criticism   *231*
Canadian Book Reviews Abroad   *235*
The Analogy with Broadcasting   *236*

Some National and Regional Cultural Policies Elsewhere *238*
Parallel Between Magazines and Books *242*
Books for the Blind in Canada *243*
Canadian Manufacture and Foreign Manufacture *245*

7   *Summary of Recommendations*   *249*

Appendix   *285*

First Interim Report *285*
Second Interim Report *290*
Third Interim Report *295*
Final Report on the Distribution of Paperbacks and Periodicals in Ontario *302*
Guidelines re Applications for Guaranteed Loans *327*
Briefs Received *331*
Copyright Act—Excerpts *336*
Photocopying in the Ontario Educational Market *341*
   (Kates, Peat, Marwick & Co. Report)
Readers' Club of Canada Questionnaire *347*
Net Book Agreement *352*
Bankruptcy Act—Excerpts *355*
Analysis of Magazine Sales in Ontario *356*
Bibliography *359*
Acknowledgments *368*

1
Book Publishing in Canada Today

When this Commission was appointed, there were fifty-three publishers in this country – not including government departments – who claimed to have fifty or more Canadian books in print and for sale. Among them they accounted for 10,431 titles in a total of 15,299 Canadian books in print. The balance of the latter production was spread thinly over several hundred small publishers and publishing houses, including associations, societies, and private presses. Indeed, the median number of Canadian books in print for all publishers in the country, big and small, full-time and part-time, was a mere five titles each.

The cumulative cultural contribution of most publishers in Canada was therefore fairly modest. It would appear even more modest if a more restrictive definition were used of what is a Canadian book. In the annual analysis from which these figures are taken, any book of forty-nine pages (the UNESCO standard) carrying a primary Canadian imprint is interpreted as Canadian. Thus even a foreign book by a foreign author – provided that the address in the imprint reads "Toronto and London" or "Montreal and New York" rather than "London and Toronto" or "New York and Montreal" – is counted as a Canadian book. The total book output of Canadian authors was buried in the median cumulative figure of five Canadian books in print per publishing house – regardless of who owned the latter, and regardless of where the books were manufactured.

Of the fifty-three publishers in Canada who in 1970 did offer fifty or more Canadian books, broadly defined as above, twenty-two firms were based in the Province of Quebec, thirty in Ontario, and one in New Brunswick. (There are indications that in the future Alberta and British Columbia will also be represented in this grouping of more productive publishers.) Understandably, all but two of the Quebec houses publish primarily in French; only one of the Ontario firms does not publish chiefly in English.

Almost all of the French-language houses in this group of most productive Canadian publishers were principally owned in Canada (in Quebec, as a matter of fact). But a substantial majority of the corresponding group of active English-language publishers of Canadiana were branch plants of foreign publishing firms, a situation that has not changed during the past two years. The implications of foreign versus Canadian ownership will be discussed later in this report, but it is noteworthy that a significant proportion of Canadian publishing in English is being done in Canada by non-Canadian publishers.

OWNERSHIP OF THE 53 PUBLISHING HOUSES CLAIMING 50 OR MORE TITLES IN 1970 CANADIAN BOOKS IN PRINT

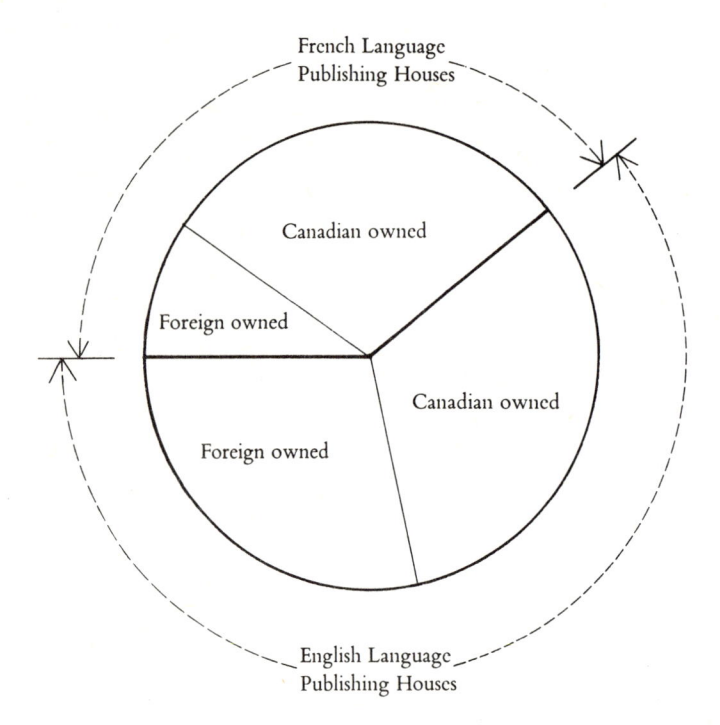

There are many ways of looking at the condition of an industry at any particular time. But an analysis of book publishing which takes into account the relative numbers of books published by different firms is more meaningful than one which bases its statistics of ownership and operating experience on a mere nose-count of individuals and firms that class themselves as publishers. There are hundreds of publishers, even in Canada, but the real contribution of most of them in Canadian books published is as small as the figures already given indicate. This is not to justify indifference towards the smaller, younger publishers of Canadiana. Among them lies the hope of the future, as this report will make clear. But before deciding where publishing in this country is headed, or how fast it is going there, we must look hardest at those firms with established track records.

Shortly before the appointment of this Commission, the Federal Department of Industry, Trade and Commerce issued a statistical and economic analysis of the Canadian book publishing and manufacturing industry prepared by Ernst & Ernst Management Consulting Services. While some of its conclusions were controversial, this study brought together for the first time a useful range of Canadian publishing statistics. If the figures were not hard in every case they were at least more relevant than any that had hitherto been available. The appearance of this study could not therefore have been more timely.

The Ernst & Ernst estimate of the contribution of the total book industry to the national economy had a special relevance to this Commission's ordering of its own priorities. "The Canadian book publishing industry's contribution," they stated, "to the national economy of 0.06% is significantly lower than the United States book publishing industry's value added which accounted for 0.22% of the United States G.N.P. in 1969. Revenue of United States publishers accounted for 0.26% of total G.N.P. In addition, statistics in other countries who have a well developed book industry show that the latter contributes from 0.21% to 0.24% of G.N.P." Whether or not it follows, as Ernst & Ernst say it does, that the Canadian book publishing industry has a market potential for Canadian books equivalent to three or four times its present annual sales will depend on whether or not the market situation in Canada is similar to market situations elsewhere. This Commission has been given good reason to conclude that the Canadian market for books is unique,

POPULATION BY MATERNAL LANGUAGE FOR CANADA, 1971

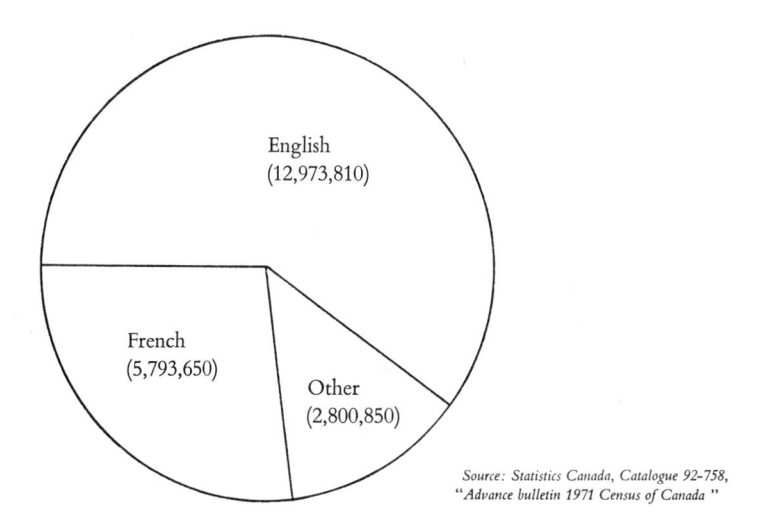

English
(12,973,810)

French
(5,793,650)

Other
(2,800,850)

Source: Statistics Canada, Catalogue 92-758, "Advance bulletin 1971 Census of Canada"

one which must not only take into account linguistic and communications barriers, but also differences in channels of supply which are not shared by any of the foreign markets with which it is usually compared.

The finding by Ernst & Ernst that the Canadian book industry's contribution to the GNP is microscopic strengthens, however, two of this Commission's premises. (a) Relatively minor economic barriers or break-throughs – the latter made possible artificially if need be – will exert disproportionately powerful forces for the breakdown or progress of the book publishing industry in this country. (b) The cultural implications of book publishing far outweigh the economic implications to society, whether the latter are measured in jobs or in cost of possible measures to preserve the industry. Thus although many of the problems that face Canadian book publishing may be economic, the issues to be weighed are cultural, and so will be the dividends that can flow from sensible solutions.

LIST OF PUBLISHERS CLAIMING 50 OR MORE TITLES IN CANADIAN BOOKS IN PRINT 1970

Publisher	Province	No. of Titles
University of Toronto Press	Ont.	992
McGraw-Hill Co. of Canada Ltd.	Ont.	719**
The Macmillan Co. of Canada Ltd.	Ont.	656
McClelland and Stewart Limited	Ont.	576
Coles Publishing	Ont.	422
Editions Fides	P.Q.	410
Gage Educational Publishing Ltd.	Ont.	389
Editions Beauchemin	P.Q.	324
Les Presses de l'Université Laval	P.Q.	309
Clarke, Irwin & Co. Ltd.	Ont.	283
The Copp Clark Publishing Co.	Ont.	279
Editions du Jour	P.Q.	275
Longman Canada Ltd.	Ont.	267
Editions de l'Homme	P.Q.	265
Forum House Publishing Company	Ont.	253
Editions Pauline	P.Q.	250
Centre de psychologie & de pédagogie*	P.Q.	245
Holt, Reinhart & Winston of Canada Ltd.	Ont.	239***
J. M. Dent & Sons (Canada) Ltd.	Ont.	218
Editions Lidec	P.Q.	216
Editions Bellarmin	P.Q.	194
Cercle du Livre	P.Q.	170
Thomas Nelson & Sons Canada Ltd.	Ont.	162
Editions de l'Université d'Ottawa	Ont.	160
Les Presses de l'Université de Montréal	P.Q.	133
Oxford University Press	Ont.	131

Publisher	Province	No. of Titles
Editions H.M.H.	P.Q.	119
Editions du Renouveau Pédagogique*	P.Q.	113
Ginn & Co. Educational Publishers	Ont.	105
Brunswick Press	N.B.	87
Sir Isaac Pitman (Canada) Ltd.	Ont.	86
Editions Leméac	P.Q.	83
Canadian Welfare	Ont.	83
Service des cours par correspondance*	P.Q.	82
McGill-Queen's University Press	P.Q.	74
The Book Society of Canada Ltd.	Ont.	73
Centre éducatif et culturel	P.Q.	71
Doubleday Canada Ltd.	Ont.	70
Editions du Lévrier*	P.Q.	68
The Carswell Company Limited	Ont.	65
C.C.H. Canadian Limited	Ont.	63
Little, Brown & Co. (Canada) Ltd.	Ont.	61
Editions du Phare	P.Q.	58
Canadian Tax Foundation	Ont.	57
Reader's Digest Association	P.Q.	56
Canadiana House	Ont.	55
Bellhaven House Ltd.	Ont.	55
Ontario Institute for Studies in Education	Ont.	53
Canadian Library Association	Ont.	53
Random House of Canada Ltd.	Ont.	52
Librairie Garneau	P.Q.	52
Burns & MacEachern Ltd.	Ont.	50
Bélisle Editeur*	P.Q.	50
	Total:	10,431

*Not members of Conseil Supérieur du Livre
**Includes books published by Ryerson Press
***Includes books published by HRW in Toronto and Montreal
–Information Canada, the Queen's Publisher (Ontario) and the CBC not included.

LIST OF PUBLISHERS CLAIMING 50 OR MORE TITLES
IN CANADIAN BOOKS IN PRINT IN 1971

Publisher	Province	No. of Titles
University of Toronto Press	Ont.	1013
McGraw-Hill Co. of Canada Ltd.	Ont.	763
McClelland and Stewart Limited	Ont.	702
The Macmillan Co. of Canada Ltd.	Ont.	668
Coles Publishing	Ont.	427
Editions Fides	P.Q.	367
Gage Educational Publishing Ltd.	Ont.	364
Editions du Jour	P.Q.	343
Les Presses de l'Université Laval	P.Q.	326
Editions Beauchemin	P.Q.	324
The Copp Clark Publishing Co.	Ont.	291
Holt, Rinehart & Winston of Canada Ltd.	Ont.	286
Clarke, Irwin & Co. Ltd.	Ont.	272
Editions de l'Homme	P.Q.	270
Forum House Publishing Company	P.Q.	254
Editions Pauline	P.Q.	247
Longman Canada Ltd.	Ont.	235
Editions Bellarmin	P.Q.	211
J. M. Dent & Sons (Canada) Ltd.	Ont.	209
Editions Lidec	P.Q.	207
Cercle du Livre	P.Q.	187
Editions de l'Université d'Ottawa	Ont.	158
Editions H.M.H.	P.Q.	156
Ginn & Co. Educational Publishers	Ont.	155
Thomas Nelson & Sons Canada Ltd.	Ont.	154
The Book Society of Canada Ltd.	Ont.	153
Les Presses de l'Université de Montréal	P.Q.	146
Centre de psychologie & de pédagogie	P.Q.	139
Oxford University Press	Ont.	134
Sir Isaac Pitman (Canada) Ltd.	Ont.	122
Editions du Renouveau Pédagogique	P.Q.	115
Editions Leméac	P.Q.	111
McGill – Queen's University Press	P.Q.	98
Brunswick Press	N.B.	86
Centre éducatif et culturel	P.Q.	85
Doubleday Canada Ltd.	Ont.	84
Service des cours par correspondance	P.Q.	75
The Carswell Company Limited	Ont.	73
Ontario Institute for Studies in Education	Ont.	72
C.C.H. Canadian Limited	Ont.	69
Editions du Lévrier	P.Q.	66
Prentice-Hall of Canada Ltd.	Ont.	65

Publisher	Province	No. of Titles
Reader's Digest Association	P.Q.	64
Fiddlehead Books	N.B.	63
Canadian Tax Foundation	Ont.	61
Editions Pédagogia	P.Q.	61
Editions du Phare	P.Q.	60
Librairie Garneau	P.Q.	60
Little, Brown & Co. (Canada) Ltd.	Ont.	59
Bellhaven House Ltd.	Ont.	57
Canadiana House	Ont.	56
Harvest House	Ont.	53
Canadian Library Association	Ont.	53
Mitchell Press Ltd.	B.C.	52
Royal Ontario Museum	Ont.	52
Bélisle Editeur	P.Q.	50
M. G. Hurtig Publishers	Alta.	50
Peter Martin Associates Limited	Ont.	50
New Press	Ont.	50

Note: Information Canada, the Queen's Printer, and the CBC not included.

LIST OF PUBLISHERS CLAIMING 50 OR MORE TITLES
IN CANADIAN BOOKS IN PRINT IN 1972

Publisher	Province	No. of Titles
University of Toronto Press	Ont.	1122
McClelland and Stewart Limited	Ont.	784
McGraw-Hill Co. of Canada Ltd.	Ont.	772
The Macmillan Co. of Canada Ltd.	Ont.	682
Editions Fides	P.Q.	464
Coles Publishing	Ont.	434
Editions du Jour	P.Q.	390
Gage Educational Publishing Ltd.	Ont.	387
Les Presses de l'Université Laval	P.Q.	337
Editions Beauchemin	P.Q.	328
Holt, Rinehart & Winston of Canada Ltd.	Ont.	321
Editions de l'Homme	P.Q.	312
Editions Pauline	P.Q.	308
Clarke, Irwin & Co. Ltd.	Ont.	278
Forum House Publishing Company	Ont.	269
The Copp Clark Publishing Co.	Ont.	253
Longman Canada Ltd.	Ont.	246
J. M. Dent & Sons (Canada) Ltd.	Ont.	238
Editions Bellarmin	P.Q.	212
Editions Lidec	P.Q.	208
Cercle du Livre	P.Q.	201
Thomas Nelson & Sons Canada Ltd.	Ont.	191
Editions H.M.H.	P.Q.	188
Editions Leméac	P.Q.	166
Editions de l'Université d'Ottawa	Ont.	165
The Book Society of Canada Ltd.	Ont.	159
Ginn & Co. Educational Publishers	Ont.	158
Les Presses de l'Université de Montréal	P.Q.	156
Centre de psychologie & de pédagogie	P.Q.	147
McGill-Queen's University Press	P.Q.	140
Oxford University Press	Ont.	122
Sir Isaac Pitman (Canada) Ltd.	Ont.	122
Editions du Renouveau Pédagogique	P.Q.	113
Centre éducatif et culturel	P.Q.	106
Doubleday Canada Ltd.	Ont.	99
Fiddlehead Books	N.B.	96
Reader's Digest Association	P.Q.	94
Ontario Institute for Studies in Education	Ont.	89
Brunswick Press	N.B.	86
New Press	Ont.	84
Prentice-Hall of Canada Ltd.	Ont.	82
Service des cours par correspondance	P.Q.	71

Publisher	Province	No. of Titles
C.C.H. Canadian Limited	Ont.	69
The Carswell Company Limited	Ont.	68
Canadian Tax Foundation	Ont.	66
Editions du Lévrier	P.Q.	66
Librairie Garneau	P.Q.	64
Talonbooks	B.C.	63
Editions du Phare	P.Q.	62
Mitchell Press Ltd.	B.C.	61
Harvest House	P.Q.	60
Little, Brown & Co. (Canada) Ltd.	Ont.	58
Bellhaven House Ltd.	Ont.	57
Simon & Schuster of Canada Ltd.	Ont.	57
Canadiana House	Ont.	56
Royal Ontario Museum	Ont.	56
Peter Martin Associates Limited	Ont.	54
M. G. Hurtig Publishers	Alta.	53
Education Nouvelle	P.Q.	52
Editions Parti Pris	P.Q.	52
Pontbriand	P.Q.	52
House of Anansi Press	Ont.	50

Note: Information Canada, the Queen's Printer, and the CBC not included.

THE PUBLISHING FUNCTION

Publishing is the interface between a nation's writers and readers. Beyond question, and this point of view will be reiterated throughout this report, it is the climate for authorship that must concern this Commission in the end. But there can hardly be a prosperous, productive, and effective writing community unless it is assured of adequate publishing facilities, good distribution channels, and an interested and informed audience. Too often each of these groups competes with rather than supports the others in the book production chain. This happens even when members of each group are not occupied with criticizing or are just being indifferent to one another. Being indifferent is a too-frequent preoccupation of authors, publishers, booksellers, book wholesalers, librarians, educationists, and even readers.

If writing is labour-intensive (it is wholly so), publishing is capital-intensive. This suggests that the latter is a business rather than a craft or profession. But this is precisely the paradox of publishing. Publishing is indeed a business, but only up to a certain point. From the standpoint of cultural value to the community, financial profitability is not the principal criterion of a publisher's success, although it may be one criterion. If profitability were all that counted, the best publishers would be those who imported the greatest dollar volume of books and incurred the lowest overhead in reselling them, whether or not they issued much or little original Canadian writing. They might even do no original Canadian publishing at all – we shall draw attention to some so-called publishers who do not.

The effectiveness of publishing is measured qualitatively more often than quantitatively – at least by the reading public and by those who are competent to judge books. Indeed, the impact and influence of a publisher is measured and judged in many ways – by the importance and quality of authors he has been the first to publish, by the imagination of his programs, by what authors think of his books, by what critics say of them, and only rather farther along by what the banker concludes.

Original publishing is done by widely differing kinds of publishers. Some are highly creative in their selection of projects and authors. Some show great critical discernment regarding the literary abilities of the authors whose manuscripts they foster. Some are inventive, and seem to be able to incite the right author to write the right book at the right time. Some practise their profession passively, waiting for publishing opportunities to present themselves, while still others go out and stir up projects. But most successful publishers are creative editors at heart, and contribute more than risk capital and marketing expertise to the books they publish. Sol Stein of Stein and Day put it aptly when he said recently: "If a publisher does not add value to what he publishes, he's a printer, not a publisher."

Understandably, this most unbusiness-like of businesses encourages a mixture of qualities among its leaders that ranges from genuine financial acumen to what must be regarded as commercial irresponsibility. No apologies and no excuses should be allowed to turn the latter trait into a virtue. We have heard of authors whose books have been published and sold but whose royalties remained unpaid – on the excuse that the publisher's working capital was tied up in unsold inventories and in other accounts payable. Do not these publishers recognize that royalties are not a production expense but a selling expense, incurred at the moment books are sold and therefore covered by moneys already received by the publisher and held in trust by him for transmittal to his authors on the due dates? Publishers who do not have the money to pay royalties that have been earned are guilty of conversion. It is therefore hard to understand the logic behind proposals for publicly funded programs of support to publishers which the latter intend to use merely to help them pay royalties which the sales of their authors' books have already financed. Nevertheless, we were told that this was to be the basis of some of the first book publishing grants considered by the Province of Ontario Council for the Arts (hereafter referred to as the Ontario Arts Council).

A large and strong backlist is undoubtedly one of the greatest steadying influences that any publishing house can enjoy. But a warehouse full of unsaleable, or only slightly saleable, previous publications obviously should not be counted as an asset – although it mistakenly often is. Such inventories should be realistically valued (using the lower of cost or market), and the most appropriate of the standard accounting formulas that are used to provide for depreciation should be selected (and adhered to) with a view to establishing the true value of books in stock.

The cost of editing, designing, typesetting, printing, and binding a new book in Canada can be as high as it would be in the United States. This may be true even for first printings of equivalent size. There can be no comparison, however, between the size of the Canadian domestic market for a schoolbook, for example, and that of the United States market. (In any event, the latter may well include, in addition to its home market, much of the Canadian market and other export markets as well.) The same is true for children's books, for many reference books, and for most college textbooks – especially college textbooks. Thus the economies of scale possible for original Canadian publishing and original American (or British) publishing are weighted heavily in favour of the foreign product. Because of the difference in size of potential markets, the unit cost of a book originated in this country tends to be high, while the traditional price levels are set by imported books, chiefly by those from the United States. Thus the same percentage of publishing misjudgments is more costly in Canada and the same percentage of publishing successes provides less income with which to underwrite the mistakes.

The competition of the market-place, too, works a little differently in book publishing from the way it does in other fields of industry. This is because copyright gives each new book a uniqueness that cannot be precisely imitated by competing

COMPARATIVE HOURLY WAGES IN VARIOUS CENTRES IN NORTH AMERICA
(NOT INCLUDING FRINGE BENEFITS)
Base: Toronto January 1, 1972 = 100

Centre	Compositors	Lithographers	Cylinder Pressmen	Bookbinders Male	Female
Toronto	100	100	100	100	100
Cleveland	92.1	108.4	95.3	98.7	88.7
Montreal	95.0	100	94.4	101.1	91.9
Seattle	106.3	110.7	122.9	129.8	121.8
Chicago	124.8	108.1	131.1	131.1	125.9

Courtesy Council of Printing Industries of Ontario and Printing Industries of the Pacific.
Lithographers' wage rates comparable for January 1, 1971.

manufacturers. This does not mean that a book will sell regardless of its price – as already observed there are traditional price ranges and only a very special kind of purchaser will not be prompted by too high a price to turn to another title and another author when deciding which book he wants to buy. But, admittedly, within a broad range price is secondary to content and presentation, both for trade books and schoolbooks.

There are some exceptions to the tendency of the average book buyer to shop for titles rather than for best buys in books, and these will be discussed later in this report. They include the educational textbook aimed at a particular course of study; however, we shall see that this is becoming an ever rarer species. On the other hand, there are definitive reference works and certain kinds of scholarly books whose audiences are reached chiefly through public and academic libraries; these may carry substantially higher prices and carry them successfully because they are unique and have no competitor. Not infrequently they belong to the category of publishing that requires subsidization in order to be undertaken at all. Notwithstanding the fact that the market for these books is less price-sensitive than that for other kinds of books, the extent to which institutional purchasing budgets can thus share in the subsidization of works of high unit costs is limited, no matter how essential the books may seem to be. Specialized publishing at quite high prices occurs in the United States and Great Britain as well as in Canada, although in the first two markets books enjoy much higher average sales because of the larger markets available.

One often hears the question, "How many copies of a book must be sold if the publisher is to break even?" As the discussion of costing and pricing later in this report points out, the variables are far too many for a general answer to mean much. What the publisher knows, or should know if he is going to stay in business, is that for a particular kind of work of so many pages, and selling at a given (acceptable) list price, a minimum firm sale of three thousand, four thousand, or five thousand copies will be required. If the work is a textbook illustrated in colour, his minimum sale may have to be tens of thousands of copies; if it is an illustrated children's book, the market will lie somewhere between these extremes. He will, of course, often be wrong, probably wrong more often than right. The favourable surprises will have to recoup not only their own costs but also the losses incurred on the disappointments.

This balancing of the bitter with the better in the course of an ongoing flow of judgments regarding what the public will or will not buy is fundamental to book publishing. Many inferior books are being published in Canada, no doubt, but this simply means that there are many areas in which more good books need to be written. Publishers are inhibited when they know from experience that cost recovery is impossible, or unlikely, or when they do not have the working capital available to undertake projects that are little better than marginal economic risks at best. Some publishers plunge ahead without the necessary capital, but in the end their bad business judgment is likely to be exceeded only by what was also their bad critical judgment.

THREE KINDS OF PUBLISHING

The two kinds of publishing most widely practised in Canada are agency publishing and original publishing, regrettably in that order. In addition, some books are produced by simultaneous co-publication with a publisher outside Canada. For every original Canadian publication, perhaps fifteen or twenty are distributed, or "published," through so-called exclusive agents who have imported these books from the original publishers abroad. Agency publishing and original publishing, and also co-publishing when it occurs, tend to overlap, often to the point of becoming interdependent.

This does not mean that every publisher of original Canadiana acts as an agent, although in fact there are only a few exceptions among English-language publishers. Even less does it mean that every exclusive agent is an active publisher of original Canadiana; some publisher-agents have no editorial staff at all. What is important about the overlapping is that all three kinds of publishing require parallel fulfilment and promotional facilities, including warehousing and shipping, invoicing, accounts receivable, plus sales departments to advertise and catalogue, provide travelling representatives, and supervise general marketing and planning.

What really distinguishes original publishing from agency publishing is that the former requires speculative commitments in units so large that they often lead directly to substantial operating losses, while the latter requires investment in a great many inventory units each of relatively modest size. Spread over a great many titles, the cost of sales to sales ratio in agency publishing is determined principally by the jobbing discount available from the original supplier, and by the degree to which the latter may mark up the price in Canada. Thus the agent's unit cost for imported books will be a more or less fixed ratio of selling cost, whether he brings them in in quantities of six copies, fifty copies, or two hundred and fifty copies. (If his services as a stockist are rated unduly high, it may mean that he imports more inventory than he can sell. If his reputation is low, it may be because he underbuys, or purchases too many titles that are not wanted and too few of those that turn out to be in demand. The best-run agencies will inevitably make some of these misjudgments respecting some of the titles they carry; for the poorly-run agency, miscalculations may be the norm.)

Thus the publisher of original Canadian editions is committed to costs related to minimum sales of several thousand copies, commitments which must be assumed in full at the moment of the decision to publish. This is vastly different from the activities of an agent importing a wide range of books from publishers abroad in dribs and drabs, as often in response to demand as in anticipation of it, with all that this implies for the quality of his service to the ultimate purchaser.

Canadian publisher-agents who do support programs of original Canadian publishing have long asserted that their continuing ability to do so depends on the security of their agency business. This contention will have to be looked at more closely a little later; it has special implications for publisher-librarian relations, as we shall see. But whatever the degree of interdependence, it does not follow that if original Canadian publishing requires assistance in order to survive, so does agency publishing. And even if the survival of original Canadian publishing can be shown to be in the public interest (this, too, need not be taken for granted), it does not follow that the survival of agency publishing is equally important to Canadians. Perhaps it is and perhaps it is not. On the other hand, agency publishing is not automatically unimportant or contrary to the public interest. A good deal of spurious reasoning has long gone on, in defence as well as in criticism of the agency system. Some of those who would jettison it altogether have forgotten to consider the added costs and added dissatisfactions that would accompany the chaos they would so cheerfully allow to replace it.

The fact is that in 1971, fifty-seven publishers in this country claimed to be the exclusive Canadian agents for five hundred and forty-three foreign publishers. That is to say, they claimed to carry stock of all, or at least all of the commonly required titles published by their principals, whether the latter were located in the United Kingdom or the United States. Interestingly, ten years earlier the same number of Canadian publisher-agents claimed to be the exclusive representatives of six hundred and twenty foreign publishers. The decrease during the decade could be explained in other ways than by publishing mergers abroad. There is some evidence, for example, that under the pressure to provide improved service and to reduce unnecessary overheads, a number of the less important foreign agencies were dropped by their Canadian representatives. But the agency system

COMPARATIVE NUMBERS OF PUBLISHERS AND AGENTS

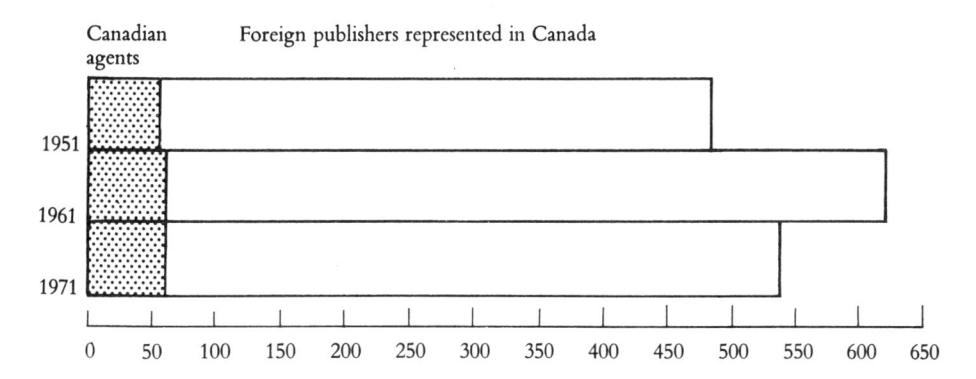

	Canadian agents	Foreign publishers represented in Canada
1951		
1961		
1971		

has by no means been generally abandoned in Canada.

One Canadian publisher-agent claimed to represent exclusively no fewer than thirty-six foreign publishers, two others claimed representation of thirty-three, while the remaining fifty-four agents shared the balance of the imported lines somewhat unevenly among them. As we intimated earlier, several of the overloaded agencies just referred to undertake almost no original Canadian publishing. Perhaps it is not surprising that they were among those that maintained the lowest profiles during our hearings.

Just as there are different kinds of publishing, there are also different kinds of publisher-agents in Canada. Some are completely independent of the publishers they represent; often, but not always, being Canadian-owned corporations. Others are incorporated subsidiaries of their parent firms, which sometimes represent other foreign publishers also. The actual number of publisher-agents in Canada has hardly increased in the last twenty years (fifty-six in 1951; fifty-seven in 1971). It would be incorrect to assume that this indicates that competition has not grown in Canadian publishing in the same period. Not only has the number of firms engaged in educational publishing, for example (including both Canadian-owned and foreign-owned), increased substantially but the complexion of textbook publishing has changed in a way that greatly broadens the competition, as we shall see later.

The functions of order fulfilment and promotion are common to both agency and original publishing, but the overlap stops there. The expensive overhead of operating an editorial department as well as the cost of carrying inventory of new publications is peculiar to original publishing. These and the other problems which we shall find are the chief financial burdens for indigenous publishing beg the question, why do any publishers choose to become engaged in Canadian publishing? Are publishers being disingenuous when they keep telling us that Canadian publishing just doesn't add up financially?

One traditional response to this question has been that schoolbook publishing pays its way and carries the cost of whatever trade-book publishing is done as well. Or at least it is supposed to have done this – in company with agency sales – until recently, when several simultaneous developments contributed to a marked adverse trend in the educational market. But like most other generalizations about the book publishing industry, this one does not stand close scrutiny. McClelland and Stewart began to take educational publishing seriously only in fairly recent times, while a good many firms (admittedly the smaller ones, chiefly) have yet to publish their first schoolbook. There have been some notable trade publishing successes, and there have been some notable failures.

Perhaps the best explanation of the attraction of trade publishing is that it can bring immense satisfaction, even if not prosperity, to those who undertake it. For those publishers who feature fiction or poetry, this explanation will almost have to do; some of them have no better reason to offer, it would seem. If this sounds cynical, it is necessary to add that we shall find that educational publishing may no longer be the complete solution to the trade-book publisher's problems.

The title of the Commission's final report on book publishing in this country, *Canadian Publishers and Canadian Publishing*, is intended to highlight two activities that are often misunderstood, if not outright confused. Canadian publishers, meaning Canadian-owned publishers, are one thing; Canadian publishing quite another, for the latter means the planning, editing, and original publication of new books in Canada, usually books written by Canadian authors, although not exclusively so.

But if our concern is to nurture a firm sense of Canadian identity at home and to project the Canadian identity abroad, our first regard should be for Canadian authors, or at least for Canadian subject-matter. We could take still further satisfaction from Canadian publishing if, in addition to serving Canadian authorship well, it could gain international acceptance on its own merits – if it were able to establish itself in the literary market-places of the world as an original outlet for foreign authorship. It is clear that Canadian publishing should mature to the point at which it could publish all the best and most popular of its authors in its own name, and do so throughout the world. It will be an even greater accomplishment if it can attract important authors from abroad to publish originally in Canada, confident that by doing so their interests will be as well served as if they had signed contracts with British or American houses. Such ambitions will remain dreams, of course, for a long while yet. But in one limited area the pattern is already emerging: more than one Canadian university press has followed the lead of major foreign scholarly presses by contracting with senior authors abroad to publish original editions of some of their most important works, which the presses then sell internationally.

THE DEPARTMENTS OF BOOK PUBLISHING

As in the United States and Great Britain, book publishing in Canada is made up of specialized branches. The most important are trade, educational, reference book, scholarly, religious, and government publishing. In each of these departments, books may either be published originally in Canada or imported from abroad. Each is distinguished from the others by the kinds of books handled and also by the channels of supply through which these books normally reach their readers and the prices and discounts at which they are sold.

Many trade-oriented publishers have educational departments as well, although the converse situation is less common. Reference-book publishing, as the term is used here, involves selling encyclopedias directly to private consumers and libraries; most sets of this kind are imported, although there are a few important exceptions. Religious publishing is usually associated with denominational support. Government publishing covers all books distributed by or on behalf of federal and provincial government departments and government agencies, including Information Canada, the National Film Board, the Canadian Broadcasting Corporation, and the various Queen's publishers and printers.

TRADE BOOKS

Not only are the different kinds of books sold in different ways and to different groups of consumers; they are also packaged and advertised quite differently. Thus the trade book, as its name implies, is primarily intended to be merchandised by trade booksellers. It is consequently priced at a level that is broadly competitive within the traditional ranges for a work in its particular subject classification, length, and quality of production. It is equipped with a colourful, somewhat informative, and highly ephemeral paper jacket. It is wholesaled at a discount and on terms sufficiently attractive to permit the bookseller to buy it on speculation and display it in his store. In Canada and the United States (but not in Great Britain), this discount is normally forty per cent off the list price, usually with shipping charges added, payable within thirty days.

The bookseller enjoys return privileges on almost all of the trade books he stocks; these privileges permit him to return within prescribed time limits unsold stock in good condition. Some publishers limit returns to a stipulated percentage of the books purchased from them. Additional discounts may be given by publishers to wholesalers of trade books when the latter purchase in large quantities for resale to libraries, and occasionally to local retailers; these supplementary discounts are usually also available to retailers for orders of equivalent quantities, meaning orders for a hundred or so copies placed before the date of publication. Such incentives are intended to maximize the distribution and display of the book at the

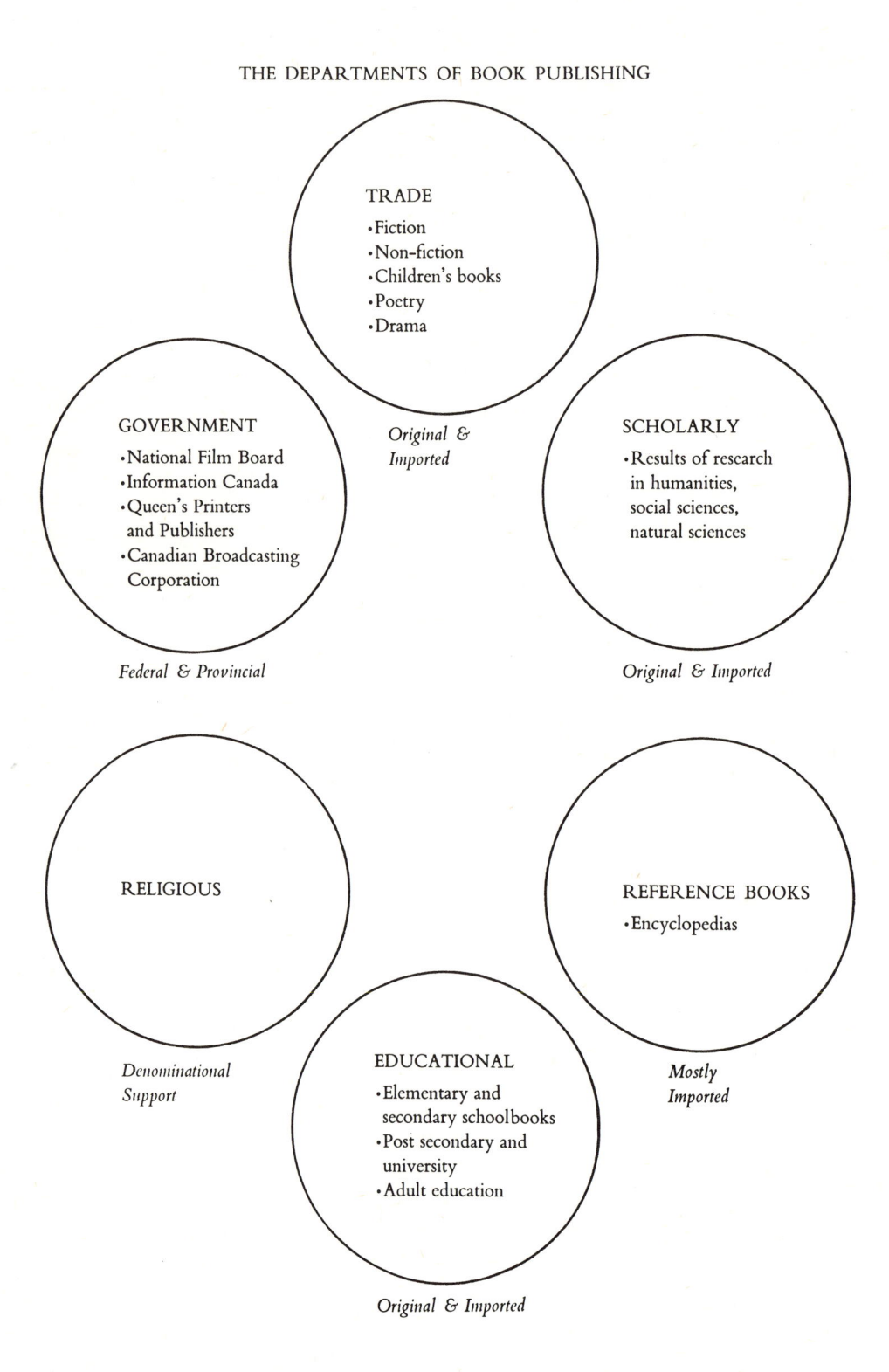

THE DEPARTMENTS OF BOOK PUBLISHING

TRADE
- Fiction
- Non-fiction
- Children's books
- Poetry
- Drama

Original & Imported

GOVERNMENT
- National Film Board
- Information Canada
- Queen's Printers and Publishers
- Canadian Broadcasting Corporation

Federal & Provincial

SCHOLARLY
- Results of research in humanities, social sciences, natural sciences

Original & Imported

RELIGIOUS

Denominational Support

REFERENCE BOOKS
- Encyclopedias

Mostly Imported

EDUCATIONAL
- Elementary and secondary schoolbooks
- Post secondary and university
- Adult education

Original & Imported

moment it is made newsworthy by reviews and advertising, rather than to assist the publisher in calculating his initial printing order. The latter deadline is usually long past when the bulk of such trade-book orders come in.

Trade-book publishing includes the following principal subdivisions, to which a few others could be added: fiction, non-fiction, poetry, drama, arts and crafts, children's books, and paperbacks of many kinds. Non-fiction has been the most dependable product for trade-book publishers and booksellers in recent years, although there have been some notable fiction successes – often imported from abroad, even when the author has been Canadian. If the sales possibilities for Canadian fiction have on the whole been marginal, the markets for poetry and drama have been for the most part sub-marginal. Children's books have been expertly discussed by Shiela Egoff in her background paper and will be touched on again in Chapter 4.

EDUCATIONAL, REFERENCE, AND SCHOLARLY BOOKS

Although most publishers have long claimed that all books are educational, educational book publishing is still a clearly defined department of the industry. (We shall see that this may not continue to be so.) Educational books are subdivided into elementary and secondary schoolbooks ("elhi"), post-secondary, and university. There should also be specialized Canadian books to serve the broad field of continuing education, or adult education; however, we have heard persuasive evidence that some of the most active educational publishers seem indifferent to this market in both their editorial planning and their sales promotion.

No department of publishing in Canada has been subjected to so many pressures and changes in so short a time as has educational publishing, and its problems will command major attention in this report.

Reference-book publishing normally involves the selling of relatively large sets of books at relatively high prices to individuals, schools, and libraries. The unit investment for the consumer is so great that sales to individuals through the normal trade channels (e.g. bookstores) would not be sufficient to sustain the business, as the encyclopedia publishers point out. Consequently the latter employ or commission large staffs of sales agents who can afford to devote considerable time – often several hours – seeking to persuade each prospective purchaser to subscribe. Much of the advertising done by such publishers is aimed at procuring "leads", which the commission agents follow up in person. In addition, reference-book publishers sell their products directly to schools and school boards, sometimes at special net prices, as well as to public and university libraries. The latter are likely to order established encyclopedias for their reference shelves more or less as a matter of routine; accordingly, they usually receive the most attractive prices.

Since the publication of *Canada and Its Provinces*, *Chronicles of Canada*, and

Makers of Canada forty or more years ago, relatively little reference-set publishing has originated in Canada. An important exception is *Encyclopedia Canadiana*, which was published in 1957. Even the latter, however, drew upon the material contained in W. S. Wallace's *Encyclopedia of Canada*, published many years earlier.

Because the original editorial and production investment in large encyclopedic works is necessarily very high, substantial markets have to be cultivated to support them. As a rule, these need to have international dimensions; even *Encyclopedia Canadiana* is but one item in a catalogue of many international reference works sold by the Grolier Society. Consequently, not only do most reference-book sets originate abroad (usually in the United States), but also their publishers are most often American subsidiaries. Some of these, such as *Encyclopaedia Britannica*, have diversified their publishing activities and are now issuing individual educational books as well as a wide variety of other kinds of learning materials. Thus for the most part, encyclopedia publishing in Canada means regional marketing of sets of imported books rather than original Canadian publishing. This situation is unlikely to change fundamentally, although Canadian branches of encyclopedia publishers will probably expand their programs to include more Canadian schoolbooks if they are able to procure adoptions for them.

Scholarly publishing may also be treated as a department separate from educational publishing because it is not concerned with the production of textbooks, not even of university textbooks. It does not normally include the publishing of theses and dissertations, although a good deal of popular misunderstanding exists on this point. (A thesis is written to persuade the examiners that a student has done his research well; a scholarly book is written solely to inform, i.e. to supply its readers, who usually are scholars, with new knowledge derived from basic research.)

Scholarly publishing has a critically important relationship to a nation's output of trade and educational books. This is because the true scholarly books is a seminal work, on which the writing of many secondary works may depend. Scholarly publishing can report the results of responsible research in every field of the humanities, social sciences, and natural sciences. In the social sciences, in particular, it has been the foundation of every unique Canadian contribution in book form, whether we are speaking of studies in economic planning, popular works on ecology or sociology, or histories of the CPR.

The volume and quality of the scholarly publishing output of a particular university press need not be closely related to the institution's student enrolment, undergraduate or graduate, nor even to the volume of research being undertaken at that institution. (However, a good scholarly publishing program may indirectly influence the quality and momentum of an institution's research, by helping to attract the best qualified scholars to its faculty.) Nor is the publishing of the results of research restricted to university presses; in Canada it is not even confined to

Canadian-owned publishers, as some of the important historical biographies issued by Macmillan in Canada so clearly testify.

A great deal of international scholarship is imported into Canada either directly or through Canadian publisher-agents, although we shall see later that this is the area where the latter find it most difficult to provide acceptable service in this country. Similarly, original Canadian scholarly publishing is marketed abroad on a scale unmatched as yet by any of the more popular departments of publishing in this country.

This international acceptance of Canadian scholarly publishing must be explained by the fact that the latter recognizes standards that are international. True, more often than not a Canadian scholarly work will be concerned with Canadian subject-matter, but, equally, it will be able, along with its foreign counterparts, to make contributions to specialized studies of other times and places. Scholarly publishing is discussed further in Chapter 6.

GOVERNMENT PUBLISHING

Book publishing by federal and provincial governments occurs in many forms and under many different policies. Federal government publishing, which in recent times has been channelled through Information Canada, remains the object of evolving and uncertain policy, although this characteristic does not distinguish it from the publishing programs of the various provincial governments.

But one notable feature of federal government publishing is that both its annual output and its backlist are by a substantial measure the largest in the Canadian book publishing industry. This fact alone makes the federal government's publishing program of serious significance and considerable concern to the rest of the Canadian book publishing industry. The latter advances several complaints, chiefly based on the kinds of publications and policies that have been announced from time to time by the Queen's Publisher (Information Canada's precursor) in recent years.

The publishers point out that some government publications – a rather small minority but one that includes some very important books just the same – compete unfairly with their own publications. Sometimes there is direct collision between books in a particular subject area, sometimes the government is said to be publishing works which might better be left to the established book industry. Almost invariably, the book industry points out, pricing of government publications is not realistic, often reflecting a desire on the part of Ottawa to make a book more generally available by reducing its list price. This can only be done, it is claimed, by subsidizing the publishing costs, thereby deceiving the public with the public's own money into believing that Canadian publisher's books are overpriced luxuries. As a rule, it is said, the production costs have been heavily subsidized at the government publishing level, as in the case of such books as *Canada, a Year of the Land*.

(Nevertheless, when this beautiful book was reprinted, it was issued by special arrangement through one of the commercial publishing houses.) Sometimes the subsidy required for government publications is furnished by the department of government which employs the author. The publishers point out that this may include artwork as well as research time and expenses on a scale that no ordinary publisher could possibly underwrite out of sales revenues, and that the government cannot and does not recoup such costs.

Exhaustive studies have been under way within and in relation to Information Canada for several years, partly aimed at arriving at a constructive accommodation with the Canadian book industry, English as well as French. Just what form this will take is still not clear, but a much closer liaison between the book industry and this government publishing department has been anticipated for some while. Co-publishing by Information Canada with selected book publishers chosen ad hoc for their particular competences is a possible development, and may extend to the support, or at least encouragement, of coordinated cataloguing by subject areas and other kinds of promotional activities on behalf of the whole industry. This cooperation may involve a successor body to Information Canada if the latter does not continue in existence, or it may involve individual government departments. For some years now, government initiative and support has made possible major Canadian exhibits at some of the international book fairs, including Frankfurt, Brussels, Nice, the American Library Association, etc. But unrest continues in the industry regarding the future of Information Canada, one of the concerns being that government publishing might be extended to creative writing by authors outside the government service. The fear is that if this kind of publishing competition should arise, the rest of the industry would suffer seriously in the ensuing competition for authors and markets. We agree that this would have serious consequences for the development of Canadian book publishing. Even where direct competition had not occurred, the existence of a government publishing policy that would admit it could inhibit many private publishing initiatives. The same danger applies to publishing by provincial governments, it need hardly be added.

In recent years the Canadian Broadcasting Corporation and the National Film Board have each developed coordinated publishing programs of their own. Many of the concerns of the Canadian book industry in relation to Information Canada (or its successor, if any) apply to these federal agencies also. In this connection, publishers seem not to fear so much direct competition for specific manuscripts, since the texts and illustrative material are generated as a by-product of other activities, as that the competition possible from such organizations, carrying as they do both government subsidies and government authority, can easily change the public's sense of values with regard to the products of publishing available elsewhere. We have even received complaints regarding the advertising of books (published by regular book publishers) when this advertising has been subsidized by educational television authorities such as OECA and thus competes with the normal channels of distribution. Some of these concerns of the industry were reflected in the *Report of the Task Force on Government Information* (Ottawa, 1969).

The coordination of publishing activities through the Office of the Queen's Printer and Publisher in Ontario, for example, has not evolved nearly as far as it has in the case of Information Canada, although it may be that federal restructuring of publishing responsibilities is not yet complete. Until recently, provincial and federal publishing programs seemed to be proceeding along roughly parallel lines, marked by similar uncertainties with regard to policy. Then in December, 1969, a Committee on Government Productivity was established, and given a broad mandate to undertake a comprehensive management analysis of the administration and operation of the provincial government and to recommend and implement changes where necessary. In its First Interim Report (December 15, 1970) this Committee took notice of the "supply function" discharged by the Division of Supply and Services in the Department of Public Works (now the Ministry of Government Services). The Queen's Printer and Publisher's branch is housed administratively within this Division, and it was decided that the operation of a central print procurement agency (Queen's Printer) and the function of a central publisher (Queen's Publisher) should be examined within the broad context of the supply function. A special committee was appointed to establish priorities and initiate studies relating to central supply and services, and this committee (known as the Committee for Development of Supply Policies and Procedures) undertook, among other things, a study of government printing and publishing. This project had as its scope the whole of government printing and publishing, although it focussed particularly on the role of the Queen's Printer and Publisher's branch as a central agency.

In the summer of 1971, the Committee on Government Productivity initiated a new task force study on Communications and Information Services. This surveyed the role of the Queen's Printer and Publisher in relation to the broad function of the government's communication services. The report on the role of the Office of Queen's Printer and Publisher has now been issued. This report assumes – correctly, we think – that printing and publishing are distinct and separate activities and should be treated and administered accordingly. The report goes on to examine the special requirements for centralized service in each of these two areas of activity.

Because the procurement of printing is recognized as essentially a matter of supply acquisition in a specialized commodity field, the report recommends that the print procurement function should be carried on as a central service in a new Printing Services branch, with a larger area of responsibility than was traditionally vested in the Queen's Printer. This new service would be involved in the proper identification and collection of all government printing costs for the advice of the

Management Board, which would exercise control over these costs. The branch would also be responsible for developing guidelines and procedures respecting print-tendering practices, pre-print planning and copy preparation, and standards for costs and graphic quality for repetitive publications issued by the government, including annual reports. It would, however, cease to be a centralized print procurement office, responsible for processing all orders for such work. Instead, it would be expected to develop as a specialized technical resource unit, equipped to offer advice to other ministries on new graphic arts technology and to establish a working liasion with the graphic arts industry throughout the province. It would in addition establish operating criteria for all internal printing facilities and provide expenditure controls, integrated procedures, and standardization for all legislative printing, including Hansard, Bills, Statutes, etc. The title Queen's Printer would be retained as an imprint to secure and hold Crown copyright on all legislative publications and other material printed by the ministries of the government, control over the use of the imprint being vested in the Deputy Minister in the Ministry of Government Services.

The future organization of publishing services on behalf of the government is of greater concern to this Commission than the coordination of government printing requirements reviewed above. We shall point out later in this report that the Canadian graphic arts are inextricably linked with Canadian publishing, even though there is no more need for the two to be consolidated as a single industry in this country than elsewhere in the world. Yet the separation of the printing and publishing functions is often imperfectly understood, especially by institutions and public bodies who too often assume that to print is to publish. For this reason we are pleased to note that the task force's report on the role of the Office of Queen's Printer and Publisher makes a clear distinction between the two functions, and also is aware how important it is that publishing as such, when it is required by government, should be articulated with the publishing industry in a way which will strengthen and complement the latter rather than expose it to misleading competition subsidized with public money.

The report recognizes that most of the creative aspects of the publishing process when embarked upon by government are the responsibility of the operating ministries concerned. These include both the publishing initiatives and the planning of the vehicles of publication to be used. It is the operating ministries which must identify publication requirements and determine the audiences to be reached and printing runs needed; indeed, it is the operating ministries which usually should discharge the responsibility of making the primary distribution, if the objective of establishing communications in specialized areas is to be realized. On the other hand, the task force recognized the need for standards and guidelines governing many publishing practices, e.g. editorial style and consistency in pricing policies. It also noted the desirability of coordinating inter-departmental publishing projects, and of providing criteria for the measurement and evaluation of government publications generally. It recommended that these important aspects of government publishing be undertaken centrally from the Management Board Secretariat as special assignments or as contract assignments to consultants from the private sector.

The report pointed out that the urgent and immediate requirement for a common publishing service occurred in the technical areas, especially in those which we would describe as production supervision and marketing. Apparently to this end it recommended that within the office of Printing Services there should be established a documentation centre, which would ensure complete cataloguing of all government publications to proper bibiliographical standards and which would be responsible for the production of monthly checklists and annual cumulative catalogues. These would constitute a source of much-needed information for the public, a management tool for the use of government itself in planning new publications, and a basis for an effective depository library system. The report also recommended that an effective inventory control and management system be established within this unit in order to control inventories of government publications in the interests of economy as well as efficient distribution, and that the government's order-fulfilment system be improved. The need for such developments was reflected in many of the comments we heard from booksellers and others in the course of our work, and are described in some detail by Mrs. Beverley Moore in her article, "College Bookstores", included in the background papers of this Commission, already published.

Under the plans recommended by the task force, both the documentation service and inventory management would rest basically on an effective intent-to-publish notification system which would be supported by all government ministries, and which would be mandatory. Such a resource unit would be expected to operate a supporting warehouse facility, improving its order-fulfilment system on a continuing basis, and expanding the depository service to public and academic libraries. This unit's program would assume tangible form in the Ontario Government Bookstore, which it would operate with the assistance of the improved cataloguing and warehousing service.

The Commission generally endorses the report of the task force, although it does not underestimate the challenge involved in setting up some of the services envisaged. But these are greatly needed, as is also the clarification of policies and purposes in government publishing which the report promises to accomplish. We therefore support the task force's not surprising counsel that its recommendations should begin to be implemented immediately, because they are appropriate to the changes in the structure of government already underway. An implementation team, generally involved with the improvement of information services, has now been established and the organization of the new Printing Services branch and its support units has been developed. The former Queen's Printer and Publisher has been transferred to a new appointment in the Legislative Services area of the government, and we understand that it is the intention to recruit technical and professional staff to supervise the new areas of activity within this branch.

In the course of the hearings representations were made that the copyright resources of government agencies such as the Canadian Broadcasting Corporation and the National Film Board should be more easily and freely available to other publishers of schoolbooks and learning materials. Admittedly, implementation of such proposals might create new problems, not the least of which would be the increased fees that might be expected by authors, photographers, and the like if their work were to be opened to secondary exploitation in this way. On the other hand, these same agencies have already mounted substantial book publishing programs and the possible interaction of the latter with other writing and book publishing is therefore a concern of this Commission. Obviously, any recommendations regarding the publishing programs or policies of federal bodies will have to be limited to advising the provincial government regarding recommendations it might make to the appropriate departments of the national government.

DEVELOPMENT OF CANADIAN SCHOOLBOOK PUBLISHING

Some publisher-agents seem to have succeeded almost too well on behalf of their foreign principals. Among the most prominent subsidiaries publishing Canadian books today are several which at one time were handled in this country by publisher-agents. The books of Macmillan, Collins, Wiley, Heath, Holt, and many other internationally known imprints could be included in this list. Indeed, the cancellation of some of the most successful agencies and their conversion into foreign-owned subsidiaries was an early phenomenon, not just a recent one.

But it is one thing for a foreign publisher to drop his Canadian agent in order to set up in this country on his own, and quite another for him to swallow his Canadian agent whole at the same time, as happened to Gage's Textbook Division. No doubt the loss of important agencies can be a serious setback to a Canadian publisher, as Jack McClelland has affirmed. However, when these set up independently they can actually add to the volume of original Canadian publishing, as the history of Macmillan in Canada demonstrates so forcibly. But one must ask all the same whether original Canadian publishing would gain or lose if every last Canadian-owned firm of importance were to fall into foreign control. This is a crucial question, and will be examined further in Chapter 2.

By international standards, Canadian publishing has markedly matured in the past decade or two. It is therefore ironical that at the very moment that Canadian books are for the first time beginning to take their places beside the finest foreign publications on the bookshelves of the world, the future of the Canadian book industry as a native enterprise seems to be in doubt. Of course, while Canadian publishing has been growing up, it has been strongly influenced in literary style as well as in format by British and American publishing – chiefly by the latter. British and American books have influenced each other, too, as anyone who has watched the impact of American packaging on British books or the migration of quality paperback publishing from Great Britain to America knows perfectly well.

Little wonder then, and no harm either, that Canadian publishing has been so responsive to publishing patterns set by the New York houses. How could it be otherwise, when Canadian intellectuals, creative people, and the reading public in general have had no national literary yardstick of their own? It would be tiresome to recite the cultural influences flowing northward across the border; this has been done adequately in countless previous studies of this subject. What we should realize is that most kinds of Canadian books (fiction, poetry, school textbooks, and the like) are written by people and addressed to readers who are, to put it mildly, very well informed indeed regarding the last word in America.

Canadian schoolbook publishing had fallen far behind its American counterpart by the eve of World War II. In 1938, Ontario replaced its Grades III and IV readers with Canadian-edited, largely Canadian-written and Canadian-designed books which, although entirely new productions, were hardly forward-looking in comparison with American standards of the time. When the decision to follow these with a new reader for Grade II was made in 1939, a number of four-colour lithographed reading series, which by then were in general use across the United States, seemed to justify a special Canadian manufacturing effort to offer equal quality of production in this country. In the event, an arrangement was made through the Copp Clark Co. Ltd. to "Canadianize" the Grade II reader in the Alice and Jerry Books (published by Row, Peterson of Evenston, Illinois). In the event, fifty per cent of the content of the American series was replaced by Canadian and British narratives and poems, many of the former specially written. The controlled vocabulary structure of the American series was totally discarded in the editorial process, although much of the specially constructed "child-experience" story material required to support this new reading philosophy was maintained, along with a high proportion of the colourful illustrations. (The films for the latter, which were about the only item that could be physically imported, were touched up by the Canadian art department, Captain Sandy's pipe being erased wherever it appeared in his mouth and the American flag being replaced by a Union Jack or eliminated altogether. Each of the changes required was listed by an editorial committee appointed by the Ontario Department of Education.)

The result was a Canadian book, of a sort. Certainly in comparison with the readers that had been available for basic use in the schools up to that time it was a production masterpiece, although hardly a pedagogical one. The door was now open – a little distance anyway – for the re-publication in this country of other

"Canadianized" readers of many kinds and levels, but especially for the elementary grades.

The same process of adapting and adopting American books was also gaining momentum in the secondary school. For the black-and-white high school textbooks (colour was not countenanced at so senior a level), it was customary to import duplicate copper electroplates, and to revise these as inexpensively as possible by welding in Canadian spellings, place names, and other references where necessary. A considerable degree of technical skill was achieved in this process, the printed result being almost indistinguishable from the original, although it was usually printed on poorer paper (made in Canada) and bound in a Canadian pyroxylin-coated cloth of stodgy appearance, carrying an unimaginative Canadian cover design.

The copyright in Canadianized editions such as the above remained vested in the United States (occasionally British) publisher, who received a royalty based on the list price (or net price) of all copies sold in this country. Sometimes an additional royalty was paid to the Canadian editor, the work of revision occasionally extending to substantive re-writing of large sections of the books concerned. At other times editorial payments were made on an hourly basis, which made it possible to sell the book a little more cheaply.

The list prices of these Canadianized editions of American textbooks were a considerable achievement in themselves, being often only a fraction of the catalogue prices of the original editions. Although the day of subventions by the Department of Education was almost over, exclusive contracts of authorization for periods of up to seven years were still the order of the day. Highly efficient inventory-planning was therefore possible, and except in the closing year or two of an authorization contract the publisher was able to go to press each year with relatively substantial printings, and with a feeling of security regarding their saleability based on the latest statistics of enrolment obtained from the Minister of Education himself.

True, the textbooks thus produced were duller in appearance than the foreign editions on which they were based. But the curriculum was being revised at various levels, and it was a time for experimentation in book-making not previously paralleled in this country. Only a proportion of the new books were derived from American editions; others were reprinted from British publications, often imported for the purpose in the form of cumbersome stereoplates. Many other books were written, edited, designed, and manufactured wholly in Canada, often furnishing their own regrettable proof that this was so. Of course, not all books that were wholly created in Canada were that much worse than the imported product, whether the latter was Canadianized or not. For in their time they set their own standards, and were warmly enough appreciated by teachers eager to find something specific on the life of the Canadian trapper, on prospecting in the Canadian

North, or on everyday life in other lands. The curriculum set forth the topics to be studied, and the content of these new textbooks was tightly packaged for teaching and for testing.

Things had moved so far forward from the old Eaton's Readers that the progress in Canadian textbook-making must have seemed self-evident to many. Colourful American textbooks, some of them embodying wholly new approaches to learning, could be seen at regional book displays. But they were priced so far out of reach, and there was so little budgetary and curricular provision for their use in the classroom, that even a basic series of unit readers in general science looked at best like extravagant possibilities for the school library – or perhaps only as possibilities for the public library.

The whole process of editorial and technological development in schoolbook publishing was, understandably, greatly slowed by World War II. Shortages of paper and of binding cloth forced frequent substitutions; sometimes a single reprinting of a schoolbook had to be bound in two or three different colours of cloth. Drastic shortages were avoided, however, because essential supplies of raw materials were made available as a matter of government policy; at the same time a certain amount of new textbook writing and publishing continued even during the War years. If there was any experimentation at all, it took the form of exploiting the discovery of seat-work exercises, published as work textbooks, text workbooks, and just plain busywork workbooks, distributed literally in carload lots.

One advance of real significance had been made by Canadian book publishers during the period leading up to the War, and was consolidated immediately afterwards. This was the building of editorial and production (including design) sections within the publishing houses. Until the late 1930s many publishers had no editorial personnel on staff at all – at least no full-time editors charged with planning the textbooks to be issued in particular fields, and with working closely with authors at the manuscript stage. Apart from a process of editorial selection which in many instances could only be described as intuitive, most if not all of the responsibility for manuscript editing, production planning, proof-reading, and sometimes even author liaison, devolved upon the foreman of the printer's composing room or his equivalent. There were exceptions, of course – including Clarke, Irwin, Macmillan, Dent, and Ryerson (to name most of them). But even in firms such as these, much of the specialized editorial function was supplied by senior executives in their spare time. Field editors, or what are now sometimes called procurement editors, were either unknown or were relatively uncreative businessmen who were better acquainted with per-page costs of typesetting than with the editorial, pedagogical, or aesthetic planning of the books they offered to publish or were called upon to produce.

The embryonic state of the editorial and design capacity of Canadian publishing began to change rapidly after the War. Competition among publishers, an increasing awareness of international standards by both publishers and educationists, and a fresh surge of curriculum revision from coast to coast accelerated the change, long overdue. New basic Canadian reading series were planned by several publishers, first in Grades IV, V, and VI, then in Grades VII and VIII, and finally in the primary grades as well. Almost all the provinces began to show active interest in the creative efforts of the several publishing houses who had entered this field. New Canadian arithmetics and new Canadian spellers were developed and soon were widely adopted.

A particularly refreshing development was the arrival in Canada, over several years following the War, of several capable and imaginative young book designers from abroad. To the influence of this group was added the momentum of a growing number of Canadian artists and typographers who chose to concentrate on book design. At first most publishers were indifferent, but one by one they came to realize that professional design and production standards required the services of specialists. A new dimension, and a new cost, had been added to Canadian book publishing.

An interesting anecdote relating to the development of a wholly Canadian primary reading series involved the Canadian publisher of the Dick and Jane Series, originally published by Scott, Foresman in the United States. When approached by the Ontario Department of Education with the suggestion that his firm consider the development of a new basic Canadian series at the primary level, the publisher made the point rather forcefully that Dick and Jane already enjoyed virtual dominion over Grades I to III in Canada and that it would therefore be economic nonsense for him to have anything to do with such a project. Thereupon the Canadian branch of an American publisher stepped into the breach by financing – with no little difficulty – the research and development of a basic Canadian series of primary readers. It was a decision that demanded considerable imagination, conviction, and dedication, because the publishing challenge involved uncertainties that would have warranted discretion even if the whole of the American market had been waiting. A publishing decision of this kind can involve risking hundreds of thousands of dollars – several years' net income at least. It was a difficult decision at that time and would be still much more difficult today because of market changes that have taken place, as we shall see. Suffice it to say that in this case the leadership came from an American subsidiary, using capital which became more easily available in the course of the project as a result of a merger in the United States between its parent company and two other major publishing firms. The results were wholly Canadian, and found widespread approval throughout the country and, in due course, stimulated healthy competition from other publishers in Canada as well.

One result of the trend toward multiple classroom books in place of the tra-

TOTAL ANNUAL SCHOOL ENROLMENT IN PUBLIC AND ROMAN CATHOLIC SCHOOLS IN ONTARIO FROM KINDERGARTEN THROUGH GRADE 13, FROM 1938 TO 1970

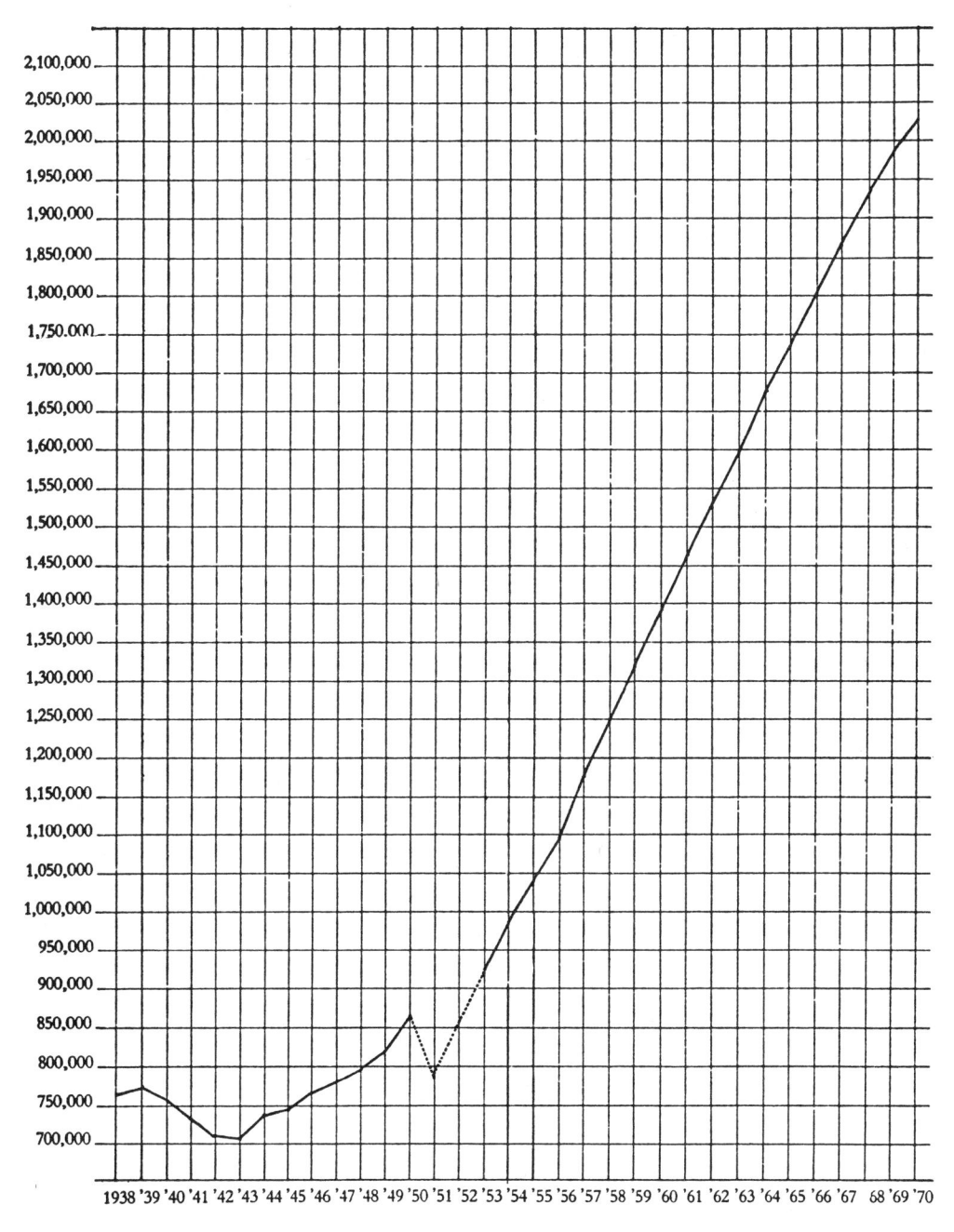

•1938 to 1950 figures taken from the annual report of the Minister of Education
•1951 to 1970 figures taken from the 1970 Minister of Education's report. The apparent drop from 1950 to 1952 could be attributed to the change in the method of calculating enrolment.

ditional set of a single textbook has been a blurring of the distinction between schoolbooks and library books. Thus children's trade books and educational books seem to be converging, and if this does occur, the schoolbook authors of the future may not necessarily be professional educators as customarily heretofore. One aspect of this process was graphically described by Sol Stein of Stein and Day in a recent interview in *Saturday Review*, in which he addressed his fellow publishers as follows:

"Ten years ago all the smart money in Wall Street was saying that what you fellows need is more textbooks, that they are the bread and butter, and that the riskiest things are trade books – and the riskiest part of trade books is fiction. Well, let me tell you something – ten years from now there won't be any textbooks."

It was our turn to whew. You mean, we said, it will all be all this damn audio-visual stuff? He quoted us. "No," he said, "it will be books – real books, paperbacks of regular trade books. What the kids will be reading is the real firsthand stuff, instead of all the secondhand stuff they've always had to read after it's gone through all those dull textbook writers."

A CRISIS IN EDUCATIONAL PUBLISHING

Although the school population has increased substantially during the past fifteen years, the prospects for individual creative publishing projects on the grand scale of the basic elementary reading series of the 1950s have not improved. On the contrary, they have recently diminished sharply.

During the same period, the number of competing texts published and the number approved for use, in Ontario at least, have both continued to increase far more rapidly than the school population. In 1968, the basis of financing the purchase of approved textbooks was changed. Alongside these developments a shift away from the traditional use of basic textbooks in full classroom sets has occurred, and the preference has grown for the introduction of a variety of books in every subject, if not indeed on every topic.

At the same time that these changes have been taking place, the book itself has encountered a new kind of competition. This comes from a vast array of new kinds of learning materials, ranging from film loops to audio cassettes, video tapes, and

ONTARIO ELEMENTARY AND SECONDARY SCHOOL ENROLMENT
PROJECTIONS 1971-1975

	1971	1972	1973	1974	1975
Elementary	1,443,155	1,420,993	1,394,145	1,368,777	1,347,456
Secondary	583,861	605,832	625,696	645,798	662,104
Total	2,027,016	2,026,825	2,019,841	2,014,575	2,009,560

educational kits of every shape, size, and price. Curricula have become flexible and their detailed planning has been largely decentralized. In short, the textbook industry that had been rapidly expanding its lines has been brought up short by a sudden and unanticipated shrinkage in the market for its products.

As a result, by 1971, textbook publishing departments were not so often financing publication of the occasional novel or book of poems, as they had for many years. Instead, some educational publishers were beginning to look to their trade departments (and to their college departments) for projects which could be counted on to improve the cash flow so that they could pay their printers' bills as well as the invoices for shipments from their principals abroad.

The Commission has had confidential access to the audited financial statements of a wide range of Canadian publishers, and it is perfectly evident that publishing in this country is experiencing a general crisis. The production of trade books has always been close to marginal. Put another way, most trade-book publishers who are at all active tend to bring out about as many books as their finances permit, if not sometimes a few more. The agency system based on sales of imported books has been leaking like a sieve as more and more foreign jobbers woo Canadian library purchasers and make inroads on this market. And educational publishing itself – long the most secure department in book publishing – has been in an economic cul de sac since 1968, its fuel running lower and lower, and unable to reverse gears.

ORGANIZATION OF THE CANADIAN BOOK INDUSTRY

The Canadian Book Publishers' Council had its beginnings in 1910 when a group of five publishers founded the Book Publishers' Association as a branch of the Toronto Board of Trade. When the Council appeared before our Commission early in our hearings, its membership comprised forty-five competing publishing houses which supported a large secretariat headed by a full-time Executive Director.

Book publishers, because of the changing and portable nature of their products, find that participation in educational and general book exhibits in various parts of the country (they also attend selected meetings abroad) is one of the most valuable methods of sales promotion available. This situation has not changed in several decades, although the number of displays mounted has greatly increased. Exhibits, however, can also be one of the most inefficient and expensive means of advertising, if they are not wisely chosen and carefully coordinated. Ideally, a substantial number of publishers (of books in relevant subject areas), are represented at the same display, in order to spread costs and maximize interest. Although the program of the Canadian Book Publishers' Council extends considerably beyond cooperation in book displays, the strongest single bond of this association over the years has probably been the need of its members for coordinated exhibits programs

CANADIAN BOOK PUBLISHERS' COUNCIL
LIST OF MEMBERS
August 1972

Addison-Wesley (Canada) Limited	D. C. Heath Canada Limited
Thomas Allen & Son Limited	Holt, Rinehart and Winston of Canada
Bellhaven House Limited	Limited
The Book Society of Canada Limited	Longman Canada Limited
Burns & MacEachern Limited	The Macmillan Company of Canada Limited
William Clare Manitoba Limited	McClelland and Stewart Limited
Clarke, Irwin & Company Limited	McGill-Queen's University Press
Collier-Macmillan Canada Limited	McGraw-Hill Ryerson Limited
Wm. Collins Sons & Co. Canada Limited	George J. McLeod Limited
The Copp Clark Publishing Company	Methuen Publications
J. M. Dent & Sons (Canada) Limited	Nelson, Foster & Scott Limited
Doubleday Canada Limited	Thomas Nelson & Sons (Canada) Limited
Educational Progress Co. Limited	Oxford University Press
Encyclopaedia Britannica Publications Limited	Palm Publishers Limited
Fitzhenry & Whiteside Limited	Prentice-Hall of Canada Ltd.
Gage Educational Publishing Limited	Random House of Canada Limited
General Publishing Company Limited	Saunders of Toronto Limited
Ginn and Company	Scholastic Tab Publications Limited
GLC Educational Materials and Services Limited	Science Research Associates (Canada) Limited
	University of British Columbia Press
Gray's Publishing Limited	University of Toronto Press
Griffin Press Limited	Van Nostrand Reinhold Limited
Harvest House Limited Publishers	John Wiley & Sons Canada Limited

and policies. We were told that during 1970 approximately two hundred requests for displays in various parts of the country were processed. Fifty-seven of these were implemented by the Council itself; sixty were given qualified approval and referred to member firms for individual direct action; the others were declined for various reasons, including insufficient time for planning, inadequate display space, and lack of certainty regarding the possible interest of visitors, or the condition of book purchasing budgets.

The Council has also undertaken preliminary experiments in joint cataloguing, and in cooperation with other associations has developed the annual volume known as *Canadian Books in Print/Catalogue des livres canadiens en librairie*. This bibliographic tool, which complements the British *Whitaker's* and the American *Bowker* indexes, fills a gap in reference literature for booksellers and librarians that had existed since Canadian book publishing began. The Council has also organized annual professional study seminars for its own members in recent years. Various public relations and communications programs are also undertaken, including

Catalogue des publications du Ministère des richesses naturelles depuis 1883
Québec. Ministère des richesses naturelles; E.O.Q., 1968 $3.00

Catalogue des publications périodiques universitaires de langue française
Association des universités partiellement ou entièrement de langue française; A.U.P.E.L.F., 1969 $5.00

Catalogue of Canadian fossil fishes
Gardiner, Brian George; Royal Ontario Museum, 1966 $3.50 paper (Life Sciences Contribution)

Catalogue of films on world development. Annual
Canadian Council for International Cooperation; C.C.I.C., 1970 $2.00

Catalogue of Italian plays, 1500-1700, in the library of the University of Toronto
Corrigan, Beatrice; U.T.P., 1961 $5.00 [0-8020-1151-9]

Catalogue of non-ferrous metal alloys and specifications
Canada. Department of National Defence; Information Canada, 1953 $15.50

Catalogue of paintings and sculptures, Vol. I: older schools
Hubbard, R.H. (ed.); U.T.P., 1957 $7.95 [0-8020-1073-3] (National Gallery of Canada Catalogues)

Catalogue of paintings and sculptures, Vol. II: modern European schools
Hubbard, R.H. (ed.); U.T.P., 1959 $12.50 [0-8020-1095-4] (National Gallery of Canada Catalogues)

Catalogue of replacement books for children's library collections
Toronto Public Libraries; Toronto Public Libraries, 1970 $10.00

A Catalogue of the Burney family correspondence, 1748-1878
Burney family; Hemlow, Joyce (ed.); McGill-Queen's, 1970 $22.00

Cataloguing for school libraries
Scott, Margaret B.; Fennell, Doris P. and Bagshaw, Denis G.; Pergamon, 1970 2nd ed. Approx. $5.95 paper [0-08-016509-5]

Catastrophic advance of the Steele Glacier, Yukon, Canada
Bayrock, L.A.; Boreal Institute, 1967 $1.50

Catch me if you can
Franklin, June; Centennial Press, 1963 $4.80

The Catcher in the rye, Nine stories, notes
Coles, 1968 Revised. $1.25 paper (Coles notes & translations)

The Catcher in the rye, Nine stories, notes
Hunter, John L.; Forum, 1968 $1.25

Catching the sun's fire
Fleet, Brenda; Fiddlehead, 1969 $.50 (Fiddlehead poetry books)

Catching up with our children: new perspectives in sex education
Rich, John; McClelland, 1968 $5.00 cloth; $2.50 paper

Catéchèse biblique (Ancien Testament)
Laforest, Jacques; Laval, 1963 Tome 1 $2.25

Catéchèse biblique (Nouveau Testament)
Laforest, Jacques; Laval, 1964 Tome 2 $3.00

Catéchisme Biblique
Fides, 1966 $1.50 net

Le Catéchisme biblique des enfants
Fides, 1962 $1.25 net

Catégories non-abéliennes
Hilton, Peter et autres; Univ. Montréal, 1967 2e éd. $2.50 (Séminaire de mathématiques supérieures)

Catenary through the counties; the story of Montreal and Southern Counties Railway
Clegg, Anthony and Lavallée, Omer; Trains & Trolleys, 1966 $5.95 [0-919130-08-9]

Catholic education in French speaking Quebec
Lussier, Irénée; Gage, 1960 $3.75 (Quance lectures in Canadian education)

The Catholic revolution
Roche, Douglas J.; Musson, 1968 $7.95 (Limited Edition Military Series)

La Catoche orange
Geoffroy, Jacques; Parti Pris, En préparation

A Cat's christmas tale
André, Gérard; André, 1968 $2.70

Causal thinking in the child
Laurendeau, Monique and Pinard, Adrien; Recherches psychologiques, 1962 $8.25

Causes and issues in current labour unrest
Brookbank, C.R.; McGill Industrial, 1966 $.50; $.35 each for 4 or more

The Cave
Newlove, John; McClelland, 1970 $4.95

Cave Springs farm
Rannie, William F.; Rannie, 1968 3rd. ed. $.75

Cavelier de la Salle
Viau, Roger; H.M.H., 1960 $1.00 (Collection: 'Figures canadiennes')

La Caverne des Rocheuses
Achard, Eugène; Lib. générale, 1954 $1.50 (Les grandes aventures)

Cazou ou le prix de la virginité
Ferron, Jacques; Orphée, 1966 $2.00 (relié) (Théâtre)

Ce combat qui n'en finit plus
Stanké, Alain et Morgan, Jean Louis; Homme, 1970 $2.50

Ce matin, le soleil
Malouin, Reine; Fides, 1962 $1.25 (Collection 'Rêve et Vie')

Ce pour quoi il faut contester
Robichaud, Emile; Beauchemin, 1970 $1.75

Ce que Jésus doit à sa mère selon la théologie biblique et d'après les théologiens médiévaux
Spicq, C., O.P.; Etudes médiévales, 1959 $1.25 ('Conférence Albert-le-Grand')

Ce qu'en pense le notaire
Senay, Alphonse; Homme, 1969 $2.00

Celebrate the sun: a heritage of festivals interpreted through the art of children from many lands
Nickerson, Betty; McClelland, Forthcoming $6.95

seminars with provincial Department of Education officials and the presentation of briefs and submissions to government and public bodies such as this Commission.

The Canadian Book Publishers' Council comprises several special interest groups, and also maintains several standing committees. In August, 1972, these included a Canadian educational publishers' group, a university and college publishers' group, and Standing Committees on Bookseller Relations, Exhibits, Information and Statistics, Library Relations, and Program and Professional Development, among others.

Apart from the Canadian Book Publishers' Council, but overlapping it in the case of several of its memberships, is the Independent Publishers' Association. This is a recently convened group of publishers whose principal condition of membership is Canadian ownership. This new association, which is at an embryonic stage, has yet to develop the cooperative display, promotion, and marketing programs to which it referred in its submission to this Commission.

When the Independent Publishers' Association appeared before us, it claimed to have twenty-three charter members, five of the largest of these being and continuing to be members of the Canadian Book Publishers' Council. (A downward revision in the fees structure for smaller firms by the latter body resulted in several additional dual memberships after the Independent Publishers' Association was called into being.) In August, 1972, there were seven dual memberships, as reflected in the accompanying lists of member firms in each.

INDEPENDENT PUBLISHERS' ASSOCIATION
LIST OF MEMBERS
August 1972

Black Rose Books	Ladysmith Press
The Book Society of Canada Limited	Learning Concepts Ltd.
Burns & MacEachern Limited	Peter Martin Associates Limited
Clarke, Irwin & Company Limited	New Press
Coles Publishing	New Press Educational
Delta Canada	Oberon Press
Fiddlehead Books	Prism International
General Publishing Company Limited	Progress Books
Griffin House	Sono Nis
A. M. Hakkert Ltd.	Talon Books
Harvest House Limited Publishers	Tundra Books of Montreal
House of Anansi Press Limited	University of Alberta Press
M. G. Hurtig Ltd.	University of Toronto Press
Ingluvin Publications	Vancouver Community Press
James Lewis & Samuel Publishers	Weedflower Press

CANADIAN BOOK PUBLISHERS' COUNCIL

August, 1972

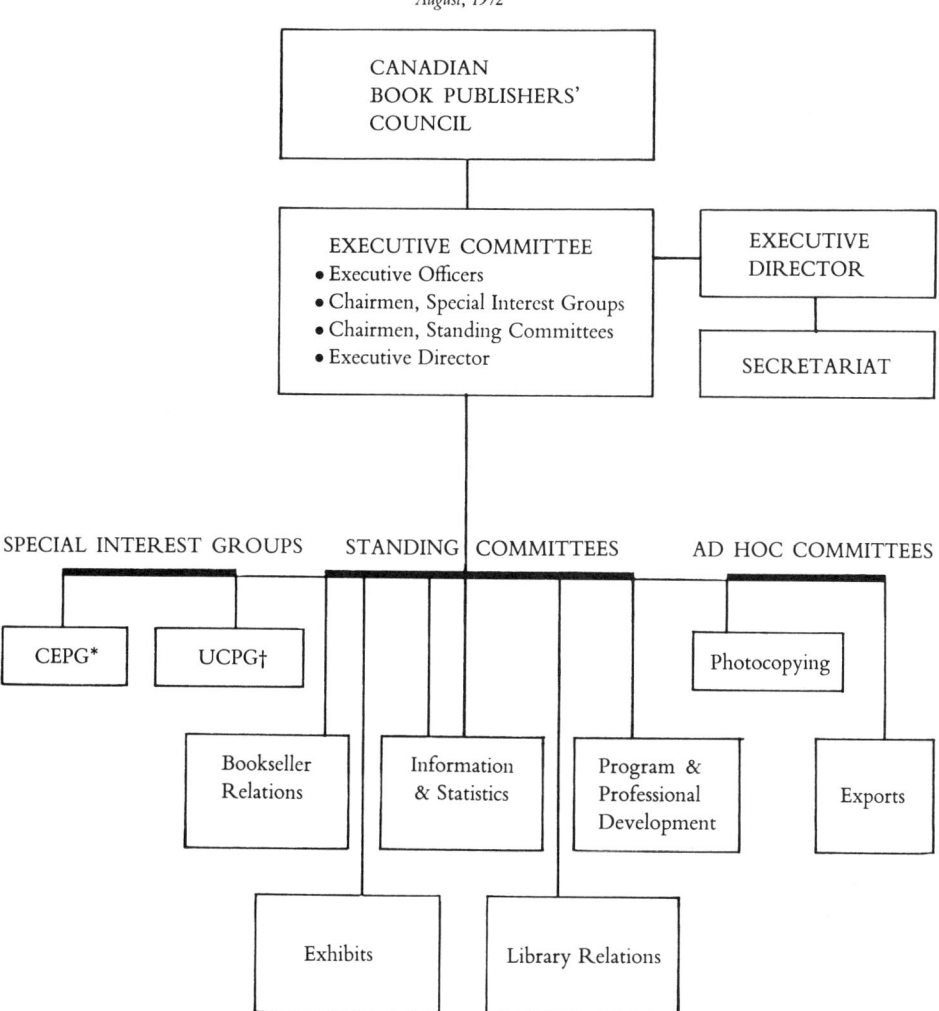

```
                    ┌─────────────────────┐
                    │      CANADIAN       │
                    │  BOOK PUBLISHERS'   │
                    │      COUNCIL        │
                    └──────────┬──────────┘
                               │
     ┌─────────────────────────┴──────┐    ┌──────────────┐
     │       EXECUTIVE COMMITTEE      │────│  EXECUTIVE   │
     │  • Executive Officers          │    │   DIRECTOR   │
     │  • Chairmen, Special Interest  │    └──────┬───────┘
     │    Groups                      │           │
     │  • Chairmen, Standing          │    ┌──────┴───────┐
     │    Committees                  │    │ SECRETARIAT  │
     │  • Executive Director          │    └──────────────┘
     └────────────────┬───────────────┘
```

SPECIAL INTEREST GROUPS   STANDING COMMITTEES   AD HOC COMMITTEES

| CEPG* | UCPG† | | | | Photocopying |

| Bookseller Relations | Information & Statistics | Program & Professional Development | Exports |

| Exhibits | Library Relations |

*Canadian Educational Publishers' Group
†University and College Publishers' Group

NUMBER OF CANADIAN TITLES IN PRINT PUBLISHED BY MEMBERS OF CBPC & IPA
(as of December 31, 1971)

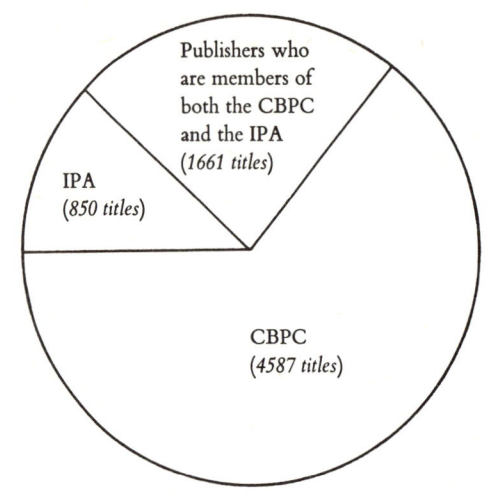

- Publishers who are members of both the CBPC and the IPA (1661 titles)
- IPA (850 titles)
- CBPC (4587 titles)

With very few exceptions, chiefly confined to publishers holding dual memberships in the two bodies, the firms in the Independent Publishers' Association are still at a comparatively early stage of their history, most having been founded within the past very few years. Understandably, therefore, they lack the fully developed marketing facilities of most members of the Canadian Book Publishers' Council.

What the members of the Independent Publishers' Association lack in selling organization, and often in capital, is, however, often compensated for in critical editorial competence and willingness to experiment. A number of them have shown special interest in Canadian fiction and Canadian poetry, not necessarily to their financial profit, admittedly. But few (disregarding those which have long been members of the Canadian Book Publishers' Council as well) have really entered educational publishing, one of the two traditional props available to support the issuing of original Canadian books. The representation of foreign publishers in Canada (the other way of acquiring publishing revenue) is also eschewed by almost all firms which are exclusively members of the Independent Publishers' Association, although not by all of them.

Nevertheless, the formation of the new Association and its early unwillingness to affiliate or otherwise identify itself with the Canadian Book Publishers' Council, does focus attention on the issue of Canadian versus foreign ownership. This is because a significant majority of the member firms in the Canadian Book Publishers' Council are now foreign-owned, a trend which had been apparent for some years before the appointment of this Commission. Nevertheless, by far the greater proportion of Canadian books in print at the end of 1971 were published by CBPC members.

Yet another publishers' trade organization is the Educational Reference Book Publishers Association, membership in which is open to any company which markets multi-volume educational reference sets. The emphasis in these qualifications is on marketing rather than publishing, which makes it not surprising that without exception its eight member firms are Canadian subsidiaries of foreign companies, or depend on imported books for their stock-in-trade. The Educational Reference Book Publishers Association is not affiliated with the Canadian Book Publishers' Council, although common membership does occur. The members of the Educational Reference Book Publishers Association are concerned, as the name implies, with marketing books by subscription selling, selling directly to the consumer (with institutional exceptions) via commission salesmen.

In January, 1972, a new special-interest group of Canadian publishers met for the first time. These were the scholarly presses of the country, which had been multiplying since the first of their number had been established at Toronto at the turn of the century. No fewer than eleven individual Canadian presses were represented at the meeting, which had been called to discuss problems peculiar to scholarly publishing. Several of these publishing institutions already were active members of one of the other Canadian publishers' associations, i.e. the Canadian Book Publishers' Council, the Independent Publishers' Association, or the Conseil Supérieur du Livre; at least one (in Toronto) was a member of two. But not surprisingly, perhaps, a decision was taken to form yet another association, this time professional rather than trade, with the result that later in the year the Association of Canadian University Presses/l'Association des Presses universitaires canadiennes was being called into being. As its name indicated, this was to be a completely bicultural organization, the first of its kind in Canadian publishing. The draft constitution of the new body (adopted in October, 1972) made clear that its purposes were to serve the special professional needs of non-profit scholarly publishing programs fostered by Canadian universities, French as well as English, and that

ASSOCIATION OF CANADIAN UNIVERSITY PRESSES
LIST OF MEMBERS

University Press	Year of Founding
University of British Columbia Press	1971
Les Presses de l'Université Laval	1950
University of Manitoba Press	1967
McGill-Queen's University Press (McGill University Press in existence since 1960)	1969
Les Presses de l'Université de Montréal	1962
Ontario Institute for Studies in Education	1965
Les Editions de l'Université d'Ottawa	1936
Pontifical Institute of Medieval Studies	1933
Les Presses de l'Université du Québec	1969
University of Toronto Press	1901
University of Windsor Press	1965

NUMBER OF CANADIAN BOOKS IN PRINT
PUBLISHED BY UNIVERSITY PRESSES
(as of December 31, 1971)

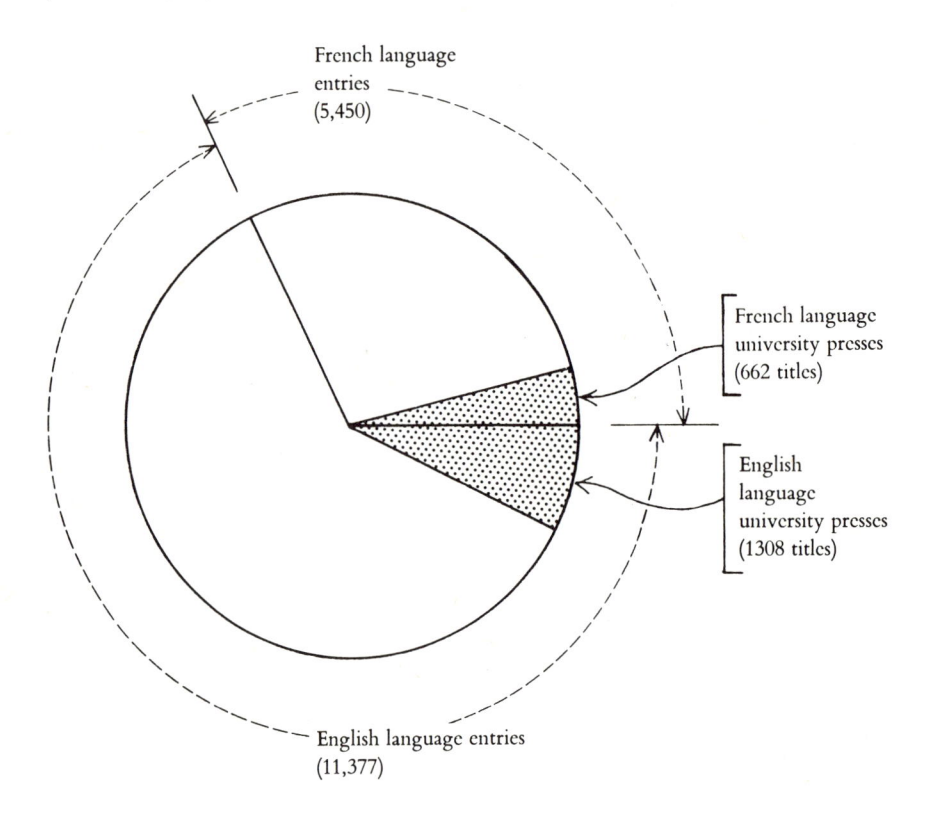

French language entries (5,450)

French language university presses (662 titles)

English language university presses (1308 titles)

English language entries (11,377)

participation by its members in forwarding the interests of Canadian publishing through active membership in other existing trade association was encouraged. The substantiality of the contribution of university presses to the total number of Canadian books in print is indicated in the accompanying graph. The seminal nature and cultural importance of scholarly publishing are discussed elsewhere in this report.

Whether or not the question of Canadian ownership should be considered a real or a phony issue, at least from the standpoint of the cultural well-being of the Canadian public, had a good deal to do with the decision to appoint this Commission. It is an issue which will be faced in the next chapter and alluded to again throughout this report.

French-language book publishing in Canada, which for practical purposes means in Quebec, is coordinated by the Conseil Supérieur du Livre, whose secretariat is in Montreal. Its affiliated bodies include the Association des Editeurs canadiens (publishers), the Association des Libraires du Québec (booksellers), and the Société des Editeurs de manuels scolaires du Québec (schoolbook publishers). In many respects its operations parallel those of the Canadian Book Publishers' Council, and in certain projects of national concern it collaborates with the latter, and with the new Independent Publishers' Association. The Conseil Supérieur du Livre receives substantial grants from the Canada Council as well as from the Ministère des Affaires culturelles du Québec for the operation of its permanent secretariat and for its various programs. (A parallel series of grants by the Canada Council to the Canadian Book Publishers' Council was terminated about two years ago. The CBPC had understood that the grants would continue if it offered low-cost memberships to the very small Canadian firms which could not afford its cooperative marketing costs. A revised fee structure to make this possible had been introduced, but up to the time of the writing of this report the grants had not been renewed. However, major grants have since been made to the Independent Publishers' Association for administrative and conference purposes.)

English-language bookselling in Canada finds its forum in the Canadian Booksellers Association. At the end of 1971 this body counted one hundred and twelve trade stores and ninety-eight university bookstores in its membership. In addition,

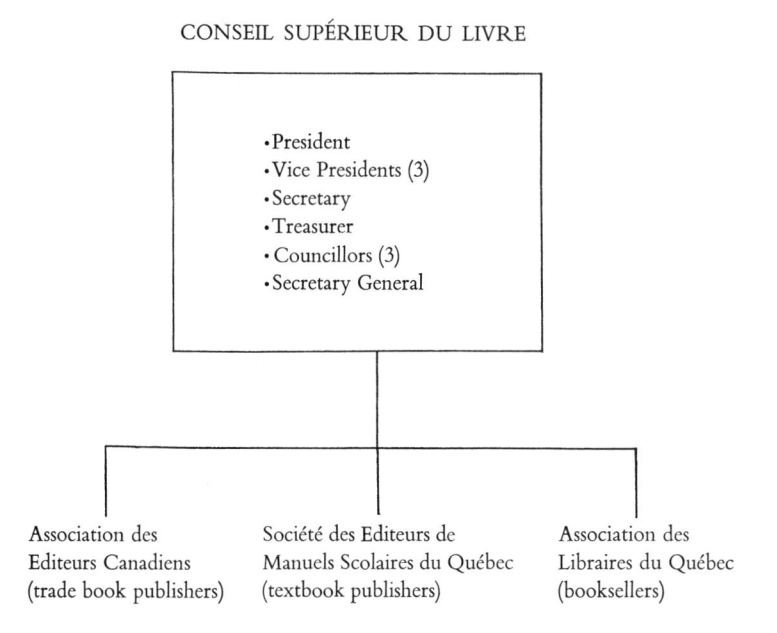

CONSEIL SUPÉRIEUR DU LIVRE

- President
- Vice Presidents (3)
- Secretary
- Treasurer
- Councillors (3)
- Secretary General

| Association des Editeurs Canadiens (trade book publishers) | Société des Editeurs de Manuels Scolaires du Québec (textbook publishers) | Association des Libraires du Québec (booksellers) |

MEMBERSHIP OF THE CANADIAN BOOKSELLERS ASSOCIATION, 1971

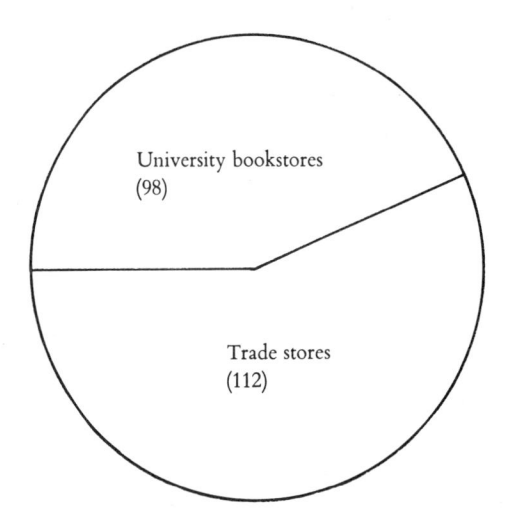

University bookstores (98)

Trade stores (112)

it included seventy-eight associate members consisting of publishers and suppliers, although the most significant figure is the total of two hundred and ten booksellers that are represented. A few important book outlets are not included in the membership of the Canadian Booksellers Association, but it does count among its members a good many establishments whose facilities could not by any stretch of the imagination be described as those of a "comprehensive bookseller." This is no discredit to the Association, whose success in coordinating the interests of bookselling across Canada stems from the imaginative leadership of a relatively small number of its members, as is so often true in trade associations. What is impressive is that the total number of comprehensive booksellers is minute in relation to the physical extent of the Canadian market, as well as in comparison with the sixty-three English-language publishers represented in the combined membership of the Canadian Book Publishers' Council and the Independent Publishers' Association. It is significant, too, that almost half the booksellers in Canada are university and college stores – a fact that has considerable bearing on the kinds of books originating in this country.

As any publisher will affirm, the diminutive extent of the retail book trade is no proof that here are untapped opportunities for retailers. Rather the opposite. Not only do most Canadian booksellers depend on other lines of retailing than books in order to stay in business, but the total absence of bookstores in many centres of population shows what a marginal enterprise bookselling normally is.

Many booksellers say that publishers are largely to blame for this condition because they support numerous channels of distribution of books that compete with the regular trade. Publishers, they point out, leap at the opportunity to distribute their books through book clubs based either abroad or in Canada (but with very few exceptions owned abroad). And publishers, the booksellers say, deal directly with schools and school boards as well as with every kind of library – except when the latter buy their imported books through yet other channels, to the chagrin of publisher and bookseller alike. Indeed, a substantial majority of the books that are accessible to Canadian readers have never seen a bookseller's shelf at all. Some of the implications of this paradoxical situation will be discussed in more detail later in this report.

No group among the many that constitute the book industry in this country has a greater stake in original Canadian publishing than Canadian book manufacturers. Unfortunately, they find themselves in competition not only with one another but also with printers abroad. Except where preference for Canadian manufacture is established policy, as in the case of educational books listed on Circular 14 in Ontario, perhaps the only factor that is operating in favour of the Canadian producer of books is his greater accessibility and resulting better service. His wage scales, and certainly his normal production costs, are in the same range as those in many major printing centres in the United States, while some classes of printing can be done more cheaply in the latter country than in Canada. The reasons why this is so require a little explanation; suffice it to say that they are largely concerned with relative size of markets, non-tariff trade barriers confronting Canadian exports to the United States, and consequent underdevelopment of printing technology in this country. The chief non-tariff barrier to the American market is found in the manufacturing provisions of the United States Copyright Law, the subject of W. E. Curry's background paper which is referred to again later in this report. Even better bargains may await the publisher who is willing to go to Great Britain, Holland, Italy, Japan, or Hong Kong for his manufacturing requirements. If a book is listed on the curriculum of any university college or school in Canada, all copies of the edition may enter Canada free of duty; in the case of book imports from Britain there would be no duty anyway, under the British Preferential Tariff.

In view of the disabilities under which it must operate, it is some wonder that Canada has a highly skilled book manufacturing industry at all. Without easy access to the continental market, which would permit it more often to set up for longer printing runs, the pressures against the full technological development of book manufacturing in this country have often been oppressive. It is hardly surprising that the number of comprehensive book manufacturers in Canada has dwindled in recent years. ("Comprehensive" in this context means those who provide a total book manufacturing service – composition, printing by letterpress or offset, as well as edition binding.) Although not all eligible firms were represented in its membership, the Canadian Book Manufacturers Institute numbered in 1960 only fifteen members. Instead of growing, this number gradually decreased, largely as a result of closings, sales, and mergers, until by 1971 its membership had shrunk to five firms in all. At that time it was reorganized as a special interest group within the Graphic Arts Industries Association and its rules of membership broadened to include firms which offer even a partial book manufacturing service. The membership of the new group, which is known as the Canadian Book Manufacturing Association, was reported in April, 1972, to total fifteen active members and seven associate members.

CANADIAN BOOK MANUFACTURING ASSOCIATION
LIST OF MEMBERS
April 1972

Active Members	Services Offered	Location
Alphatext Systems Ltd.	C	Ottawa
T. H. Best Printing Co.	CPB	Toronto
The Brown Bros. Ltd.	B	Toronto
Bryant Press	CPB	Toronto
Pierre DesMarais Inc.	CPB	Montreal
John Deyell Co.	CPB	Lindsay
Evergreen Press Ltd.	CPB	Vancouver
Hignell Printing Ltd.	CPB	Winnipeg
The Hunter Rose Co.	CPB	Toronto
Quebec Newspapers Ltd.	CP	Quebec
Richardson, Bond & Wright Ltd.	CP	Owen Sound
Stroud-Bridgeman Press Ltd.	CP	McKellar
University of Toronto Press	CP	Toronto
Web Offset Publications Ltd.	CP	Toronto
York Litho Ltd.	CP	Toronto

Associate Members

Abitibi Provincial Paper Ltd.		Toronto
Anglo Paper Products Ltd.		Toronto
Columbia Finishing Mills Ltd.		Don Mills
Domtar Fine Papers Ltd.		Montreal
Kruger Pulp & Paper Ltd.		Scarborough
The Sheridan Company		Don Mills
Spicers International Ltd.		Scarborough

Note: The services offered are: composition (C), printing (P), and bookbinding (B).

PUBLISHERS AND AUTHORS

If the public has an interest in the welfare of Canadian book publishing (one of the central questions before this Commission), its first concern must be for Canadian authors. If books are to define the Canadian identity in the future and embed it in the national consciousness, Canadian authors must write them. If these books are to command the love and interest of Canadians and the respect of readers elsewhere, only the literary competence of their authors will bring this about. We shall serve ourselves poorly if we do not create a climate for Canadian authorship in the future that will stimulate the best talent and hold it in this country. Promising authors are going to have to be given the incentive and the opportunity to write. R. M. Farr's background paper discusses the programs of assistance now available to Canadian authors.

One of the most important incentives that an author can have, of course, is the assurance of competent and reasonably prompt publication on fair and just terms, and of effective marketing by the publisher thereafter. This is not to be achieved merely by legislating a doubling of royalties or an increase in advances to authors or by requiring that books be kept in print when they will not sell in sufficient quantity to repay the cost of doing so. On the other hand, it is too easy to take the view that if Canadian publishers are looked after, Canadian authors will be able to look after themselves.

Probably no publisher is indifferent to authorship in general, although many publishers are so preoccupied with the purely commercial activities of their businesses that they grow out of touch with the creative individuals on whom their industry depends. This is more likely to occur in very active, heavily sales-oriented firms than in small houses in which the chief executive may be field editor, manuscript editor, production manager, sales manager, shipper, and accountant all in one. But it does not follow that the last situation is the best one for the author. Our investigations have brought home the fact that a publisher who does not manage his business well is not likely to look after his authors' interests well either. And when communications between publisher and author languish, or when the former encourages his authors by his behaviour even to suppose that they are being exploited, the whole fabric of the Canadian book industry is weakened.

We have carefully examined the standard author-publisher agreement forms issued by twenty-six of the better known publishing houses operating in Canada. What is striking is the high degree of similarity of the conditions set forth in most of them; however, there are important differences, and it may be useful to comment briefly on some of the more controversial provisions.

Fourteen of the author-publisher agreement forms give the publisher the right to make editorial revisions to render the finished works suitable for publication; the others do not consider this question. In some cases this right is qualified by the addition of the phrase "subject to the author's approval" or words to that effect.

No generalization can easily be made regarding the royalty rates stated in these contracts, which vary from one type of book to another as well as from publisher to publisher. Sliding scales on trade books beginning at 10 per cent and reaching 15 per cent after five thousand copies are apparently not uncommon. Royalties on trade books are likely to be based on list price, but on educational books it is becoming more common to relate such percentages to the net or wholesale price. The basis of royalty payments on bound copies or sheets sold for export is usually stipulated in the agreements, as a rule being calculated on the net price actually received by the publisher when a special discount is given to the foreign purchaser.

In the contracts examined, the division of income from subsidiary rights, such as fees for the right to quote excerpts or to serialize in newspapers or periodicals, usually involves an equal split between publisher and author. However, in some cases a higher share is provided for the author, ranging up to 75 per cent. Income received in a lump sum or royalty for the right given to other publishers to issue the book in foreign countries calls for varying divisions between the original publisher and the author; most provide for division on a 50-50 basis but some transfer to the author 75 per cent and several as much as 90 per cent. Almost all the agreement forms contemplate an even division of subsidiary income resulting from book club adoptions. Film and TV revenues are distributed on the same basis as income from foreign re-publication rights; income from translation rights varies from 50 per cent to 90 per cent to the author.

Several of the forms contain some variation of the following additional clause: "If at any time after one year from the date of original publication of the said literary work, in the judgment of the publishers the publication of a cheap edition should be deemed advisable and desirable then the publishers may lease the plates or otherwise conclude arrangements for the publication of such an edition in Canada sharing equally with the author all royalty or other income derived from such sale, or the publishers may publish their own cheap edition and shall pay to the author a royalty of $7\frac{1}{2}$ per cent on the retail price of each copy sold." The alternatives provided for here would yield roughly comparable income to the author, assuming the same sales.

A termination clause, to be invoked in the event that a work goes out of print and the publisher does not wish to republish, appears in some form in most of the contracts, although four seem not to contemplate this contingency at all. Section 14 of the Copyright Act would be applicable in the event that a book becomes out of print; this is discussed in Chapter 3.

The termination clauses follow different wordings, but they normally confer on the author the right to enter into a new contract with another publisher after his book has been out of print for a given length of time and after due notices have been exchanged. However, in some cases the publisher retains an option to republish in such circumstances, a privilege which seems difficult to justify even though it is unlikely that it has ever been exercised.

Only one publisher stipulates that the agreement should be interpreted in accordance with the law of a jurisdiction other than the Province of Ontario. This is an American subsidiary, whose contract states that the agreement should be interpreted and governed by the laws of the state in which its head office is located.

Twelve of the agreement forms contain a clause requiring the submission of the author's subsequent work or works to the same publisher, i.e. a "first refusal" clause. Most of these state that the publisher should have the first option to publish the author's next work, although four firms require that the author should submit his next two works, such publication to be on fair and reasonable terms. This clause can be said to be controversial, although it appears frequently in publishing contracts in most countries. Publishers argue with some justice that for certain kinds of works, such as poetry and first novels, the speculation on an author's first book is almost hopeless unless offset by the prospect, however remote, of being assured an interest in possible future successes. On the other hand, it is difficult to see any justification for this restriction in connection with a publication which is clearly expected to repay its costs. Such works would include school textbooks and many kinds of non-fiction. The appearance of such a clause in contracts for the latter classes of books, therefore, is probably not seriously supported by the publishers concerned and its deletion could and probably should be requested and granted automatically.

One reason for reviewing normal publisher-author contractual provisions in even this slight detail is to highlight the fact that the decision to publish is a critical one in the publishing process, and involves weighing by the publisher of the prospects of commercial profit versus the prospects of failure. The operations of the market-place are such that every author must auction his copyrights for the most advantageous agreements he can procure. This does not mean that he should always shop around before signing, or he may indeed be left unpublished. What it means is that the author is able to command terms and conditions, as well as to limit any agreement to specific markets, in accordance with the apparent commercial value of the manuscript he has created – and which he owns absolutely until he enters into a contract concerning it. A Farley Mowat or a Pierre Berton may be able to sign separate contracts with different publishers in different markets, but for every Mowat or Berton there will be dozens of authors who will find it necessary to share the uncertain returns from sales of subsidiary rights with the originating publisher if their work is to be effectively published. With the certain best sellers necessarily set aside, the average returns for Canadian authors and Canadian publishers will be meagre in any event, to judge from the operating trends that this Commission has examined.

Some publishers display a tendency to overload their programs, to make commitments beyond their editorial and financial capacity to implement. It is clearly unethical and indefensible for a publisher to enter into arrangements under which authors are committed but the publisher is not. This raises the question of how long authors should be kept waiting before their accepted manuscripts are produced in book form. It is impossible to generalize, although some of the admissions made by publishers to this Commission regarding delays forced by lack of available publishing capital cause one to wonder about the bona fides of the original publishing agreements. There may often be extenuating circumstances, but what publisher can defend his signing a contract to publish in the full knowledge that he lacks the capital to do so?

Another area for potential exploitation of authors has been brought to our attention indirectly by publishers and others who have complained that the Ontario Department of Education will not announce the eligibility of a book for inclusion on Circular 14 until after it has been published. They point out that substantial savings could be achieved if they were advised of a decision not to list a new work in advance of its publication. At whose expense? one must ask. If such a policy were adopted by the Ontario Department of Education, would it not invite an increase in the number of irresponsible publishing proposals, leading to serious investments of time and effort by authors but involving minimal risk for the publishers? The latter could then withdraw or defer or provide only token publication in the event of a failure to secure a prescription. Of course, the present procedure may not be ideal either, involving as it does a heavy financial loss for the publisher if his book is not approved. But any modification of it will have to take into consideration the interests of the author and guard against any possibility that he might go unpublished as well as uncompensated if his book is not prescribed.

Although some professional organizations exist in other fields of creative writing, the only organization that even pretends to coordinate the interests of book authors in this country is the Canadian Authors' Association. In 1971 its paid-up membership was 650, of whom 212 were members of four branches in Ontario. But of the 650 members only about two-thirds were regarded as active, or regular, members, i.e. members who have produced a body of work of at least 25,000 words through normal publishing channels (not vanity publishers). Unfortunately, a number of the most successful Canadian authors are not members of the Canadian Authors' Association. Many of the latter seem to eschew any kind of professional organization, and some of them take the position that the existing national association serves social rather than purely professional ends. Eleven such authors appeared before this Commission at its final regular public hearing to announce their intention of forming a new authors' union. However, as the different members of the group voiced their opinions, one by one, the policies and attitudes of this new body turned out to be considerably less than unanimous. Indeed, disagreement among them became so outspoken that two of their number expressed their protest by withdrawing even before the group submission had been completed, and before the Commission had fully entered the discussion. There is a moral in this, surely.

It is unlikely that the urge to write will ever be closely harnessed by any kind of collective bargaining procedure, at least not across the whole spectrum of authorship. Doubtless there are areas and specific issues on which authors may succeed in organizing and should try to organize, if only to establish fair standards of employment. Specialized fields of writing, such as radio and television, are the most likely to see such standardization of rates and conditions of use, and a considerable measure of organization has already occurred in these areas. But authorship everywhere in the world is a profession that is only partly employed, and those of its members who do publish regularly are often very unevenly remunerated. However, even if only a small percentage of the book manuscripts that are published can be really profitable to their creators, the same must be said for the institutions that publish them, i.e. the publishers. When best sellers are being discussed, it is often forgotten that many books are subsidized by their publishers, however unintentionally.

INTERNATIONAL STANDARDS

Publishing is after all an international profession and those who are most interested in its products tend to judge all of it, Canadian books included, by international standards. This is so whether they are measuring literary excellence, design and format, pedagogical soundness, or whatever. In the end there can be no such thing as Canadian publishing flourishing in isolation from all other publishing in the world.

Canadian works must stand comparison with foreign works if they are to find a market abroad. Even more important, they must measure up to foreign books available in this country in literary quality, physical format, interest, and imagination. If they do not, they will not find readers. Even in Canada, these international critical standards are supported by international reviews, meaning foreign reviews, as well as by foreign advertising including some of the most elaborate and sustained programs of all, such as those of the Book-of-the-Month Club. They are also applied by domestic reviewers, who only reflect public literary interests when they choose to review important foreign books as readily as Canadiana.

We have been told in some of the hearings that we should recommend embargoes, or at least quotas, on the importation into this country of books from abroad. Some of these recommendations have come from individuals and firms who have demonstrated by their editorial postures and preferences that they abhor every kind of restriction on their own freedom to speak, to listen, and to demonstrate, whenever they wish to do so. It is difficult to imagine how much intellectual censorship is really wanted, therefore, by those who advance such incongruous proposals. It is even more difficult to reconcile their recommendations with what publishing is all about.

2
The Question of Ownership

There has been much talk about the number of "foreign takeovers" of Canadian book publishing firms which are said to have happened over the years. But contrary to popular supposition, very few of the numerous foreign-owned book publishers in this country ever were Canadian-owned. Of about twenty-seven such subsidiaries in English-language publishing, probably not more than three or four came to this country by buying out existing Canadian concerns.

Most non-Canadian publishing houses are branch plants of long-established British or American houses that first sold their books here through Canadian publisher-agents. We have been reminded frequently that representation of foreign principals has always been an important prop to the creative side of our country's publishing industry; we have also been told that such agencies face many problems. We have come to think that one of these must be that if a Canadian publisher-agent does not succeed in selling his principal's books he may lose the agency, but if he sells them too successfully he may lose the line anyway when his principal decides to open up here on his own. After all, the foreign publisher says, my books are being purchased by bookstores, schools, and libraries across Canada. Why should they be promoted and billed in the name of another publisher, perhaps half-heartedly (he may suppose) alongside a number of lines other than my own? It's hard enough to earn a single profit in book publishing; it is even harder to earn two profits – one for an agent and one for a principal. And if original publishing is what is wanted in Canada, he rationalizes, all the more reason for me to open up there so that I can do my share of it.

CANADIAN AND NON-CANADIAN PUBLISHERS

It is easy to say that competition in book publishing is just like competition in any other type of industry. But there is an important difference, one which makes book publishing satisfying for most people engaged in it in spite of its frustratingly low return to investors. For unlike the goods of competing manufacturers of plastics, home appliances, textiles, electronics, and farm implements, every new book is an exclusive product available only from its publisher, who works under an agreement with the author. Because copyright is involved, no one else can produce the same item for sale in the same market. In other fields of enterprise, competition turns almost exclusively on price, quality, and service, but for books there is this added quality of uniqueness. If this uniqueness could not be assured, there would be vastly fewer books written and published. This is a characteristic of book publishing which should be kept in mind when considering the comparative effectiveness of Canadian and foreign publishers, in Canada or anywhere else.

If importation of foreign books into Canada were to be prohibited, or were placed on a quota related to the volume of original Canadian books issued by the importing publisher (as was seriously recommended to us), the reading public would be unlikely to accept the enforced substitution of one title for another that such a system of control assumes would happen. It might be argued that in other fields of manufacturing, tariffs successfully give protection to the home product, either reducing or excluding competition from abroad. But if restrictions are placed on the brands of foodstuffs, televison sets, or clothing that may be freely bought in Canada, similar Canadian-made commodities are available as alternatives. A regulation that means that certain books must be read instead of other books is entirely different. The intellectual censorship inherent in such restrictions would be rejected by Canadians, as it would be by any other free society. And it would not reassure them to say that "important" world literature would be permitted to enter the country, while controls were imposed on the rest in order to stimulate domestic book production. Just what kind of selective censorship are proponents of this plan calling for? Advocates of such a simplistic solution are reasoning emotionally, not logically, if they are thinking at all.

Beyond question, the foreign subsidiary has many things going for it in this country which the Canadian-owned publisher lacks. To begin with, the branch plant enjoys from the outset the momentum of the backlist of its parent company. Sometimes the latter is both lengthy and prestigious, thereby providing assured sales volume. Hence the newly established subsidiary in Canada often offers a wider range of saleable books than a Canadian firm of many years' standing. Booksellers, educationists, and librarians are aware of this, and respond accordingly.

In most fields of publishing, the international momentum of information and promotion favours imported books, or favours the best of them at least. The score is written for their popular acceptance in Canada by the great review media such as the *New York Times Book Review* or *The Times Literary Supplement*, by promotion in periodicals of every kind which flow or seep into this country, by book club adoptions or listings which pour into Canada in tens of thousands of copies,

APPROXIMATE NUMBER OF TITLES IN PRINT BY A
REPRESENTATIVE GROUP OF CANADIAN PUBLISHERS – 1971

Company	Ownership	Approximate number of titles in print
Clarke, Irwin & Company Limited	Canadian	272 (*Canadian Books in Print* 1971)
D. C. Heath Canada Ltd.	British	3,000 (including non-book materials)
Holt, Rinehart and Winston of Canada Limited	American	9,602 (including 2% non-book materials)
McClelland and Stewart Limited	Canadian	702 (*Canadian Books in Print* 1971)
McGraw-Hill Ryerson Limited	American	10,500-10,800 (including non-book materials)
Oxford University Press	British	18,000
Van Nostrand Reinhold Ltd.	American	4,520 (including non-book materials)

Note: Approximate figures for D. C. Heath Canada Ltd., Holt, Rinehart and Winston of Canada Limited, McGraw-Hill Ryerson Limited, Oxford University Press, and Van Nostrand Reinhold Ltd. were supplied on request by those companies.

by prospectuses which announce institutional adoptions earned by new college textbooks, and in countless other ways. Canadian book reviewers are bound to take imported books seriously. With so few reviewers and so many immigrant books, the wonder is not that original Canadian books are reviewed but that they receive as much time and space as they do. This question is examined further in Chapter 6.

The cost advantage enjoyed by the foreign publisher operating in Canada is as overwhelming as the economics of his advantage are easily explained. Fixed costs in book publishing are small in comparison with many other industries – but then so are the markets. A new title can be put out for a tiny fraction of what it costs to add a new product line in other enterprises, but in book publishing the proportion of fixed costs to variable costs in each unit produced is very much higher. In this sense, every new title corresponds to an additional line of inventory, and in proportion to its turnover the number of such inventory lines in publishing can be staggering. It may be misleading to convert sales figures into averages because they vary vastly for different kinds of books, but more often than not original editorial, typesetting, and design costs of upwards of ten thousand dollars must be written off over sales of three, four, or five thousand copies. Obviously, availability of a continental or international market can reduce these unit costs significantly. But if all the output must be disposed of in a national market as small as the Canadian one, the unit costs will inevitably be higher, sometimes uncompetitively so.

A reduction in unit costs makes a lower unit selling price possible, although in publishing the saving may not be passed on to the consumer quite so directly. The nature of the industry is such that expansion of gross sales often depends on the speed with which it is possible to expand the lines carried, i.e. the number of titles in a given list. This does not always happen; an encyclopedia publisher may diversify his enterprises by entering other fields than book publishing, instead of expanding the actual number of books he publishes. But in most publishing situations, expansion means constantly adding titles, allowing slow-sellers to go out of print if necessary, all with a view to exerting a stronger and stronger influence in the market-place and to increasing profitability through what is essentially the same selling organization – the latter expanded perhaps, but not in proportion to increasing sales. This is an extremely capital-intensive procedure, one which cannot very well be carried out on a small scale in a purely regional market. Thus a Canadian-owned publisher, issuing Canadian books only and for the Canadian market primarily, can hardly hope to generate enough working capital to permit large-scale healthy expansion of his book publishing program in the face of foreign or foreign-owned competition which is largely based on run-on costs of editions first published abroad.

Canadian executives of foreign-owned publishing firms in Canada have been heard to say that publishing is a business which can be begun with less capital than most enterprises. There is truth in this, because publishing is composed of as many product lines as there are titles, and additional capital goes into expanding the number of titles rather than into seeking economies by printing longer runs. Thus it is not difficult to buy a small piece of the action. But this does not mean that it is easy to sustain an unwarranted level of expansion. In fact, as we shall see later, the small publisher – who may on occasion deserve the epithet of dilettante – sometimes seems to be able to afford almost anything except sudden success. That is to say, he may be able to survive publishing up to half a dozen books a year, but as soon as he expands his list to ten or fifteen new titles per season he incurs increased costs for order processing, invoicing, accounting, warehousing, and shipping, and these costs are likely to be disproportionate to his previous fixed overheads. This is because he can no longer provide the services personally, or perhaps at artificially low real wages paid to other members of his family or to an equally dedicated partner, and he cannot borrow the working capital he needs to support his growing inventories – however realistic his depreciation policy may be. When he has to go out and hire help in the market-place, he may discover for the first time that he cannot afford to do so. Book publishing does not require as much capital to enter as do other lines of enterprises. But it is a capital-intensive business from first to last.

No doubt the foreign subsidiary enjoys some advantages in available marketing expertise, too, although these are sometimes exaggerated. It is easy to overlook the fact that the largest and strongest foreign subsidiaries in Canadian publishing are, with one or two exceptions, managed by Canadian executives. These Canadians served their apprenticeship mainly in Canadian publishing. The answers to our questions in the hearings confirm that many subsidiaries enjoy a considerable degree of editorial autonomy, although there may be exceptions. When Mr. Campbell Hughes, President of Van Nostrand Reinhold Limited (a recently established Canadian subsidiary of Litton Educational Publishing Inc. of New York), was before us, we asked him specifically where the decision to publish a Canadian book was made – a question that we addressed to others as well. Mr. Hughes' reply is interesting:

> In fact, what happens in our particular organization is that we are really sharing a computer service, a discount flow analysis of what is going to happen to money that is placed or invested in a book ... The computer happens not to be in the parent company but they have the contract through which this service is obtained. We submit certain figures arranged in a way that makes very little sense to me except that we fill in certain boxes. This is fed into a computer and it comes back telling me precisely how long the break-even point is away ...

The decision to publish, even in the United States, may still be made with more of a wet finger in the wind than the above procedure would suggest, but it does point to interesting developments in the future.

Some publishers, notably those who cultivate international markets, support some institutional advertising programs aimed at strengthening their corporate image. Nevertheless, most of the advertising dollar in book publishing everywhere is spent directly to obtain sales. And whether it is or not, all promotional costs must be recouped from the gross margin on sales. Thus, on a title-by-title basis, the foreign subsidiary in this country cannot justify spending much more on advertising original Canadian works than can the indigenous publisher. On such books, manufacturing and promotional costs will be much the same for both. We have seen little evidence that foreign firms, staffed and operated as they normally are by Canadians trained in Canadian publishing, have any expertise in advertising which is not shared by Canadian firms. If they have, they must acquire it by coincidence, not by importation.

Where the subsidiary often does surpass the Canadian firm, however, is in the size and sophistication of its sales organization. But even this distinction is not wholly valid, as the comparison is itself unsound. The great majority of Canadian book publishers are at an early stage in their development. No foreign publisher would think of opening a branch in Canada with sales and resources as small as those of the average Canadian house. History has shown that until his business in Canada has been established at a considerable level, it pays him to let someone else assume his sales promotion and order fulfilment responsibilities – usually a publisher-agent, as we have seen. Thus a large foreign publisher who has opened a branch in Canada may employ several dozen representatives in various parts of the country, while some of the smaller independent Canadian publishers still cannot afford a single full-time salesman. The difference is to be explained by economies of scale available to the subsidiary with the longer list and the resulting larger sales volume, not to lack of adventuresomeness on the part of the small Canadian houses. After all, McClelland and Stewart has a large sales force, too.

On the other hand, the branch publisher in Canada usually (although not always) has access to cheaper operating capital than does his Canadian competitor. The capital may be borrowed locally, but the parent firm's credit (and often the parent firm's guarantee as well) will ensure a comparatively favourable interest rate, even when rates are as high as they have been in recent years. This places Canadian-owned publishers under a distinct disability in this capital-intensive industry, for reasons which we discussed in our Third Interim Report (see Appendix). That report noted that Canadian book publishers are normally unable to borrow from commercial lending institutions on the collateral of the unsold but saleable portion of their inventories of publications. Foreign subsidiaries, however, can often secure guarantees from their parent companies, making possible not only bank loans but loans on relatively favourable terms. Our Third Interim Report recommended a procedure whereby this comparative disability could be offset through a system of government guarantees of bank loans and partial subsidy of interest costs, to be available to Canadian-owned, Ontario-based book publishers only. The report, the main provisions of which have already been implemented by the Government, included a set of guidelines designed to minimize cost and provide maximum security to the public in connection with these loans. These guidelines have since become part of the loan-guarantee application procedures which this Commission was requested to administer during the initial stages of the program.

Another respect in which Canadian publishers operate at a disadvantage in comparison with foreign publishers is not so much related to foreign subsidiaries as such. It has to do with the right to share (with the author) in income from subsidiary rights, including the revenues that may sometimes come from book club adoptions and movie and television adaptations. Canadian publishers' contracts normally do provide for such participation, but in practice the licensing of rights is likely to yield modest and irregular revenues at best, perhaps from Canadian television and radio services. The author with an established international reputation will usually have a separate New York contract, and just possibly a British one as well. In such cases, any publisher-sharing of the proceeds from Hollywood or major network rights will be spelled out in these foreign agreements, not in the Canadian one.

Sometimes the Canadian publisher's contract will not be with the Canadian author directly anyway; instead he will become the Canadian licensee under an agreement with the foreign publisher usually American. In this way the royalty he pays on his sales to the primary publisher abroad becomes itself a kind of subsidiary income which the latter shares with the author. His licence to publish the work in Canada may preclude his sharing in American book club rights, even though he may have to contend with the competition posed by many thousands of copies of such a club edition being mailed to Canadian members. In ways such as these, the Canadian publisher's sources of revenue are limited while his unit costs are sharply increased in comparison with those of foreign publishers issuing similar kinds of books.

The economies of scale available to the foreign subsidiary have, surprisingly, not been pursued by Canadian-owned firms even as far as they might have been. This failure on the part of Canadian publishers is noticeable in two areas at least. First, even established Canadian publishers, with sales of, say, more than $500,000 (of whom very few remain), have not up to this time succeeded in broadening their market base by developing significant markets for their books abroad. There are isolated exceptions (one is compelled to mention the scholarly publishers, all but one of whom is smaller than the figure mentioned, who do export an important proportion of their books), but the average Canadian author must either be sufficiently popular internationally to be able to command a separate contract with a foreign publisher, or remain virtually undistributed outside his own country.

There is another underdeveloped area in Canadian publishing, represented by the smaller, and usually more recent, independent houses including such imprints as Anansi, New Press, Oberon, Sono Nis, Fiddlehead Books, and others. Many of these firms have up to this time specialized in the most limited, least remunerative, and in many ways the most difficult markets to promote of all, namely fiction, poetry, and occasionally even drama. Not that these fields are without value to this country; it would be difficult to name any of greater cultural importance. But some of these firms are, administratively anyway, at so early a stage of evolution that they can hardly afford the luxury of expanded sales; as has been explained, they can draw on no more free or underpaid labour to provide the additional service that more orders and more customers require. Several of these publishers have issued important non-fiction works, frequently concerned with current social issues, but few have published any Canadian schoolbooks up to this time. It may sound paradoxical, but this situation may change automatically. As we shall see in Chapter 5, the transformation of schoolbook publishing now occurring suggests that the classroom may absorb, in part at least, what these houses are already publishing, and they may become schoolbook publishers by accident rather than intention.

Export sales and schoolbook sales, then, are two areas which Canadian book publishers have left underdeveloped until now. Export sales of course do not particularly concern the foreign subsidiary in Canada; his parent house has shown itself sufficiently interested in these already, or he would not be here. He may offer, indeed he may exaggerate, the international marketing services available from his home office on behalf of prospective Canadian authors; the latter's consequent decision to publish with an American or British house may reflect an undue optimism regarding the export sales that will follow. In fact, publishers abroad will tend to take about the same speculative interest in new Canadian books whether the latter are sold to them by an independent publisher here or by their Canadian subsidiaries. And there is no good economic or publishing reason why it should be otherwise.

THE SUBSIDIARY AS PUBLISHER AND AS AGENT

It is sometimes forgotten that if the subsidiary were not here to act as agent for his parent company's books, someone else would be selling them anyway. The Canadian reading public expects to have access to the books it wants, and it will not readily be denied the right to read those of foreign origin – which means now and in the future the great majority of all books in English. Canadian book consumers will always want to be able to read the best-known fiction and non-fiction, and will require a broad range of other books as well for special purposes, including college and university courses.

If foreign books are going to come into this country anyway (and short of some kind of intolerable censorship this is going to happen) our concern regarding the ownership of publishing houses in this country can be focussed a little more sharply. It becomes a concern for the quality of service rendered by publishers to the creative authors of Canada, and for the impact of the competition by foreign subsidiaries on indigenous publishing enterprises. There may be areas, of course, where the national origin of books used and read may be controlled, as in the case of schoolbooks purchased with public funds. What has been done and may reasonably be done in the future to make Canadian authorship and manufacture a condition of such purchase will also be discussed later in this report. But how well is the foreign subsidiary supporting Canadian authorship, and to what extent does his presence in this country impair the Canadian-owned publisher's ability to do so?

In the first place, there are several Canadian-owned publisher-agents the amount of whose original Canadian publishing in recent years falls far short of that of the average foreign subsidiary. Some of the former enjoy very substantial sales, but almost wholly in books they import from abroad. As noted earlier, these firms include some of the Canadian publishers who stayed well in the background during the hearings of the Commission. If there is any validity in the argument that agency publishing helps to sustain original Canadian publishing, companies such as these do nothing to support it. Many of the books they sell in the course of their importing business may have cultural value, but they themselves make almost no creative contribution to the Canadian publishing scene. How could they, when they have no editors or designers or book production persons on their staffs? If there is an indigenous publishing industry worthy of public concern and possibly of some measure of public support, the so-called publisher who imports but does not publish can claim assistance as a publisher only as a freeloader. Under its terms of reference, this Commission can have no special concern for his welfare, a point to which we shall return later.

Slightly more than half of the English-language book publishers in the country when this Commission was appointed were principally Canadian-owned. But the ratio is misleading because it does not reflect the proportionate volume of sales of Canadian and non-Canadian firms, nor even their relative activity as publishers of original Canadian books.

This Commission was appointed at the end of 1970. The accompanying chart shows the output of new Canadian books published in that year by 40 members of the Canadian Book Publishers' Council and by 17 publishers who became charter members only of the Independent Publishers' Association when the latter was founded in 1971 (disregarding IPA members who continued also as members of the CBPC). It also indicates the subject classifications of the titles issued by each. The firms whose principal ownership is counted as Canadian (for the purpose of this comparison only) are marked by an asterisk. Thus 345 of 631 Canadian books were published by Canadian-owned firms (140 of these by only two houses). But 286 original Canadian works were published by firms controlled (at the end of 1970) either in Britain or the United States. This was a formidable contribution to Canadian publishing by non-Canadian publishers; indeed, as a percentage of dollar sales it is substantially higher than these figures indicate. It is a disservice either to deprecate it or overlook it, both of which some critics would have us do.

The relative activity of foreign- and Canadian-owned publishers differs somewhat from the above pattern when one compares their outputs in Canadian literature, including fiction, poetry, and criticism. Only 46 of 170 new Canadian books in this category were published by non-Canadian firms in 1970, an output that is smaller proportionately than the latter's share of the total number of new Canadian books, but a respectable contribution nonetheless.

This contribution to Canadian publishing by foreign subsidiaries appears smaller still if only works of fiction and poetry are counted – "works of the imagination" as they are sometimes described. The fact is that, with the exception of Macmillan and to a lesser extent Oxford University Press, almost all Canadian creative writing of book length in these fields is being issued by the wholly Canadian publishing houses. By doing this they stimulate more writing of the same kind, and thereby provide a valuable cultural service to the Canadian community. That foreign subsidiaries (as well as many other Canadian firms) do not participate actively in this kind of publishing does not indicate their anti-Canadianism so much as their

CANADIAN PUBLISHERS AND CANADIAN PUBLISHING – CANADIAN BOOK PUBLISHERS' COUNCIL
Subject Classification (Dewey decimal classes)

Company	No. of new Canadian books published in 1970	General-ities	Philosophy Religion	Social Science	Language	Pure Science	Technology Arts	Literature & Rhetoric	General Geography & History
Abelard-Schuman (Canada) Ltd.	0								
Addison-Wesley (Canada) Ltd.	1						1		
Allen & Son Ltd., Thomas*	0								
Bellhaven House Ltd.*	15			3		3		1	8
Book Society of Canada Ltd., The*	2	1				1			
Burns & MacEachern Ltd.*	2								2
Clarke, Irwin & Co. Ltd.*	28			2		1	4	4	17
Collier-Macmillan Canada Ltd.	2				2				
Collins Sons & Co., William	1	1							
Copp Clark Publishing Co., The	31	1		2	2	12		9	5
Dent & Sons (Canada) Ltd., J.M.	9	1		5				1	2
Doubleday Canada Ltd.	2	1						1	
Encyclopaedia Britannica Publications Ltd.	0								
Fitzhenry & Whiteside Ltd.*	0								
Gage Educational Publishing Ltd.	78			8	41	4	4		21
General Publishing Co. Ltd.*	1						1		
Ginn & Co. Educational Publishers	11			6		1			4
Griffin House*	2	1						1	
Heath Canada Ltd., D.C.	0								
Holt, Rinehart & Winston of Canada Ltd.	13	1		5	3	2	1		1
Longman Canada Ltd.	13			2	1			9	
Macmillan Co. of Canada Ltd., The	39		1	4		3	1	16	13
McClelland & Stewart Ltd.*	71	6	1	8		2	2	25	25
McGill-Queen's University Press*	6			2				3	1
McGraw-Hill Co. of Canada Ltd.	57	2		15	6	3	22	3	5
McLeod Ltd., George J.*	1	1							
Methuen Publications	6	1		1		1		1	2
Nelson, Foster & Scott Ltd.*	0								
Nelson & Sons Canada Ltd., Thomas*	25		2	12		6		4	1
Oxford University Press, Canadian Branch	5							3	2
Palm Publishers Ltd.*	0								

Pitman, Canada Ltd. Sir Isaac	1						
Prentice–Hall of Canada Ltd.	10	2		3	1	1	1	2
Random House of Canada Ltd.	7		1	3			2	1
Saunders Co. Canada Ltd., W.B.	0							
Scholastic Tab Publications Ltd.	0							
Science Research Associates (Canada) Ltd.	0							
University of Toronto Press★	69	8	2	24	1	7	3	1	10	13
Van Nostrand Reinhold Ltd.	0							
Wiley & Sons Canada Ltd., John	0							
Total	508	27	7	105	57	46	36	10	94	125

★Counted as Canadian-owned

THE QUESTION OF OWNERSHIP   61

CANADIAN PUBLISHERS AND CANADIAN PUBLISHING – INDEPENDENT PUBLISHERS' ASSOCIATION
Subject Classification (Dewey decimal classes)

Company	No. of new Canadian books published in 1970	General-ities	Philosophy Religion	Social Science	Language	Pure Science	Technology Arts	Literature & Rhetoric	General Geography & History
Book Society of Canada Ltd., The*†									
Burns & MacEachern Ltd.*†									
Clarke, Irwin & Co. Ltd.*†									
Delta Canada*	9	1						8	
Fiddlehead Books*	21							21	
Frontier Publishing*	2							1	1
General Publishing Co. Ltd.*†									
Griffin House*†									
Harvest House*	4			2				1	1
House of Anansi Press Ltd.*	13			3				10	
M. G. Hurtig Ltd.*	14	2		1				4	7
Ingluvin Publications*	0								
James Lewis & Samuel Publishers*	8			8					
Ladysmith Press*	6							6	
Learning Concepts*	0								
Peter Martin & Associates*	6	1		2				1	2
New Press*	21	2		12				7	
Oberon Press*	6	1						5	
Progress Books*	2			1				1	
Talon Books*	5							5	
Tundra Books of Montreal*	0								
University of Toronto Press*†									
Weedflower Press*	6							6	
Total	123	7		29				76	11

*Counted as Canadian-owned
†See under Canadian Book Publishers' Council

commercial realism. Regional fiction and poetry are simply not attractive domains to the business-oriented publisher. For the latter, apparently, Canadian literature suffers all the commercial drawbacks of regional literature.

CREATIVE CRITICISM IN PUBLISHING HOUSES

Even if the publishing of fiction and poetry is poor business – and there is convincing economic evidence that it usually is – it provides more than a mere outlet for creative authorship. It also contributes to the development of a critical editorial capacity in the publishing industry – an ability to discriminate, to select, to advise, and to encourage Canadian novelists and poets. The authors who are most often helped in this way are the young, pliable writers, among whom one can confidently assume must be at least some of the important Canadian literary figures of tomorrow. This particular kind of editorial ability is needed in every literary community in the world, but is especially important in ones which do not have the inspiration of a national literature developed over centuries. Canada is a young country in this sense, and an indigenous body of competent creative editors can be one of its greatest cultural assets; the same could be said, of course, for most of the world's new countries, many of them so much younger than our own.

But there is no reason to assume because a firm publishes fiction or poetry, much less because it is small (and unbusinesslike perhaps), that it therefore automatically possesses this critical editorial competence, or that it ever will. This conclusion is jumped to rather often, sometimes with an enthusiasm that attributes to the smaller independent presses a quality of publishing judgment that surpasses that of much larger and longer established houses, including all publishers who are owned abroad. This is faulty reasoning, but one hears and reads it often enough, and from sufficiently responsible quarters, to justify our mentioning it here. In point of fact, among all the small independent Canadian publishers there are perhaps two or three editors who can be compared with the very best in the industry, and because they are publishing kinds of creative literature that most of the older publishers do not, they can rightly be called Canadian literature's hope of the future.

One of the reasons that this creative and critical editorial competence does not yet exist more widely in Canada is that it cannot flourish in houses where the publishing parameters require that every undertaking must be planned to be profitable, and where the manuscripts to struggle hardest for are those which hold the greatest prospect of being profitable. This could present an even greater dilemma were it not for an unusual feature that distinguishes publishing from most other businesses, mentioned early in this chapter. Book publishing is a business only up to a certain point, and what holds many of the best people in it is the fact that they are able to produce at least some works for the sole reason that they are ones which they believe deserve to be produced. This can be seen most clearly in the original publishing programs of such houses as Clarke, Irwin and Macmillan – the latter admittedly a foreign-owned firm. It was certainly true of McClelland and Stewart and Ryerson Press twenty years ago, and still holds – although possibly with less force – for the former. The kind of deserving authorship referred to here does not include every work that loses money – most publishers have too many books of the latter kind on their lists anyway. Rather it means those books which were originally selected in full awareness that they could not possibly pay their costs, and nevertheless were edited with the same care and produced with as much taste as though they were destined to be best sellers.

With due regard for at least one exception just mentioned, most foreign subsidiaries in Canada base their decisions to publish primarily on profitability. This is not an offence in itself, at least not under our economic system, and while adhering to their policy most such houses issue a good many works of Canadian authorship, as we have seen. And no doubt they lose money on many of them, albeit unintentionally. But they tend to publish few original creative works of fiction, poetry, drama, or criticism except in the course of their textbook programs. The subsidiaries may be correct in claiming that they are good corporate citizens; in some respects they may be too successful as corporate citizens. Perhaps it is because they are so business-minded, and because Canadian-owned firms are often less so, that the latter are experiencing a struggle for survival at this time. This is a considerable over-simplification of what is happening, no doubt. But at least some subsidiaries could broaden their programs in the public interest and most of the Canadian firms could render theirs a little more realistic. We are inclined to answer the subsidiaries' claim that they would publish still more Canadiana if good manuscripts were available by asking what constitutes a good manuscript. Our impression is that good is synonymous with saleable in this context. One can argue that it should be, we suppose.

REPATRIATION OF CANADIAN PUBLISHING

It has sometimes been proposed that book publishing should be declared a key industry and that over a limited period of time foreign-owned publishing firms should be required to restructure their ownership so as to place majority control in Canadian hands. Occasionally it has been suggested that ninety or even one hundred per cent of equity stock should be Canadian-held, although this has been the extreme view. No doubt legislation could be recommended that would impose conditions of Canadian ownership in some way, but the legislation would be difficult to implement and even more difficult to sustain.

A publisher's real stock in trade is found not in his physical inventory of books, as might readily be supposed, but in the copyright assignments and licences which permit him to produce and sell his books. If he were forced to leave the country, his copyrights would go with him. Indeed, most of a foreign subsidiary's copyrights (whether he owns them or licenses them) are administered by virtue of contracts between the writers who wrote them and his parent house, whether the latter is in Britain or the United States or somewhere else. His books are going to be in demand in Canada whether he is here as a corporate subsidiary to sell them or whether he is not. No practical legislation, and certainly no legislation that is culturally sound, is going to keep our the Hemingways and Steinbecks and Barzuns and Maughams – or any of thousands of other best-selling authors – just because their copyrights have not been assigned or licensed to Canadian-owned publishers. And any move to expropriate foreign-owned copyrights would isolate Canadian publishing permanently from the world markets it so badly needs. Only one part of the price would be the need for Canada to denounce her international copyright commitments. The importance of these will be reviewed in Chapter 3.

It will be urged that enforced Canadianization of publishing firms would not be designed to keep out good literature, but if it didn't – and it is unthinkable that it should try to – what would be gained? Some freedom from competition locally, perhaps, but would that enhance the quality of publishing in this country? One thing that would then be lost would be very large numbers of Canadian books by Canadian authors now being published by the foreign subsidiaries who operate here. Again it might be said that these could be published by Canadian-owned houses, but what is to prevent this happening now? The preference of some authors?

Only a smallish proportion of Canadian manuscripts issued by the subsidiaries are of the kind that come in "over the transom," i.e. many Canadian books would never have been written at all without the planning and persuasion that first came from their publishers. As noted earlier, a large part of the Canadian publishing done by foreign firms here is intended to be the kind that they think people want to buy rather than just the kind that authors want to write. It is difficult to see what national benefit would accrue if such Canadian books were never conceived at all – as most of them would not be if the firms who publish them were ostracized.

The argument in favour of enforced Canadianization of foreign-owned publishers in Canada has several facets, just as it has been advanced by persons of several widely different political and economic ideas. Even if not always frankly admitted, an anti-American political bias sometimes underlies the enthusiasm for emasculating the subsidiaries, although certainly not always. Some critics of the American presence relate book publishing to the rest of the communications industry, pointing out that foreign acquisition of radio, television, and newspaper publishing (to say nothing of banking) has been effectively halted and that the ownership of book publishing should be brought under equally stringent control. There can be no question that books and ideas are synonymous, but there is a vast difference between books and the other communications media. The number of radio frequencies and television channels available is severely limited for technological reasons. And the economics of newspaper publishing are weighted heavily in favour of the established enterprise with a mass distribution, with the result that foreign control of the latter would virtually mean foreign monopoly over news reporting and opinion making without the need to heed domestic competition, because there would be none. But the number of books that can be published is always completely flexible, dependent only on there being authors to write them, readers to buy them, and publishers to issue them. And books do not produce the cumulative bias that can be inculcated by the editorial policy of a single newspaper, because so long as there is complete freedom to publish there will also be freedom to read. Thus there will be a cross-section of points of view in the books available on every subject.

Of course it would be short-sighted to suppose that ownership of publishing houses in Canada is of no cultural consequence at all to our community. The dangers of foreign domination can be seen most easily in educational publishing, although they could be pointed to in other areas as well. It hardly seems necessary to argue that the history of our own country in relation to North America and the world should be presented from the perspective of the Canadian tradition. This is not to say that our schoolbooks should inculcate anti-Americanism, nor that they should preach an unreasoning kind of Canadian patriotism which could confound their readers in later years. In the social sciences, at every level of the curriculum, the issue is rather easily resolved in favour of the Canadian-written and Canadian-structured book. It is less clear in some other subject areas, such as the natural sciences. This question will be discussed further in Chapter 6, but what must be noted here is that we are considering two separate issues which are often confused. One is the question of ownership of publishing houses in Canada, the other is the question of authorship and point of view in the books published. *It is the distinction between Canadian publishers and Canadian publishing.* The importance of this distinction we have tried to highlight in the title of this report.

Canadian ownership of a publishing house will not of itself deter the house from seeking to adapt foreign-developed and foreign-owned copyrights if the latter can be made attractive to its customers. As was noted in Chapter 1, when Ontario adopted its first primary reader that had a "modern look," it adapted an American reader which the then Canadian firm of Copp Clark republished. And it was an American subsidiary that led publishers into original Canadian publishing of modern primary readers. A very large number of schoolbooks at every level were borrowed from abroad and reproduced in "Canadianized" editions both before and after that time, although in recent years the official policy in this province has been to exclude foreign-born books as far as possible.

On the other hand, we must ask ourselves precisely why foreign-owned publishers have been as active as they have been in issuing Canadian-written and Canadian-produced books in this country. Several reasons can be given, all with some bearing on this question of ownership. The obvious importance of being able to offer texts in Canadian history, geography, and related fields by Canadian authors, gives the development of projects of this kind a high priority for foreign firms opening here. But much more important has been the effect of the Ontario Department of Education's policy of preference for Canadian materials in Circular 14; Canadian authorship and manufacture have been for a number of years a virtual condition of such listings. No doubt this fact has been a commercial frustration for many subsidiaries, whose market for imported educational books has been seriously restricted by the Ontario policy. However, most of these houses have had reasonably free access to curricula in other provinces, which have put somewhat less stock in the importance of excluding useful foreign materials. We explored the attitudes of other provinces on this question of Canadian authorship in the course of visits across the country, and were repeatedly assured that content and presentation should take precedence over the nationality of the author. This pedagogical principle held some appeal for us, too, but its implications for a Canadian-owned and Canadian-oriented publishing industry did not. In the end we became convinced that the policy of Canadian preference pursued in recent years by the Ontario Department of Education is sound and that, if necessary exceptions are admitted, it is compatible with the best interests of those whom education is expected to serve.

THE COLLEGE AND UNIVERSITY LEVEL

Those firms that have college departments (as most educational houses now have) have been able to promote university textbooks without much concern for either their authors' nationality or their own. At the same time the Canadian university market has expanded to a point at which many publishers (foreign-owned or not) can afford to issue specially edited Canadian college reference works on occasion, in particular those composed of collected readings. Moreover, the subsidiaries have been able to couple with their university promotional travelling a vigorous editorial scouting activity on behalf of their parent houses, signing up hundreds of instructors at Canadian universities and colleges to write or edit books for publication abroad, usually in New York.

The result is that a very substantial marketing capability by foreign-owned firms in this country has been developing for a number of years, especially at the college level. In very recent times this has led to pressures and reactions to pressures which bear on the issues that face other kinds of Canadian book publishing today. Certainly at the university level, there has been foreign domination of the market (meaning American domination for the most part) for several decades. Only in recent times has it become economically feasible to produce original Canadian university textbooks at all, because the domestic market has been too small and is still too small in most subject areas. (It is one thing to bring out an anthology of readings in sociology for freshman use in Canada only, and quite another to develop a basic textbook in medicine, engineering, or even international affairs without access to a continental or world market.)

The shortage of Canadian academics qualified to fill the expanded faculties has lately forced the importation of instructors from abroad in substantial numbers, resulting in an imbalance which many administrators insist is unavoidable and likely to be temporary. But these visiting instructors naturally tend to turn to the textbooks and reference works they know best, prescribing them for the undergraduate courses which they give. Where such books demonstrate by their contents their authors' profound unawareness of both the Canadian scene and tradition, national emotions are understandably aroused among those who read or even hear about them. Thus there arise counter-offensives which have occupied newspaper columns, books, public meetings, and even investigations in recent times. This question is referred to again in later chapters of this report.

The easy availability of American college textbooks and reference works, vigorously promoted and eagerly adapted to every general university need, is not offset by alternative publishing done by the Canadian-owned firms that do exist. Not that there is a lack of publishing of academic research by the scholarly presses of Canada, but even this tends to be mined for inclusion in bits and pieces in the anthologies and collected readings offered by the college textbook publishers, mostly foreign, whenever a market is large enough to support a special Canadian edition. The fact is that the foreign firms enjoy a marketing momentum (based on the imported books of their parent firms) to which no Canadian-owned firm can hope to aspire, at the university level at least. What the latter would need in order to do so would be more than additional capital; they would also have to find additional markets.

Another pressure resulting from the operation of the subsidiaries at the elementary and high school levels has been for the modification or elimination of the Canadian preference policy in the Ontario Department of Education's listings on Circular 14. No doubt such a demand would arise even if imported books for the elhi levels were being sold principally through Canadian publisher-agents, as most of them used to be. But the degree to which such a demand has been proving almost irresistible, at the school level if not at the departmental level, will be discussed in Chapter 5. It is also relevant, however, to the question of ownership of publishing houses in Canada.

IMPORTANCE OF RESIDUAL CANADIAN OWNERSHIP

The foreign subsidiary's presence in Canada, then, is necessarily motivated by profitability. If the market could be rendered equally profitable and secure to the parent company without its operating a branch plant here, it would close down its Canadian office even more quickly than it opened it. For the United States publisher at least, the Canadian market would then become part of the run-on continental market. This is a condition that could very well arise if original Canadian publishing diminished further in importance, for example through the disappearance of the last of the Canadian-owned houses of any size. Then there would be no original publishing done by Canadian houses, and soon there would be less reason for foreign subsidiaries to do much either.

Here, then, lies the danger of any further foreign takeovers or business failures among the remaining Canadian-owned publishers, especially the few that have extensive Canadian publishing programs. If existing Canadian houses can continue to flourish, so will the publishing of original Canadian books – by them and also by the foreign subsidiaries who compete with them. If they should vanish, many of the Canadian alternatives to imported trade and educational books would disappear with them, and there would be little compulsion on the subsidiaries to continue to be as active in fostering domestic writing as they have been in the past. The pressures on the Ontario Department of Education to set aside its traditional Canadian preference policy would become almost irresistible, for there would be scarcely a publisher who would have business reasons to speak out in its defence.

Another serious consequence of the total disappearance of Canadian control of publishing in this country would be that certain kinds of books might not be published anywhere – inside or outside the country – in the future. For even though book publishers do not try to disseminate their own ideas through the books they issue in the same way that newspaper publishers do, it is fair to ask who – other than Canadian-owned publishers – will foster the books that will report the discussions of ownership that gave rise to this Commission, say, or that will spearhead whatever campaigns may be mounted in the future on behalf of Canadian cultural or economic nationalism. It is not necessary to be an ultra-nationalist to say that this country must always possess a publishing facility which is prepared to present, and promote if necessary, every point of view on such basic issues. A short catalogue of some of the more outspoken works on behalf of Canadian national interests published in recent years will demonstrate the point: *The New Romans; What Culture? What Heritage?; The Struggle for Canadian Universities; Gordon to Watkins to You; Close the Forty-Ninth Parallel etc.; Read Canadian; An Independent Foreign Policy for Canada?; The Wretched of Canada.* Not one of these books was issued by a foreign-owned publishing house. How many of them would have been published had there been no Canadian-owned publishers? How many of them would have been left unwritten, in such circumstances?

PARALLEL SITUATIONS ABROAD

We were interested from the outset in the possibility that other lands than Canada might have experienced foreign competition from larger and older publishing industries than their own, presumably located in countries with which they, too, have had close ties of language and culture if not of common history. We were not disappointed, although the applicability of such evidence to the Canadian situation is sometimes unclear. We were told of the influence that Paris houses have had on publishing in Geneva and Brussels, for example. Although both Switzerland and Belgium continue to have their indigenous publishing industries, important footholds have been gained by French publishers in both these countries either by acquisition of existing enterprises or by the opening and development of their own branch plants. In both these communities, with their large but not exclusively French-speaking populations, the penetration of French authors in Parisian editions has been substantial at all levels of book users, and understandably so. The impact of French publishers on the publishing industry in Quebec has had unusually interesting ramifications in recent times, and is dealt with in some detail by André Vachon and Georges Laberge in their background paper on the new *politique du livre* in that province, already published by the Commission.

The Scottish experience in recent years has not been dissimilar to that in English-speaking Canada, although the process seems to have gone farther there than here. A number of important, long-established Scottish houses – the two best known perhaps being Oliver and Boyd and Thomas Nelson – have been taken over by English firms so that now only a very few independent Scottish publishers remain. (Whether Nelson should be classed as an English or a Canadian house is an interesting question itself; the Commission received evidence that its majority control is now in the hands of members of Lord Thomson's family, who retain Canadian citizenship.) We were told that, although it is neither so articulate nor so widely shared as in Canada, concern is growing in Scotland about the future of publishing in that country and the implications for Scottish culture and society of its apparently imminent demise.

The problem is complicated by the status of Scotland in the United Kingdom. On the one hand, Scotland has a tradition and society clearly distinct from the rest of Britain and administers its own internal affairs – education, law, municipal government, etc. – separately. On the other, the country lacks the legislative autonomy which would enable it to take independent action on such an issue if it desired to do so. The recurring movement for some degree of political independence seems to be ebbing at the moment and most Scotsmen are ambivalent on the question. Nonetheless, on the problem of Scottish publishing, a strong feeling seems to exist that something should be done to preserve an independent Scottish publishing industry.

Views about how this should be accomplished vary considerably. Some Scottish publishers believe that their salvation lies in exploiting the distinctive qualities of their region, in authors as well as subjects, and in aiming to penetrate the metropolitan market selectively and systematically. The Scottish publisher, it should be noted, has readier access to an audience in England than the Canadian publisher has to a market in the United States. But it is significant also, as one Scottish publisher pointed out, that two of the most prolific and successful Scottish authors of the past twenty years, John Prebble and Gavin Maxwell, have both been published by English houses.

The other Scottish view is that government initiative and support can and must be used to ensure the survival and development of an independent publishing industry, but that this support must be provided on a different basis than in the past. The tradition has been for the government, through Arts Council grants and the like, to furnish support directly to individual authors. Too often such awards have gone to established authors, it is said, with no resulting effect on their careers. The Scottish publishers with whom we have been able to communicate seem to favour the provision of working capital to publishers in the form of grants, low interest loans, and the like. They point out that indigenous authorship would continue to be rewarded, possibly more generously overall, because such a stimulus would strengthen and ensure the survival of the Scottish publishing industry. One point on which the publishers consulted have been especially emphatic is that the government should limit its involvement to making decisions about the quality of publishing houses it might support (standards of management, past record, imaginative experimentations, etc.) and possibly, in some cases, the general class of book it might especially wish to encourage. Beyond that, decisions about particular authors and books, production details, marketing, and so on, should be left to the people best qualified to make them – the publishers.

George Ferguson's background paper on Australian publishing summarizes the recent history of foreign involvement in book publishing in that country. Prior to the 1950s, British publishers did not go beyond opening sales offices in Australia for the purpose of distributing their books, and remained generally aloof from regional publishing. Some of the American technical publishers had developed agency arrangements, but they, too, did little or no Australian publishing. But during the last twenty years, this situation began to change rapidly, and a number of Australian subsidiary corporations were established by both British and American houses. The Australian Book Publishers Association today has thus many of the cosmopolitan features of the Canadian Book Publishers' Council, being made up both of indigenous firms and of foreign subsidiaries who are in Australia to sell their parent companies' books as well as simultaneously to engage in original Australian publishing. The exclusive agency aspect of foreign book distribution in Australia has tended to work somewhat more efficiently than its Canadian counterpart because of the vast distance that had to be travelled by books being "bought around." Nevertheless there has been much seepage of orders, as agents like to describe it, from that country, too.

Australian publishing, like Canadian, is staffed in the main by nationals of the country, whether it is owned abroad or at home. This appears to be purely pragmatic policy on the part of the parent companies, where these are foreign. The interests of Australian publishing programs of overseas publishers tend to reflect their areas of specialization at home, but to make use of Australian authors. "It would be safe to say now," George Ferguson points out in his background paper, "that virtually all the books used in Australian primary and secondary schools are published in Australia by educational publishers or by the educational departments of general publishers, without much regard to the national ownership, but with regard to the publishing direction of each company."

DOES OWNERSHIP MATTER?

We have seen that there is likely to be a period following the immigration of a foreign publishing firm during which it will accommodate itself, often remarkably well, to the regional interests of the Canadian market. But this support of things Canadian can only be expected to endure so long as the requirements here remain special. During this period, the subsidiary is likely to count aloud its Canadian publishing projects (perhaps including "Canadianized" publications from its parent's list) and to profess – with absolute sincerity let it be emphasized – a desire to publish still more. "Nothing but unavailability of publishable manuscripts holds us back," paraphrases a remark that is sometimes heard. But at the same time it is likely to be boosting at every opportunity the editorial bargains that could be available if there only were a wider use made of foreign copyrights, particularly in Ontario, where Canadian preference has been strongest. It will constantly allude to publications of its home office which embody research that "cost millions." And it is likely to decry any regulations designed to create a still more congenial market for the Canadian-written and Canadian-manufactured book, even though it publishes Canadian books itself. It is this negative attitude towards Canadian preference which some defenders of foreign-owned publishing houses who themselves are in other fields have either not been exposed to, or which they conveniently overlook.

Does it all really matter? Is it perhaps correct that the imported product is likely to be the better buy, in books as in so many other things? One listens to the marketing manager of a foreign publishing firm scoff in public at the thought of Canadians trying to develop a good atlas, for example, and implying that for the same reason that this is a futile ambition for our country, most other educational needs can also be more amply served by books imported from abroad. (His selection of atlases as a category of publishing beyond Canadian competence was unhappy, because a Canadian-edited, Canadian-designed, and Canadian-produced atlas recently won first prize for design at the Leipzig International Book Festival in competition with every kind of book from every other country in the world.)

Yes, ownership probably does matter, and matter a good deal. Not that there is a foreign conspiracy to put Canadian publishing down, for we have had no evidence of anything like that. But to reiterate a hypothetical situation that would have wide-ranging implications, let us suppose that Canadian-owned and Canadian-based publishing does go down the drain in the next few years. Where then will one read the objective accounts of this cultural tragedy, and of others of similar kind (written from the Canadian point of view, that is) in time to come? It is not likely to be a particularly attractive Canadian publishing project for those firms whose books will then dominate this market, and if it ever is written it is hardly likely to hold much interest for readers abroad. If our publishing programs become totally foreign-oriented, who will then be planning and publishing books and collections at the university level, for example, dealing with the impact of American economic domination of this country?

It is important to remember that today university courses tend to be inspired by books rather than merely to motivate the writing of textbooks as they did in the past. Where courses once resulted in books, today books often create courses. And undergraduates are today reading books on a scale unimagined fifteen, twenty, or thirty years ago in the universities. This achievement is confirmed subjectively by

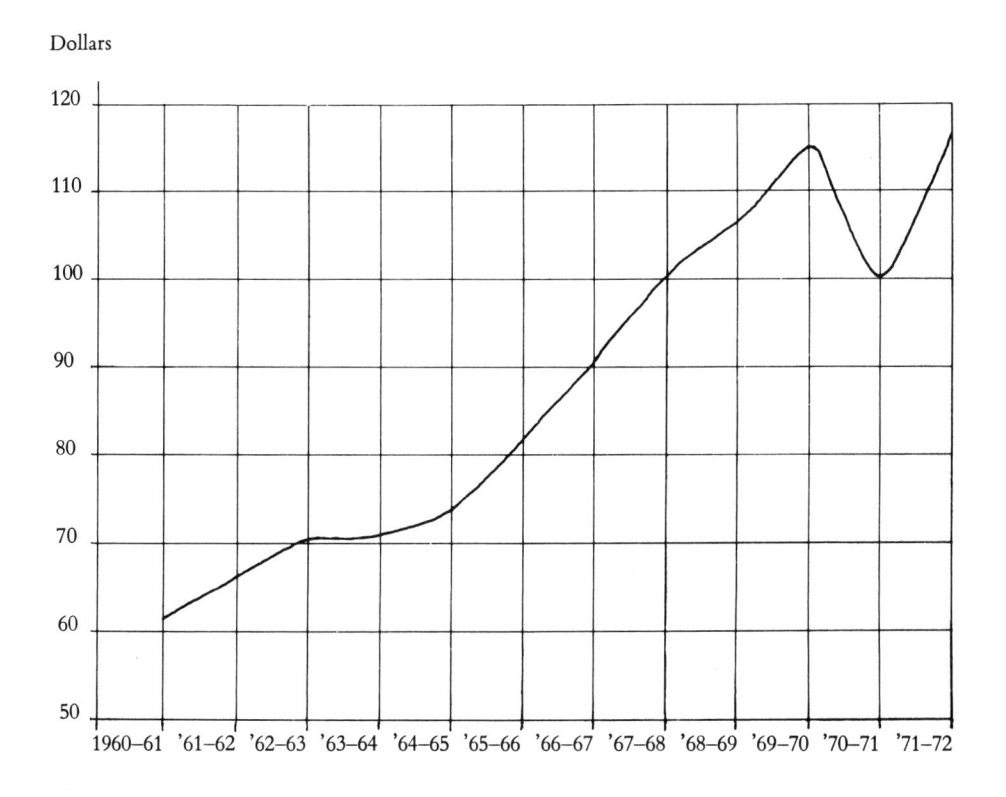

PER STUDENT TEXTBOOK EXPENDITURE AT UNIVERSITY OF TORONTO, 1960-72

almost every university administrator and instructor in a position to make the comparison, and it is supported by the sales statistics of college bookstores, even if corrected to reflect increased enrolments and higher prices. What kinds of books will these be in the future if they include no works published by firms with a completely Canadian commitment? What kinds of courses will be built upon those that are offered? And, one might add, what kinds of professors will be devising the courses?

The foreign branch plants can do good and will certainly do no harm so long as they pursue vigorous publishing programs in this country on behalf of Canadian writers. Indeed, they can help to upgrade every aspect of Canadian-owned publishing – editorial, design, and marketing. No harm at all will be done if Canadian publishers are kept on their toes in this way, and it is disingenuous therefore for the latter to call for a prohibition on Canadian publishing by foreign publishers. Canadian writers and readers have been well served in the past by the Canadian publishing programs of Macmillan, McGraw-Hill, Dent, and a number of other foreign firms which established branches here and gave leadership by originating regional publishing programs in this country. But at the point at which the branch plant seeks to substitute foreign editorial content for Canadian content, say in schoolbooks, when the latter exists or can reasonably be stimulated, it does a disservice to every creative person in this country. And it is guilty of a special kind of cultural genocide whenever it fails to reflect in its published materials that peculiar sense of common identity, be it political, historical, economic, or cultural, which is Canadian. It is Canadianism, probably more than anything else, which will be served if Canadian publishers are enabled to survive. And it is Canadianism which will suffer if they fail.

Although total domination of the Canadian publishing industry by foreign-owned firms is undesirable from the standpoint of our national culture, it should also be clear by now that it would not be realistic to aim at the suppression, enforced sale, or deportation of the subsidiaries. However, the interests of Canadian authors and readers would probably not be affected adversely by a requirement that the opening of new foreign-owned or foreign-controlled publishing enterprises in this province be approved in advance. It would be desirable if this requirement could be made nation-wide rather than province-wide, but action by the federal government would be necessary to accomplish this.

Before any such condition of approval is imposed, even at the provincial level, indeed before it can be formalized as a recommendation, it will be necessary to consider just how withholding approval could be made effective. The agency system of distribution can be resorted to by a firm that wishes to evade a requirement that it not open a branch plant without first receiving official approval. In all likelihood any firm strong enough to consider a branch operation is already effectively represented by an agent here. Would the withholding of approval to open in Canada prevent the appointment of a Canadian agent? Would it prevent the substitution of a new agency for an existing one? Would it distinguish between a foreign firm (*a*) opening on its own and (*b*) placing an agent under such stringent conditions that it could achieve virtual managerial control without owning a single share of voting stock? (The ways in which a major foreign publisher, or group of publishers, could dominate an agent here are numerous. They might include, in return for the appointment as agent, the right to nominate managers and supervisors, to approve marketing policies and sales budgets, and to determine discount and returns policies. The profits would be made on sales to the agency, with possibly greater security than there would be if a wholly owned subsidiary were set up. Here, then, are just a few of the complications awaiting the drafter of legislation or regulations on this unstable subject of ownership.)

Another question regarding such a possible control measure is the constitutional one. As we have said, it would be desirable if the requirement that approval be first sought were national rather than provincial, but this would demand federal legislation. Yet the province is not impotent in the matter by any means. After all, it funds a large proportion of the library and educational purchases made from publishers, and it can decide which orders should be eligible for financial assistance. We alluded to this provincial prerogative in our Third Interim Report. Nevertheless, acting without federal support, Ontario could not prevent the establishment of foreign publishers' branches elsewhere in Canada. It could only keep them from being established in this province, probably a dubious economic achievement to which to aspire. An embargo on new sales of Canadian-owned publishing enterprises to non-Canadians would be more important and we have already entered a specific recommendation in our Third Interim Report that further takeovers of this kind should not be allowed (see Appendix).

The freedom to read assumes freedom of access to books issued by foreign and multinational publishers. As we implied earlier it might be possible to force the branches of these firms to "go Canadian or leave," but it would not be practicable to force them to surrender their copyrights. Better far that they should publish Canadian books as well as their own than that they should get out of Canadian publishing and sell nothing but their own books here.

It must always be remembered that a foreign publisher's successful entry into the Canadian market is greatly facilitated by the backlist he has to offer for sale at the outset, i.e. he possesses copyrights to which Canadian readers wish to have access. Artificial restriction of the general public's access to such published works could constitute censorship, and we reiterate our opposition to the latter. But restricting an individual's right to select his own reading material is one thing. For the province to assume a responsibility for deciding what conditions relating to authorship and manufacture should be met by books whose purchase it is prepared to subsidize is altogether different, in our view. No more censorship is involved when a provincial authority – or a municipal or a school authority for that matter – exercises its delegated responsibility to approve or not to approve specific books according to their educational worth than when such authorities establish other broad parameters for their selection or exclusion. We see no conflict whatever in this with the all-important right of the individual to choose his own reading material. Even in the matter of textbooks and reference books, the reasonableness of this distinction is exemplified as one moves up through the educational system. The university student – more today than ever in the past – reads whatever books and articles are in his opinion most relevant to the course of study he is pursuing, and this is as it should be. But the high school pupil, and to a more marked degree the elementary school pupil, reads and makes his reading choices from books that have been selected for him by others. It is fatuous to suggest that school pupils are thereby victims of censorship.

We think that *the best way to serve the Canadian book publishing industry is to create a climate in this country conducive to more and better Canadian writing and more and better Canadian publishing*. If some of the latter is undertaken here by foreign-owned firms, no matter, provided that they help to upgrade both the quality of Canadian publishing and the demand for it. But what foreign-owned publishers must absolutely not be allowed to do is to encourage changes in the ground rules which would lead, however indirectly, to the reduction of domestic creativity in order to permit substitution of foreign products. It is one thing to deprive mature readers of access to any and every kind of reading material they may wish to have. It would be entirely different for us to shirk our responsibility to present our children with Canadian points of view on the widest possible range of subject-matter. To this end, they must have continuous access to a steady flow of new Canadian books by Canadian authors. No other kind of books can serve the same purpose.

One might expect that Ontario's long-standing preference for Canadian-written and Canadian-manufactured textbooks will, if continued, accomplish the objectives just mentioned. The problem is that this policy not only has had to contend with mounting opposition, but has apparently been widely circumvented in recent times. We shall return to a discussion of this question, which must be regarded as a crucial one, in Chapter 5. It is enough to say here that while our educational system has been developing its present admirable flexibility, the de facto displacement of Canadian textbooks in our schools by foreign learning materials of every kind has been proceeding apace. Canadian publishing has found itself under extreme practical disabilities even in the Ontario school system, and positive steps are required if it is to regain its former importance in the eyes of those whom it is intended to serve. If it cannot do this, Canadian publishers (whose original publications are almost exclusively Canadian) will disappear, and the non-Canadian publishers who remain will be more and more absorbed in marketing their home products.

Either indifference to the foreign presence in Canadian publishing on the one hand or an attitude of national extremism on the other can be detrimental to our cultural interests. What seems to be called for is a movement towards moderate cultural nationalism in book publishing. The instrument of this movement should be encouragement of Canadian publishers through a policy of public preference for books by Canadian authors, more or less without regard for the question of who publishes them. One of the purposes of this report, therefore, will be to propose a positive plan of support for Canadian books. Such a program of encouragement need not cost the taxpayer millions; some phases of it could be self-liquidating, some would demand a modest degree of pump-priming, and others might require limited direct support in the form of ad hoc grants. Our First and Third Interim Reports recommended measures of assistance which are relatively uncostly in relation to the cultural value of the national assets they are intended to conserve and stimulate.

In November, 1971, the *Report of the Interdepartmental Task Force on Foreign Investment* (Ontario) recommended a policy of "moderate economic nationalism," pointing out that "this holds the promise of a gradual reversal of present trends without at the same time endangering economic stability." This was followed by the appointment of a Committee of the Legislative Assembly to review the report and the current status of opinion and information on economic and cultural nationalism in Canada, and to provide a preliminary report by March 1, 1972, which was duly submitted. This Commission has observed elsewhere that the dollar significance of book publishing in the GNP is minuscule, relatively speaking, and that our concern with book publishing is cultural rather than economic. But the principles of the *Preliminary Report of the Select Committee on Economic and Cultural Nationalism* are nevertheless relevant. We are satisfied that our own conclusions on the question of ownership in book publishing set forth in this chapter, which are based on cultural rather than economic considerations, are consistent with the preliminary conclusions reached by the Select Committee. As the Select Committee pointed out, "The goal of centralized efficiency may conflict with the desire of host countries to gain a greater degree of self-sufficiency and self-determination. The central issue is – where does the greater benefit lie?" The Committee noted that there are no simple answers applicable to all situations; this Commission has outlined what it believes would be the best policy with respect to book publishing, and with respect to book publishing only, for the people of Ontario and of Canada.

The Select Committee suggested certain standards or guidelines to which foreign-controlled firms should conform. Again these deal with economic rather than cultural issues, but among them it is interesting that the Select Committee recommended that foreign-controlled firms should "develop exports to overseas markets" and "assure adequate levels of research and development work in Canada." And we could not agree with the Select Committee more than we do when it also states:

The development of a comprehensive national policy for all industry, including foreign-controlled industry, requires the cooperation of the federal and provincial governments. It is evident that the formulation and administration of policies on foreign investment should not be the exclusive responsibility of the federal government. The provinces have distinctive responsibilities for their own development, having regard to local and regional needs and capabilities. Ontario policy must be part of national policy, but Ontario should not wait for federal action. The federal government has central responsibility to develop and implement national policy, but the provinces must have a concurrent and direct role in both formulation and administration of such policies.

Elsewhere the Committee recognized the public concern about the quantity and quality of Canadian educational materials available for use in Ontario schools and universities and recommended that there should be an effort to develop an appropriate range and quality of educational materials for use in Ontario schools and universities. It recognized that Ontario's colleges and universities "should continue to stress intellectual and teaching excellence in faculty recruitment," and took note of the appointment of this Commission to deal with what it described as an area of "the cultural industries." We hope that the guidelines respecting book publishing that we have developed in this report, and the reasons for them, are sufficiently explicit to assist directly in the formulation of policy in the area entrusted to us.

To conclude this chapter on the question of ownership, we wish to observe that the trend toward increased domination of Canadian book publishing by foreign-owned publishers is not necessarily irreversible. But it should be allowed to reverse itself, without the kind of government intervention that would be implied by statutory confiscation or repressive legislation and regulation. Some discussions that we have had with foreign-owned publishing branches since publication of the Commission's Third Interim Report lead us to hope that a voluntary trend in the direction of Canadianization of ownership of some foreign subsidiaries may at least be in its early stages. Such developments should continue to receive every encouragement. What is required, we repeat, is not that the foreign-owned publishers should be put down, but that the climate for Canadian-owned book publishing enterprises should be substantially improved.

3
Copyright and Book Publishing

If there were no copyright protection, there could be no profession of writing. Without authorship, there could be no book industry – no publishing, no bookselling, no librarianship. Intellectual property, unlike almost every other kind of property, is vulnerable to unauthorized appropriation by anyone who wishes to use it or to reproduce it for the use of others. Only the copyright, which in most English-speaking countries vests automatically in its original creator, endows a work with pecuniary value.

Thus it is copyright that makes it possible for intellectual property to be bought and sold, or conditionally licensed by one person to another. Where the level of copyright protection is low, the incentive to write is likely to be reduced, and so is the incentive to publish original editions of new books. If the level of protection is high, the reward to creative authorship and to publishing enterprise may reach to whatever level is set by the market-place. It is difficult to see how Canadian publishing output can compete with that of other lands unless Canadian books enjoy at least as much protection in this country as foreign books receive in theirs.

This may sound like an assertion that copyright in all literary works should be expanded into a perpetual and absolute monopoly for the owner and his assigns, something which it is not now either in fact or theory. Of course we hold no such view. An absolute monopoly would be contrary to the public interest, and so the author's right to what he creates must be restricted in various ways. For example, the term of copyright in published works (although not in unpublished works) is limited in every jurisdiction in the world. Similarly, the right to exercise absolute control during the existence of copyright is modified by doctrines of fair use, either by legislation or by the courts. A responsibility of government is to ensure that the balance between the level of protection to the author and society's need to have access to copyright matter is maintained in both the short and the long term. Copyright must not impede the progress of learning on the one hand, nor the writing and publishing of more books on the other. And it must stay abreast of changing communications technology.

THE QUESTION OF JURISDICTION

Copyright lies exclusively within the jurisdiction of the federal government, and it may seem strange that this Commission has included it among its other concerns. But copyright is the life-blood of publishing, and it is difficult to consider one apart from the other. Copyright legislation carries social, cultural, and educational consequences for all Canada, and affects the books that will be written and read in every province. It is because copyright is virtually synonymous with publishing that we have agreed that we cannot fulfil our terms of reference without giving it careful consideration.

However, we have also decided that we should comment only on aspects of copyright which are of direct concern to Canadian publishing at this time, or to the writers and users of books. Where we find it necessary to make recommendations regarding existing or future legislation, we of course address these to the provincial government as a basis for possible representations by it to the federal government. Nor are the copyright issues on which we report here of uniform importance or urgency. Most of them have already been the subject of study or comment by federal agencies or departments, even of policy announcements or recommendations, some of which are indeed controversial. We believe that the latter warrant additional consideration in the interests of encouraging the development of the whole book industry in this country, and the writing and publishing of Canadian books in particular.

THE NATURE OF COPYRIGHT

A few months after the appointment of this Commission, the Economic Council of Canada issued its *Report on Intellectual and Industrial Property*. The sections of the latter dealing with copyright are likely to have an important bearing on the general revision of the Canadian Copyright Act that has been anticipated for more than fifteen years. Updating of the Canadian legislation grows increasingly desirable, but uncertainty about the time and nature of revision of the United States Copyright Law (also pending for several years) leads us to urge that only interim revisions be made in the Canadian statute until American revision policy is known much more definitely that it is now. One of our reasons for being so concerned regarding future United States legislation is the latter's manufacturing provisions, discussed later in this chapter.

The Economic Council report makes many points which this Commission can endorse unreservedly; it contains other observations, including some recommendations, which give us pause. Our concerns regarding the latter are based on the possible adverse effect their implementation could have on authorship and publishing in Canada in the future.

We support with special enthusiasm the following remarks in the Economic Council report:

> ... most Canadians desire for their country (full account being taken of its fundamentally bilingual and bicultural character) a strong and distinctive cultural identity. We have further assumed that, for this, most Canadians would be willing to pay some as yet undetermined economic price.
> ... the cultural identity sought should as quickly as possible become a sturdy and viable entity, capable of holding its own in the world without shame or inordinate special protection ... To reduce the matter to a concrete example, any decision-maker responsible for foisting upon Canadian students a third-rate textbook simply because it is written and produced in Canada should consider himself overdue for an interview with his conscience and a careful contemplation of the long forward shadow cast by the quality of education ... Low-grade cultural parochialism does no service to the cause of a durable and creative Canadian nationalism – quite the contrary ... It is particularly important that the relevance of cultural goals in a policy-planning situation should not be used as a smoke screen behind which material interests and conflicts between private and social interests are allowed to shelter unexamined.

Quoted out of context, these comments may seem peripheral to copyright, but they are so relevant to our report that one might almost suppose that they were addressed to this Commission. We have tried to make it clear elsewhere that we would never support Canadian writing, much less Canadian publishing, for its own sake. But if we can find ways to stimulate Canadian creativity of a quality comparable with that which is imported, we also have a public duty to do nothing that would hinder Canadian authorship. Unfortunately, a few of the copyright recommendations contained in the Economic Council report could in our judgment lead to just such a result.

The Economic Council report seems to base much of its reasoning on the premise that Canadian publishing, and possibly Canadian authorship too, are not in any particular need of stimulation at this time:

> A *basic* change in copyright protection should be made only if there is judged to be a large discrepancy between society's need for the copyright type of incentive and the amount of such incentive currently being provided. At the basic level, there does not appear to be in Canada any very firm evidence of a large discrepancy one way or the other. We are therefore not recommending any substantial reductions in the basic amount or kind of protection offered to holders of Canadian copyright, but by the same token we urge that there be no substantial increases either, for the existing "levels of protection" seem already quite sufficiently high, incentive-producing and costly.

The report again seems to assume a state of economic strength for Canadian publishing, which this Commission has been unable to discover, when it says:

> Authors may, of course, be directly subsidized by the State, but given the supply and demand

schedules involved, this is likely to channel appreciable benefits to publishers, who will now have more manuscripts to choose from and acquire at lower prices.

AGENCY PUBLISHING AND CO-PUBLISHING

Another area in which the *Report on Intellectual and Industrial Property* makes recommendations which could seriously inhibit the expansion of Canadian book publishing is that of territorial rights in editions co-published with publishers abroad. The report seems either to fail to distinguish between such co-editions and books imported for distribution in Canada under "exclusive agency" arrangements, or else it recognizes the distinction but proceeds to lump them together in the copyright modifications it recommends. We think that these situations should be examined much more closely before implementing the report's recommendation favouring "the removal of copyright as an import-restricting device," for example. Otherwise the development of Canadian publishing internationally could be jeopardized.

Exclusive agency arrangements normally relate to the complete catalogues of foreign publisher-principals, which Canadian agents undertake to promote and stock (with varying degrees of thoroughness) in return for exclusive rights to sell in this country. We realize that Canadian publisher-agents are jealous of the fact that these agency rights are in practice not as exclusive as their contracts assume, and that as agents they are regularly "bought around" by customers who place their orders with foreign wholesalers. Such wholesalers are often located in the principal's own country, where they may be among his major customers, although he nominally sells books to them only for resale in territories which he has not assigned. Blackwell seems to be one of the best known examples, although there are many others. Prominent international book wholesalers based in the United States include such firms as Richard Abel, Bro-Dart, and other firms which specialize in supplying libraries, and often retail accounts also, particularly for academic books. Some of these have opened branches abroad, with the result that British publisher-agents for North American principals are now finding themselves "bought around" in the United Kingdom, an interesting variation of the agency problem here.

This system of exclusive international agencies has many shortcomings, often including inadequate service on titles out of stock or not yet delivered and, as the Economic Council report mentions, a clear tendency on the part of agents to mark up prices when converting them from the currencies of the countries of origin. This practice of marking up does not follow uniform patterns, and by no means all agents can be said to overcharge. Even for some of those who do, it is necessary to acknowledge that the inefficiencies of the agency system itself contribute to the cost of handling. This is because the exclusive agent normally has the responsibility for developing market interest in Canada, including sales promotion and advertising, the distribution of copies to book reviewers, issue of news releases, and so on. At least part of the resulting orders bypass him to wholesalers who do not share in these overheads, which are often large in relation to gross sales of individual titles. A more important factor in the price differentials is the wide disparity between wholesale discounts in Canada and Britain, including library discounts especially. And because the publisher-agent normally is expected to carry most or all the titles published by his principal, the average sale of each is likely to be very small; for certain kinds of lists, the total Canadian market may be as few as twenty or thirty copies altogether. For some, it is smaller; for others, substantially larger.

Exclusive agency arrangements normally do not involve copyright assignments, not even licences in the copyright sense. They are international trading agreements between publishers, and the most that can be said for them is that over the years they seem to have been the most satisfactory system that foreign publishers have found to service the Canadian market, particularly the far-flung Canadian retail trade. The system has worked least well for library customers, as we shall see later. In our opinion, the whole exclusive agency system is becoming progressively less workable, and its demise has long been predicted, even by some publishers. But those who criticise it, including ourselves, have difficulty in proposing a system to replace it.

Several factors sustain the agency system. One is the difficulty of devising alternative systems which can cultivate the Canadian market reasonably thoroughly for foreign publishers' complete lists. Publisher-agents do assume the responsibility for stocking most current titles (if not the complete backlists) of the imprints they represent. Another reason for its survival is that many exclusive publisher-agents in Canada are subsidiaries of parent firms abroad, whose books they carry and promote in this country. When one asks whose ox is being gored if the Canadian branch of a McGraw-Hill or Prentice Hall or Oxford is "bought around," the manager of the subsidiary branch will quickly answer, "Mine!" And he will say this with a fervour that belies the overlap between his interests and those of his parent company, from whose shelves all orders are filled in the end anyway.

So much for the way in which the exclusive agency system works, or doesn't work (although its implications for libraries are discussed further in Chapter 4). The Economic Council takes into account the argument sometimes advanced by Canadian publisher-agents that "Canadian literature should be cross-subsidized out of profits on the distribution of foreign books" and rejects it:

It has been argued that some system of this kind [an agency system] is necessary for the maintenance of Canadian cultural identity and the survival of the Canadian publishing industry . . .
It is our conclusion, however, that the maintenance of prices as high as those now prevailing for many foreign books on general sale in Canada is a poor way of furthering the objectives mentioned – a way more objectionable even on cultural than on economic grounds . . . If there were some clear

association between the amount of agency business available to individual publishers on the one hand and their support of Canadian authors and production of Canadian textbooks on the other, the cross-subsidization argument might carry somewhat more weight. But no very definite pattern of this sort is apparent. Some Canadian publishers with agency business have indeed gone out of their way to foster Canadian textbooks and general literature and to "carry" native authors through some very lean years. Not all, however, have acquitted themselves on any very large scale in this way. Meanwhile, a most encouraging recent development has been the emergence of small Canadian publishing houses, with little if any agency business, specializing in the handling of Canadian writers.

It is indeed true, as we note elsewhere, that Canadian branches of a few foreign firms have set enviable records as publishers of Canadian authors, the best example over the years being Macmillan. Without its import business (and perhaps its Canadian schoolbook business), it is likely that this firm would have had to curtail its Canadian publishing long ago. Yet only one publisher in 1970 had a larger number of Canadian books in print.

There are other so-called publishers, however, which are Canadian-owned and have large import businesses, but are doing almost no original Canadian publishing at all. Examples of these are George J. McLeod and Smithers & Bonellie. Each of these two "Canadian publishers"– and there are others which rival this record – list themselves as exclusive agents for a substantially larger number of foreign publishers than they have separate Canadian titles of their own in print. The Economic Council is right in questioning the assumption that agency publishing automatically leads to Canadian publishing. On the other hand, we have no evidence that the small new Canadian publishing houses "with little if any agency business" have yet demonstrated that their businesses are viable, as the Economic Council report also implies. Certainly these are the firms that are in the front ranks of those seeking public assistance now, both in Toronto and in Ottawa. It looks rather as though agency business may be necessary for a publisher to flourish. Whether or not he also supports Canadian publishing is another matter.

If Sections 27 and 28 of the Copyright Act were revised as the Economic Council suggests "so that the law does not deny to anyone the right to purchase works protected by Canadian copyright in other countries where they enjoy copyright protection, and to import these works into Canada," it is not clear to us how the *agency* business of "exclusive Canadian representatives" would be significantly affected, or how the average Canadian book-buyer would be assisted. For all practical purposes, buying around these agents through third parties abroad is possible now, and occurs on a substantial scale. As we have noted, agents normally do not have assignments of copyright in the long lists of titles they are responsible for selling. Even if they did avail themselves of the right to add specific titles to the list of prohibited goods (Schedule C of the Customs Tariff) as provided in Section 28, there appears to be an official interpretation of that section which would then prohibit their importing such titles themselves. The reference here is to what has become known as the "Varcoe ruling," contained in a letter from F. P. Varcoe, Deputy Attorney General of Canada, to the Director of Investigation and Research, Combines Investigation Act, Ottawa, dated March 12, 1953, and quoted at pp. 91 ff. of the *Report on Copyright* submitted by the Royal Commission on Patents, Copyright, Trade Marks and Industrial Designs (Ottawa, 1957).

Where the views of this Commission depart considerably from those of the Economic Council is with regard to territorial rights, which are what make possible bonafide co-publishing arrangements between Canadian and foreign publishers. If Canadian publishing is to find an international market at all, it is going to have to become involved in co-publishing on an ever-expanding scale. In such cases, the Canadian publisher either purchases from a foreign publisher a whole edition of a new book together with the exclusive Canadian (and sometimes American) rights, or he sells the exclusive rights in defined territories abroad to regional publishers in those areas. This buying and selling of territorial rights is the life-blood of international publishing, being the main purpose of such international book markets as the annual Frankfurt Book Fair. One thing is certain; Canadian publishers will have to be prepared to buy as well as to sell regional editions if they are going to find themselves in the mainstream of international commerce in books. The question is whether or not the Copyright Act will be revised in a way that would effectively prevent their doing so.

If the co-publication of a book by a Canadian publisher does not carry with it some assurance that he will have the same exclusivity in the Canadian market as if he had published the book only in Canada, he is unlikely to co-publish. Marginal books by Canadian authors which he might market abroad in co-editions he will be less likely to publish at all, lest cheap foreign editions of the same titles find their way back into the Canadian market. Soon he will enter into international publishing commitments neither as a purchaser nor as a vendor of editions. If he fails to internationalize his business by co-publishing wherever it is economically feasible for him to do so, he has no hope at all of broadening his market base and so reducing his unit costs. In the meanwhile, the large "international" publishing houses abroad, whose ability to compete is so irksome to Canadian firms, not only have the much larger continental market to absorb their costs, but are also actively engaged in co-publishing with overseas firms.

If Canadian publishers are to participate in the publication of regional editions, therefore, they are going to require better, not poorer, protection against the competition of unauthorized editions in their home market (and also, of course, in foreign markets). Any legislative revision in Canada which might have the effect of limiting the geographical divisibility of copyright could impose disabilities on the publishers most concerned – in this case the Canadian publishers. This is perhaps the worst time in the history of book publishing in this country for additional disabilities to be placed on Canadian cultural enterprise, especially by government.

There is a further reason why protection of regional editions against competition from unauthorized imported editions should be increased rather than reduced, although it is a more idealistic one. Canadian publishing is in an excellent position to make a contribution to the educational, scientific, and cultural advancement of developing nations, either at its own cost or as an instrument of Canadian External Aid policy. This is because Canadian educational books generally meet American standards of design and educational philosophy at the same time that they reflect British traditions in spelling and in many other ways. These are features which have a special appeal to certain foreign markets. On a selective basis, it should be possible to produce low-priced editions for export (particularly to former British countries) at prices close to overrun manufacturing costs, i.e. at prices which need not retrieve their full share of preparatory costs. Whether such editions are sold commercially or supplied under government assistance programs is immaterial. What is serious, however, is the possible resale into the Canadian domestic market of any part of such editions. So long as copyright cannot be turned to "as an import-restricting device" the exploration of such special marketing possibilities is much less likely to attract the interest of Canadian publishers. And yet this is a potentially significant market, as has been clearly demonstrated by the success of many low-cost international editions of textbooks now being published in vast quantities by American publishers, for example.

For the above reasons we consider that no revision of the Copyright Act should have the effect of making lawful the importation into Canada of copies of copyright works where copies of an edition specially printed or bound for sale in Canada with the permission of the copyright owner are available in this country. The word "edition" might require definition in this context.

The procedure under Section 27 whereby the owner of the copyright may give notice to the Department of National Revenue "that he is desirous that such copies should not be so imported" and whereby they are thereupon included in Schedule C (prohibited goods) to the Customs Tariff has been applied in a way that makes it unworkable in practice, and we think that this should be reviewed and clarified. It is particularly important that co-publishing arrangements respecting individual titles be defined and adequately protected against the competition by importation which could limit the ability of Canadian publishers to participate in the publication of regional editions either abroad or in this country. We do not necessarily favour, however, that copyright sanctions should be available to importers as a means of enforcing exclusive agency arrangements respecting whole lines of titles, and it may be desirable to distinguish in the legislation between such trading agreements and bona fide co-publishing initiatives. But it could be in the public interest to protect agency arrangements, within defined limits, regarding availability and price—difficult regulations to administer, admittedly. But co-publishing certainly must be encouraged if Canadian firms are to participate in international publishing on the same basis as their counterparts in other countries.

FORMAT COPYRIGHT

We commend the decision of the Economic Council of Canada favouring statutory recognition of format copyright based on the original typographic design of a new edition of a work, regardless of the status of the literary copyright in its contents. However, we think that the recommendation is undesirably restricted in scope. We would prefer to see publishers (and book designers and manufacturers as well) protected against unauthorized photographic or other kinds of facsimile reproduction of their typography for a substantially longer period than the ten years proposed. Canadian publishers cannot always retrieve their preparatory costs in so short a time, especially for books in the public domain which they reset in type. We think they should be stimulated to undertake more publishing of this kind by making its profitability less uncertain, albeit only marginally so.

Another feature of format, or typographical, copyright which justifies its segregation from copyright in the work itself, is that it can sometimes spread the speculative risk in new ventures between publisher and printer, at least to some extent. At present, the printer who sets a work in type for a publisher must assume that he will have the right to print the work only once, however successful it may be, i.e. his typography may be photographed by a competing tenderer (who may have no typesetting capacity), if additional printings are required later. He may even be required to deliver the films to the publisher under the terms of his printing contract, which will further increase the likelihood of his typography being printed by a competitor. (Significantly, the most economical source of quality reprinting in single colour anywhere in the world is often the United States.) If the typographic design belonged to the typesetter, assuming that it was designed and executed by someone in his employ, he could either include the value of an assignment of this format copyright in the cost quotation he submitted to his publisher-customer, or he could retain the format copyright and thereby be in an improved competitive position in the event of a reprinting. In the latter event, it would be reasonable for him to offer a lower typesetting quotation to the publisher for the first printing, according to his assessment of the likelihood of the work being put on press again. It is true that the dispostion of films and plates even now depends on cost negotiations between a publisher and his competing printers; thus the right to reprint can be made a condition of the manufacturing contract without the invention of format copyright at all. But this is something that cannot always be provided for in practical situations. And to the extent that the creation of a typographical copyright may provide any incentive at all to reduce preparatory costs, or to share them between printer and publisher, it would be in the interests of book production in Canada for it to be embedded in the Act. The Economic Council has proposed that this be done.

But we think it would be desirable to extend the lifetime of format copyright sufficiently to permit recovery of costs in average situations. The term of ten years, which the Economic Council has recommended, falls far short of the term of fifty years after death that attaches to other kinds of copyright, and would be insufficient in many cases to permit recovery of original productions costs, e.g. in the case of a large and expensive work. And there are other reasons why a term of ten years seems undesirably short, as well as arbitrary. The Copyright Act of the United Kingdom creates a typographical copyright with a term of twenty-five years. While Canada is not obliged to imitate the British lead, the legislation of the two countries is closely related and there is a strong argument in favour of as much international uniformity as possible in such matters. We would therefore favour a term of twenty-five years for typographical copyright in any revision of the Canadian Copyright Act.

UNAUTHORIZED COPYING

No aspect of the oft-cited revolution in communications technology has roused greater concern among copyright owners than the mushrooming of copying methods during the past fifteen years. Beginning with the appearance of the first practical office copying machines, which yielded a wet photographic print by a mechanized method of chemical development, a growing threat to the market for published materials was sensed, even when it was not admitted, by all those involved in the new technology. And it took very little time before almost everyone in business, in education, or in office employment of any kind was involved with it it in some way. Countless hours of typing in offices "to make an extra copy" were suddenly eliminated. To say that teachers and librarians found the newly invented technology "handy" would be a considerable understatement. At the same time, those publishers who were most vocal in claiming that rigorous enforcement of copyright laws was urgently needed to save their businesses from extinction built some of the fattest files of articles on the subject of unauthorized copying – mostly in the form of xerox copies taken from trade and library journals and other professional literature. The keynote of the new copying technology was convenience, and it was on grounds of inconvenience quite as much as from a desire to avoid costs that most of its users rejected the complaints of authors and publishers or, more often, were indifferent to them.

This Commission was supplied generously with advice regarding what should be done and should not be done about copying as it is now practised, particularly in educational institutions (including libraries); surprisingly little was said about copying done in other situations such as business offices. As with other copyright problems, it would be appropriate, and invitingly easy, for us to pass the whole dilemma along to the federal authorities who have the constitutional responsibility for dealing with it. But again we felt that we must at least offer our views on the nature and seriousness of the problem from the standpoint of book publishing in

Ontario and Canada. We should admit forthwith, however, that we approached the question with no expectation of being able to resolve it to our complete satisfaction, much less to the satisfaction of either copyright owners or copyright users. Our chief concern was to decide whether or not copying as it is now practised, or as one might reasonably predict it will be practised during the next decade or so, poses a significant threat to the viability of a Canadian book publishing industry.

To begin with, we would like to make clear that we have no patience with arguments of authors and publishers who uncompromisingly demand their pound of flesh as a legal right, and are too impatient to weigh the practical consequences of seeking to enforce a permissions procedure, and possibly even remuneration, in every copying situation. Nor do we find any better reason to countenance the frequently heard argument to the contrary, viz. that in the name of non-profit education every kind of copying should be permitted. With regard to the latter position, the Economic Council's *Report on Intellectual and Industrial Property* again exhibits a point of view with which we must express our hearty disagreement, when it says:

Since it was also found, in both the American and Canadian studies, that the majority of copied works was from works published within the last ten years, it would appear that the photocopier's main use is for widespread dissemination of modern work *in the nonprofit fields of research and education* [Italics added].

We simply cannot accept the proposition that because research and education are (usually, at least) not conducted for profit, services and goods should therefore be provided to them free of charge, i.e. at the cost of the supplier. Not even professors who might urge that no charge should be made to schools and universities by copyright owners would agree that the same principle should apply to the services given by researchers and instructors. Nor to any of the other countless suppliers to non-profit institutions, including lists of occupations which it would only be tiresome to set forth as examples. And it is simply not good enough to say that if the author concerned is a member of an academic community, he should be pleased (and perhaps is pleased) at the compliment of being quoted at all. This kind of author publishers can do without, university presses included, unless the costs of publication are going to be subsidized in order to offer an economy to the public, which obviously would be absurd. Because copyright property is more vulnerable to appropriation without remuneration than are, say, the supplies used in a copying machine or the services of a teacher or a typist, it needs statutory protection if continued production of it is to be stimulated.

On the other hand, the principle of fair dealing must be allowed to cover a wide range of copying activities, even if the framers of the legislation could at no time have anticipated the technology now available to copyright users, particularly in libraries. What constitutes fair dealing is defined in Section 17(2) of the Copyright

Act (see Appendix). We do not disagree with the proposition that it should be more precisely defined than it is, but redefinition should lead to clarification and not to confiscation. For example, there are few situations where a user copying passages by hand from a copyright work could properly be claimed to be exceeding the limits of fair dealing. Why should the substitution of a faster and more convenient process of copying convert fair dealing into unfair dealing? We think it should not, even when it means that more copying of the same kind can be done, as it usually does.

There are limits to what we think should be characterized as fair dealing, however, and it is for this reason that we think that the revised Act should outline these with as much clarity as possible. For example, it is as difficult to conceive why the making of multiple copies of the same passages from a work by a copying machine should be considered fair dealing as it would be to justify the making of more than one copy manually, e.g. by using carbon paper or some other duplicating method. The example of twenty students wanting one article to which an instructor has referred them contains nothing that raises it to the level of fair dealing. In *some* way, the copyright owner should be remunerated in such a case, *and* the students should gain access to the article without delay. Most unequivocally, the making of multiple copies of any copyright work can be said automatically to exceed the limits of "fair dealing . . . for the purposes of private study, research, [or] criticism." The plea that these are required for private study by a number of students individually has been found not admissible in this context, in our view correctly. Such a practice is a substitute form of publication, even when it can sometimes be argued that it does not substitute for purchase of the published book. For example, because a book is expensive and only one chapter of ten is wanted, surely does not justify reproduction of the chapter under a plea of fair dealing. Given greater economies in the technology of copying, reasons such as these would have to be admitted as proof of fair dealing in many more situations where copying would then be substituted for purchase of the work itself. For example, if costs were sufficiently reduced (perhaps by public institutional subsidy?) a subsidiary publishing industry by college bookstores and libraries could easily develop, at first for more expensive reference works such as law books, but eventually for many other kinds of publications also. As this reached the level of "publication on demand" by someone other than the copyright owner or licensee, the effect on creative writing and publishing would surely become obvious. The problem is to devise a simple method of effecting remuneration, or to invent an equitable alternative procedure which would accomplish the same purpose.

Between the extremes that have been mentioned, a wide spectrum of fair and unfair kinds of dealing involving copying can be hypothesized, and do indeed occur. Where such copying interferes significantly with the potential market for the copyright work, we think it should be proscribed by statute and that the institutions involved should be at pains to see that the law is enforced. Where it can be shown to have no significant adverse effect on the market (of which the copying may or may not be a part) and particularly where the copying is merely a mechanized version of the kind of copying anticipated by Section 17(2) in the present Copyright Act, it might well be left in the category of fair dealing. This would include, for example, the making of copies by a librarian acting as agent for a library user as well as the making of copies by the user himself, e.g. on a coin-operated copying machine. The distinction between copying by a librarian and by the user is sometimes claimed to be important legally, but is spurious in our view.

In the interests of writing and publishing, then, we would draw the line where the copying of copyright materials for distribution to students in a classroom is concerned, or even to some students in a classroom. There can be no doubt whatever, according to the evidence we have heard, that this frequently does happen in practice. Not only is copying of this kind illegal, it is immoral and should not be tolerated, least of all by educational institutions and systems. We have been told privately by a teacher, for example, of a school board that warned its staff "not to permit the pupils to take home" photocopies of instructional materials made from copyright works. Regrettably, those publishers who do encounter such situations are too often intimidated by the fact that the offenders are their educational customers to complain directly, much less to have recourse to the courts as their solicitors often remind them they have the right to do. After all, it is a poor salesman who sues his customers, especially when the specific damages to be claimed in any one case are unimpressively small.

Studies of copying practices

Until recently there were almost no quantitative studies of the amount and kinds of copying done by Canadian educational institutions, including libraries. We were unable to find any experimental evidence concerning copying practices in elementary and secondary schools in this country, but two or three intensive surveys of copying in libraries have been undertaken since a little more than a year ago, in the main by librarians and library groups. The principal purpose of these studies has been to determine whether or not the kind and amount of copying that is done can reasonably be said to affect adversely the interests of copyright owners, including authors and publishers, as the latter claim. At least the Canadian Book Publishers' Council contended that copying had this effect in the brief it presented to this Commission.

Any review of copying practices involves problems of definition and terminology, as well as decisions regarding what practices should be measured. What distinction should be drawn between copying and duplicating? Is it right to monitor the library copying machine, even for the purpose of developing statistics, and to ignore the wholesale reproduction of chapters and selected passages from books that may be going on in the duplicating centre of the university or of one of its departments? What meaningful differences – for the copyright owner – separate copying for no charge, for recovery of costs, and for a profit? Does it matter who, student or librarian, does the copying? Should the same standard apply to copying Canadian books as to foreign books? Are any ethical considerations to be recognized at all? And so on. In this chapter we are trying to indicate our views on at least some of these issues, but it is not possible to propound all the questions that should be asked, much less to develop reasoned answers. Nevertheless the public has a duty to raise and explore all these issues, perhaps by means of wide-ranging research projects under federal auspices, in which specialists could be directly involved – specialists, that is, in the art of writing, publishing, manufacturing, bookselling, librarianship, as well as law and economics.

What has been learned from the few Canadian studies of unauthorized copying that have been made? The Commission received carefully documented reports from several library groups including the University of Toronto Library and the Committee on Copyright Legislation of the Canadian Association of College and University Libraries. Their conclusions, perhaps not surprisingly, were in strong contrast with the apprehensions expressed by publisher and author groups such as the Canadian Book Publishers' Council, the Canadian Copyright Institute, and the Canadian Authors' Association. Some of these briefs dealt also with other matters affecting library-publisher relations, but it is with respect to copying that we refer to them here.

The Canadian Book Publishers' Council based its assumptions regarding the volume of Canadian copying on an American study made by the Committee to Investigate Copyright Problems Affecting Communication in Science and Education (CICP) undertaken for the Office of Education in the U.S. Department of Health, Education, and Welfare. The Canadian situation was assumed to be proportionate to that in the United States, i.e. the American statistics were reduced in ratio to population. On this basis, the CBPC reasoned that some 40 million pages of copyrighted books were copied in Canada in 1971, and pointed out that a royalty of two cents per page would therefore yield "800,000 dollars annually."

At the present time, publishers and other copyright owners receive nothing for their works copied in this manner but most libraries charge from 5¢ to 25¢ per page for copies ... The only persons who are not paid are those most entitled to payment, the copyright owners.

The study by the Canadian Association of College and University Libraries (CACUL) indicated that university library copying constitutes only a small part of any such amount. However, the total of unauthorized copying of all kinds in Canada might reasonably be assumed to be of the magnitude suggested by the CBPC, unless university library copying as reported by CACUL constitutes a much larger proportion of the whole than our own survey, reported later, indicates. But if the gross volume of all copying is high, so of course would be the cost of administering any kind of collection system, including one proposed by the publishers.

Yet it must be recognized that we are speaking of something substantial, and we should therefore be more concerned with whether copyright owners are entitled to compensation at all than with the futility of trying to develop a system of collection. The convenience of copying or the inconvenience of paying for the right to do so are important reasons why a better approach than the negotiated permission may have to be prescribed by government. But if there is a strong moral or cultural argument in favour of remuneration being paid, it becomes a public responsibility to see that remuneration occurs. One method of accomplishing this, as has been noted by the Economic Council and others, might be to provide some kind of formula compensation from tax revenues, with attendant dangers of discrimination, or at least charges of discrimination in the allocation of payments. We are prepared neither to support nor to reject such an approach to the problem; we think it deserves more intensive study than it seems to have received up to this time, however.

The CBPC notes that it is likely to be but a matter of time before "photocopies will be produced at less than the cost of acquiring the original book or journal." We have no doubt that this will happen, and observed earlier in this chapter that even under existing costs, selective copying may already be an economical alternative to buying a complete book. But is this important in those cases where purchase of the book would not be seriously contemplated, whether or not it is conveniently at hand in a bookstore (which it certainly often is not)? On the other hand, and the CBPC brief stops short of making the point, it is likely that if and when "on demand" publication of a kind envisaged by the Economic Council becomes widespread, it will more easily occur in libraries than elsewhere. If the copyright owner is to be recognized at all in such transactions in the university community, therefore, the bench-mark for doing so can probably be looked for in the library.

The CBPC brief concludes its section on copying by advocating an independent survey of copying practices in universities, colleges, schools and libraries "to determine more accurately the nature of the material copied and the extent of the copying." A full-scale objective survey could generate additional useful information, but we were impressed by what has already been done by CACUL in this area. Nor were we convinced that a further effort to establish the exact amount of library copying being done would justify its costs at this moment, e.g. by this Commission, although we shall report shortly on one study we did make. With regard to this, we are surprised that the publishers do not give equal weight to a study of copying being done in offices and by coin-operated machines available to the public elsewhere than in libraries and other educational institutions.

It may be urged that the university library studies are not objective in the sense that neither copyright owners nor government as such participated in their planning and administration. But in our opinion they yielded valuable information, and were on the whole planned with commendable care and concern for achieving reliable results.

One of the surveys of Canadian library photocopying was undertaken by the University of Toronto Library, the (previously published) results of which are summarized in the brief received from Robert H. Blackburn (Chief Librarian) and David G. Esplin (Associate Librarian) of that institution. Although the University of Toronto Library study was based on local sampling only, an even more ambitious survey was published by the Canadian Association of College and University Libraries (CACUL) in 1971 in the latter's report entitled *Purchasing and Copying Practices at Canadian University Libraries*, prepared by B. Stuart-Stubbs. The results compiled in the Stuart-Stubbs study were drawn from 41 participating university libraries and covered 1160 copying machines at the universities represented, of which 246 machines were under library jurisdiction.

The total number of copies reported in this survey was 14,725,946. Thirty-seven of the reporting libraries then participated in an analysis of the content of the copying that was done, using a sampling technique (one per cent of the annual exposure rates of all machines under library jurisdiction). (We do have reservations as to whether the few days included in a one per cent sample of this kind would be representative of some of the practices being studied. For example, it might reasonably be supposed that the proportion of copying of lecture notes would sky-rocket in the weeks before an examination period, but would be low at the beginning of an academic year, or when published references were being collected for the preparation of essays and other study projects.) While it is not the purpose of this report to summarize the Stuart-Stubbs study, the following conclusions, which are paraphrased, are most relevant to any effort to appraise the extent and nature of copying in Canadian university libraries.

There are about one thousand copying machines at present in Canadian universities, and about one-fifth of these are under library jurisdiction. (These figures seem to exclude machines restricted to copying letters, invoices, etc., as well as microfilm and photostat cameras and microform reader-printers.) The library machines produce about 15 million copies annually for all purposes, about half of these being of published material (most of which may be presumed to be copyright, although not all). About one-quarter of the published material copied is of Canadian origin, slightly more than a million exposures per year being from Canadian books and periodicals. About half of the latter have been published since 1965, the average number of pages taken from Canadian books being about eight (and from Canadian periodicals, nine). About one-twentieth of all copying of Canadian books and periodicals involved multiple copying. The average charge made by university libraries surveyed is seven cents per exposure (as compared with the "5¢ to 25¢"

mentioned in the CBPC brief). The report concludes as follows:

A system for the collection of royalties, at present levels of copying, would be impractical and harmful to the broader interests of society in providing access to information for educational purposes. No devices are presently available to discriminate among materials being copied, to select those for which a royalty could be charged, or to identify the publishers or authors to whom payments should be made ... Assuming that royalties could rightfully be claimed on a million exposures a year, and that as much as ten cents were added to the cost of each exposure for this purpose, it is improbable that much would remain of the $100,000 thus collected, after administrative costs were paid. Further, anything remaining would have to be divided according to some formula between authors and publishers. Individual payments would be minuscule, and would do nothing to alleviate the financial problems which beset authors and publishers.

As we have said, we think that the Stuart-Stubbs photocopying study was imaginatively conceived and that the considerable effort expended on it is amply justified by the factual data it generated. We agree with the conclusion that the cost (and inconvenience) of administering a royalty collection system could not be justified. But we respectfully differ from its conclusion, implicit if not explicit, that for this reason no remuneration to copyright owners is indicated. As we have already observed, what level of remuneration should be paid and how it should be generated are questions that should be considered separately from the issue of whether or not it is practicable to effect payment, especially by traditional means.

It appears that a substantial amount of copying does take place in university libraries. Most of this probably falls within the area of fair dealing, but a significant proportion of it must not, including necessarily most of the multiple copying that is done. The hypothetical royalty rate of 10 cents per copy mentioned in the conclusion to the CACUL report may be inequitably high or low (we suspect it is high) but it would need to be verified by extremely sophisticated sampling projects which would have to consider such elusive questions as the motivation of library users, the degree to which books published essentially as textbooks were being copied instead of purchased, and so on. The Stuart-Stubbs report necessarily omits consideration of almost four times as many university copying machines outside library jurisdiction. Thus one is left to speculate on the volume of copying done elsewhere in the universities, in other educational institutions at every level, in public libraries, in offices and on coin-operated machines in public places (including post offices). In the aggregate, such unauthorized copying must be many times the volume reported in the Stuart-Stubbs survey. However, this does not detract from the importance of the latter; it only enhances the significance of the hard figures it does furnish.

Survey of photocopying in Ontario educational institutions

Some indication of the nature and extent of photocopying of printed materials in educational institutions throughout Ontario (including university libraries) was gained from a special survey undertaken for the Commission by Kates, Peat, Marwick & Co. This study had been suggested by the Commission's chairman, who took the initiative in planning the terms of reference given the consultants. One of the more indirect purposes of this study was to determine whether or not it would be practicable to look to manufacturers of copying equipment and supplies for some or all of the revenues lost to copyright owners through unauthorized copying, i.e. through some form of taxation which would presumably be incorporated automatically in the selling price of the copying equipment and materials. There would remain the question of how to distribute such revenues equitably, although consideration was given to the advisability of simply applying such revenue to some of the various programs on behalf of the Canadian book industry recommended elsewhere in this report. In the end it was decided that, while such an approach may well deserve further consideration (e.g. by the proposed Ontario Book Publishing Board), the assessment of such a tax on a sound basis would be difficult to contrive with the limited statistical information regarding copying still available. The expensive complexities of administering a licensing system in this area, too, would outweigh the early net benefits that could be anticipated for authors and publishers. Moreover, the ratio of machines that are purchased to those leased turned out to be higher than anticipated. Finally, the rationale of such an approach inevitably tends to revolve on copyright, which is a federal jurisdiction, even though the provincial right to license dealers in copying equipment and supplies is clear. Thus if budgeted revenues were to be related to estimated lost income to authors and publishers, for example, copyright infringement would have to be segregated from fair dealing and extensive sampling would have to be pursued on an ongoing basis. International copyrights would become involved, and to some degree at least it might be inferred by many interests that the licences authorized indiscriminate copying, which of course they could not. Nevertheless, the data collected in the survey deserves being summarized here. The report on which these details are based is included in the Appendix for reference.

1. There are nearly seven thousand photocopying machines in the Ontario educational market at this time, i.e. in universities, colleges, schools, and public and academic libraries. This does not include duplicating equipment.

2. There are twelve principal manufacturers of these machines. Most of these were supplied by one manufacturer.

3. Most machines are manually operated and are owned by the customer institution, but there is a strong trend toward automatic machines with a leasing arrangement based on a cost per copy charge.

4. Significant volumes of printed materials (which may be subject to copyright) are being copied, perhaps to the extent of 30 to 40 per cent of the Ontario educational market. In libraries this proportion would seem to be in excess of 50 per cent (which correlates closely with the university library study by Stuart-Stubbs).

5. The size of the Ontario educational market has grown significantly in the last three years, from $6.3 million in 1969 to approximately $11 million in 1971.

6. Although a substantial proportion of manual machines use a thermographic process, plain paper or xerographic process copiers are gradually replacing other types. Increased use of xerographic copying is expected to continue.

7. The Ontario educational market in 1971 at $10 million comprised three per cent of the total sales of photocopying equipment and supplies in Canada. This proportion is substantially smaller than the Commission had anticipated. Although nothing in this report turns on the accuracy of this figure, it deserves special scrutiny in future surveys, in our opinion. We were also told that the growth rate of the Ontario market in relation to the total Canadian market was substantially higher than in other provinces, with consequent implications for the increasing importance of the Ontario educational market.

THE PUBLIC LENDING RIGHT

The royalty system as a basis for compensating authors of books has shortcomings, although it is the method most generally in use in western countries. Elsewhere in this report reference is made to the Soviet system of making payments at the time a work is accepted for publication, which is based on length, subject classification, and size of printing (or reprintings) among other things. A few western publishers, including some in Canada, are known to purchase book-length copyrights from authors for outright payments, although the inequities possible in this procedure make one ponder. Of course, periodicals have traditionally paid negotiated amounts for the right to publish, although frequently only first serial rights are purchased in such cases. It is difficult to see how a royalty system could be applied to magazines anyway, especially when their circulations may be very large, net income from actual sales relatively small compared with advertising revenue, and a substantial number of authors included in each issue. A somewhat parallel problem can arise with certain kinds of multiple-author books, including anthologies; in such cases, payments for permissions (when required at all) are likely to be flat sums, varying in amount according to the prominence of the author and the market for which the collection is intended.

One inequity in the royalty system, the most common method of compensating authors of books, is that although it yields revenue in proportion to the number of copies sold, it does not take into account the number of times a books is read, i.e. the size of a book's audience. Of course it can be said that for given classifications of books, average readerships could be computed and that it should not matter very much whether the author is paid a certain amount per copy sold or a somewhat smaller amount each time his book is read (a reduction that is likely because presumably the market would not absorb a substantial increase in the total amount paid out in royalties). Even if some way could be invented for counting or estimating the number of readers instead of the number of purchasers, the complex computations necessary would be difficult to make accurately, and even harder to police. Readership can vary enormously from one kind of book to another, and even from one kind of edition to another. For example, it can be said that some kinds of scholarly books are sold chiefly to libraries, where they may be consulted or read by many more users than will ever purchase copies for their own bookshelves. Other more popular books are virtually ignored by libraries. For example, notwithstanding some recent changes in library buying patterns, almost all sales of paperback editions are to private purchasers, the hardback editions of the same books going to libraries, for obvious reasons.

One of the arguments put forward in favour of a system whereby library readings or "borrowings" might be weighed alongside the number of copies sold is that nothing akin to the playwright's (or actor's) performing right fee exists for books, although the playwright also receives royalties on copies sold. The late Sir Alan Herbert christened the new concept the Public Lending Right; it has been variously known as the Author's Lending Right and the *droit public payant*. In 1951, an author, John Brophy, proposed that British public libraries introduce a small charge – perhaps as little as a penny – each time a book was borrowed.

The Public Lending Right was not a new idea, having received legal recognition in the Scandinavian countries several years earlier. It has now been in force in some form in Norway, Sweden, and Denmark since the late 1940s, and has more recently been reflected in Finnish, Icelandic, and West German legislation as well. In several of these areas its actual method of calculation and administration has continued to undergo further study and revision, the method of distributing revenues and the classifications of books and rates of tax varying significantly from country to country.

Early in 1971, Lord Eccles, the minister responsible for the arts in the United Kingdom, indicated that the government was unwilling to support the costs of a Public Lending Right, but that it might be prepared to consider an amendment to the Copyright Act of 1956 which would extend copyright restrictions to lending to the public. This could lead ultimately to the establishment of some system of payments to copyright owners, or at least to authors, whose books are bought by libraries. But it was recognized also that administrative difficulties might be insurmountable inasmuch as no system introduced in the future could be allowed to involve a direct charge on library users, who should continue to be served without charge. In the spring of 1972 a Working Party was appointed to study the problem.

The copyright law in West Germany has for some years contained a requirement that if copies of a work are loaned, "the lender shall pay to the author an equitable remuneration with respect thereto if the lending was executed for the financial gain of the lender." New legislation is now under consideration there which would remove the restriction that the lending must be for the "financial gain of the lender" before compensation is payable. The purpose of the German legislation (and this is largely true of most of Scandinavian law as well) is to support a social security program for authors, as well as to enhance the incentive to write. The West German legislation is based on that of Sweden, but differs from the latter country's approach in that it makes the lending right a part of the copyright law proper. This makes necessary its enforcement with respect to the copyrights of foreign authors protected in Germany under the various international conventions to which it is a party. The method of distributing such revenues collected on behalf of foreign authors has not yet been finally determined.

In May, 1972, the Working Party which had been appointed by the Paymaster General in Great Britain submitted its report on "how an amendment to the Copyright Act 1956 which added lending to the public to the acts restricted by copyright might be implemented." The Working Party had been specifically instructed not to consider particular courses of action, but to "define possible methods by which [an amendment] could be implemented and to set forth and compare their detailed implications." Its report was further expected "to provide a basis for a decision of policy on whether such an amendment to the Act would be a practical and worthwhile step."

The Working Party's report drew a distinction between "remuneration to authors," as provided in the Scandinavian countries to their own authors only, and the concept of Public Lending Right which would require remuneration of all authors whose rights in Great Britain were subject to protection on an equal basis by virtue of international agreements. The report noted that the proportion of foreign publications bought by British libraries is small. It further assumed that net proceeds of compensation paid would be distributed to authors, and apparently would not include copyright owners (who might be publishers). Perhaps the most interesting feature of the report is the way in which it suggests that a lending right fee might be collected. Because British libraries normally purchase through booksellers, it proposed as one possible method that the retail suppliers be required to generate and insert in each book a machine-readable receipt for the lending right fee charged.

This Commission carried its review of the Public Lending Right principle to a greater length than can usefully be summarized in this report. For example, it examined the possible application of a lending right fee to books lent by Ontario libraries, and even considered whether or not it should make wider recommendations which the provincial government might forward to the appropriate federal authorities regarding possible changes in the Copyright Act. It paid particular attention to the possibility that any kind of lending right might, because of Canada's obligations under international copyright conventions, require uniform application of new regulations to foreign as well as domestic works.

In the end, the Commission decided that it would not be fruitful to recommend implementation of any kind of lending right at this time. This conclusion was reached only after weighing many considerations pro and con, however. On the one hand, it was clear from the outset that a requirement that remuneration be paid to authors, and possibly to publishers, could be developed entirely outside the Copyright Act, and could even be established under provincial jurisdiction. It might therefore be applied to any group or class of books purchased (usually with public funds, it should be noted) for lending purposes, e.g. to books by Canadian authors published by Ontario-based Canadian publishers, and lent by Ontario public libraries (including academic libraries). Even the payments might not have to be made directly by the libraries themselves, least of all from their existing budgets. Amounts payable could be established by sampling procedures, repeated at regular intervals, and allocation of revenues could be determined in a similar way, granted that some inequities would have to be accepted. (The inequities inherent in the present system are probably substantially greater.) There need be little additional administrative responsibility for the individual lending institutions, and the cost of what would be needed could be subsidized out of the revenues obtained, provided that genuinely streamlined procedures were established.

Another reason why we were attracted to the lending right principle – although surprisingly this argument was not put forward in any of the briefs – is that it might help to equalize the cost to authors and publishers of a free textbooks program. When the latter was introduced in Ontario as a by-product of the book stimulation grants program (discussed in Chapter 5), all books were retained by the school boards at the end of the school year, and recycled in succeeding years to new students until they were worn out. This practice was economically justifiable, although it did lower the overall number of copies of each prescribed title sold over the years, and so contributed to some increase in prices when preparatory costs had to be retrieved through smaller total editions. But schoolbook costs were now equalized throughout the community, and the expense of producing books that formerly disappeared into the homes of their owners was thus eliminated. (It could be argued, with some justice perhaps, that these were almost the only books on the shelves of many homes, and in this sense the change may not have been an unmitigated cultural blessing.) But even if the publisher raised his prices to cover the increased write-off of preparatory cost required by the shorter editions, the author was not proportionately compensated for the lessened distribution of his books. This was because only a nominal price increase sufficed to distribute preparatory costs over a shorter run, and the author's royalty share of this increase was necessarily negligible. Thus there were some cogent arguments in favour of the adoption of some kind of lending right, preferably on a selective basis, within the province and under provincial regulation.

On the other hand, we had to agree that no lending right system could be administered in a way that would yield across-the-board benefits directly to Canadian authorship and Canadian publishing as effectively as some of the alternative assistance programs that could be proposed, and which we are recommending in this report. That is to say, even the most streamlined system could entail administrative expenses quite out of proportion to the benefits, which in any event might not be applied to furnish the greatest stimulation to the book industry, at least not the Canadian book industry. To be as equitable as possible, a lending right principle, once introduced, should apply to all books lent, by whatever author and whatever publisher. To confine it to Canadian books (or some narrower group than this) would not automatically mean that substantial net revenues would be generated for their assistance; its selective application might even reduce sales, and on the same selective basis. If it were applied as an extension of the copyright (by the appropriate authority) to all books lent, then this book-importing nation would export the vast bulk of the revenues so collected. And as just mentioned, if it were applied as a means to assist Canadian copyright owners only, there are more direct ways of accomplishing the same end.

We are not opposed to the Public Lending Right principle as such, and we anticipate that some day it may be embedded in the Copyright Act. The changing technology of communications is sufficient reason to ensure that copyright owners will not have to watch their markets shrink in the face of expanding information retrieval systems which – let it be emphasized – are likely to be heavily subsidized by public funds. Most of the apprehensions regarding possible recognition of a lending right by this Commission have been expressed by librarians, probably because they expect that they would have to subsidize its administration and even deduct compensation payments from their existing budgets.

One argument we heard was that because most of the market for certain kinds of books, including some scholarly and reference works, is furnished by libraries, to recognize a supplementary lending right would be illogical. But where the nature of a book is such that the public's need to consult it will be satisfied principally by libraries, its attractiveness as an item to be stocked by booksellers is diminished. This fact will be given due consideration by the publisher when he is establishing its price and discount (which is when he is also deciding whether or not it is economically feasible to publish it at all). If a lending right were recognized for such books, more works of the same kind could be written and published. And in some cases at least, the publisher would be encouraged to reach out for the wider market made up of private consumers at home and export sales abroad by lowering his price, which he can do only if the income from the book can be increased without a corresponding increase in overhead.

We do not think that the arguments in favour of maintaining the status quo are valid if what is happening now is unjust to private authors and publishers. But neither do we think that this province, nor even this nation, can afford to take the lead in adjusting what may be an inequity, but one in which Canada is involved more peripherally than other countries such as Great Britain and the United States. Even the dimensions of the problem are uncertain. The most we would recommend is that the federal government be earnestly requested by the provincial government to keep under continuing review the advisability of following any clear leads given by such countries as Great Britain and the United States with regard to embedding in the copyright law a lending right of the kind discussed above.

THE UNITED STATES MANUFACTURING PROVISIONS

We have had occasion to review in some detail the history and the impact on Canadian book publishing and manufacturing of the manufacturing provisions contained in the United States Copyright Law. Put briefly, these provisions deny United States copyright to any book in the English language whose author is an American citizen or American domiciliary unless the book is wholly manufactured in the United States. (A temporary copyright can be procured, for five years only, permitting the import of up to 1500 copies during this period, under ad interim copyright provisions.)

The impact on Canada of these provisions has been summarized by W. E. Curry in his background paper on the subject. In addition, numerous references to the problem have been made in briefs received, and many of these we have pursued in interviews, correspondence, and in other ways. We note that in response to concerns we expressed to the provincial government regarding this matter, there have already been communications between the Premier of Ontario and the Prime Minister of Canada on the subject; we hope that it will be possible for intergovernmental review within this country to continue, and that the federal authority, in whose jurisdiction this copyright question falls, will be able to negotiate an end to the disability which these non-tariff barriers work on the Canadian graphic arts and book publishing industries. As Mr. Curry states in his background paper:

... Canadian book publishing is engaged in a fight for survival against great odds, and ... the manufacturing provisions lengthen those odds considerably:

1. Canadian publishing's main competition comes from the world's largest and most sophisticated graphic arts industry, located next door in the United States.

2. The U.S. industry has inherent advantages in size of runs, access to greater variety of papers and bindings, and availability of a variety of manufacturing facilities.

3. The same unions and wage scales apply on both sides of the border, giving an automatic cost advantage on plate and set-up costs to the United States.

4. Books and printing of all kinds enter Canada relatively freely from the United States. This is somewhat of a one-way street, because the manufacturing provisions prevent Canadians from competing for the requirements of U.S. publishers.

5. As a result Canadian publishers, to stay competitive, must consider manufacturing in Europe, Asia, or the United States, while their domestic printing sources are effectively prevented from expanding to a more economical scale of operation.

With regard to the final two paragraphs just quoted, it should be noted that most books other than prescribed textbooks enter Canada from the United States subject to a duty of ten per cent, at least when they are imported in bulk through normal wholesale channels and not delivered directly to customers by the Post Office. On the other hand, duty is no longer imposed on foreign books entering the United States. But the competition does not lie at the level of trade in each other's copyrights, a fact which nullifies any countervailing effect that might be expected to flow from the seemingly favourable customs balance. The real barriers are of a non-tariff kind as Mr. Curry and others have pointed out. And the whole effect of the United States manufacturing provisions is to make Canadian production for Canadian publishers less competitive than it would otherwise be.

It is sometimes asked whether the sales volume of Canadian book exports, particularly to the United States, is large enough to attract American authors to this country for first publication in any event. Yet one of the reasons why export volume is low is that the manufacturing provisions exclude from Canadian catalogues almost every original work that might have sufficient relevance to the American scene to make a more expensive sales effort there viable, i.e. the very works about which the question is asked.

But if Canadian book publishing is injured directly by the United States manufacturing provisions, it suffers indirectly from the even greater harm which they work on the Canadian graphic arts industry. As we say elsewhere, we do not believe that a healthy national book industry can be achieved if the growth of any of its main branches is impeded; yet the United States Copyright Law has exerted a strangling influence on Canadian book manufacturing up to this time. Mr. Curry offers a number of examples, but one has only to think of the "Printed in USA" label which is omnipresent in this country to appreciate the significance of Canadian manufacturers being virtually denied the right to tender on American book requirements of any kind, for copyright reasons. Neither magazines nor books, including instruction manuals, annual reports, directories, and book club selections – even where an important part of the edition is to be distributed in Canada – may be imported into the United States if the authorship is American and United States copyright protection is wanted. But Canadian copyright is available regardless of the country of manufacture.

In 1971, book exports from the United States were valued at 177 million dollars of which Canada absorbed 45 per cent (with the United Kingdom next at 12 per cent). In the same year American book imports were 101 million dollars, of which Canada supplied only 11 per cent. Periodical exports by the United States in 1971 were 87 million dollars, of which Canada was again the largest purchaser, acccounting for 68 per cent. But total American periodical imports were 16 million dollars, with only 20 per cent of this value coming from Canada. (The value of other kinds of printed matter is not included in these U.S. Department of Commerce figures.) As Mr. Curry says, Canada buys more printing from the United States than do all other countries in the world combined. It is not without some reason, therefore, that the special thrust of the non-tariff barriers contained in the United States Copyright Law has been said to be against Canada, not against the lower wage countries of Asia and Europe.

We consider that the manufacturing provisions impose totally unjustifiable disabilities on the book manufacturing and publishing industries of this province and this country. They limit technological and economic growth in areas of Canadian enterprise which must be developed if our people are to have the incentive and the means to express their cultural identity in the future. Book publishing and book production are too intimately related for one to flourish while the other is forced to languish. And we do not believe that the solution is to seek extreme measures of reprisal, such as including corresponding manufacturing provisions in a new Canadian Copyright Act (a suggestion that is often heard). Such a move would only penalize successful Canadian authors, as well as alienate them, and we have too few of these to spare.

Apathy and unawareness must explain the fact that this inequitable situation was endured for so many years with so little outcry. It is hard to believe that almost all books produced in Canada before August 10, 1962 (when Canada's ratification of the Universal Copyright Convention became effective) were – and *still are* – in the public domain in the United States. It is just as hard to accept the fact that the copyrights of Canadian authors who are published and produced in the United States are protected in Canada, while the tender of a Canadian manufacturer to produce a Book-of-the-Month Club international selection of American authorship cannot be accepted without throwing the U.S. copyright into jeopardy.

Revision of the American legislation has been actively anticipated for many years, but for various reasons (apparently not related to the manufacturing provisions themselves) enactment of a new Copyright Law by the United States Congress has been deferred from session to session since 1965. An important stage in the consideration of new legislation was a revised Copyright Bill reported by the Senate Copyright Subcommittee in December, 1969, which was referred to the Committee on the Judiciary. This Bill included a specific exemption for Canada from a modified but fundamentally unchanged set of manufacturing requirements. Since then, action on the new copyright legislation has continued to be postponed, notwithstanding general support for its enactment on the part of American publishers, manufacturers, printing trade unions, and other interested constituencies in the United States. Although the exemption for Canada is incidental to the interests of these groups, the desirability that such an exemption should be granted has been recognized and formally supported by them since early in 1968, as explained by W. E. Curry in his background paper where he discusses the Agreement of Toronto signed in January of that year.

The economic and cultural consequences of a prolongation of the present situation are bound to become increasingly serious, especially in view of the many other problems that surround book publishing and book manufacturing in Canada today. It might be unrealistic to expect that the trade imbalance in printing which now favours the United States in a ratio of something like thirty to one can be equalized; as we have said elsewhere we are actually much more concerned with the cultural than the economic implications of the situation.

It grows increasingly clear that this imbalance must not continue to be shielded by international copyright agreements which contain exceptions and conditions that are not mutual. This is a position which could be greatly strengthened not only by leadership from the federal government, which we have been assured has been given, but by support from the public at large, on both sides of the border. This might well be forthcoming, and in meaningful measure, if the apathy and unawareness just mentioned could be dispelled by a responsible public information program carried forward on a sufficiently broad scale. The industry which this Commission was appointed to study is operating under a serious disability in the international field, the very area in which it must expand if it is to survive. We have considerable confidence that if present hopes for relief are not realized, an accurately informed public opinion could be induced to demand it.

OTHER DESIRABLE STATUTORY REVISIONS

Unpublished letters and other unpublished manuscripts held by libraries and museums are normally the subject of perpetual copyright. This is so even though they may be open (in the absence of instructions to the contrary) to examination by the public. It follows that they may therefore be published only by permission of the copyright owner. These and other restrictions on the lawful use that may be made of such materials by library users suggest revisions that would seem desirable in the Copyright Act. Some of these changes could facilitate the writing and publishing of new books which make use of such materials without abridging the rights of the original authors, whom it indeed may not longer be possible to identify, much less to locate.

Publication by library exposure

It would be helpful, we think, if the public exhibition of manuscript materials by a library or other public institution, when such exhibition is authorized, could be deemed to constitute publication, and if the Copyright Act were revised accordingly. This would mean that public circulation would require the permission of the copyright owner, or at least an effort by the institution to find the copyright owner for the purpose of seeking permission (perhaps by discharging some simple conditions prescribed in the legislation itself). Several advantages might accrue to the public, including authors and publishers, if materials freely available for use in libraries could be deemed to have been published in the absence of specific notice to the contrary.

Most important is the right to quote short passages under the provisions of Section 17(2). These permit fair dealing with any work for the purposes of private study, research, criticism, review, or newspaper summary. "Fair dealing" has been defined by the courts, and clearly includes the right of an individual to make a single copy of an extract of a work, possibly of the whole of a work, in the course of any of the activities just listed, assuming that they are bona fide. But fair dealing is not permitted with respect to an unpublished work, granted that in practice unpublished works in libraries are exposed to being dealt with in a host of ways. (It would be manifestly unfair if an unpublished literary work could be made, without the consent of its creator, the subject of criticism or review, much less of newspaper summary.) Once the copyright owner, meaning usually the author in the first instance, authorizes publication, he also opens his work to fair dealing, and rightly so. Nor is there any valid argument why publication in any way of a work which an author did not intend to publish (that is, make available to the public) should constitute fair dealing if it means publishing it without the permission of the author.

The revision of the Act to accomplish the above would not normally deprive a copyright owner of his right to leave his material unpublished, and therefore unquoted, if he were not yet ready to give the public access to it. But he does this, it seems to us, when he authorizes its circulation by a library, even though he may not authorize anyone to print copies for sale or public distribution. From the standpoint of the library user, it is desirable that dissertations and theses, for example, should be open to fair dealing in the same way as other books in a library's holdings. (The fact that commonly they may be erroneously thought to be subject to fair dealing is irrelevant.)

To sum up, we think that it would be in the interest of all concerned – the public, the author, and possibly publishers – if (a) the statutory definition of publication were extended to include the authorized exposure to the public of even one copy of a manuscript continuously over a reasonable period of time, and if (b) libraries and other institutions were therefore required on deposit of the manuscript to secure permission from the copyright owner to publish it in this way, whenever the latter is know or can with reasonable diligence be established. There could be a statutory conversion to published status of manuscripts deposited for circulation in the past, in order to clarify their situation and to minimize the administrative problems that would be involved in securing permissions retrospectively.

Such a statutory revision would for the first time make possible fair dealing with manuscripts hitherto considered unpublished, but available to library users. It would also legitimize whatever degree of photocopying ought to be permitted under the head of fair dealing. This would be an accomplishment, for there can be no lawful photocopying of unpublished manuscripts at present. This is because there can be no fair dealing with them within the meaning of Section 17(2), whether by photocopying or any other means. If the existing situation does not in practice inhibit the creative use of library resources – including such items as unpublished letters let it be remembered – it does so in law at least. We have considered instances of correspondence being available to biographers, but not available for quotation in the course of research writing except through tortuous and uncertain inquiries by correspondence. Moreover, the technological advances which have so vastly increased the accessibility of library holdings to an ever-expanding body of users, often at different institutions simultaneously, make it undesirable to distinguish (from the standpoint of published status) between the deposit of one copy of a manuscript in a library and the deposit of a number of copies in a number of libraries.

If authorized exposure of manuscript material were to constitute publication, the term of the copyright would begin to run with the death of the author (or with the act of publication in this manner), whichever occurred last. Universities can procure the right to publish theses and dissertations from the latter's authors as a condition of enrolment, granted that such students limit the scope of the assignment or licence to fair dealing of the kind already described. The fact is that if such manuscripts are not deemed to have been published, many of the normal activities of research being conducted today respecting them are unlawful.

At the same time, copyright owners of important archives could be assured of privacy when they wish to defer publication, but wish nonetheless to place valuable source materials in the professional custody of an institution. That is, they would be less inclined, perhaps, to destroy important letters and similar materials than they are now, because the illegality of unauthorized publication by photocopying and other forms of reprography would no longer be cloaked by an ambiguous status of the item being copied. This should be an added incentive to people in public life, for example, to entrust their files to libraries subject to whatever conditions regarding publication they wish to place upon them; it is quite true that responsible libraries already respect scrupulously conditions of gift or assignment, but it would be well to add this assurance that recovery or injunctions could be sought in the event of inadvertent publication.

There are other breaches of confidence that can occur by unlawful publication, including even the "leaking" of classified documents. Regardless of one's views on the desirability of openness in all such matters, it is difficult to argue that the right to privacy should be wrested from copyright owners, whether the latter be private individuals or governments, whenever confidential letters can be placed in front of a xerox duplicator. Official examination papers are another example of confidential material whose misappropriation in any way should be capable of being controlled. It is not satisfactory, we think, to have to rely entirely on other remedies, including sometimes criminal law, to restrict their unlawful reproduction.

The United Kingdom Act of 1956 provides, in Section 7(6), that after fifty years from the death of an author and after at least one hundred years from the creation of a work which is in copyright but has not been published, and where the manuscript or a copy of the work is kept in a library, museum or other institution where it is open to public inspection, then copyright in the work is not infringed by a person who reproduces the work for purposes of research or private study, or with a view to publication. The suggestion we have made, however, would include current works by living authors. By extending the definition of publication in the way we have proposed, including appropriate legislation regarding existing manuscripts lawfully being made available to the public at present, the problem of perpetual copyright in library materials is eliminated. The few exceptions would perhaps include original documents entrusted to institutions under the condition that they not be published for a fixed number of years, and new additions of manuscripts added to the physical inventory of a library without permission from the copyright owner to reproduce; the latter might well include ancient documents. These exceptions could easily be covered in revised legislation, in our view, in ways that would serve the public interest fully.

Compulsory registration of copyright

If the authorized exposure of manuscripts to the public were to constitute publication, the latter would doubtless carry (or should carry) notices of copyright ownership as a matter of course. It would be in the interests of authors if this normally took the form of the Universal Copyright Convention notice. Then the procedure for researchers wishing to procure permission to publish beyond the limits of fair dealing would be immediately apparent. Indeed, the desirability of streamlining the process of identifying the copyright owner was neatly advocated by the Economic Council *Report on Intellectual and Industrial Property:*

Today, with communications and other information technology greatly improved and with governments more continuously in touch with each other on copyright matters, formal national and international registration of copyright in works could be carried through much more quickly, cheaply and certainly. The United States, it may be noted, already has a national copyright registration system. The advantages of general compulsory registration, which if the system were well-designed would be primarily those of more rapid identification of owners and securing of rights, now appear to exceed the disadvantages. Canada should . . . be prepared to set an example in her own domestic system . . .

Provided that the system of registration could be truly simple and uncostly to users, we think that this recommendation has great merit at this time in history. It is difficult to see how it could be applied retroactively to existing copyrights, and these of course should not be prejudiced in any way. However, it might well be possible to require all assignments (although not necessarily all licences) to be registered under the same system.

We offer the further suggestion that for books the International Standard Book Number system be used for the purpose of identification; if this could be done, it would be all the more desirable that the latter should be given official recognition and made an administrative responsibility of either the National Library or the Copyright Office, under statutory authority, as discussed elsewhere in this report. It is assumed that if registration were introduced in this country, it would relate to Canadian works only, of course. Anyone who has had to locate the copyright owners of all passages to be included in a complex anthology will appreciate how much expense could be saved by an efficient registration system, granted that such advantages could be realized only gradually as all new Canadian copyrights were brought within its purview. But savings at the editorial stage in publishing can stimulate publication itself, and consequently the proposal is of much interest to this Commission. It is hardly necessary to add that it has a special value in a world in which communications technology is undergoing the most radical revolution since the day of Gutenberg.

Protection of extemporaneous lectures and commentaries

The mere delivery of a lecture or live address on radio or television probably does not constitute publication within the meaning of the present Act. Apart from certain special rights granted to newspapers to report public lectures, it seems that when a lecture is delivered without notes and without having been expressed to some extent at least in a material form that has reasonable substance, it is vulnerable to copying and possibly even to formal publication by a second party who would thereupon enjoy copyright protection in it (even though he might acknowledge the authorship accurately). It does seem that authors should be protected against every such possible misappropriation of their creative works, especially in this day of omnipresent and highly portable tape recorders.

Apart from the right of a newspaper to report a public lecture, therefore, which no doubt should be retained, it seems unthinkable that important lectures – which are more and more likely to be related to subsequent creative works of literary criticism and political commentary (to name just one kind of ensuing publication that is possible) – must be "read" in order to be capable of protection, or must be cast in a form that can be read. We think that the present statutory protection should be extended to include the content not only of lectures but of interviews and discussions, including those on radio and television. Otherwise there is a danger that a parasitic publishing industry could be developed to publish books based on the informal, but frequently highly informed, comments by public figures. It does not tax the imagination to think of books made up simply of news photographs of such personalities, held together by a substantial text derived from recordings of their public interviews and news conferences, and attributed firmly to them as authors. Conceivably, the extemporaneous comments of prominent journalists or commentators might also be collected over a period of time and republished as new copyrights by those who did the collecting, assuming that the recording was done from live broadcasts and telecasts. Another apparent copyright exposure arises where research workers interview individuals in the course of field studies, or even where a Royal Commission such as our own holds a public hearing and transcribes the best thoughts of a dozen Canadian authors on the subject of writing and publishing. The degree of control over publication which can be exercised by the authors in such cases should hardly turn on whether or not a written manuscript exists. Nor would the author's droit moral ensure more than accurate transcription. In this day of multi-media, when librarians are found in resource centres and are as likely to be tangled in miles of audio tape as weighted down with armfuls of books, issues such as these become serious.

We believe therefore that Section 2 of the Copyright Act should broaden the definition of a "work" to include speeches, lectures, and interviews whether or not these exist in manuscript form, so long as their form is tangible, e.g. a sound recording made by anyone. The ability to prove authorship of the verbatim text would in practice be as feasible for the author as for the copyist, and the right of the author to restrain the latter could be assured. Section 3(2) of the Act should also be revised to extend the meaning of "publication" to include creative work of the kind just described.

Compulsory licences under present Copyright Act

There is adequate provision in the Copyright Act, and the Canadian statute seems to be unique in this regard, to require copyright owners to reprint out-of-print publications or to allow others to reprint them under a compulsory licence on equitable terms. Thus the situation does not arise in this country in which a work is no longer in print but remains in copyright with the copyright owner barring its being reprinted although the demand supports such action. It might be supposed that this is an unlikely situation as it would not be in the copyright owner's financial interest to stand in the way of a reprint under such circumstances. However reprinting technology has moved rapidly forward in recent years, and copyright owners – including the heirs of authors – are sometimes loath to see earlier works reappear, especially without revisions and updatings, which may be expensive and impracticable. There is a new interest in the history of scholarship in many fields, including Canadian studies of all kinds, and we do not think that harm is done to an author's reputation by the reprinting of a work whose publication he authorized previously. At least the harm done to the cause of scholarship would be greater if permission to do this could be withheld. Therefore we do not think that the compulsory licensing provision included in Section 13 of the Act should be rescinded, as has sometimes been proposed.

Section 14 of the Act provides that any person may apply to the Minister for a licence to print and publish in Canada any book wherein copyright subsists, if at any time after publication and within the duration of the copyright the owner of the copyright fails to produce copies in Canada or to supply by means of copies so produced the reasonable demands of the Canadian market for such a book. These provisions have rarely been invoked, but careful thought should be given before they are removed from the Act when it is being revised. At least, Section 14 provides a useful bargaining point in international copyright negotiations; it ensures availability in a Canadian edition, where this is important, of any copyright work whenever the demand is sufficient to justify its reprinting here; and it is distinguished from the manufacturing provisions in the United States Copyright Law in that it guarantees a royalty to the copyright owner and does not impair the copyright. It is possible for a work to go out of print abroad and, although a marginal demand sufficient to cover the costs of a reprinting might continue in Canada, its being withheld from republication by the foreign publisher would make it inaccessible to Canadian readers. (This situation is most likely to arise regarding a work about Canada, of course.) The feasibility of reprinting a book for the Canadian market only, albeit in so small an edition that there would be little financial incentive to a foreign publisher to undertake it, is increasing as reprinting technology advances. It is now technically possible to reproduce library editions of as few as fifty copies at reasonable prices, for example. As a result, the time should be approaching when there will be few books indeed, particularly in Canadian studies, that need to remain out of print if even a modest library demand for them exists. Therefore we think that Section 14 should be retained, notwithstanding the pressures that have arisen to have it removed from the Act.

Reproduction twenty-five years after author's death

Section 7 of the Copyright Act provides that after the expiration of twenty-five years from the death of the author of a published work, copyright in the work shall not be deemed to be infringed if the person reproducing the work proves that he has given the prescribed notice in writing of his intention to reproduce the work and that he has paid in the prescribed manner to or for the benefit of the copyright owner royalties in respect of all copies sold by him. This section clearly depreciates the value of the original copyright by limiting the exclusive term for the owner or his assigns. We think it should be removed on the grounds that instead of encouraging publication of further editions, which would seem to have been its intent, it is likely to discourage publication in the first place by reducing the speculative attraction of the author's manuscript, if it has any effect at all.

Doubtless few works are undertaken on the assumption that costs will be recovered over a period of as long as twenty-five years. But in addition to occasional encyclopedic projects that do fall into that category, it is not necessarily in the author's interests for his work to fall virtually into the public domain (except for a royalty requirement) at the end of such a period. That is to say, the loss of exclusivity of the right to reprint is more likely to dissuade publishers from republishing than to encourage them to do so in competition with one another. There may be some rivalry in the race to be the first to reprint important items of Canadiana; however, the prospect of being the second or third is generally unattractive to publishers. A literary property will attain its greatest value if the exclusivity of the copyright in it can be assured for the full normal term of life of the author plus fifty years.

Section 12(5) provides for the reversion to the legal representatives of an author's estate twenty-five years after his death of any assignment made by him for any longer period, except in the case of collective works. This section is difficult to reconcile fully with Section 7, discussed above. Its purpose must have been to give the heirs of an author an opportunity to renegotiate the publishing agreements entered into by him during his lifetime, although Section 7 says that they could not offer exclusive rights anyway. As with Section 7, we think this provision probably causes a greater devaluation in the total value of all original copyrights than it increases the value of the few that may still be in print at the end of the twenty-five year period. At least the effect of Section 12(5) seems likely to be either negative or negligible; whichever is so, we recommend that it be rescinded.

INTERNATIONAL COPYRIGHT

Canada's principal international copyright commitments have been summarized in the Economic Council report previously referred to, in a background paper by Roy C. Sharp, Q.C. already published, and in many other sources; there is no reason to review them here. Suffice it to say that this country has long been a member of the Berne Union, having ratified the Rome revision of the latter treaty in 1928. It also ratified the newer Universal Copyright Convention in 1962. Most western nations with which Canada has active cultural relations share its membership in both agreements with a few significant exceptions including the United States. The latter country has never become a member of the Berne Union, although in 1956 it ratified the four-year-old Universal Copyright Convention, well ahead of Canada which did not follow suit until six years later. The Soviet Union has until now stood apart from both agreements.

This Commission takes the view that Canadian publishers must join the mainstream of international commerce in books if they are to find the markets they need in order to produce competitively. If they are to succeed in this, it is essential (among other conditions) that Canadian legislation impose the smallest possible number of unique copyright disabilities on works published in this country. That is to say, it must be as advantageous for authors to publish in Canada as anywhere else in the world, at least in so far as the legal protection afforded their works by Canadian legislation is concerned. Works of American authorship published in Canada are under a disability which has already been adequately commented upon. Yet incredible though it seems, until Canada ratified the Universal Convention in 1962, and thereby was able to benefit from United States adherence to it, this disability included works by Canadian authors as well.

If publication (or republication) in Canada involves a lesser degree of protection for the author than publication elsewhere, it will be more difficult for Canadian publishers to obtain contracts from authors or, in the case of co-publishing arrangements, from foreign publishers. If, for example, there were a copyright advantage for a British author or publisher to arrange for a North American edition to be published in the United States instead of Canada, the choice is a foregone conclusion. In the marketing of international rights that is always going on, decisions of this kind have to be taken constantly. Until now, the only authors from abroad who are likely to seek initial publication in Canada are those with scholarly manuscripts. This is because scholarly publishing is international in nature and distribution. Even so, prominent American authors can be persuaded to publish in this country only if the American manufacturing sanctions can be avoided. This can only be done by manufacturing their books, under Canadian imprints, in the United States, unless the import ceiling of 1500 copies under ad interim copyright is adequate for the American market.

It has occasionally been suggested, sometimes even in government circles, that there might be a net advantage to Canada if this country were to withdraw from all international copyright agreements and protect its own authors by domestic legislation only. We think it is doubtful if Canadian authorship, let alone Canadian publishing, could ever live down the stigma that would be earned internationally if such a step were ever taken, or even openly contemplated. Having regard for the concerns that led to the appointment of this Commission, we think that any kind of denunciation by Canada of her international copyright agreements would be the quickest kind of cultural suicide that could be devised. Canadian authorship of every kind – academic, journalistic, or whatever – would then find itself left in a cultural backwater by its own government.

One context in which retrogressive action in relation to general international copyright commitments has been contemplated has been with regard to the proper term of copyright. The revised Copyright Bill reported by the United States Senate Copyright Committee in December, 1969 (discussed earlier) provides a term of life of the author plus fifty years, generally accepted by other western countries and made mandatory under the Brussels revision of the Berne Convention (which Canada did not ratify). If Canada were for any reason to adopt a shorter term than this, it would only contribute to the imbalance that marks this country's present international commerce in copyrights. Or if the right of Canadians to reproduce foreign works without permission were extended beyond their present limits, the attractiveness of Canada as a possible publishing scene would be further reduced.

Our domestic book market is too small now, and the acceptability of our books abroad could be permanently prejudiced if this country were even to toy with playing the role of a Taiwan in international publishing. Canada should resist every temptation to abandon any of its international agreements in order that its publishers and printers may pirate the works of others, whether for use here or for export abroad. If we were to debase the value of Canadian copyright in any of these ways, we would quickly drive our best authors elsewhere, and earn the condemnation of every literate nation.

THE COMPETITION ACT (BILL C-256)

The tabling of Bill C-256 in the House of Commons on June 29, 1971, had repercussions in many segments of Canadian industry, and it may not be surprising that we heard numerous comments regarding its possible impact on creative authorship and publishing in Canada. These comments were made by authors and publishers in briefs and informal submissions to this Commission. We were wary about being influenced by the fact that virtually every assessment of the proposed Act reflected apprehension that the Bill not only dealt with business practices which are contrary to competition policy, but that it isolated copyright as a specified area of concern. However, as we studied the provision of the Bill in relation to our terms of reference our own misgivings regarding the suggested legislation mounted.

We cannot be certain of the future status of the Competition Act, although Bill C-256 (as we shall continue to describe it here) has at this time been withdrawn pending reintroduction later. But we feel obliged to report briefly on it, strictly from the standpoint of writing and publishing, for the guidance of the provincial government in any further representations the latter may wish to make to the federal government concerning the Bill. We do not necessarily accept as valid every criticism that has been put forward (according to our understanding) by such groups as the Canadian Book Publishers' Council, although we note that some of the fears expressed by that body, by the Canadian Copyright Institute, and by individual authors and publishers do run parallel with our own.

Clause 37 of Bill C-256 provides for orders of prohibition to be issued by the proposed Tribunal against "a person or persons ... in a monopoly position within the meaning of section 41." The latter section reads as follows:

41. For the purposes of section 37,
   (a) a person is in a monopoly position when he, or
   (b) two or more persons are in a monopoly position when they, acting in concert or apparently in concert,
either
   (c) completely or substantially controls or control, in a market, a class of business in which he is or they are engaged, or
   (d) accounts or account for all or substantially all of a commodity or service that is supplied for or in a market,
whether or not such position results in whole or in part from ownership of or the right to use any patent, trade mark, copyright or industrial design.

This Commission is not concerned with patents, trade marks, or industrial designs, but the inclusion of *copyright* in this definition of monopoly position is another matter. It appears to place both authors and their assignees in a hopelessly ambiguous position, if indeed it does not seriously limit the value of the only stock-in-trade they possess, viz. the statutory copyrights they acquire in their works by virtue of the Copyright Act. Copyright is by its nature an exclusive right, and the copyright owner either possesses this right or he does not. If he does not, he has no right that that he can enforce, and his effort to do so can be upset by ordinary civil process. There is no reason to suppose, as the Bill seems to, that he will be able to enforce rights he does not enjoy. From what we have seen, he is more likely to fail to enforce rights he possesses.

Sections 48 and 51 of Bill C-256 describe orders that may be issued by the Tribunal to void copyright altogether, or to require the grant of a compulsory licence to other persons "on such conditions as the Tribunal considers appropriate."

It seems to us, as it apparently has to Canadian authors and publishers, that a copyright owner is usually – by virtue of the exclusive rights conferred by the Copyright Act – in the position of accounting for "all or substantially all of a commodity or service that is supplied for or in a market" and is ipso facto in a monopoly position within the meaning of Section 41. We do not believe that it can be argued, on the basis of the legislation as drafted, that the monopoly position so defined arises only when the normal privilege of copyright is exceeded by its owner. Even if no action by the Tribunal should be anticipated except where the copyright privilege has been exceeded, we fail to perceive why the remedial action should under any circumstances extend to the setting aside of the statutory copyright itself, or to limiting its value by requiring the granting of a compulsory licence. It could be argued that in such circumstances the Tribunal might be empowered to issue some kind of cease and desist order respecting the unenforceable claim of copyright, but the latter can be set aside quite effectively by ordinary court procedures now available, or be ignored without resort to legal process at all, which is what usually happens in such situations.

Surely copyright is either created by the appropriate statute, the Copyright Act, or it is not. The copyright owner should not be put in the position of having to speculate regarding the legal propriety of his exploiting the copyright in his own interest or, in the case of a publisher, in the interests of his author as well. Indeed, if Canadian cultural interests are to be served fully by our writers and publishers, it is desirable that the latter should be encouraged to create and exploit to their maximum legal value copyright material of every kind. Neither authors, nor publishers – on whom the ambiguity in the Bill seems to weigh most directly – can be expected to expand their services if at the same time a new statute makes it advisable for them to pull their punches.

Clause 41 defines the conditions under which a monopoly position arises, and Section 17 prohibits the monopoly position so defined:

17. No person and no affiliated companies, partnerships or sole proprietorships shall, ...
    (b) wilfully engage in behaviour that is intended to place him, either alone or together with one or more other persons, in a monopoly position within the meaning of section 41.

Section 73(1) prescribes penalties as follows:

73. (1) any person who violates ... section 17 is guilty of an indictable offence and is liable
    (a) for a first offence, to imprisonment for two years or to a fine not exceeding one million dollars or to both; and
    (b) for each subsequent offence, to imprisonment for five years or to a fine not exceeding two million dollars or to both.

Even a remote possibility that these provisions might be applied to efforts to control the exclusive right to market copyrights cannot seriously be contemplated by anyone who is acquainted with the practicalities of book publishing in this country. And yet Section 41 would seem to do precisely this when it says that "*a person is in a monopoly position when he ... accounts ... for ... substantially all of a commodity ... that is supplied for or in a market, whether or not such position results in whole or in part from ownership of or the right to use any ... copyright ...*" [Italics added]

In our efforts to rationalize the specific inclusion of copyright in Bill C-256 we have asked ourselves how the public interest has been adversely affected by copyright privilege as it has been exercised in Canada in the past, or as it might be improperly exercised in the future. Not for the first time we have concluded that so long as a distinction is made between short-term public convenience and long-term public interest, the normal methods of marketing copyright matter should encourage the creation of more, not less, original publishing.

This is not to say that revisions in the Copyright Act are not desirable in order to bring its principles into line with user requirements and modern technology. We have offered a number of suggestions for such revisions already and doubtless many other changes are under consideration. Perhaps the right to withhold licences that would permit use of copyright information in retrieval systems should be restricted. Compulsory licences should perhaps be called for in other situations. It did not seem to be the responsibility of this report to develop more suggestions than we have. But these and other limitations on copyright belong in our opinion to the Copyright Act, and not to the discretion of a tribunal appointed under a completely separate statute.

In speculating on possible copyright abuses which might warrant separate statutory supervision of the kind contemplated by Bill C-256, it has occurred to us that the framers of that legislation could have had in mind the exclusive agency system whereby most foreign-published books are distributed in this country. This system was discussed by the Economic Council in its *Report on Intellectual and Industrial Property*, and reviewed earlier in this chapter. We have already pointed out that (*a*) with regard to the distribution of foreign publishers' complete lines of publications this system does not turn on copyright so much as on trading agreements in which no equitable interest in copyright is assigned; and (*b*) the Economic Council did not distinguish between such exclusive agency arrangements respecting whole lists of titles and co-publishing arrangements respecting specific works in which territorial copyrights may be assigned. If it should be the intention to limit the right of Canadian publishers to buy and sell territorial copyrights by means of the powers to be vested in the Tribunal under Bill C-256, then the expansion of Canadian publishing into international markets will be effectively halted by the same legislation. It is not good enough, we repeat, for the administrators of the proposed Act to say that they would not enforce it in this way; the inclusion of copyright as a specified area of concern of the proposed Act strongly suggests that it would be best for Canadian publishers not to run any risks.

The Economic Council observed that

> ... the Canadian copyright system should be aimed as exclusively as possible at its primary incentive function. It should not be used as an economic and informational trade barrier between Canada and other countries nor be extended beyond its basic grant of right into a vehicle for practices contrary to competition policy.

We reiterate our concurrence that copyright should first and last aim at furnishing incentive to Canadian authorship, which necessarily includes the marketing of copyright materials through publishers in Canada and, hopefully, abroad. But we also repeat that the incentive function will be compromised if we deprive the Canadian author or publisher of the right to market his copyrights as advantageously as he can, both in Canada and throughout the world. If we say, and we pointed this out earlier, that he may not sell or license a cheap overrun edition for sale abroad without permitting that edition to come back into the Canadian market, we shall merely be ensuring that foreign marketing of this kind will not be attempted. Not by Canadians, at least.

The reference in the last quotation to "practices contrary to competition policy" adds a pejorative dimension to copyright that may appear to make the recommendation self-justifying. Section 41 of Bill C-265 virtually casts every copyright owner "in a monopoly position" by including in that definition any person who "accounts ... for all or substantially all of a commodity or service that is supplied for or in a market." Why should it not be said that most practices related to the exploitation of a copyright are therefore contrary to competition policy, when Section 41 makes the normal marketing of a copyright a self-incriminating act? Again it will be urged that Section 41 would not be invoked unless there were abuse of the copyright privilege. But in our view there is no way at all for a copyright owner to know how far he may go in exploiting his copyright property in the marketplace, be it manuscript or published book.

Section 51(3) of Bill C-256 provides that no order may be made under that section (e.g. voiding the copyright or requiring the issue of competing licences) that is at variance with any treaty or convention between Canada and any other country. It is understandable that the legislation should aim at avoiding conflict with Canada's obligations under the Berne Convention and the Universal Copyright Convention. But our concern is that these international agreements do not necessarily prevent the kind of intimidation of domestic writing and publishing that the proposed legislation threatens to accomplish. If publication in Canada implies reduced copyright protection, or if it places the copyright owner in an ambiguous position with respect to his right to market copyrights anywhere, then Canada will be placed under a disability in comparison with other possible countries for original publication, and also for co-publication. This is because what applies to original publication of Canadian and non-Canadian manuscripts applies also to the international buying and selling of territorial editions of works of domestic and foreign authorship.

One of the principal reasons for the appointment of this Commission was that the Canadian book industry appeared to be approaching an economic crisis that could have serious cultural consequences, and the evidence we have gathered and the recommendations contained in this report do not contradict that assumption in any way. There has not been a time in recent publishing history when government action of a kind that could inhibit book writing or book publishing in Canada, even to the slightest degree, would be more inappropriate or when it could have more far-reaching undesirable consequences.

Most authors featured by Canadian-owned publishers are themselves Canadians, and this is a time when the survival of our original publishing can depend on straws, even if we hope that it will be proffered more. It is a time when too few of the best-known Canadian imprints of the past continue to appear on new books, at least on behalf of Canadian-owned publishers. And yet a substantial number of eager, small Canadian firms are seeking opportunities to enter the mainstream of publishing. It is therefore decidedly not a time to introduce avoidable restrictions or uncertainties into Canadian publishing, or to ask the industry to operate within parameters which are either too constricting to encourage the kind of creative cultural speculation we need or too ambiguous to be easily understood by all concerned.

This Commission is strongly of the opinion that, regardless of other considerations concerning the proposed legislation, neither Bill C-256 nor any successor Bill respecting monopolies should contain any reference to copyright as such, and that the rights and privileges of copyright should be defined in the Copyright Act, amended as may be necessary, and nowhere else.

THE NEED FOR RESEARCH

We think that the various segments of the Canadian book industry – including authors, publishers, manufacturers, librarians, booksellers, and many related groups and sub-groups – have individually been so defensive in their dealings with one another that they have sometimes retarded rather than given collective momentum to the literary development of this country. Individual bodies will doubtless protest their being joined in any such indictment, saying that they have always acted for the literary enrichment of the country, although agreeing cheerfully that indifference if not downright selfishness has marked the policies of other groups of bookmen. A substantial aroma of distrust usually fills the air whenever two or more professional and/or trade organizations do sit down together, and the fact that such joint meetings seem to be extraordinarily rare affairs only adds to our concern. There has been an obvious failure on the part of those who create and handle books to rationalize their programs in the common cultural interest of this country.

This is no plea for stronger or more active associations, either trade or professional; the book industry is well enough endowed in this regard already – possibly too well, to judge from the redundant membership fees which many of its members pay. But what the industry does require, in our opinion, is access to a central information and research facility operating independently of any constituent interests. Its function would be to conduct surveys and foster research projects regarding as many as possible of the copyright issues that concern the writing and use of books in Canada. The long-term public interest, that is the long-term Canadian public interest, should be the sole criterion by which such a research organization should determine priorities in its many possible programs.

It should be clear by now that this Commission considers that copyright – a federal jurisdiction – is virtually synonymous with books, whether one has in mind how they are written, how they are manufactured and published, or how they are marketed through the many alternate channels through which their contents become accessible to the public. The mere fact that this provincial Commission has heard as much about copyright as it has from authors, publishers, printers, booksellers, and libraries, highlights our contention that it is copyright that should bring the book world together. It is regrettable indeed that its different branches have too often approached copyright as special pleaders, and so have allowed it to divide them.

A simple list of typical copyright "topics" can precipitate as many points of view as there are disparate interests in the Canadian book world. Territorial rights; the agency system; the right to copy; the right to produce multiple copies; the public lending right; the definitions of publication and of fair dealing; the right to manufacture abroad; assignment versus licence; the proper term on copyright; format copyright; the issue of compulsory licensing; information storage and retrieval; microform publication and republication; the problem of permissions; the right to quote – can there be any question that these are topics that more often arouse emotions than logical thought? No one group whose vital interests seem to be brought to the stake by the above brief catalogue of copyright issues can, with the best will in the world, respond with solutions that will convince the rest of the book community, not even if its proposals are given statutory sanction. A government-sponsored copyright research organization (necessarily federally sponsored) on whose council all interested bodies could be represented alongside government, but which would not answer to any special interests in the conduct of its research or in the publication of its findings, might command the respect of all segments of the industry. At all events, it should.

The Canadian Copyright Institute has lacked the broad support that would qualify it for a role such as the one just described. Although its brief, referred to earlier in this chapter, lists some nine sustaining members, four associate members, and "several private fellows," it is not financed and therefore it is not governed in a way that permits it to give objective leadership in exploring controversial issues of the kind described a little earlier. The brief from Robert H. Blackburn and David G. Esplin speaks for itself when it says, "Unfortunately, as a mere associate member of the Canadian Copyright Institute our Library has had no access to the Institute's brief or any discussions on which it may be based . . ." In our view, Canadian libraries in general should be as completely involved in the work of this kind of body as any other book interests, and the Institute should not be beholden to anyone but the public. If this kind of relationship could be established, we think it might serve a valuable purpose both in resolving domestic issues and by permitting Canada to give international leadership in the field of copyright reform. We do not believe that government can do this, even with the advice of the Economic Council, unless the practical problems of those who create, deal in, and lend books can be fully taken into account.

We have learned from our own experience as a Commission that even public hearings of invited briefs serve to enhance rather than modify an adversary relationship among interested parties, and it is this which we think should be eliminated so that policies can be arrived at which are convincing, even if not pleasing, to all. A government-sponsored copyright research organization could accomplish this if it planned its research projects independently and openly, turning only for broad advice to a council representative of all book interests, including appropriate civil servants. It should guard against pronouncing judgments which are not based on thorough field studies, when these are applicable, and it should ensure that the advice from constituent bodies on the council is shared by and, if necessary, commented upon by all of them. Neither the research body nor its advisory council should be called on to make representations to government, but it would be hoped that the studies it might undertake would be fully reported and that its findings would carry weight with government. Finally, such a research organization should be as sensitive to the cultural implications of copyright as to the economic ones, and its terms of reference should be explicit on this point.

4
Book Markets and Book Marketing

The financial troubles of Canadian book publishers have sometimes been attributed to poor marketing, but we received much evidence that an unanticipated deterioration of the market itself is a more reasonable explanation. That is not to say that the distribution of books in Canada is as efficient as it might be; our attention was drawn to many shortcomings in the system, some of which we shall return to in this report.

Educational publishing in particular has suffered from changes in grants policy, from the sudden flourishing of non-print media, from a trend away from the use of basic textbooks in classroom sets, from a weakening (in practice if not in theory) of the policy of Canadian preference in schoolbook selection, and from other related developments of the past very few years. At the same time, publishing of original Canadian trade books has shared with educational publishing the dilemma of spiralling increases in manufacturing costs, while every direct expenditure on promotion from advertising to prospectuses and mailings has also involved paying much more to obtain much less.

As noted in Chapter 1, the most meaningful statistics regarding the size and breakdown of the market for books are those contained in the Ernst & Ernst report prepared for the Department of Industry, Trade and Commerce. Even though it offers many "soft" statistics, some of the critically important figures it uses having had to be based on estimates, its importance lies in the value of its quantitative reporting rather than its qualitative evaluation of the problems of publishing and their possible solutions. The analysis was timely, even if a much greater range of statistics would make it correspondingly more useful to the industry. It is to be hoped that this study will be continued and broadened in scope, and that the industry will be fully involved in its planning and conscientious in providing the necessary returns. Obviously a survey of this kind would have to continue to deal

BOOK MARKETS AND BOOK MARKETING 123

with the total Canadian book industry; thus it is not a suitable provincial undertaking. Such an expanded study should be published annually, or biennially at least. And participation in it should be mandatory for all publishers and manufacturers. Probably this could be achieved under existing statutes if the project could be undertaken by Statistics Canada.

The Ernst & Ernst report establishes the Canadian consumption of books in 1969 at 222 million dollars, of which approximately 191 million were English and 27 million French. It was also estimated that of the total consumption, about 161 million dollars' worth was sold by publishers in Canada, 77 million being chiefly manufactured in Canada and 84 million imported from publishers abroad. Some 61 million dollars' worth of additional books were imported directly by customers, not through publisher-agents, presumably largely by or for libraries. Against these import figures, approximately 5.5 million dollars' worth of books were exported from Canada. Low though it is, this last figure could be misleadingly high, because it may include some mass-market paperback (and conceivably periodical) manufacturing for publishers located in the United States. There is little enough of the latter, however, by virtue of the manufacturing provisions in the United States Copyright Law, which are discussed in William Curry's background paper and in Chapter 3 of this report. Still more important, export sales of this kind do not

ORIGIN OF BOOKS SOLD IN CANADA IN 1969

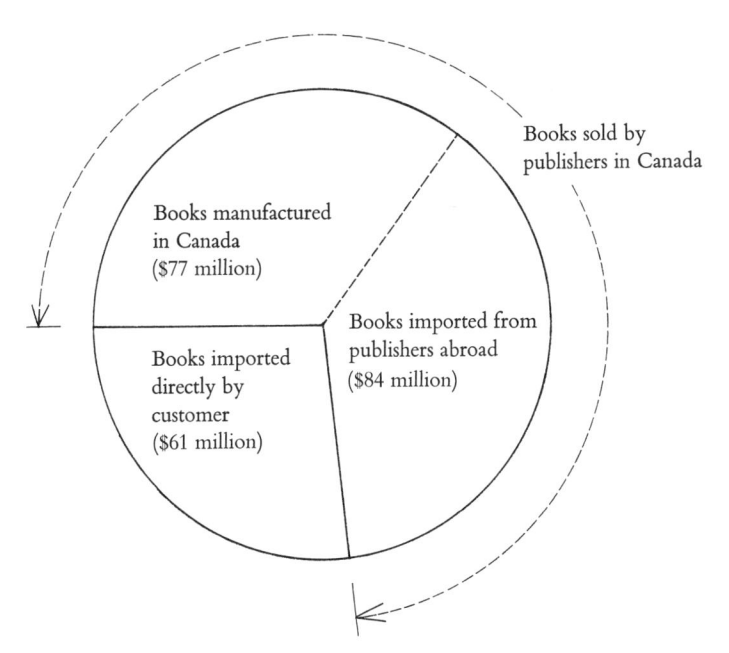

- Books sold by publishers in Canada
- Books manufactured in Canada ($77 million)
- Books imported from publishers abroad ($84 million)
- Books imported directly by customer ($61 million)

Courtesy Department of Industry, Trade and Commerce, Ottawa form part of the consumer market available to Canadian book publishers, because they are related neither to original Canadian publishing programs nor to books imported for sale in this country. Ernst & Ernst place the percentage of exported original Canadian works at 73 per cent of the 5.5 million dollars. In fact it is doubtful if the value of exports of original Canadian books, in English at least, could exceed 2½ million dollars, and a significant portion of this figure comprises sales of scholarly publications.

A few other statistics developed by Ernst & Ernst are relevant to this part of our report. Textbooks accounted for 50 per cent of publishers' sales in 1969, trade books for 27 per cent, specialized books for 19 per cent, and "other" books and near books for 4 per cent. Specialized books were defined to include professional, scientific, and religious books principally designed for use by people with a common basic purpose, e.g. doctors, engineers, architects, etc., and also included dictionaries, directories, and encyclopedias. Domestically produced books, including original publishing and foreign editions republished with adaptations, accounted for 35 per cent of the total available market of 222 million dollars. The breakdown of these sales by customer category is shown in the accompanying table, reproduced by permission.

1969 ESTIMATED CANADIAN CONSUMPTION BY LANGUAGE OF
BOOKS CONSUMED

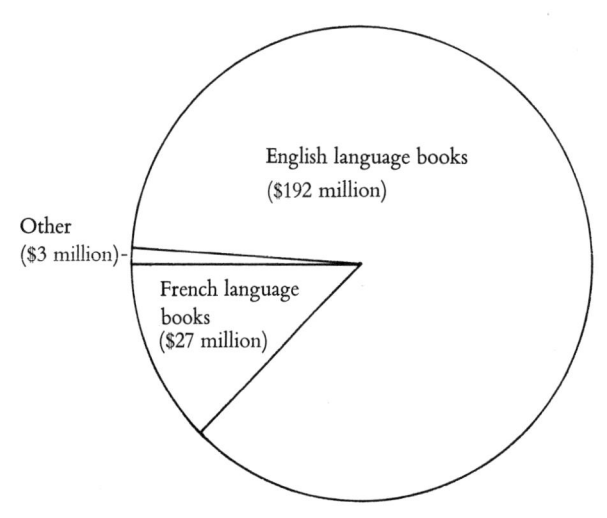

English language books ($192 million)

Other ($3 million)

French language books ($27 million)

Courtesy Department of Industry, Trade and Commerce, Ottawa

SUMMARY OF SALES BY CUSTOMER CATEGORY

(in $ millions)

Market	Estimated Market Size	Publishers' Sales Value — Domestic Publishing	Publishers' Sales Value — Adapted Rights	% of Available Domestic Market Served
School Agency	88.8	32.1	14.7	53
Library	40.0	6.0	2.0	20
Wholesale and retail	40.0	12.2	1.2	34
University bookstore	33.4	1.6	1.0	8
Mail order and book club	17.6	2.0	3.0	28
Other	2.2	0.9	0.5	68
Total	222.0	54.8	22.4	35

Courtesy Department of Industry, Trade and Commerce, Ottawa

THE ECONOMICS OF CANADIAN PUBLISHING

Of all the challenges that confront original Canadian publishing programs, the relative smallness of the market is certainly the most serious. Admittedly, smaller populations than either the English- or French-speaking sectors of Canada are able to support indigenous writing and publishing activities; the Scandinavian countries offer vivid proof of this. Thus the book-buying markets in Canada's two linguistic areas are not small, they are only relatively small – small in relation to English-language and French-language publishing communities in other parts of the world. The concern of this Commission is primarily, although not exclusively (because of the Franco-Ontarian situation), with publishing in English, but the corresponding industry in Quebec has faced many parallel problems. Quebec's publishing problems, and the solutions being attempted in that province, are discussed in the background paper by André Vachon and Georges Laberge, already published.

The exports of the two dominant English-language publishing communities abroad, Great Britain and the United States, overlap in Canada. Here they vastly complicate the marketing system not only for their own books but also for those of the relatively diminutive Canadian publishing industry. Nowhere is this interaction more apparent than in pricing and discounting, where Canada must try to rationalize two incompatible traditions in a single system, and adapt its own publishing program to them at the same time. However justifiable, the demands of booksellers, librarians, and consumers cannot always be reconciled, although the Canadian publisher must try to do this. Moreover, he must price his own new publications, produced for what in world terms is a regional market, to reflect traditional price levels for books of a similar size and complexity that are addressed to a continent-wide or international market. The result is understandable; manuscripts that are only marginally publishable in Canada would be eminently publishable if translated into their American or British equivalents. And the book that is marginally publishable abroad finds no place in original Canadian publishing at all. A good book published in the United States on the flora of Texas or the fauna of California can perhaps do well; first-rate equivalent books in Canada on the birds of Manitoba or arctic wildflowers are likely to need subsidies if they are to be published without a loss, as experience has often demonstrated. The prospects for Canadian fiction and poetry and drama and for other writings of the imagination are generally even more dismal.

In noting these disabilities of Canadian publishing, we are speaking of relative markets, not relative quality in writing. But do not printing and binding in Canada cost about the same as in the United States? Of course they do, and so do typesetting, artwork, designing, and production – which is where most of the costs come from. These last are the one-time preparatory costs which in Canada must be written off over very much smaller average sales than in the United States. As observed earlier, this means much higher unit costs, on which the selling prices must be based. When there is a policy of Canadian preference in selection, as for educational books listed on Ontario's Circular 14 (assuming that the provisions of that circular are closely adhered to), the disability can be partly offset. Or if Canadian books could enjoy much better distribution abroad than they do now, unit costs would be reduced. Or if the domestic market could be stimulated to expand, the cost threshold of publishability would be lowered and the number of new Canadian books thereby increased. Publishing itself cannot spend more on sales promotion and market expansion than it does at present, although areas may exist in which it could spend its promotional budgets more effectively. The importance and possibilities of export development will be dealt with in Chapter 6. We are concerned here chiefly with the markets and marketing problems in this country for various categories of Canadian books.

1969 SOURCE OF SUPPLY TO CANADIAN BOOK MARKET

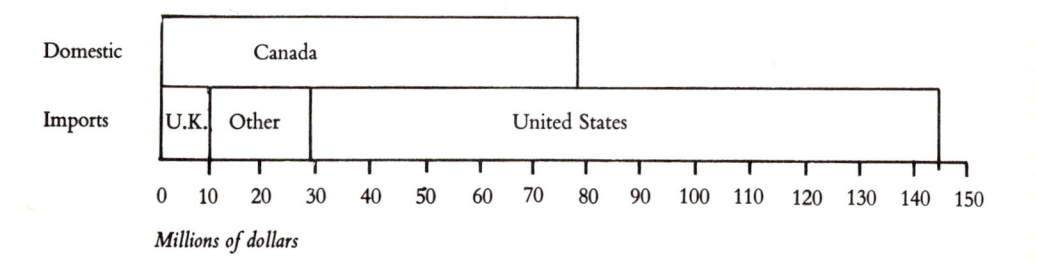

Domestic: Canada

Imports: U.K. | Other | United States

0　10　20　30　40　50　60　70　80　90　100　110　120　130　140　150

Millions of dollars

ESTIMATED 1969 CANADIAN BOOK IMPORTS BY COUNTRY OF ORIGIN

Country of Origin	Publishers' Sales Value (Million $)	%
U.S.A.	115.0	80
France	12.0	8
United Kingdom	10.0	7
Other French language suppliers — principally Belgium and Switzerland	3.0	2
Other countries supplying linguistic books — principally Italy, Germany, Holland	3.0	2
Other English language book suppliers (includes reprints)	1.8	1
	144.8	100

Courtesy Department of Industry, Trade and Commerce, Ottawa

Discounts granted and royalty rates promised in contracts are not part of a publisher's unit costs, but they have a profound bearing on his selling prices. They can influence his costs indirectly, because if his books are priced too high they will certainly sell less well, and so he will print smaller editions (which will mean higher unit costs), if he decides to publish at all. Unless Canadian publishers are profiteering, and we have had little evidence that they have done so successfully in recent times, those who undertake to pay higher than standard royalty rates to authors whose books have normal sales prospects are likely to have to inflate their selling prices, with consequent adverse effects on the sales of the particular titles and on their own financial position generally. This consideration is relevant to this inquiry, because most of the authors we heard from voiced greater concern for royalty rates and contract terms than for the survival of the Canadian publishing industry.

On the other hand, a provision for escalating royalties for a particular book as its sales increase is a logical and not uncommon feature of publishing contracts, at least for trade books. Such escalation clauses are not as likely to be applicable to educational books, which are more often priced on the basis of a low preparatory-cost/running-cost ratio. Whether or not an educational book is priced low enough will be decided by the market-place. That is to say, the one-time costs involved in the production of a schoolbook are normally written off over a relatively large anticipated total sale; in educational publishing, therefore, the preparatory expenses do not bear so heavily on the selling price. But royalty and discount rates do, and with important competitive implications.

CHILDREN'S BOOKS

There are some areas in which international publishing houses are much more active than are Canadian firms. Partly as a consequence, Canadian authors are also relatively inactive in these fields, lacking as they do the incentive of easy publication. One such area is children's books (apart from those works written and produced primarily for the classroom). Most of the factors that influence the volume of Canadian publishing for children done in the past and that may be done in the future have been expertly reviewed by Sheila Egoff in her background paper on the subject, which has already been published; only a few observations need be added. An aspect of the problem that may have deserved greater emphasis than Miss Egoff gave it is again the small size of the market in this country. The total Canadian demand for even the most popular children's books imported from Great Britain and the United States would not begin to support their original production costs if they had to recover these wholly from their Canadian sales.

Neither the fact that a children's book is written in this country, nor that it is produced here, will in itself inspire a sufficient increase in its Canadian sales to render its publication economically viable. For example we are quite certain that a maple leaf on every Canadian book would hinder rather than stimulate sales. Historically, of course, Canadian children's books have earned at least a modest degree of recognition abroad through export sales, as the successes of such earlier writers as Sir Charles G. D. Roberts, and Marshall Saunders testify. Occasionally the size of overprintings for foreign markets has been large enough to reduce unit manufacturing costs significantly, and a definite interest does exist overseas in stories about the Canadian North, the Royal Canadian Mounted Police, and the native peoples of this country. But sometimes the Canadian juvenile is also distinguished in international book markets such as the Frankfurt Book Fair by its overly conservative and budget-conscious design and production, which too easily screen good writing from serious consideration by prospective publisher-purchasers abroad. The relatively depressed market in Canada for children's writing is illustrated by the Ernst & Ernst conclusion that sales of juveniles account for 22 per cent of the market in the United States, but only for 6 per cent of sales in this country – with domestic and imported children's books both added in.

The brief that shed as much light as any on the difficulties of marketing children's writing in Canada was submitted by M. O. Edwardh, President of Gage Educational Publishing Limited. He reviewed for us how, a couple of decades ago, his firm had sought to expand the supply of published children's authors from whom it could draw for its educational publishing program, i.e. for its basic Canadian reading series then in preparation. He told us that, during the early 1950s

... stop-gap solutions had to be found. Established writers in the field of adult literature were commissioned to write selections. Experts in science, geography, history, and other disciplines were asked to write essays about Canada. Selections written for adults were simplified and adapted. Hardpressed editors frequently became instant authors, writing selections designed both to teach a skill and make children aware of Canada. None of these solutions could possibly create first-rate children's literature.

In 1960 his firm announced a program entitled "Writing for Young Canada." Under this program, manuscripts were solicited for short stories, essays, biographies, one-act plays, and poems. Only Canadian citizens or permanent residents of this country were eligible to submit manuscripts. All works accepted were to be published in a new two-stream series of children's anthologies, *Nunny Bag* (for six- to nine-year olds) and *Rubaboo* (for ten- to twelve-year olds). Adequate payments and additional stimulation awards were offered. The advertising program and design budgets were generous, and the physical production of the resulting books compared favourably with similar anthologies being produced abroad. The program continued for about six years, and led to the publication of ten annual anthologies, five in each series. A total of 114 Canadian authors were represented in a total of over 200 selections, all previously unpublished material. Not surprisingly, the quality of the writing was uneven, but the experiment was an imaginative one, and the finished products would have been a credit to any publisher anywhere. Mr. Edwardh went on to tell us that while

. . . the anthologies were being produced, very little recognition came in Canada. However, the work did not go entirely unnoticed. Textbook firms in the United States became aware of the collection and requested permission to reprint some of the selections. In the visual arts field, *Rubaboo 5* was selected as an award winner in the *47th Annual of Advertising, Editorial, TV Art and Design* in the United States. Since 1966, when the program ended, many selections have been reprinted by Canadian publishers.

. . . An enormous effort had been made and a substantial sum of money had been invested. But the sale of the books had been disappointing.

Teachers said that they preferred small paper-bound volumes of individual stories for the classroom. Libraries said small paper-bound books were not suitable for a library shelf, where the title must be seen on the spine . . .

Marketing also presented problems. Individual textbook publishers do not have the sales staff to visit public libraries and bookstores, because sales are not high enough to justify the expense. So it was difficult to distribute in "trade" outlets.

Whatever the reason for the low sales, W.J. Gage Limited had to face the fact that a program to develop Canadian literature for children would have to be heavily subsidized. Requests for support from government agencies such as the Canada Council were refused. So, regretfully, the "Writing for Young Canada" program was discontinued.

In 1971, the textbook publishers in Canada face the same problems they faced in 1950 and 1960. They can produce excellent Canadian readers only if they have a body of published Canadian selections for children. The problem is so fundamental and so enormous that one publishing firm cannot assume the burden of creating the material. It requires a nation-wide effort at the governmental level.

THE UNIVERSITY AND COLLEGE MARKET

Another field in which international publishers dominate the Canadian market is that of universities and colleges. Many of the reasons for the imbalance between foreign and domestic publishing at this level were discussed in Chapter 2. Whereas the market in this country for children's books is small but in no way restricted in subject matter, the university market is substantial but highly specialized. From the standpoint of individual titles, the effect is much the same; the Canadian market will not, except in a few special areas, support the costs of developing original university textbooks.

The exceptions to this market limitation, as noted elsewhere in this report, are found for the most part in the Canadian social sciences, where there are few foreign-published books because there is little foreign market for them. Here we find the collections of Canadian readings, drawn largely from creative academic writing in scholarly books and journals and in other periodicals concerned with social and political affairs. Ernst & Ernst report the division of the university market as 87 per cent imported books and 13 per cent domestically produced. There are few Canadian-written university textbooks in mathematics, science, and engineering apart from those first published by the international textbook houses, usually based in New York. But of these foreign-published textbooks by Canadian authors there is indeed a profusion.

Beverley Moore has traced the development of college stores in Canada in a background paper on that subject; her explanation of what books they sell, where they obtain them, and how these specialized retail outlets have grown over the years assists in understanding the nature of the college market for books of all kinds. As we have already seen, serious non-fiction in almost any subject area is

SALES BY COLLEGE STORES IN CANADA 1969-1970

Province	Net Sales
Prince Edward Island and Newfoundland	$ 568,000
Nova Scotia	1,283,000
New Brunswick	975,000
Quebec	4,975,000
Ontario	14,505,000
Manitoba	1,822,000
Saskatchewan	1,727,000
Alberta	3,765,000
British Columbia	3,782,000
Total Sales:	$33,402,000*

*Textbook and trade book sales account for 80% of total sales; stationery, supplies and miscellaneous sales account for other 20%.
Source: *Dominion Bureau of Statistics publication 63-219, "Campus Bookstores."*

likely to be relevant to university courses at some point, and there is an increasing tendency to offer a wide range of such materials for sale to faculty and student bodies. This market is particularly open to serious Canadian non-fiction works, including both anthology-type publications and original books.

Mrs. Moore's background paper underlines the seriousness of the problem of estimating inventory requirements resulting from the trend away from single prescribed textbooks (to which might be added the increase in the number of optional courses that undergraduates may elect). An instructor at Toronto, estimating his department's freshman enrolment in zoology for the following autumn, is said to have shown on his spring estimate to the college bookstore: "I estimate textbook requirement for September between 50 and 500 copies." To his credit be it said that he had no information on which to base a more precise forecast. The resulting shortages of supplies at the time that they are needed is complemented by the extremely heavy returns of unsold books which have occurred in recent years, a problem that has grown to crisis proportions according to several publishers. In some cases returns are said to have amounted to 20 per cent of sales. These difficulties contribute in a marked way to marketing inefficiency in the book industry, and affect foreign subsidiary and Canadian-owned publisher-agent alike. They are most serious, of course, in relation to imported books where delays in replenishing supplies may be great and where overstocks cannot easily be returned to the originating publishers. But they are costly also for the publisher of original Canadian college textbooks, even if he is able to dispose of his returned books in subsequent years and to other institutions. And while textbooks may be sitting unsold at one institution, another may be in a state of crisis for want of the same titles. The inconvenience to student consumers is thus only another aspect of the same serious problem.

As Mrs. Moore points out, an important distinction between the college stores of today and of two decades ago has been their evolution from simple textbook depositories to professional merchandising operations. A major contributor to this change was the advent of the quality paperback. Paperback books are normally wholesaled at the trade discount of 40 per cent instead of the traditional textbook discount of 20 per cent. Because an increasing proportion of their business is now being done at the higher trade-book margin, college stores are finding it feasible to support Canadian (as well as imported) publishing of serious non-fiction on a scale hitherto impossible, and to serve a constituency that has an elasticity of demand never known in the past. While an overwhelming proportion of college stores' book business is still done in short discount titles, as community colleges, including especially the Colleges of Applied Arts and Technology in Ontario, expand their enrolments and bring their more diversified interests to bear on the retail stores that serve them, the importance of these channels of distribution will continue to mount. We have ample evidence, for example, that college stores are already proving to be important outlets for Canadian fiction and poetry of the kind issued by some of the newer independent publishers.

THE PAPERBACK MYTH

It is not infrequently suggested by otherwise well-informed laymen that the market for books would really open up in this country if only publishers would learn to issue them always in paperback editions. Coupled with this notion is a good deal of confusion, or unawareness, regarding the distinction between first editions and reprint editions, and between quality paperback editions and what are generally known as mass-market paperbacks. The two principal costs in publishing a new trade book are the one-time typesetting, design, and production expenses (as opposed to the run-on costs) and the sales promotion budget. The latter is sometimes the larger of the two, and may include space ads, trade journal ads, colourful prospectuses and related costs of mail campaigns, distribution of review copies and news releases, special travelling expenses, pre-publication offers, and the like. Almost all these costs are eliminated when the same book is later offered in a paperback reprint, as it often is after it has proved popular. And if the paperback edition can be fitted into a well-established series of paperbacks, the need for individual title promotion will almost be removed, because the series will be promoted as a unit.

It is also often supposed that the difference in price between a hardback edition at seven or eight dollars and the paperback reprint at two dollars, more or less, is to be explained by the economies achieved in binding. Actually the latter savings are likely to be nominal – amounting perhaps to fifty or seventy-five cents per copy, depending on the length of run and lavishness of design. Most of the savings occur in the virtual elimination of preparatory production costs and direct sales promotion costs, and because these savings bear on the unit costs of the publisher they make possible reductions in the selling price. A first edition of a trade book may be as small as three thousand copies, yet it must regularly absorb one-time production costs of three or four thousand dollars plus direct selling expenses of almost as much, depending on the importance and potential of the book. As a result, the unit cost to the publisher of the same title in a paperback reprint will be reduced by two dollars or more, plus the saving in binding costs. The list price can thus be reduced by four or five dollars by the time that discounts and royalties are taken into account. McGraw-Hill Company of Canada, in their brief to this Commission, referred to the popular misconception of paperback publishing as the "paperback myth"; it is an apt term.

It does not follow that no original publishing can be done in paperback, but when it is it must contend with the one-time preparatory costs just discussed. Moreover, the price ceiling for an original paperback is often pressured downward by traditional price levels of paperback reprints of the same format, and this involves its own publishing disability. Although any saving, even the reduction in binding costs already mentioned, can have a disproportionate effect on the selling price, there are good reasons why hardback editions normally continue to be issued first. Most libraries prefer hardback editions, and they are an important sales nucleus for any book. Although more and more such institutions are introducing paperback departments, in which the books are considered to be consumable items, the fact is that a huge library rebinding business exists in this country (as it does elsewhere) for the purpose of reinforcing library books, repairing and rebinding worn copies, and in some cases even converting paperback editions to hardback. The cost of these services varies according to the work involved, but commonly runs to several dollars per book processed and the books are taken out of circulation for several weeks on the average. It is not difficult to see why original hardback editions are likely to continue to have a special attraction for such institutions as compared with paperbacks.

QUALITY PAPERBACKS AND MASS-MARKET PAPERBACKS

Canadiana is being offered more and more often in paperback reprint editions, and several of the indigenous book publishers in this country have established series of their own. Some of these, such as the Carleton Library of McClelland and Stewart, are reset in type in uniform formats and supplied with special introductions. Others are straight reprints of serious non-fiction previously published in smaller editions at much higher prices. Some paperback editions are issued apart from series altogether, including reprint editions of many popular original Canadian publications. Also in this category are some original works of fiction and poetry of such firms as Anansi, New Press, Peter Martin, and others. Foreign subsidiaries in Canada have also published extensively in paperback, especially in the social sciences at the university level.

Along with this considerable array of Canadian paperbacks, of course, are displayed countless paper editions imported from abroad. These tend to divide themselves into two groups, the so-called quality paperbacks and the mass-market paperbacks. The latter can be distinguished by their lower price levels, by the series in which they appear, by their uniform formats, and by the channels through which they are distributed to most retailers who handle them – the latter often not being bookstores. Mass-market editions are addressed to a different audience from that using the regular editions. This is pointed up by the fact that when bookstores do carry mass-market paperbacks, they may at the same time successfully carry some of the same titles in hardback, and even in quality paperback editions as well. In most other outlets the contrasting editions do not have so much opportunity to compete with one another, because only the mass-market lines are stocked.

Mass-market paperbacks tend to concentrate on best sellers and near-best sellers. There have been two firms in Canada (General Publishing and Harlequin Books) who have been publishing less well-known books, often including light fiction (not necessarily by Canadian authors), on a mass-market basis. But in general the only way for an original Canadian book to be offered in a mass-market edition is for it to be republished (by arrangement) by a mass-market paperback publisher in the United States. This happens, but it happens no more often than Canadian books become best sellers in the North American market. It is probably almost as difficult for American books whose authors are not already widely read to be selected for inclusion on mass-market lists, a fact that can be overlooked when one is considering the implications of this kind of edition to our national literature.

Mass-market publishers normally rent the exclusive right to publish their paperback edition of a popular book for a limited period of time – usually four or five years only. As noted earlier, this licence will not necessarily require withdrawal or suspension of other editions in print with the original publisher, although it may. The consideration for the right granted is most often a royalty (which will then be shared with the author under the original publishing agreement), often coupled with a substantial advance – which may be anything from five thousand to a hundred thousand dollars or more, depending on the sales anticipated and the size of the edition planned. But the key to mass-market paperback publishing lies in large printings and the efficiency of a marketing system built upon rapid turnover of cheap editions. Initial press runs of a hundred thousand copies are common, and first printings of several times this quantity are not infrequent.

MASS-MARKET PAPERBACKS

The Commission's *Final Report on the Distribution of Paperbacks and Periodicals in Ontario*, submitted on March 27, 1972, reviewed the process whereby selected books, usually best sellers, may sometimes be offered in what are known as mass-market paperback editions, which are distributed not only through bookstores but through a wide variety of supplementary channels as well. Because that report is included in the Appendix to this volume, only a few additional comments regarding the mass-market paperback industry need be added here.

As explained in the earlier report just mentioned, the phrase "mass-market paperbacks" normally refers to special paperback editions issued by specialist mass-market paperback houses. These usually comprise only reprints of fast selling, if not best selling, books originally issued by other publishers in traditional formats. The rights to issue mass-market editions are normally leased from the original publishers, even when the latter may already have issued the same works in paperback editions of their own, i.e. in editions known as "quality paperbacks." Because the mass-market editions are produced in much larger printings, sometimes as large as several hundred thousand copies, unit costs are substantially reduced. Sufficient margin can thus be generated between cost and a comparatively low list price to permit a chain of discounts to support the fairly complex distribution network. The latter may include, in addition to the original publishers and the mass-market publishers, a national distributor who sells to geographical or regional wholesalers, and the latter in turn may sell through rack jobbers (for small accounts) to retail newsdealers, who sell to the ultimate purchaser. Not surprisingly, the marketing system best suited to the needs of mass-market paperback publishers on this continent is the one which has developed for the marketing of most periodicals, not including newspapers or magazine subscriptions. In addition to newsdealers, mass-market paperback publishers also distribute their products through bookstores. The Commission's *Final Report on the Distribution of Paperbacks and Periodicals in Ontario* discusses some of the problems that result from the effort to integrate the two channels of distribution, notably with respect to discount and service.

Because mass-market paperbacks are on sale in such a wide variety of retail stores, and because they obviously sell in substantial quantities, some well-wishers of Canadian publishing incorrectly conclude that publishers have been remiss in not exploiting the same marketing technique. It is probable that more money has been lost than earned by Canadian publishers when they have tried to develop sales for their own paperback editions, and this may have been because they, too, failed to take full account of the economics involved in mass-market publishing. Most successful mass-market paperbacks are titles in successful mass-market paperback lines. They are neither advertised nor reviewed individually in their mass-market editions; they have already received these vital promotional services from their original publishers before they were selected for republication as part of a mass-market paperback list. Either their titles or their authors, or both, have a high recognition-value, or they are closely associated with other books in the same line which do have. They thus have a built-in promise of rapid turnover, and if they do not fulfil this promise they are promptly removed from display. And most important, they require a substantial market base – usually much larger than can be developed efficiently in Canada, much less Ontario, alone. There are exceptions to these rules, the PaperJacks of General Publishing Co. Ltd. being one; but even here the ratio of Canadian paperbacks to books by foreign authors is limited, and is likely to remain so.

We studied with interest the effort by McClelland and Stewart to establish a Canadian Bestseller Library series of mass-market paperbacks, which has now been discontinued. Perhaps no other Canadian publisher has been in so favourable a position for exploiting his own list of popular Canadian titles, but the experiment proved unsuccessful. There were not enough good titles; new possibilities for inclusion did not appear with sufficient frequency; the sales of the less successful paperback editions fell far short, in the limited Canadian market, of covering the costs of producing them; cooperation from wholesalers was uneven and sometimes nonexistent; booksellers resented the competition from newsdealers in titles which they felt they had launched, and they complained particularly about the limited discounts they were offered, especially at first.

All this is not to say that the paperback does not have an important role to play in Canadian publishing, but it is unlikely that mass-market paperbacking will have a profound influence on its development. Quality paperback editions will doubtless continue to be offered, e.g. the Carleton Library of McClelland and Stewart and the Canadian University Paperbooks of University of Toronto Press. These will find their customers gradually, over many years in all likelihood, chiefly through the better stocked booksellers (of which there are too few) and through college stores. But they should not be confused with mass-market paperbacks, from which they differ in size of editions, readers addressed, methods of distribution, and list prices.

BOOK PUBLISHERS AND BOOKSELLERS

It is possible to point to a few bookstores serving English-speaking Canada which enjoy a reputation for knowledge of books, conscientiousness, and good service that would earn them public esteem in London or New York if they were located in the latter centres instead of here. But generally speaking the retail bookselling industry in Canada is woefully underdeveloped in relation to the geographical extent of the country and to the disproportionately large number of publishers seeking to sell their books through it. There are many reasons for this imbalance, but certainly one of them is not that numerous opportunities to open thriving new businesses are being neglected. Not under the existing system of book distribution, at least.

At the end of 1971 there were in the whole of Canada 112 trade bookstores and 98 college stores that were members of the Canadian Booksellers Association. This association is representative enough of the English-language industry for these figures to be accepted as close to the total number of full-time important English booksellers. Some book outlets, largely of the shopping centre variety, are not members of the association; on the other hand, the CBA includes more stores for which bookselling is a secondary activity than there are serious booksellers whom it omits. The number of non-overlapping memberships in the Canadian Book Publishers' Council and the Independent Publishers' Association totalled 63 in the same year, meaning that there were barely two booksellers per publisher in English-speaking Canada. One might leap to the conclusion that the number of publishers ought to be decreased rather than the number of booksellers increased, were it not that there are so few Canadian publishing enterprises anyway. The great majority of the books that are sold through Canadian booksellers are imported, and would be published whether or not there was a Canadian-based publishing industry.

It is difficult to determine exactly the Canadian-produced portion of sales made by booksellers, setting sales of mass-market paperbacks aside. However, estimates made by some of them in answer to our questions support calculations based on Ernst & Ernst figures, which show that between 20 per cent and 25 per cent of trade sales are of books of Canadian origin. If this is so, it is a respectable and important proportion, having regard for the minuscule number of Canadian titles that exist in comparison with the vast number of other English-language books in print.

A short history of Canadian bookselling is given in the background paper by June Whitteker, including a reference to the controversy out of which the present discount structure for books was born. Perhaps the important consideration is that a trade discount, which is now normally 40 per cent, is given to a bookseller in recognition of the fact that his bookselling contribution is vital to the sale of the book. The same logic restricts educational discounts to booksellers to the generally prevailing rate of 20 per cent, i.e. it is assumed that where the bookseller handles these he is providing a distribution service for "adopted" textbooks, and not a display service whereby he will seek to stimulate demand. Just why the same discount should be given to educational authorities (and even to individual teachers) is hard to rationalize, if it can be explained at all. Sliding scales of discounts according to quantity purchased apply to some quality paperback lines, where unit prices tend to be low and processing of single copy orders is usually uneconomical for both publisher and bookseller. (In a few cases, retail customers are apparently not able to purchase mass-market paperbacks from the Canadian publisher-agents, but are referred to the news company who is the geographical wholesaler. The latter supplies such books at a 30 per cent discount, compared with the 40 per cent given by the publisher-agent to other booksellers. This is discussed in the Commission's *Final Report on the Distribution of Paperbacks and Periodicals in Ontario* (see Appendix).)

Generally, Canadian retail discounts correspond with those granted in the United States, on whose marketing structure the Canadian one is closely based. On the other hand, the distribution system in these two countries is unlike that which prevails through most of the rest of the English-speaking world, including Great Britain. The British domestic trade discount is normally between 30 per cent and 35 per cent, the distinction between trade and educational discounts is much less sharp than in North America, and yet the bookselling trade flourishes in a way that often makes bookmen on this continent envious. Mrs. Whitteker alludes to the reason why circumstances are so different in the two markets. In Great Britain, the book industry generally supports the Net Book Agreement, under which orders, even from libraries and educational authorities, are normally channelled through accredited retailers. In this way bookselling expertise is stimulated and a proliferation of bookstores is encouraged, many of the latter specializing in particular areas of publishing. We are obliged to ask ourselves whether the institution of a similar system in, say, Ontario would help book publishing and bookselling more than it would hinder library and educational purchasing.

This is more than vague speculation, too; it is already the subject of an official experiment in Quebec, outlined in the background paper by André Vachon and Georges Laberge. The legislation and orders-in-council which set forth the new *politique du livre* of Quebec have as their objective nothing less than the channelling of almost all publicly funded book buying through accredited booksellers, and include a declaration that the establishment of retail stores with defined minimum inventories should be encouraged throughout the province as a consequence. Without prejudging this Canadian experiment, it is obvious that it deserves to be closely monitored by this province during the next year or two. It may have to be modified in the light of experience; certainly there are equally strong conflicting pressures to uphold it and to abandon it, and compromises will probably have to be reached.

Booksellers have various interfaces with the book publishing industry. The most frequent – at least for major retailers – is through periodic visits made by publishers' sales representatives. Very often the relationship between publisher and trade store thus devolves, as in so many lines of business, into a personal one between the salesman and the bookseller. Where friendship is mutual and confidence is high, the interchange of information and problems will be frank and valuable. The salesman may not be able to resolve every local difficulty, for example when over-extension of credit is one of them, but he can and does carry many first-hand reports back to his home office. He sometimes can facilitate special arrangements regarding returns to be made immediately or deferred until later, and he is always an eager listener to plans for expansion or changes in retail selling policy. One call by an informed and trusted salesman can bring a publisher more business than scores of circulars and catalogues, however lavish the latter may be. Even sample copies, which might be considered an economical substitution for a day's stopover on a long and expensive sales trip, do not command the attention that those outside the industry may think they should.

The importance of the sales representative in the distribution of books through retailers is relevant to this review. Some of the more remote centres see book salesmen far too infrequently. Outside Toronto, even fewer sales calls are made on behalf of the books of the very small Canadian-owned publishers, who (wisely or not) restrict their activities to selling Canadian books, as was noted earlier. It is true that the bookselling trade in this country is not so prosperous that sales through it could be very greatly multiplied if all the new books could be brought to its notice by personal calls made at the right time each season. But it is equally certain that the proportion of Canadian-produced books in bookstores will remain smaller than it might be so long as they are not adequately promoted in the flesh to those who alone can display them to the public, i.e. to Canadian retail booksellers.

Although we reiterate that there are a few important exceptions, retail bookselling in Canada is in a pitifully underdeveloped condition in comparison with bookselling in most other countries, particularly in Europe. To be able to browse through a representative collection of recent Canadian books should be the privilege of every citizen in this country, or at least of everyone who lives in a built-up area. In fact the facilities to do this are inadequate in most large urban areas, a condition which is greatly exacerbated for people who live in smaller centres. And it is pointless to blame the booksellers for this cultural deprivation; our whole economic system ensures that there will be about as many bookstores distributed through the community as can hope to survive, and possibly a few more. And while the bookstores that do exist are bound to exhibit varying degrees of expertise and efficiency in their management, their state of development will by and large be determined by the importance that society attaches to them, and by the way in which they are fitted into the cultural traffic of the community. Too often, in the opinion of the Commission, they are accorded no particular cultural status at all, as is demonstrated by the infrequency with which booksellers are invited to participate either as advisers or as suppliers in connection with regional literary activities of any kind, including those connected with school and public libraries, to mention the most obvious examples.

A good bookseller is a cultural asset to any community, and this fact should be recognized more widely than it is. As the narrowly textbook nature of the books used in classrooms softens so as to embrace many kinds of children's and even adult books not previously used for teaching situations, the bookseller might well be given an expanded opportunity to assist in their presentation and distribution to schools. (In Chapter 5 we shall examine more closely the transition that has taken place in educational materials.) What is potentially important to the bookseller is that many of the new books of the schoolroom are trade books in the broadest sense, including the feature of being available to him at the full trade-book discount. Educational authorities should welcome the opportunity this fact gives to them to patronize a local bookseller where one exists, and to encourage the establishment (or improvement) of such services where necessary.

THE PROMOTION OF TRADE BOOKS

With average sales per title small and unit manufacturing costs relatively high, the gross margin available for promotion of trade books in Canada – as in other countries, for that matter – is limited. Of course one can ask whether sales might not be drastically increased by means of more ambitious budgeting of advertising of all kinds, and there is evidence that they sometimes can be. But not often to the point at which increased advertising costs are reimbursed, which suggests that advertising alone is not the solution. On a highly selective basis, a publisher can plan to mass-market a particular title or group of titles, possibly even bypassing the normal trade channels of distribution and depending on coupon advertising or book club memberships, for example. Such approaches to marketing are standard for certain kinds of subscription books, including encyclopedias and similar works which in the end are sold by canvassers working on commission. But even for more ordinary kinds of publications, there have been some important experiments at specialized selling techniques in the history of Canadian publishing, and doubtless there will be more. Most of them have ended unsatisfactorily, and some of them disastrously, but they are all worth the time of study.

McClelland and Stewart, possibly the most imaginative and easily the most adventurous of Canadian publishers, sought without success to enter the mass-market paperback field with its Canadian Best Sellers Library, as mentioned earlier in this chapter. The same firm launched the Canadian Centennial Library in collaboration with *Weekend Magazine*, a venture ambitious in scope and design and supported by a major advertising campaign aimed at procuring direct orders from customers. But in due course the periodical publisher exercised his option to withdraw; more books had been sold than normal bookseller channels could ever have hoped to dispose of, but the cost of selling them was inflated beyond commercially acceptable limits.

Occasionally a new reference work with a widespread reputation – or capable of earning one – can be successfully promoted on a scale that outstrips normal sales development costs and yields appropriately increased sales, but it is not easy to make such publishing experiences routine. A publisher issuing a very few, carefully selected works each year might be able to apply new marketing techniques successfully, but the firm that publishes fifty or seventy-five new Canadian books cannot hope always to publish the kind of book that is susceptible to this level of promotion. Even if he could do so, such a list would quickly lose its momentum with the reading public anyway. In the end, the promotional costs of new books, whether they are Canadian or not, must be related directly to realistic forecasts of the sales that are possible.

What are the normal techniques and media for sales promotion of books? There can be no pat formula, and the publisher who believes he has found one will decide soon enough that a change of pace is necessary. But the most important is clearly personal selling, already discussed; this of course is an operation that is limited by the number and location of bookstores in the country. To personal selling should be added wise and prompt distribution of review copies, really newsworthy news releases issued in various forms, informative cataloguing in advance, distribution of appropriate prospectus material as well as posters in some cases (not all), and discriminating and soundly budgeted space advertising programs in both trade and popular media. The effective sales manager looks on all these routines as mere overtures which may open other opportunities to be exploited promptly and by skilled personnel, including radio and television appearances or reviews, autographing parties (often more valuable for the news that they are happening than for the direct sales they bring, and so on).

Val Clery has examined the impact of the media on book sales in *Promotion and Response*, sponsored by the Canadian Book Publishers' Council with assistance from the Canada Council. This study was completed in the month that this Commission was appointed. In it he reports opinions as well as facts gleaned from a representative range of publishers, reviewers and critics, broadcast media, booksellers, librarians, and "readers." The publishers' own order of value for promotional expenditures (apart from personal calls on booksellers) assigns first place to general and special catalogues, and then in descending order to review copies, direct mail promotion, space advertising, press conferences and receptions, authors' tours, display kits and posters, and finally TV and radio advertising. But as Mr. Clery points out,

> ... exposure on TV is going to become increasingly the decisive factor between a book that is merely successful and a best-seller. It is not going to supplant the book-review in print, or provide the creative element of criticism, but it can, by relating books to the humanity of their authors, catch the attention of a larger Canadian audience that would not ordinarily read reviews or book-pages.

Provided the larger audience is one that will buy books, or at least read books, one cannot help but concur with this. But it would be a mistake to assume that even intensive news coverage on radio or TV provides any assurance of reader demand regardless of topic. An example of when it did not can be cited.

For several successive years in the early 1960s, the proceedings of the Summer Conferences of the Canadian Institute of Public Affairs at Lake Couchiching were broadcast "live" on the CBC national radio network each evening during the week of the meetings. Every broadcast opened and closed with an announcement that the complete proceedings could be procured in book form directly from the publishers, whose address was given, at a modest price (modest because the book was partially subsidized, although the announcement did not explain this). In one year when an attempt was made to isolate the impact of this radio coverage by deferring all other publication announcements concerning it, the total orders that had accumulated one month after the series was finished totalled fewer than fifty copies. Thereupon the publisher issued his usual prospectuses to libraries as well as other announcements to the trade and review copies to critics, and a typical sale of about 1500 copies was generated – still smaller than the interest in the Conference justified, but nonetheless the kind of sale that normal promotion for a book of this kind was budgeted to produce.

The limitations of size of the potential market make meaningful statistical sampling impossible in many areas which would be test-mailed first in other countries such as the United States. Nevertheless, there is a desperate need for more and better statistics to guide publishers in their marketing programs, and the desirability of a coordinated regular survey being centred in Statistics Canada was mentioned early in this report. In the meanwhile, the lack of statistical data does not in itself justify the assertion sometimes heard that the marketing of books in this country should be regarded as an art rather than a science. If useful conclusions based on statistical sampling cannot easily be reached in Canada, at least it should be possible to apply here many of the marketing principles developed scientifically in other comparable countries. For most kinds of book promotion, although admittedly not all, the marketing challenge in this country is not so different from that in the United States that we can afford to disregard the ever-changing commercial priorities that are recognized there, making adjustments where they obviously do not apply here. Canadian publishers need not be slavish imitators of Americans in their book promotion techniques, but they must be fully conversant with them if they expect to emulate them in this market.

David McGill, in his background paper on the marketing of trade books, takes note of the importance that most publishers in this country attach to exploiting all possible channels of distribution, even when this means bypassing the bookseller. As we have already observed, this leads to one of the dilemmas that publishing both in the United States and Canada has built for itself, as it has substituted volume of books ordered for the function of the purchaser when determining discount applicable. Thus some publishers extend full trade discounts, sometimes even jobber's discounts, to ultimate consumers including institutions and libraries, and force themselves to raise list prices all around in order to make this possible. The equivalent of a British Net Book Agreement cannot even be discussed by trade associations without at least a feeling of concern that the Canadian Combines Investigation Act is being violated in some way. It does seem, therefore, that nothing less than some form of government intervention is likely to permit the Canadian book industry as a whole to rationalize itself. Apart from the British Net Book Agreement, one has the orders-in-council respecting book distribution announced in Quebec in 1971 as an interesting alternative model. As pointed out earlier, this new *politique du livre* should be allowed to prove itself before Ontario either tries to imitate it or to improve upon it.

Mr. McGill's background paper on the marketing of trade books also discusses their distribution to libraries and adoption by book clubs, relations between publishers and wholesalers, and the place of trade organizations such as the Canadian Book Publishers' Council in assisting in the orderly and efficient development of sales. Similarly, the marketing of educational books in Canada has been intensively examined by S. J. Totton in a separate paper on that subject. But more remains to be said regarding the opportunities that exist for coordination of marketing efforts in these two areas – areas which in the past have represented almost separate book publishing worlds, but which in very recent years are overlapping more and more and even show signs of merging with one another.

COORDINATION OF MARKETING

One would think that the physical expanse and financial limitations of the Canadian book market would have encouraged a higher level of coordination of non-competitive services among publishers than has thus far been achieved. At the same time, Canada's ambiguous position in the English-speaking world spells a need to improve information to customers regarding titles whose rights overlap or collide. The importance of coordinated exhibits programs has long been recognized by publishers in Canada, and the ways in which these operate are discussed elsewhere in this report and in the background papers which accompany it. But the mounting of displays is only one facet of the total marketing responsibility, which normally is taken to include all activities connected with the movement of goods from the time they are produced until they reach their ultimate consumers.

Specifically, most economists would say that the total marketing function in book publishing embraces design and production; selling and distribution; transportation; warehousing; cataloguing, promotion, and advertising; invoicing and operation of accounts receivable; credit control; and provision of working capital. Some of these functions (such as design) are creative; others depend upon the differing capacities of individual competitors (such as the furnishing of working capital). Where marketing operations are strictly competitive, they of course cannot be pooled. But is there any reason at all why an industry faced with as many marketing challenges as Canadian book publishing should try to maintain so wide a range of separate but redundant non-competitive operations? Is it necessary that twenty, thirty, forty or more publishers in this country should each operate separate warehouses, separate order fulfilment centres, separate invoicing and accounting departments, and conduct totally independent promotion and cataloguing programs?

In most industries, any tendency toward over-duplication of facilities which are used at an inefficiently low level is self-limiting. Competition soon weeds out the weakest and the productivity of those that survive is enhanced, with corresponding benefits to the consumer. Paradoxically however, much of our concern with book publishing has been to preserve the weaker firms, if only because of the unique cultural benefits they can bring to our society. Too many of the underdeveloped publishers are Canadian houses, specializing in Canadian lists, and Canadian book publishing would suffer if they disappeared.

The difficulty could be alleviated somewhat if there were meaningful coordination of those marketing functions which are essentially non-competitive, and which each firm now tries to discharge independently. Some publishers are already using their available facilities in an efficient way, but it is hard to believe that most of them would not be able to reduce their costs if the economies of larger-scale operation could be exploited.

In addition to the trade association programs of organizations such as the Canadian Book Publishers' Council there has, of course, already been one major effort at cooperative marketing of books by English-language publishers. In 1953, plans were made to incorporate a cooperative wholesaling centre through which libraries could procure consolidation of their invoices and shipments of books from all publishers in Canada, with a view to discouraging the growing tendency of such institutions to "buy around" the exclusive publisher-agents in this country and to deal with jobbers and other suppliers abroad. Although it was a significant experiment in coordinated marketing, the Co-operative Book Centre of Canada Ltd. never did establish itself as a stockist for books; instead its services were limited in the main to acting as a clearing house for library orders, procuring books through the publisher-agents as required. To too great an extent, perhaps, it became an extra stage in the distribution process, sometimes even experiencing criticism and competition from the publishers who supported it financially. Its need for working capital increased steadily with its business and with the number of its employees, and an ever-growing share of its efforts had to be devoted to services which could not recover their own costs, such as searching titles and maintaining back-order files of crushing dimensions. Over a period of some sixteen years of active existence it was only partially successful in attracting library goodwill and in maintaining the support of its publisher-members. In the end it went into receivership and its assets were acquired by Maclean-Hunter Limited.

But the Co-operative Book Centre did not really replace other publishers' marketing mechanisms in Canada; it had merely added to them. The business it was invented to capture was business that was not being done in this country anyway; in the event, it did not so much divert buying around from foreign suppliers to Canadian channels as it inserted itself into the domestic distribution system already in existence. Thus it did not really eliminate or significantly reduce the overheads of publishers in Canada, because the latter had to continue to preserve their fulfilment services practically intact – including invoicing, accounting, warehousing, shipping, sales promotion and the like. Indeed, not even the number of invoices was significantly reduced for most publishers, who often found it necessary to process separately each customer's order received through the Co-op, because the latter was generally unable to consolidate them in advance.

The coordination of marketing services which it might be worthwhile for the industry to explore today should have as its immediate purpose the reduction of existing overheads and the improvement of fulfilment services rather than the establishment of a duplicate facility such as the Co-operative Book Centre. It would not need to embrace the whole industry; it might be best if it were first attempted by a few publishers of approximately the same size and with somewhat similar lists, even if this meant that parallel programs would be undertaken simultaneously by more than one separate group of publishers. Two or three cooperative fulfilment centres would be more reasonable than forty or fifty independent ones, granted that no voluntary program of coordination is likely ever to attract the participation of all publishers. Indeed, it would doubtless be vigorously opposed by some. Those who would be least likely to approve such a trend would be the large firms which believe they exceed the critical size below which serious operating inefficiencies need be accepted. In spite of such likely opposition, one or more complete fulfilment centres might arise, furnishing the full range of non-competitive marketing services described earlier. In each, the participating publishers would still be able to retain and strengthen their individual identities and develop their separate publishing programs and policies for better or worse. But the substantial overheads that must be added to manufacturing costs in order to distinguish publishers from printers would for the first time be shared, presumably on a proportionate use basis related to space required and volume of turnover.

During the course of the Commission's work, we have noted some exploration of possible areas of cooperation, at least among some of the Canadian publishers. The Commission has been party to some of these discussions, but not to all of them. It understands that as of August, 1972, three firms – Anansi, James Lewis and Samuel, and Peter Martin – had taken steps to set up joint warehousing and shipping facilities, and were investigating the possibilities of consolidating invoicing and operation of accounts receivable as well. By this time, too, at least one full-time sales representative was acting for several Canadian publishers in Southern Ontario, and there were signs of further consolidation of this kind continuing. The Commission considers that it would be in the interests of Canadian publishers and of the Canadian publishing they do if they were to expand their cooperative efforts in every way possible, expecially in the non-competitive areas of order processing and fulfilment.

We have also studied carefully the advisability of recommending some degree of government sponsorship of a program of coordination of the kind envisaged above on behalf of Canadian-owned publishers, or possibly of all Canadian books regardless of who publishes them. We have however regretfully concluded that the practical problems outweigh the stimulus that such a scheme could be expected to give to the publishing of Canadian books. It would be possible to propose, for example, that physical space to house the necessary accounting, shipping, and warehousing facilities on an adequate scale be provided by the government, perhaps for a temporary period, on the condition that the fulfilment centre it housed would be used exclusively for Canadian books (the definition of which should not be too restrictive). The advantages of participating in such a centre could be made sufficiently attractive that every Canadian-owned publisher who had no agency commitments would have good reason to participate, even to the point of discontinuing his existing fulfilment services. The problem arises when one tries to integrate the stocking and processing of all orders for all Canadian books through such a centre, even on a customer-option basis. Publishers of Canadian books (whether Canadian-owned or not) who have agency franchises could not easily channel orders for their

Canadian publications through the centre and at the same time handle orders for imported books separately, even if they wished to do so (there is no reason why they would). Although customers might continue to deal with each publisher as in the past, and the centre might be related to each publisher just as his own order-processing and fulfilment centres are related to him now, the confusion that would occur in the administration of orders and returns and stock inquiries involving a mix of domestic and imported books could become insurmountable. But the fact that such a mechanism has been studied should be noted for reference, because it would have offered a series of important advantages for the Canadian book over imported books (without imposing any restrictions on the latter).

It is worth considering what some of these advantages might be and whether it might be possible to achieve them in some other way.

A CANADIAN BOOK CENTRE IN ONTARIO

It is to be hoped that the federal government will proceed rapidly with the long-discussed proposal that Canadian Book Centres be established abroad, e.g. in London, Paris, and New York. By late 1972 the establishment of such a system of fulfilment centres outside the country, to operate in the interests of Canadian publishing rather than just Canadian publishers, appeared to be imminent. In the case of Great Britain, it seemed likely that a high priority would also be given to the establishment of a retailing capacity, which is necessary in that country if all Canadian books are to be promoted actively and in full perspective, i.e. if it is to be possible to present and to supply (to libraries as well as to private customers) all Canadian best-selling authors, many of whom must be read in Great Britain in separate British editions. A wholesale facility alone could not do this – first, because it would not have access to Canadian editions that lacked British rights, and second, because the British Net Book Agreement (see Appendix) has strengthened a tradition whereby libraries purchase through retailers rather than from publishers.

We have indicated why we have not recommended the establishment in Ontario of a central wholesale fulfilment centre, which could stock and supply all Canadian books in print as required. But we do strongly recommend the establishment of a Canadian Book Centre in this province, as a provincially sponsored program, which could do for the Canadian book at home as much as the federally sponsored Canadian Book Centres abroad will be able to do for it outside the country. Indeed it would become the mechanism through which a whole series of activities and programs on behalf of Canadian publishing could be mounted in support of the Canadian book as such, and bring to these programs a greater efficiency and a better coordination than they could be given in any other way.

Canadian publishing (meaning the publication of original Canadian books by any publisher) would benefit enormously from a strong and sustained public information program aimed at its special benefit, and the latter could best be coordinated through a Canadian Book Centre in Ontario. Such a Centre could also house a major Resource Reference Centre, perhaps oriented in favour of Canadian educational books but not confined to them, in which educationists representing the Boards of Education from across the province, as well as the public, could be assured of being able to examine in one place all the Canadian materials available at any time. That is to say, it could be the physical embodiment of both Circulars 14 and 15 as they are now known, and much more as well.

Such a Canadian Book Centre in Ontario might at first have to be located only in Toronto, but it could serve as the administrative centre for several smaller regional resource centres elsewhere in the province in the future. There need not be many of these, and they might be opened seasonally, in some cases only for limited periods of time, in order that at least half a dozen regions could benefit from having access to their facilities, and plan accordingly. To be specific, one of these should be accessible to educationists in the Lakehead area, another in Northern Ontario, and others in the Ottawa, London, and Windsor areas, in rotation, if they cannot operate simultaneously.

What would the retail functions of the Canadian Book Centre, and to a lesser degree the regional resource centres, be over and beyond the display of available Canadian books? We think that they should be given the added attractiveness and value of being encouraged to sell over the counter as well as on special order where large quantities are involved, but it would be imperative that the interests of the bookselling trade not only be respected, but that they be served in the course of doing this. As we explained earlier in this report, the danger of the sale of educational books interfering with the sales of trade books by booksellers would have been unimportant in the past because short discounts and direct purchase by boards have kept schoolbooks out of bookstores. But as we have also pointed out, educational and trade publishing seem to be gradually merging, if not in discount structure yet, at least in content.

As this process goes forward, the Canadian book trade should be drawn into the supply cycle – in the interests of Canadian publishing among other good reasons. This could be accomplished if the Canadian Book Centre as well as the regional resource centres it administered sold books at list price or (to educational bodies) at a limited discount only, and if in all cases they made a practice of procuring the name of the purchaser's preferred regional bookseller, to whom credit could be given for a calculated proportion of the gross margin earned. This might be small, and in the case of short discount books it would be minuscule for individual items, but the net costs would be worth incurring if an intelligently planned service could be mounted. In this, the Ontario Book Publishing Board would obviously play a key role. And even though early returns might be modest for booksellers, if a modern data processing system were used to support the procedure it need be neither cumbersome nor inequitable. And the whole thrust should be in the direction of strengthening the future role of the bookseller – and of future booksellers – in providing books of all kinds for examination and purchase by educational bodies. We think it is premature to legislate booksellers into the supply cycle, especially when they do not exist yet in sufficient numbers, much less in sufficient size. However, we have noted with interest the effort to do this in Quebec and we have recommended that the latter program be monitored carefully. We think that regional facilities must come before it is decreed that they should be used, but as the practice of examining available materials (always Canadian) in regional resource centres and in the Central Canadian Book Centre grows, educationists' awareness of the retail book trade should also expand.

Special exhibits and displays of Canadian books, at educational conventions as well as at gatherings open to the general public, could also be arranged and coordinated through a Canadian Book Centre, making use also of the regional resource centres when they are formed later. An efficient and active exhibits program is now conducted by the Canadian Book Publishers' Council, and what is proposed here need not seek to compete with it so much as complement it. And inasmuch as the volume of imported books tends to put Canadian publications in the shade in many situations, notwithstanding Circulars 14 and 15, this new central display service would ensure the continued consideration and appreciation of Canadian books as such.

The Canadian Book Centre in Ontario would also act as a launching pad for an expanded Canadian book export program, which the federal government has announced its intention of fostering, as noted earlier. In some respects this activity would simply be an enlargement of the regional display coordinating function discussed above. Canadian books in English submitted for exhibit at the annual Frankfurt Book Fair could be assembled, judged, catalogued, and shipped by the Centre; this would involve only a very small proportion of English books published outside the province, although it would have a moral responsibility for these in connection with national projects it was fostering. As noted earlier in this report, Canadian book publishing in English tends to be Ontario book publishing to an overwhelming degree, and it is desirable that a corresponding assumption of responsibility for the industry take place at the provincial level. Thus the planning of Canadian book export projects, by the industry, could be focussed in the Centre, which could bring together appropriate publishers (from whatever association), arrange publicity, consult with the relevant departments in the federal government, and mount a sustained follow-up program abroad regarding Canadian rights and books for sale during the many months each year when individual publishers have other priorities to concern them. To the extent that the federal government will assume or assist in costs related to the Canadian book export program – and it appears likely that substantial assistance is about to be forthcoming – the value of having a central Canadian Book Centre in Ontario will be all the more apparent. Indeed, almost any program intended to assist Canadian books which this Commission might recommend to the Government of Ontario could be administered more easily if, in addition to federally assisted Canadain Book Centres abroad, there were also a provincially assisted Canadian Book Centre in Ontario.

That the interests of the Canadian book are central in the concerns of the Canadian Book Publishers' Council as well as the Independent Publishers' Association has been asserted by both bodies, but we would like to see a much closer cooperation between the two groups to this end. We endeavour to make clear in this report that it is only the interests of Canadian publishing, meaning of Canadian authors, which we feel have a legitimate claim for public support. But this leaves a large area of common concern for the two trade organizations in English-language publishing in this country, and we would like to see them cooperate in their efforts to serve it. We categorically reject any suggestion that the work of a Canadian author published in Canada by a non-Canadian firm should be placed under any kind of disability; in saying this we are not contradicting the conclusion we express elsewhere that Canadian-owned, Ontario-based publishing firms will be needed in the future if the long-term interests of Canadian authorship are to be served, and our recommendations are intended to corroborate this view. But in no way do we support the narrow, ultra-nationalistic view that Canadian authors should in some way be denied the right to publish with whom they please, or that their works should not be recognized in exhibits of Canadian books at home or abroad. A Canadian book is a Canadian book is a Canadian book.

In the context of expanded cooperation between the Canadian Book Publishers' Council and the Independent Publishers' Association, we would reiterate that a coordinated public relations program on behalf of all Canadian books is long overdue in this country. It is hard to conceive of a more logical base for such a program, on behalf of English-language books, than a Canadian Book Centre located in this province. The maintenance of good mailing lists for the purpose, and just possibly the provision of certain mailing services as well – within budgeted limits – would form a natural part of such a public relations program.

Although many additional joint activities on behalf of the Canadian book could also be proposed, the great value of a Canadian Book Centre in Ontario would be as a gathering place for all bona fide Canadian bookmen, whether they be authors, publishers, booksellers, librarians, or simply people who feel that they have a stake in books written and published in this country. Provided that it could be assured that all the social and quasi-social uses to which such a Centre might be put would be self-costing, and this would have to be established firmly in advance, the psychological stimulus that the physical existence of such a Centre would bring to Canadian publishing could be important and lasting. This is not a proposal that another building should be constructed, least of all another government building.

It is rather an acknowledgment of the fact that there has been too little coordination of marketing effort on behalf of the Canadian book as such in the past, and a recognition of the broad interpretation that any such marketing program should be given if one is attempted.

The primary purpose of a Canadian Book Centre would be to provide a place where coordination could take place of all commercial efforts on behalf of Canadian books wherever these can be more efficiently conducted cooperatively than separately. If conflicts of interest, real or imagined, are to be avoided and if the unbusinesslike decisions that so often characterize creative enterprises are to be neutralized, it is obvious that the Centre itself would have to be administered with uncompromising business efficiency. This could be accomplished best if the Centre were independently incorporated and managed, and if relations with participating publishers (and other groups of bookmen) were made the subject of annual contracts. These contracts would have to stipulate with considerable precision the coordinated services that would be undertaken, the areas in which there would be consultation, and the conditions under which no consultation in advance should be expected. They would have to be explicit regarding charges to participating organizations, and the day-to-day management of the premises would have to be clearly vested in the corporation and its appointees and respected on all sides.

Once the basis for cooperation had been determined but before the corporate mechanism had been called into being, there should be a thorough exploration of the possibility of providing to appropriate organizations full-time and part-time office, conference room, and general meeting space within the future premises. Such tenants would need to have no added authority in the Centre because they were tenants, and their participation would not be a condition of its viability. On the other hand, the greater the concentration of book-related groups possible, the more efficient the total budgeting would be. In the first instance, the establishment of such a cooperative enterprise would have to be decided upon by a voluntary group convened for the purpose. Presumably the charter members would be publishers of Canadian books rather than associations or other groups and enterprises not directly involved in creative publishing. But as has been pointed out already, there should be room for a wide range of cousin enterprises and organizations once the primary purposes of a Canadian Book Centre had been provided for.

There remains the question of how such a Canadian Book Centre would finance itself. If it were able to realize its goal of coordinating many marketing services now either being provided independently (or unwisely being overlooked) it could of course expect participating publishers to furnish all the financial support necessary; after all, they would be the first to reap any economic dividends to be derived from a coordination of marketing services. There are several reasons why such a conclusion would have to be qualified, however. First, not all publishers of Canadian books could be counted on as participants, although some of the projects (special subject catalogues, for example) could be expected to serve them all, and could not be modified to serve fewer. Second, some of the publishers of Canadian books who would stand to gain most, relatively speaking at least, are the small independent firms, chiefly of recent vintage, which still survive largely on the free or underpaid labours of those who administer them. Some of these firms stressed that this was the situation in the briefs they submitted to us. So long as they operate in this way, they can hardly afford to grow larger, paradoxical though this may seem.

The establishment of a Canadian Book Centre in Ontario would implement the third recommendation contained in *Promotion and Response*, the study by Val Clery sponsored by the Canadian Book Publishers' Council and submitted in December, 1970. Although the Commission does not endorse every aspect of this recommendation, its relevance to our proposal for the establishment of a Canadian Book Centre justifies our including it here without further comment:

RECOMMENDATION THREE

That an initiative be taken towards the establishment of a non-profit organization with the following aims:
(a) To serve as a meeting-point for the several components of the book industry in Canada,– publishers, booksellers, librarians and writers;
(b) To assemble and disseminate general information about books and literature, and to further and develop the cultural objectives of the book industry;
(c) To promote, primarily, Canadian books, and to encourage Canadian writing and a creative criticism of it; to promote also appreciation of other literatures and their books in Canada;
(d) To assemble current information about all forthcoming books in Canada and to circulate a bi-monthly list, categorized under subject and country of origin, to booksellers, librarians and the media; list to include details of authors' tours, press receptions and conferences, and other special promotions;
(e) To subsidize by joint industry/government grant an independent national book magazine...
(f) To promote continuing research of media outlets about books; to disseminate current information about media to the book industry;
(g) To provide a central service for clipping and filing of book reviews, and of national and international news about books;
(h) To assemble and facilitate the production of non-commercial tape film and v.t.r. programs on books and writers for use by libraries, schools, e.t.v. & cable outlets;
(i) To organize and support lectures, seminars, conventions and courses relating to books and literature.

THE SMALL PUBLISHER

We have a special interest in the small, new, Canadian publisher, for as we implied earlier, he is the sine qua non to the preservation of a substantial domestic publishing industry. This does not mean that we believe that every private individual who wishes to declare himself a publisher deserves public confidence, much less immediate public support. We have already spoken of the capital-intensive nature of publishing, and explained that this characteristic does not conflict with the fact that it does not take much capital to enter the business. But to expand in publishing can be entirely different.

Jack McClelland described the plight of the small independent Canadian publisher in a hypothetical illustration included in his brief to the Commission. Not everything about the model he developed can in our opinion be applied to all such enterprises, but the contributions and the scope of these small publishers is so frequently misreported – sometimes by their own members – that we think that Mr. McClelland's words should be allowed to speak for themselves:

> The implementation of the Third Interim Report of this Commission has gone a long way towards making their survival feasible. It is our opinion that further steps are needed to encourage more firms to enter the field. Even with the assistance already available only a few of the existing firms will survive. More are needed if we are to achieve a proper level of Canadian ownership.
>
> We believe it may be useful to demonstrate why survival is so difficult for a small publishing house and why the system of Government-backed bank loans is so essential. The Commission does not need this instruction. The public probably does. Let us attempt to explain the paradox that the greater the success of a small book publishing firm, the more certain its failure.
>
> To start, let us examine the economics of the simplest possible publishing transaction. A, an author, who is extrovert with some imagination, energy, a little money, no job, completes a novel and decides after a number of rejections, to publish his own book. In fact he starts a new publishing company.
>
> His manuscript of 75,000 words which will make a book of 224 pages with a good type page, ample prelims, 2-colour jacket and a simulated cloth over board binding, would sell today for $7.95 if published by a typical general publisher. (3,000 copies)
>
> To publish and market the book himself, provided his own time is not accounted for, "A" will encounter the following costs:
>
> | | | |
> |---|---:|---:|
> | Editorial (a good moonlighter) | $ 300 | |
> | Designer (overseas manufacture and includes jacket) | 300 | |
> | Manufacture (3,000 copies) | 4,500 | $5,100 |
> | *Promotion & Sales* | | |
> | 1. Three week sales and promotions across country | $ 500 | |
> | 2. Two mailings to stores and libraries | 100 | |
> | 3. Invoicing | 200 | |
> | 4. Phone | 100 | 900 |
> | | | $6,000 |
>
> For $6,000 he is able to sell 2,900 copies (he gives away 100 for review and promotion) so his unit cost is $2.07. He decides that if he doubles his money, he will do very well indeed. He rounds this out and he needs to get $4.00. This means if he gives a 40% discount (which he is told is standard) he can sell for $6.95 and do even better. ($1.00 less than the commercial firm would charge.) He calculates that if he sells out he will make 2,900 x $2.10 = $6,090.

He calculated his personal publishing time-involvement as one month before publication, two after, and decides if he sells out he will have earned $6,000 in three months. Not bad. That's $24,000 a year if he does four books; maybe much more if he does six or eight.

As it happens, his own book does well. All the media automatically support a new house and a colourful figure. He gets lots of space. The book trade, too, is sympathetic. Within one month of publication he is sold out.

He reprints 2,000 copies. This time his cost per unit is only $1.30 everything included and his profit is $2.87 per copy. He sells out and adds $5,700 to his $6,000 with a little additional effort (equivalent to one month's work) so he has made $11,700 in four months or $35,000 a year.

For certain he is going to be a publisher. He signs up six books (five already been rejected by many commercial firms). He decides to spend a year publishing six books (his spare time writing another novel). He has his original $6,000 plus $4,000 saved out of earnings. He will edit the books himself. He will not use a designer, copy other books, buy only jacket designs.

The media reacts well to his announcement but when the books come out he gets less cooperation. Also he can't afford the time to travel or call on stores, etc. He also has to pay royalties. Some of the books are badly treated by reviewers and the public; others have costly mistakes in manufacture.

RESULTS AT END OF ONE YEAR

	Print	Cost	Sell	Net Sales
Book 1	3,000	$2.00	2,100	$ 8,400
2	5,000	2.00	5,000	20,000
3	2,000	1.50	600	1,800
4	3,000	2.00	1,200	4,800
5	5,000	1.80	2,600	9,360
6	1,500	2.50	300	1,500
		$32,350.00		$45,860

His investment in the year (disregarding his own time) is $32,350. His sales are $45,860 but he can't collect 5% – say $2,360 so his cash income is $43,500 out of which he must pay royalties of $7,500 which leaves $36,000. Also he has had to acquire a typist-bookkeeper type for say $3,650 per annum (to keep things neat) which means his earnings in cash, net, are $32,350 so he pays his bills and still has his original $10,000. Unfortunately, life as a publisher is fraught with obligation and he took an income of $15,000 during the year and ended up $5,000 in debt.

In fact, though, he has an inventory of $15,620 on hand so he made a profit in his company of $10,620 and paid tax of $3,700. Thus he ended up with a cash debt of $8,700.

By this time, however, things looked quite good. He had paid himself $15,000. He had a profit (after tax) of $12,000. He had 15 books signed up for the next year. He paid moderate advances on these (a going concern but still growing so don't press) – an average of $250 or a total of $3,750 – except on one sure-fire book he paid $1,500, because of an offer from a commercial house. Cost $5,000. Total debt in cash at year end $13,700.

To cut a long story short, only 10 of the 15 books were published the next year because authors failed to deliver and because of other problems. Nevertheless he did well, sold 70% of all books printed and several had long-term potential. Tally at end of year:

    Investment $60,000
    Sales $84,000

Therefore he almost doubled his sales and sold 70% of all books printed. His gross profit was $24,000. Out of this he paid $8,400 in royalties, his girl was increased to $5,000 because she was working about 70 hours a week; his bad debts were $4,000; his tax on his inventory profit was $3,600 including his personal income of $15,000 and his advances on next year's books ($5,000), his total cash outlay for the year was $41,000 (after manufacturing costs) and his cash income was $24,000 so he added $17,000 to his debt which after two years was $30,700. To this he had to add $5,000 for an editor and $6,000 for a sales and promotion manager so he was actually $41,700 in debt. However, he now had an inventory of $27,000 (he had sold 25% of the first year's inventory which is not bad). Although he was $41,700 in debt his apparent loss was only about $14,000 and next year looked really good.

The real problem in the foregoing is the steadily increasing need for working capital. This is further compounded by the need to keep earlier titles in print.

Frequently this can be done only by printing a very small quantity (which in turn means a very high unit cost and subsequent loss of operating margin). Even the smallest economical printing can mean a five year inventory at this stage.

The limited capital is needed for new books but no backlist will be developed if books are allowed to go out of print. Nor will authors continue to publish with a firm that fails to keep their books actively available. The problems of the small publisher begin to compound themselves but the crucial issue is still lack of working capital which won't have been attracted by the earnings record to this point...

New publishing houses, publishing only Canadian books, have little hope of survival unless
(a) they are lucky or brilliant beyond reason,
(b) unless they are subsidized by volunteer help,
(c) unless they have unlimited cash resources or,
(d) unless they stay very small.

    It is not necessary to accept all the hypothetical calculations quoted by Mr. McClelland, but they do illustrate a key aspect of the problem, and are sensibly related to actual figures we have studied. However, the final two conditions of possible survival which he cites are particularly relevant: *New publishing houses, publishing only Canadian books, have little hope of survival unless they are subsidized by volunteer help . . . or . . . unless they stay very small.* Some of the small firms which would stand to benefit immensely from a coordinated public relations program on behalf of Canadian books through a Canadian Book Centre could not afford to pay their proper share of its costs because they are not buying equivalent services commercially now.

    For the reasons just outlined, and because in the survival of Canadian publishing the cultural interests of the Canadian community are at stake, some degree of public financial support to such a Canadian Book Centre in Ontario is indicated. The amount need not be large, and its effectiveness should be the subject of review and report. Such review should be one of the numerous functions of the Ontario

Book Publishing Board, the need for which was anticipated in this Commission's Third Interim Report. The provincial investment would in all circumstances be modest in relation to the cultural value of the promotional programs which such a Canadian Book Centre in Ontario would coordinate and foster.

INTERNATIONAL STANDARD BOOK NUMBERS

A proposal for a system of International Standard Book Numbers (ISBNs) grew out of a British proposal made in 1965, and has since received widespread support internationally. Its main purpose is to establish a computer-compatible identification number for every distinctive edition of every book published, with each publisher assigned a prefix of his own. In its first form, nine digits were used but the prefix was subsequently expanded to ten (and in some cases eleven) digits when it was decided to make provision for books published in other than English-speaking countries. A typical ISBN would be:

$$0\ 8020\ 1526\ 3$$

The number 8020 identifies the publisher, the number 1526 the book as well as the precise edition of the book, and the final digit 3 serves as a check against the possibility that any of the preceding digits have been transposed either by the customer or by the publisher's order department. The method whereby this check is made is of some interest in that it illustrates again the close relation between publishing developments in the future and the new technology. It has been summarized by Harald Bohne as follows:

The digits in the ISBN are multiplied in order by the numbers 0, 9, 8, 7, 6, 5, 4, 3, and 2. After the multiplications have been completed, the results are added, and the total divided by the modulus 11. On the principle that the total of all multiplied digits (including the check digit times one) should be divisible by 11, the difference between the remainder resulting from the above calculation and the modulus 11 is the check digit.

Example:

```
    0           8  0  2  0           1  5  2  6           3
    X           X  X  X  X           X  X  X  X           X
    0           9  8  7  6           5  4  3  2           1
    ─           ──────────           ──────────           ─
    0           72+0+14+0      +     5+20+6+12 = 129 ÷ 11 = 11[+8]
```

Because the division leaves a remainder of 8, and the difference between 8 and 11 is 3, the check digit must be 3 to make the total of all products divisible by 11. When the book is processed by ISBN numbers, automated equipment makes the calculation instantaneously, and rejects the item if the ISBN does not check.

The signficance of the ISBN system to this Commission is that at the present time Canadian participation in it is voluntary (as is true of the participation of publishers in other countries up to this time). Moreover, it has been administered in Canada by a senior official of one Canadian publishing company (Harald Bohne, Assistant

Director of the University of Toronto Press) without compensation for more than four years. Because the importance of this numbering system will obviously grow in the future, it is desirable that Canadian publishers should adopt it not only for new titles but also for all Canadian books in print, in order that the advance of Canadian publishing into international markets may go forward unimpeded. To this end, the Commission is of the opinion that the use of ISBNs should be made mandatory by federal statute, and that the administration of the system should be vested in an appropriate office in Ottawa, e.g. the National Library or the Copyright Office. In any event it is imperative that the office administering the system be in a position to issue ISBNs instantly – by telephone in the first instance, if necessary – although in practice continuous series would presumably be made available to individual publishers as at present.

PUBLISHERS AND LIBRARIES

The agency system, whereby many foreign publishers appoint exclusive Canadian publisher-agents for their complete catalogues, was outlined earlier in this chapter and needs little further explanation here. Suffice it to say that its feature of exclusivity has invited considerable criticism, at least by certain categories of book purchasers in this country, to the point that some of the latter have elected to operate as though the agency system does not exist. In protesting the resulting "buying around," the Canadian publisher-agents point out that they have the exclusive responsibility for encouraging the interest of Canadian readers, whether by personal sales promotion, advertising, or the distribution of copies for review, and that they are therefore morally as well as legally entitled to process the orders that result. The university librarians say they are not influenced by sales promotion, not by promotion in Canada, anyway.

Because the foreign principals respect their exclusive agency arrangements in Canada, whatever buying around there is takes place through third parties – usually through international book wholesalers. These wholesalers do not share in the costs of promotion and display, which are an important part of the overhead of the publisher-agent. Such competitors, whether their offices are located in Canada or abroad (or both), are in a particularly advantageous position to supply most of the needs of certain kinds of Canadian book purchasers, especially those who place a premium on receiving consolidated shipments of books from many publishers ("one order, one invoice"). Although large retailers, especially chains, sometimes join in decrying the agency system, saying they would prefer to purchase directly or through their own offices abroad, the customers who seem most unwilling to deal through so-called exclusive Canadian representatives are libraries. And among libraries, those to whom the agency system seems to have least to offer are clearly the college and university libraries. Perhaps this is because the book requirements of the latter, although substantial in value, are farthest removed from works of popular interest, i.e. they tend not to be the books which agents stock first for promotion to bookstores, nor even to libraries serving more general interests. Certainly academic reference works, and foreign books of non-fiction generally, are the ones whose sales in Canada can be least accurately predicted, and which therefore are imported speculatively with greater reluctance.

At all events, the publishers contended and the university librarians demonstrated that an overwhelming proportion of the holdings of the latter are in fact purchased otherwise than through Canadian publisher-agents. The evidence from the librarians seemed to show that most of the books they buy could not be purchased from agents anyway. At least they often cannot be purchased from stock on hand with Canadian agents; the librarians also told us that most of the books they buy come from catalogues which are not even represented in this country. The reasons for such lack of representation are numerous. Many books required for university reference are antiquarian or foreign-language editions, or government publications, or are published uncommercially by associations and societies, or are produced by publishers so specialized that commercial representation of them in Canada is impracticable. These are important considerations, although we are of the view that in assembling their statistics of proof the librarians perhaps laid undue stress on what is not available rather than on what is available through agents.

In protesting their loss of business through buying around, the Canadian publisher-agents emphasized that such purchases were made with funds chiefly provided from public tax revenues. They told us that the resulting loss of business seriously compromises their ability to publish original Canadian works. We listened to this argument carefully, because it impinges on an area of special concern to us under our terms of reference. We also noted the librarians' repeated observation that there is not necessarily any connection between the agency business and Canadian publishing. Some of the reservations with which such a claim must be considered have already been discussed; certainly some so-called Canadian publishers have no right to make or join in this plea at all, to judge from their low outputs of Canadiana, as the librarians also observed. Nevertheless, it is necessary to acknowledge that those publishers who have been active in issuing original Canadiana have indeed required income from other sources than publishing Canadian trade books. We had little evidence that programs of general Canadian publishing can be profitable in themselves, much less furnish the working capital needed for their expansion. Even McClelland and Stewart is able to spread its fixed costs over the revenues it earns from administering several valuable import lines, in addition to an educational publishing department.

If we could be assured that Ontario libraries could afford to support Canadian publishing without compromising the effectiveness of the services to their users that they are expected to provide, and if we could be assured that the resulting added revenues would in fact play a proportionate role in enhancing both the quantity and the quality of original Canadian publishing, we would not have much difficulty in resolving such conflicting considerations as those mentioned above, and in framing a recommendation. Without doubt, the latter would be that public moneys should be spent in the way that will best serve the public interest, and that inasmuch as the latter embraces the continued development of original Canadian publishing, Canadian publisher-agents should be supported so long as doing so results in no significant impairment of library services or a counterbalancing increase in library overheads. The argument that university libraries also receive support from private endowments is not a compelling one in this context, we think. *But the assurances just mentioned were not forthcoming* during any of our public or private hearings, nor in the course of any of the concurrent studies we undertook – the latter involving numerous meetings with publishers and university librarians, individually and in groups, as well as protracted correspondence in many directions.

We have weighed the advisability of reviewing and commenting in detail on the many briefs dealing with the agency question which we received and studied. These are matters of record and we have concluded that it would only be redundant to recapitualte their contents here. Instead we shall summarize briefly our reasons for concluding that no additional restrictions on library ordering procedures can be recommended at this time, while we do recommend that a particular kind of ongoing review of the subject under appropriate independent auspices be provided for.

As was true with regard to library copying practices discussed in Chapter 3, by far the most precise information we received regarding existing practices was contained in the brief we received from the Canadian Association of College and University Libraries. This included the results of a systematic survey of purchasing practices among Canadian university libraries embodied in the report by B. Stuart-Stubbs mentioned earlier, *Purchasing and Copying Practices at Canadian University Libraries*. Reference should be had to the report itself for information regarding the scope and nature of this study, as well as for an understanding of some of its limitations. Separate statistics regarding purchasing practices at the University of Toronto Library were also furnished in the brief from Robert Blackburn and David Esplin of that institution. Several additional library briefs, as well as a number of publishers' briefs, dealt vigorously with the subject of buying around, but although they helped to clarify points of view, few of these submissions offered statistics on which to base a judgment of the dimensions of the practice.

The Commission considered expanding the quantitative studies that were received from librarians, as mentioned above, but in the end decided that to do so would not be helpful at this time. This decision was reached because it seemed clear that the issue should not turn on the amount of buying around, but rather on what conditions would have to be achieved before libraries could be said to have viable alternatives.

The library studies themselves amply demonstrated that the proportion of books purchased by university libraries through other channels than the so-called exclusive agents is probably smaller in proportion to total purchases than the publishers at first surmised, a fact which came to be acknowledged by the publishers in the course of our discussions with them. However, in absolute terms, the value of books thus bought around is substantial enough to warrant being taken seriously by anyone studying the Canadian book trade; it probably runs to several million dollars annually.

At the present time at least, the quality of service available from publisher-agents for university reference books is more often inferior to than better than that furnished by other channels of supply. As we have said, any recommendation to restrict library purchasing to authorized agencies would have had to be conditional on our receiving convincing assurance that there would be no important disability worked on libraries in the form of a deterioration in the quality of the service already available to them. We saw no reason to believe that present service by agents would improve to the extent necessary.

Much of the attention of the Commission was taken up with efforts to propound a compromise procedure which for the libraries would meet the condition regarding service, and at the same time measurably improve the position of the authorized agent. For example, the Commission was told by the representatives of the Ontario Council of University Librarians that if a library could know in advance of ordering that a particular book was actually available in Toronto, this would bear on how the institution would prefer to order. The Commission explored at some length the practicability of a system under which library orders might be "exposed" in advance of being placed. Specifically, it seemed possible that a clearing-house acting in Toronto for the Canadian agents might determine whether or not the required agency books were actually in stock in Canada, using simple computer techniques to locate them, advise the library (or Canadian wholesaler, if preferred), and if necessary even reserve copies against confirmation of order. Thought was also given to the possibility that, assuming competitiveness in price, such orders might be filled automatically if stock were available. Unfortunately there appeared to be a preference among some publisher-agents, perhaps among most, for a system that would ensure their being called on automatically to fill all orders for all books of their principals, even when stock might have to be specially imported. That this would often be necessary in the case of university library requirements was obvious, and was further corroborated by this demand. A sophisticated order referral system making full use of computerized data transmission techniques, whereby orders for books would be transferred to overseas publishers whether or not they were represented in Canada, was proposed tentatively by the publishers and carefully examined by the Commission. However, we decided not to commend it to the university librarians, at least not in its then rudimentary form.

In a meeting between representatives of the Canadian Book Publishers' Council and the Ontario Council of University Librarians, held under the auspices of the Commission on March 30, 1972, the librarians made clear that they would consider favourably any proposal whereby availability of the books from the Candian agent at competitive prices could be confirmed within ten days to two weeks. However it also became clear at this meeting that any system based on the exposing of orders being placed by libraries would not accomplish what the publisher-agents wanted, viz. the exclusive right to import if the book were not in stock in Canada. Assuming that a title being ordered has been published for a sufficient length of time for the agent to have received it (we do not think the latter can be held responsible for not having stock on hand in advance of publication, of course) we believe that acknowledgment that it frequently is not physically available in Canada but must be specially ordered lends much weight to the librarians' contention that they must be free to procure it in the most efficient way they can. That they are legally free to import themselves is of course assured by Section 28 of the Copyright Act. To subject them to any purchasing restrictions at the provincial level in such cases would only exacerbate the problems inherent in an exclusive agency system that did not provide the service which many libraries require, and which they have therefore had to develop for themselves. (Although we believe that this summarizes the history of the present situation, we hope that statements such as the preceding will not be attributed to the Commission out of the full context in which they are made.)

We recognize that if all orders for agency books could be channelled through the exclusive agents concerned, the efficiency of the agency system itself would be bound to improve, through use if nothing else. Moreover, substantial additional gross income would be available to the publisher-agents (as well as to some agents who now do almost no publishing). And we recognize – although the librarians have not – that additional gross income would be even more important than net profit, because it would help to carry many fixed costs of publishing in Canada, when the latter is done at all. Such a re-directing of business could increase processing costs for libraries, even if the agency system could be made to work well. It should not, however, add significantly to the prices paid by libraries for the books they buy, at least not if the pricing structure were supervised to prevent inordinate mark-ups in some cases. (One system of supervising price conversion rates is implicit in the new *politique du livre* in Quebec, it should be noted.) We note that existing price conversion rates did not figure significantly in any of our discussions, service apparently being the key issue in the opinion of librarians. The

Economic Council's *Report on Intellectual and Industrial Property*, on the other hand, seemed to be preoccupied with price differentials between foreign-and domestic-purchased copies of selected titles, without regard for variations in marketing costs between the territories compared.

To recapitulate, the Commission is not willing to concede, at least not on the basis of any evidence which it has seen, that any requirement that Ontario libraries should channel all orders for agency books through the Canadian representatives of the publishers concerned would improve the service which the libraries must procure, or that it would not impair the levels of service which they must now give to their users. Certainly we do not believe that the efficiency of libraries would be enhanced in any way if they were required to secure reports on unstocked titles from a multiplicity of exclusive agents in Canada that were not able to furnish accurate information, were not in a good position to procure it, and which had something less than their existing competitive incentive to do so. At the present time, most reporting on unfilled orders placed with agents is unacceptably bad, granted that there are a few happy exceptions. We have received ample evidence for this statement.

We have mentioned that the publishers tentatively proposed a system whereby library orders might be consolidated and referred (if the book were not in stock locally) to the foreign principals, using computerized data transmission techniques. Under this procedure, consolidation of shipments would also occur abroad, for forwarding by air where necessary, and prompt reporting would take place through the same channels. This proposal was not fully developed, and we think that it will have to be pursued – if it is at all – by the publishers themselves, and that it is now incumbent on them to persuade the librarians of its competitive advantages. But let us add that we also think that it is incumbent on the librarians to join constructively in any such discussion.

At the public hearing of the brief from the Ontario Council of University Librarians we explored the possibility of more extensive cooperation between the Canadian publisher-representatives and the university librarians. Mr. Redmond, speaking for OCUL, answered, "I am absolutely sure that the Council will be willing to cooperate. I would point out that Council has stated its policy that it does not hear commercial representations so that we would want such a discussion to be under the auspices of the Commission." As intimated already, the Commission gave a substantial amount of time to exploring with both groups the matters reviewed above. In concluding the last joint meeting with the publishers and librarians, held on March 30, 1972, it was stressed that "once the Commission had gone this did not mean this particular issue could be forgotten." We would like to conclude our comments on this topic by reiterating our view that the conversations between librarians and publishers should continue, either bilaterally or under the auspices of the Ontario Book Publishing Board. Every effort should be made to articulate the interests of the two groups in the Canadian book industry most concerned with the issues discussed above, issues with which the public of this province should also be concerned. These groups are, first, the university librarians and, second, those publishers who, in addition to acting as agents for foreign imprints, issue a significant volume of original Canadian books themselves. In such cooperative explorations, we would be willing to give only limited attention to agents who call themselves publishers but rarely publish, as well as to those wholesalers whose operations weaken rather than strengthen original Canadian publishing.

READERS' CLUB OF CANADA SURVEY

Surveys of personal reading habits and preferences constitute a kind of market research which can be difficult and costly to undertake, and are likely to yield uncertain results; the Commission was cautious about launching such projects. In a market in which "trade book" sales account for less than three dollars per capita according to Ernst & Ernst, any kind of community cross-section sample is likely to lead to misleading conclusions, especially when the data must include subjective judgments of large numbers of individuals who probably never purchase books of their own volition. Explorations we made of student groups showed that their habits, too, varied enormously. Because their book selections often, although not always, reflected curriculum interests, the problem of distinguishing between leisure reading and reading for information appeared likely to invalidate most conclusions that might be drawn from a knowledge of what they read.

When it was proposed to us that we might conduct a survey of the reading habits of members of the Readers' Club of Canada (whose book selections are all Canadian), we were doubtful that a sufficiently large response could be generated to justify studying a group of such limited numbers – slightly more than two thousand in all. However, it seemed that such a study might tell us something about the kind of individuals who have a special interest in Canadian books and who elect to support them in the course of whatever other reading they do. Because the membership was at least of manageable size, we decided to find out what information we could glean from this group. We recognized that the Readers' Club was not representative of any larger Canadian body of readers than its own membership, but a questionnaire was devised and mailed to the complete list of members, kindly furnished by Peter Martin, President of Readers' Club of Canada. In the event, we were much surprised by the high percentage of replies received. Although the questionnaires (see Appendix) were mailed out by the Commission and were to be returned unsigned, albeit in stamped envelopes provided, no fewer than 1498 replies were received in reply to 2020 questionnaires distributed in this way. The percentage of spoiled questionnaires returned was insignificant, and in

PROFILE OF READERS' CLUB OF CANADA MEMBERS

	Number of books read per year				
	1-11 books %	12 books %	13-51 books %	52 books %	52 + books %
1. Sex					
male	69	69	65	59	55
female	31	30	34	40	44
2. Age					
15-25	8	6	9	9	9
25-35	23	20	27	20	28
35-45	24	30	26	27	26
over 45	44	43	38	44	37
3. Education					
elementary	1	1	—	1	—
some high school	6	5	4	4	4
high school graduation	6	11	7	7	6
some post-secondary	17	21	19	22	18
B.A. or equivalent	27	23	24	25	21
some graduate	7	11	16	16	15
graduate degree	36	29	30	26	36
4. Family Income					
under 5000	7	3	4	6	7
5000-7500	3	6	7	4	5
7500-10000	12	10	9	13	8
10000-15000	22	25	26	25	29
15000-20000	26	22	21	20	19
over 20000	30	34	32	31	31
5. Occupation					
student	8	4	5	9	10
labourer or semi-skilled	—	1	1	1	1
skilled	1	1	1	3	1
clerical	1	5	3	1	3
sales	1	1	2	2	1
semi-professional	5	6	6	4	4
professional	50	46	46	42	41
executive	10	15	12	13	11
housewife	8	11	13	15	14
retired	5	4	5	6	7
other	9	5	6	5	7

	Number of books read per year				
	1-11 books %	12 books %	13-51 books %	52 books %	52 + books %
6. Distance from nearest bookstore					
less than 1 mile	9	16	17	17	18
less than 2 miles	22	16	23	24	20
less than 3 miles	20	23	18	16	15
less than 4 miles	8	10	9	10	7
less than 5 miles	5	7	3	4	6
less than 6 miles	5	5	7	5	6
6-10 miles	8	8	8	6	7
11-20 miles	7	5	5	5	6
21-50 miles	5	5	3	6	5
more than 50 miles	10	3	6	7	8
7. If a bookstore in community, book selection is considered					
no bookstore	28	17	16	17	18
poor	8	5	7	11	12
fair	10	19	16	19	17
good	23	26	29	28	24
excellent	27	31	29	22	26
8. Visits bookstore					
every week	2	9	11	17	32
1-2 times monthly	17	20	40	39	32
monthly	48	51	35	33	26
rarely	33	19	13	10	9
9. Books ordered from Readers' Club					
fewer than 1 per month	94	87	83	80	74
about 1 per month	6	11	14	16	22
more than 1 per month	—	1	2	3	3
10. Other books purchased					
a) hardcover–					
fewer than 1 per month	81	69	52	46	35
about 1 per month	15	18	26	28	23
more than 1 per month	—	8	21	24	41
b) paper backs–					
fewer than 1 per month	66	41	23	16	11
about 1 per month	21	32	30	27	15
more than 1 per month	9	23	44	54	71
11. Membership in other book clubs					
Book-of-the-Month	26	31	32	30	40
Literary Guild	12	9	12	14	19
Doubleday Dollar	3	3	4	5	5
Book Find	1	1	3	2	4
Readers' Subscription	2	2	1	2	3
History Book Club	3	1	4	6	8
other	15	11	13	15	16

BOOK MARKETS AND BOOK MARKETING 165

	\multicolumn{5}{c}{Number of books read per year}
	1-11 books %	12 books %	13-51 books %	52 books %	52 + books %
12. Newspapers read daily					
none	6	3	5	3	5
one	52	42	45	45	42
two	37	52	44	46	47
two +	5	1	4	3	4
13. General interest periodicals read regularly					
Maclean's	56	78	78	72	78
Chatelaine	28	32	34	34	36
Saturday Night	35	46	50	52	58
Atlantic Monthly	5	11	15	14	21
Reader's Digest	17	26	24	19	22
Weekend Magazine	56	68	66	71	72
Canadian Magazine	58	54	60	52	59
Life	9	14	12	13	13
Newsweek	5	5	9	6	11
Time	37	48	44	48	46
Harper's	2	8	7	6	12
14. Preferred departments in newspapers and magazines (first choice only shown)*					
book reviews	7	4	5	7	12
editorials	21	20	16	19	18
comics	—	1	—	1	1
sports	1	3	2	2	3
business	7	6	8	4	4
"women's"	5	1	1	1	2
international	26	35	32	32	30
feature articles	14	14	20	19	18
15. Daily TV viewing					
0-1 hr.	50	51	52	51	48
1-2 hrs.	35	37	36	31	32
2 hrs. +	10	9	7	9	10
never	5	3	5	8	9
16. Preferred TV sources*					
CBC-TV	78	80	79	78	74
CTV	17	15	18	14	14
American	8	9	14	7	10
ETV	7	3	6	4	3
17. Daily radio listening					
0-1 hr.	50	44	41	41	41
1-2 hrs.	37	37	36	36	32
2 hrs. +	10	18	22	22	25

166 CANADIAN PUBLISHERS AND CANADIAN PUBLISHING

	Number of books read per year				
	1-11 books %	12 books %	13-51 books %	52 books %	52 + books %
18. Preferred radio sources*					
CBC (AM)	51	56	59	58	58
CBC (FM)	12	15	16	19	16
private Canadian AM	37	31	26	23	23
private Canadian FM	16	15	20	16	19
U.S.	5	2	2	2	2
19. Book-reading motivation (only "most frequent" shown)					
newspaper reviews	19	21	24	28	26
general magazine reviews	14	22	20	26	27
professional magazine reviews	24	21	33	32	46
news stories	1	3	6	3	5
recommendations of friends	12	22	24	27	23
radio reviews, interviews	5	7	10	6	11
TV reviews, interviews	3	6	6	4	6
20. Mother tongue					
English	88	92	93	92	95
French	2	3	2	2	1
other	9	5	5	6	3
21. Other languages spoken	ambiguity in replies — results invalidated				
22. Public library member?					
yes	56	54	70	72	74
no	44	45	30	27	26
23. If a library member, frequency of visits					
every week	—	3	6	9	25
1-2 times per month	9	16	25	33	25
a few times each year	33	28	29	23	19
infrequently	14	9	11	7	6
no reply	44	45	29	27	26
25. Preferred general reading					
fiction	8	19	18	23	28
non-fiction	85	71	70	65	53
irrelevant	7	7	9	9	16
no reply	—	3	3	3	3
26. Authors read most					
Canadian	51	46	36	28	22
Foreign	45	45	58	63	70
irrelevant	2	4	5	7	5
no reply	1	5	1	2	3

★Where returns do not total approximately 100%, attribute to some respondents not indicating order of first preferences or indicating more than one preference where only one requested.

almost all cases each respondent supplied answers to each of the 32 separate items which made up the questionnaire, an exercise that we estimated required an average of about fifteen minutes per respondent. Because the return was so high, and because they provided more than sixty thousand bits of information from a demonstrably interested segment of the community, a fairly complete tabulation of replies received is included herewith. Omitted from this report are the opinions regarding the Readers' Club of Canada itself, which information has been made available to Mr. Martin. Also omitted are some second- and third-choice answers, and information in reply to questions that appear to have been ambiguous. All percentages shown are rounded to eliminate decimals.

It was decided that Question 24 ("How many books do you read?") should be the basis for grouping replies and calculating percentages, on the ground that it was the most significant question, however subjective the answers to it necessarily were. It would, of course, have been equally possible to analyze all the returns under the headings male or female, family income, occupation, etc. But relative activity in reading seemed to commend itself as the market division to which other habits might most usefully be related.

5
Educational Publishing

All books may rightly be described as educational. But it has always been easy to distinguish books produced primarily for schools and colleges from other kinds. Certainly, the dividing line has been clear enough in the past, although one has to agree that the problem of classifying many children's books as well as many serious non-fiction adult books increases as the two main branches of publishing – educational and trade – continue to merge in the ways already explained.

THE VANISHING TEXTBOOK

Traditionally, the differences between schoolbooks and general books have been found in the motivation behind their writing, the ways in which their authors find publishers, the manner of their editing and design, the prices and discounts at which they are sold, the channels through which they are distributed, and the average sales of the two kinds of books.

For general books, moreover, the decision to read has always been made by the reader himself. Until recently, at least, educational books have normally been selected by someone other than the reader to whom they are addressed. Consequently, textbooks have been planned and promoted with the purpose of persuading instructors or other educational authorities to prescribe them, while the preferences of the pupils and students for whom they are ultimately intended have of course concerned the publishers, but only indirectly.

This situation is indeed changing, and that it is changing more or less simultaneously at every level from the primary grades to university is especially significant for educational publishers. To an increasing degree the basic textbook, so long the backbone of the curriculum in the classroom, is giving way to a much more individualized selection of resource materials. This selection is being made from a wider range of books and other kinds of educational media than was ever listed in publishers' catalogues in the past, and from a vastly wider range than was ever before available in any one educational institution.

Not all curriculum areas lend themselves to so flexible an approach. But even though classroom sets of a preferred mathematics series are still standard equipment in many institutions and at many levels, other subjects such as history and science and literature are now served in the same classes by a rich variety of different books, as well as by other kinds of learning materials. These are likely to be purchased in quantities of from one to five or six copies rather than in sets of thirty-five or forty copies. Moreover, the books themselves more and more often resemble the "trade" books described in Chapter 4 rather than the traditional kind of textbook. Many deal with only a few topics or possibly with just one aspect of the year's curriculum, but they are likely to deal with it in greater depth, and usually in a more interesting way, than did the formal textbooks which they have replaced.

What has been happening in the elementary grades is paralleled in the high school grades, and even at the university level. The pedagogical reasons may not always be the same, but there are striking similarities in the results. The basic textbook shows a tendency to be displaced in an increasing number of situations, if not always by new kinds of topical books, then by other media altogether. This is because new techniques of instruction and study have opened up important classroom markets for film strips and film loops, audio tapes and cassettes, specially prepared sets of pictures or informally collected clippings and travel posters, off-the-air video tapes and multi-faceted portfolios of background information on specific topics. Indeed, the range of non-book media already in use is surpassed only by the range of print and non-print media being planned for publication tomorrow.

Even in many university courses, particularly in the humanities and social sciences, the very thought of a basic textbook on which students will be examined at the end of the year has become anathema. There always were recommended reading lists, of course, but until very recent years these have tended to be supplementary lists of books to be read in the library (selectively, if and when available) rather than of books to be owned. The advent of the quality paperback is not the only reason for the change that has taken place in readership and ownership habits in the universities, although it doubtless made a revolution possible. In the social sciences particularly, relevance of curriculum content has become increasingly important, and this has placed a premium on the topicality of what is studied and read about.

Lists of recommended books are now taken seriously, and especially in the universities equipped with adequate college stores, students and faculty alike are avid customers for new books on Canadian affairs, particularly when they are offered in paperback. At the same time, books on literary, art, and musical criticism abound, while some publishers have mined the scholarly journals for years back to produce omnibus collections of readings on topics and sub-topics of literature, history, sociology, and every other discipline represented by a sufficient undergraduate population. Non-book media at the university level have chiefly taken the form of closed-circuit television experiments, microform publishing of various kinds including microfilms and microfiche, and a generally greater emphasis on audio-visual aids of every description.

Thus instructors at all levels, and in the elhi grades particularly, have been coming into possession of a new and ever-changing arsenal of resource items in which books are one item – still an important one but nevertheless just one item. The educational publisher must now present himself as a publisher not of books but of learning materials. The school library has been converted into a resource centre, and its holdings are no longer merely books but multi-media of every kind, two-dimensional and three-dimensional, opaque and transparent, print and non-print.

This latest revolution in the classroom was neither an Ontario nor a Canadian phenomenon. As with so many other developments affecting education (and therefore educational publishing), it was foreshadowed in the United States, although only by a couple of years or so. And it is probably incorrect to say that pure schoolbook publishers, either there or here, benefitted more than they suffered from the changes that took place. The transition, which developed fairly rapidly, opened up competition from too many new sources, some already highly experienced in their own fields (as were the audio-visual producers), some finding themselves in the school market for the first time.

IMPLICATIONS FOR CANADIAN PUBLISHERS

But if foreign book publishers had to scramble to keep abreast of the new market, it is true that the few Canadian-owned publishers of schoolbooks were quite unprepared either financially or organizationally to cope with the changes that suddenly gathered force at the end of the 1960s. In every way they were at a disadvantage in comparison with the Canadian branch plants of foreign publishers, again chiefly American branch plants. The latter's experience with multi-media publishing was limited, and still is, but the Canadian-owned publisher had none at all.

A totally new marketing approach was required in order to present and procure orders from most of the non-book media, some examples of which have already been mentioned. Required, that is, when the Canadian publisher could offer the new tools of education at all, which he often could not. The foreign-owned firms cataloguing film loops, transparencies for overhead projectors, and other items that made up the new miscellany of the classroom were often not publishers at all, or were publishers only peripherally. A few of them were Canadian branches of visual aids and visual aids equipment companies; others were spin-offs from highly specialized departments of foreign book publishers (including encyclopedia publishers), separately organized to develop and promote the new non-book learning materials.

The new approach to equipping a school with appropriate resource materials demanded a new flexibility in selecting what those materials should be. The only tools of this kind which could be used effectively were ones which teachers understood. Because the variety was great, and rapidly increasing, this meant that only those media were selected which could be fitted to specific needs and opportunities. That is to say, almost all the decisions regarding what to use now had to be made by the teacher rather than by someone making value judgments on behalf of the teacher. Neither principal nor regional supervisor, and certainly not a still more remote provincial department of education, could pick and choose the resource materials which individual teachers could use to best advantage. Information regarding the new media was eagerly sought after, but a restrictive list of approved media was not. No such list could be kept up to date, and the more selective it was the less flexible it would be, until it might even contradict the purpose of the new multi-media approach to learning.

In Ontario, the Department of Education's policy of publishing annually a list of those approved textbooks eligible for support from provincial per-pupil grants stood directly in the way of the classroom teacher's access to the new media. So long as these provincial stimulation grants were not equally available for non-book resources, the latter had to be purchased from other regional educational budgets, none too easily procured. Moreover, the new media tended to be much more expensive than textbooks, with the result that what money was available for them would not go as far anyway. But at best the regional budgets for such purchases were usually too limited, too difficult to tap, and too unpopular with finance committees who could not easily distinguish between the new media and textbooks. After all, the province offered grants of upwards of three dollars per pupil (considerably more at the higher levels), often with equalization grants to be added, for the purchase of any textbooks on Circular 14; if teachers were going to add non-book materials to the expendable equipment of the classroom, perhaps the provincial grant should be applied less restrictively, and include every kind of miscellaneous educational requirement along with approved textbooks.

In the end – and it was not long in coming – that is exactly what happened.

TEXTBOOK STIMULATION GRANTS POLICY

A system of stimulation grants, to apply separately to textbooks and library books, had been authorized by legislation as early as 1951. This system continued to function with various revisions and expansions until 1969 when the costs of books were again grouped with other operating costs and stimulation grants ceased to apply to their purchase, as will be explained shortly.

The 1951 grant regulations provided that the board of a public or separate school should be paid a grant equal to the amount actually expended in the current year for the purchase of textbooks, up to a maximum of $3 per pupil computed on average daily attendance in Grades I through VIII during the previous year. The library book grant paid to the boards was computed in the same way but with a ceiling of $1 per pupil. During the next two years the grants were extended first to include Grades IX and X, and later also kindergarten. Average daily enrolment replaced average daily attendance in the calculation of textbook grants in the 1967 grant regulations. In this same year a supplemental grant known as an equalization grant was extended to some boards. The chief factor in determining the applicability of this additional grant was the municipal assessment in relation to the number of classroom units under the jurisdiction of the board.

In the case of an elementary school board, the textbook stimulation grant of $3 per pupil continued. If the assessment per classroom unit of the board was equal to, or greater than, $1,500,000 (this amount representing the assessment of a board of above average wealth), it was not entitled to an equalization grant. If, however, its assessment was less than this figure the board received a percentage of an additional $3 per pupil. The percentage could be as low as .1 per cent and could go as high as 57 per cent.

Secondary school boards continued to receive the basic stimulation grant of $6 per pupil for textbook expenditure in Grades IX and X and a stimulation grant of $10 per pupil in Grades XI and XII. If the board had an assessment per classroom unit equal to, or greater than, $4,410,000 (considered to be an assessment of a board of above average wealth), it was not entitled to an equalization grant. If its assessment was less than this amount the board received a percentage of an additional $3 per pupil. The minimum percentage rate was .1 per cent and the maximum was 55 per cent.

In the case of library books, boards might either receive $2 per pupil for library book expenditure, or a percentage (the percentage could be as low as 35 per cent and as high as 95 per cent according to the assessment per classroom ratio) of actual expenditure up to $9 per pupil. As with the textbook grant there was an expenditure tie-in. The board received the greater of these two amounts – the determining factor being its actual per pupil library book expenditure.

The only change in 1968, the last year these grants were in force, was related to library book expenditure. In that year it was provided that boards might receive a percentage of up to $10 per pupil for library book expenditure.

DISCONTINUATION OF BOOK STIMULATION GRANTS

In February, 1969, the Canadian Textbook Publishers' Institute wrote to the Department of Education urging an increase in the amount of the per-pupil textbook grant, particularly for elementary schools. This letter claimed that school authorities were reluctant to increase local taxes as would be necessary if purchases of textbooks exceeded the $3 per pupil "which they know will be refunded in full"; it pointed out that since the establishment of the $3 subsidy in 1951 the cost of manufacturing texts had steadily risen; it noted that print runs of texts were growing smaller in the face of expanding competition, with the result that unit costs were rising, and that under the existing grant structure only a small part of the increase could be passed on to the purchaser; and it concluded with a request that the $3 per-pupil grant be increased to $10 per pupil on the basis of average enrolment, plus an additional incentive grant of $5, adding that it was hoped that this latter grant "might cover those printed materials now being required in the resource centres which form part of most new schools."

On April 8, 1969, the Deputy Minister replied in part as follows:

I have your letter of February 26, 1969, in which you urge, on behalf of the Canadian Textbook Publishers' Institute, an increase in the amount of the textbook grant, particularly in the case of elementary schools.

No doubt you are now aware that the Grant Regulation for 1969 has been issued, and that there is no longer a specified stimulation grant for textbooks. This is not to say that no longer will boards receive grant assistance for the purchase of textbooks, as well as those other expenditures which formerly were subject to stimulation grants, e.g. evening courses, home economics and industrial arts, library books, larger units of administration, milk, municipal inspectorates, special fees, special education programs and services, and Ontario School Trustees' Council fees. Rather, boards now have greater freedom to apportion to these expenditures as much as they see fit of the grants received for ordinary expenditure.

The former stimulation grant of $3.00 per pupil of average daily enrolment, although not intended to cover total annual expenditures for textbooks, was, in many instances, the amount expended annually by school boards, as you have noted.

It is hoped that the removal of a stated amount of grant for textbooks will eliminate the element of restrictiveness and encourage boards to make more realistic expenditures according to needs. This is a natural outgrowth of the creation of larger units of administration which demands more planning and decision-making at the local level, and gives to locally-elected trustees and appointed education officials greater freedom to effect economies in some areas and approve additional expenditures in others.

The desegregation of the textbook grant reported above was referred to repeatedly in the briefs we received as a factor which made an important contribution to the serious plight in which textbook publishers have recently found themselves. We were urged to accept the proposition that regardless of the size

COMPARISON OF NUMBER OF "PUBLISHER UNITS" LISTED ON CIRCULAR 14
1893-1972

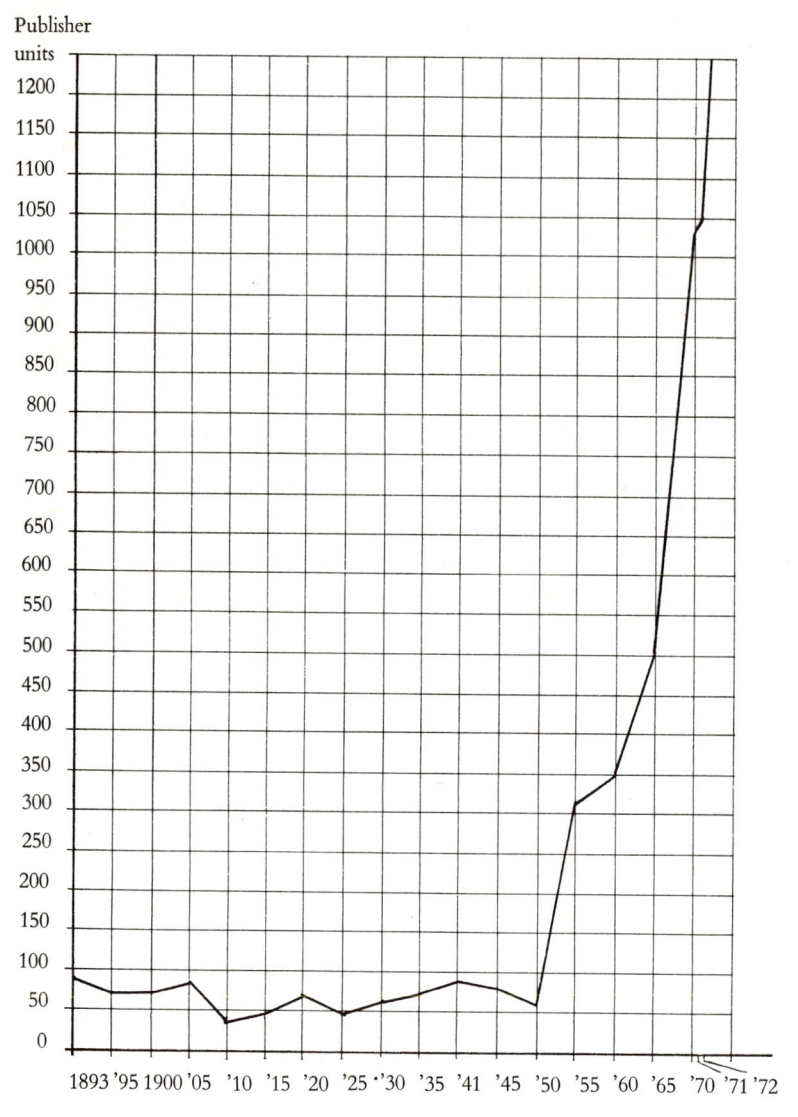

Note: One "publisher unit" is one entry of a book, or a related series of books that appears under one heading.

of the general educational grants, the elimination of the specific stimulation grants for textbooks exposed an already depressed industry to still further losses of business as a result of budgetary shuffles made to accommodate increasing expenses elsewhere, including teachers' salaries and general maintenance, as well as the purchase of non-book media.

If the situation was exactly as it was being depicted to us, the pure educational publisher was being buffeted from a number of directions simultaneously. More money was being spent on non-book media and less on books – on textbooks, possibly much less. Even if the provincial stimulation grant of a fixed amount per pupil earmarked for the purchase of approved textbooks had continued, inflating costs meant that it could not buy as many books. Circular 14 itself, although still essentially a list of Canadian-written and Canadian-produced textbooks, seemed to be growing in size to the bursting point. (It had expanded from 87 titles in 1951-52 to 743 titles in 1967 to almost 1650 titles in 1971.) And even the listing of a new book or series on Circular 14 had ceased to be a guarantee of widespread sales in classroom sets. The trend toward multiple selections meant that the function of a textbook was growing more and more like the function of a library reference book, and the latter could be purchased without regard to Circular 14 if funds were available.

Perhaps the most serious consequence of the consolidation of the per-pupil textbook stimulation grants with the general per-capita education grants at the beginning of 1969 was that the precise significance of Circular 14 became less clear in relation to texts that were not being purchased in sets for basic classroom use. And the total demand for the kind of basic classroom textbook which had to be purchased in this way was diminishing.

ESTABLISHMENT OF COUNTY SCHOOL DISTRICTS

Almost concurrently with the developments just described, school administration in Ontario had come to a turning-point in its history. On November 14, 1967, the Premier made the following public statement:

We believe that . . . our objective should be to reduce the number of administrative units to approximately 100 boards of education [compared with more than 1000 previously] . . . It is the intent of the Government of Ontario that these boards be established on a county-wide basis in Southern Ontario. These units will include the cities and separated towns within the county. However, there will be a few exceptions. For example, this development will not affect the existing system in Metropolitan Toronto. A few other large cities will have their own boards of education . . . Legislation is in preparation . . . so that this reorganization of school units can become effective on January 1st, 1969.

Under the promised legislation, all boards in Southern Ontario, with the exception of five urban areas, were to be consolidated into 38 county boards of education. Northern Ontario was to be reorganized into boards of education according to territorial units prescribed by regulation. In all, the legislation and subsequent regulations established 77 boards of education and retained 48 public school boards, for a total of 125 boards replacing 1010 which had existed in 1968. In addition, discussions with separate school interests resulted in legislation providing for 61 separate school districts to replace 499 existing in 1968.

The administrative, educational, and ultimately the economic advantages of this sweeping consolidation have become increasingly obvious in the short time that has passed since it took place. If this report were concerned with broader issues than it is, it could dwell on these benefits here, but the terms of reference of this Commission are much too specific. The face of local school administration in Ontario had been radically altered in character. So had the market for schoolbook publishers. At first glance, it might seem that the educational market itself should have remained substantially unaltered, and that at most only the channels of distribution and perhaps the addresses of the purchasing agencies would change. Not so. The impact on publishers of educational books, and particularly on Canadian-owned publishers of educational books written by Canadian authors

NUMBER AND TYPE OF SCHOOL BOARDS IN ONTARIO, 1969

Boards of Education		
	County	38
	District	28
	City	10
	Metropolitan	1
		77
Combined Roman Catholic Separate School boards		
	County	28
	District	18
	City	3
		49
Isolated boards		
	Public	48
	Separate	12
Protestant Separate School boards		2
Special boards (appointed)		
	Canadian Forces	16
	Ontario Hydro	5
	Hospitals	19
	Indian schools	2
		42
Grand Total		230

and produced in this country, was much more far-reaching than this.

The early stages of the transitional period were marked by exceptional efforts on the part of the newly established school boards to minimize the first regional educational budgets under the new system. Their anxiety to achieve such economies was stimulated by their desire to offset local tax increases which occurred in some areas as a result of unevenness in the previous distribution of educational costs, or because of needed improvements in other educational services. Of course, these educational improvements were among those which it was the intention of consolidation to achieve. Even the efforts at economizing in schoolbook expenditures could have been termed commendable, had they not in many cases offered short-term savings, possibly at the cost of long-term standards. Every educational system possesses at all times the option of achieving short-term economies by postponing equipment replacements or by deferring the addition of new equipment, but the saving is temporary while the disadvantage to the community being served may take much longer to repair.

Officials of the Department of Education told us of one measure of economy widely adopted at this time. This took the form of a partial moratorium on further expenditures on schoolbooks until existing inventories could be physically pooled and reallocated under the new county board system. The desire to economize at that time can hardly be faulted, but the transition could not be compressed into a single week or even into a single schoolbook-buying season. It does seem that as a result there occurred the equivalent of a year or more of greater retrenchment in the buying of educational publications than individual classroom needs and resources actually justified. Doubtless the fact that there were deferrals of textbook ordering, even where they were short term, had a long-term impact on the inventories of some publishers. Some of the delay may have been sound economics from the standpoint of the boards concerned, but some of it must have reflected mere administrative convenience at a time of fundamental change. Where this was so, it must have resulted in a reduction in textbook supplies which was undesirable educationally, however temporary it was. At all events, to whatever extent the delay took place, it spelled a setback for education publishers who had not anticipated this adverse fluctuation in sales.

The combined impact of consolidation and other influences on the demand for textbooks is reflected in the accompanying graph of comparative sales figures for twelve of the largest schoolbook publishers in Canada for the years 1967 to 1971. This graph shows an actual drop in net sales in 1969 and a substantial flattening of the growth rate thereafter. The arrested growth pattern becomes significant when one considers that printing costs continued to mount, as indicated in the comparative tabulation later in this chapter. (The graph depicting comparative textbook sales over the five-year period includes educational sales throughout Canada; thus the impact of consolidation in Ontario cannot be definitely isolated. But we are

COMPARATIVE SALES FIGURES FOR EDUCATIONAL BOOKS

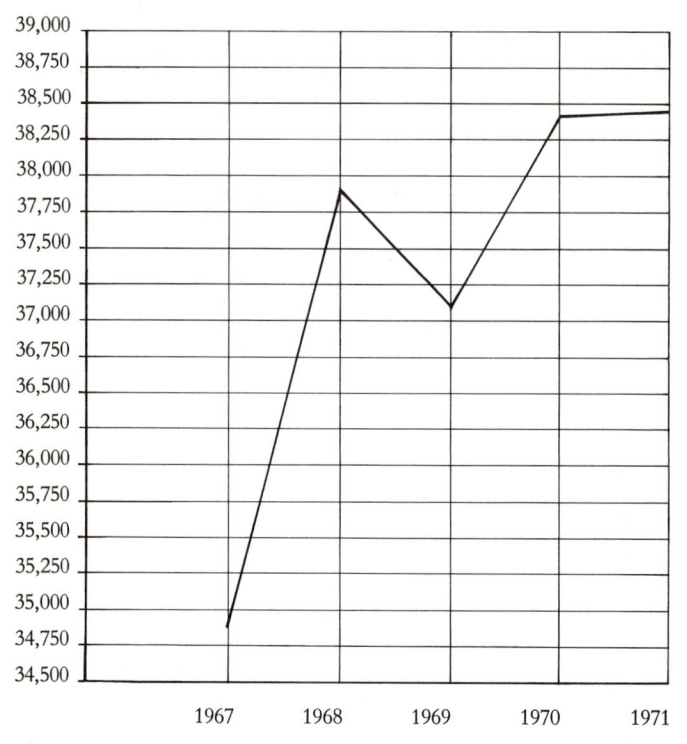

Total sales
(in thousands of dollars)

Note: These figures represent the total sales figures of twelve of the largest schoolbook publishers in Canada

satisfied that no factors in other provinces exerted an effect of comparative magnitude. For accounting reasons it was not feasible, we concluded, to obtain separate sales figures for Ontario only, except from a few publishing houses.)

The Commission was as interested as were many publishers – to say nothing of other educationists – in making direct comparisons between textbook purchases by Ontario school boards before and after consolidation. This proved to be immensely difficult, because available records did not separate accounts on a uniform basis, and central reports which listed textbook expenditures separately ceased to be maintained by the province after consolidation took place. However, we did devise certain studies aimed at relating global expenditures on textbooks and library books before and after establishment of the new county board system, and more particularly before and after elimination of the per-pupil stimulation grants. Let us look at what these studies disclosed.

We have already noted that the comparative graph of sales of educational books made by twelve of the principal schoolbook publishers over a five-year period shows a flattening of the growth pattern, but not an actual decline in net sales except in one year. Publishers, as well as others who came before us, claimed that the integration of per-pupil textbook grants with the general educational grants at the beginning of 1969 led directly to significant cutbacks in book expenditures across the province. This new funding policy, combined with the policies of retrenchment already mentioned, may partly explain the drop in total educational sales in 1969, assuming that most of this drop occurred in Ontario. Interestingly, however, the Commission did not find unequivocal evidence that the elimination of the stimulation grants was itself accompanied by any significant cutback in schoolbook purchasing.

In order to establish as accurately as possible the impact of the change in grants policy on the acquisition of educational books, the Commission undertook a widespread survey by questionnaire to 214 boards of education (public, separate, and "other"). This was followed by an extensive program of personal visits and interviews which will be described later.

Textbook and school library book expenditures before consolidation were available in the Department of Education, although it was necessary for the Commission to piece the figures together from nearly 1400 reports from individual school boards. Following consolidation, the equivalent figures ceased to be reported, and the Commission therefore made its comparisons with the figures provided on the questionnaires returned by the individual consolidated boards, in order to obtain global "before and after" figures showing per-pupil expenditures. The results were interesting, even if not at first convincing.

Among the boards to whom questionnaires were sent were 76 public school boards and 49 separate school boards. Replies were received from 66 and 42 boards, respectively, or 86.8 per cent and 85.7 per cent (figures which are typical of the close cooperation the Commission received in most of its surveys). The figures for average per-pupil elementary book expenditures in the public schools developed in this way were $3.59 in 1965, $4.29 in 1969, and $4.12 in 1970. Per-pupil expenditures on textbooks by separate school boards were $3.78 in 1965, $4.88 in 1969,

AVERAGE PER PUPIL BOOK EXPENDITURES BY BOTH PUBLIC AND
SEPARATE BOARDS IN 1968, 1969 AND 1970

	1968	1969	1970
Elementary Textbooks	$ 3.54	$ 4.55	$ 4.84
Elementary Library Books	$ 5.08	$ 5.46	$ 6.11
Secondary Textbooks	$11.45	$11.89	$11.22
Secondary Library Books	$ 6.71	$ 7.99	$ 7.71

Note: "Other Boards" have been omitted.

and $5.79 in 1970. Similarly, between 1969 and 1970 per-pupil expenditures on library books in public schools had grown from $5.72 to $6.29, and on library books in separate schools from $5.11 to $5.87. As the accompanying table shows, the average per-pupil expenditures on textbooks in 1968, 1969, and 1970 followed similar patterns.

Although these results were surprising in the light of the evidence we had heard, it seemed possible that the figures furnished in answer to the questionnaires were unwittingly optimistic for the two years of consolidated board operation. We therefore arranged for an extensive audit of the replies received to be made by the firm of chartered accountants who were acting as our consultants (Clarkson, Gordon & Co.). The following comments are excerpted from their report:

Our tests indicated that the per pupil textbook expenditures reported by the boards are understated as: (a) some of the questionnaires only included the costs of textbooks listed in "Circular 14" as the total of book expenditures, and (b) in practically all cases the cost of textbooks included in departmental expenses were omitted.

The consultants' report went on to explain that it had been practicable only to audit returns made for the year 1970, and to list the boards at which audits were made. The report continued:

Our audit tests consisted of: (a) agreeing the textbook expenditure figure as shown on the questionnaire to the textbook expense accounts, (b) scrutinizing these accounts for charges of a non-textbook nature, (c) examining some of the invoices supporting the charges in the textbook expense accounts, and (d) checking the calculation of the per pupil expenditure figures.

The comparative analysis could have been carried farther, but the Commission concluded that it had gone far enough to determine that overall policies respecting the value of educational books purchased per pupil were probably not going to be substantially different under the consolidated board system than they had been in the past. Nor did it appear that textbooks as such, certainly not classroom books as such, had suffered wholesale cutbacks in favour of other kinds of educational media, although there was much evidence that expenditures on the latter had climbed greatly. (Comparative tabulations of expenditures on non-book media proved impossible to make on a meaningful basis because of the variety of accounting heads under which the latter are reported; these varied from board to board and no reliable basis of comparison of figures before and after consolidation could be established. But such comparisons did not seem to be of crucial importance.)

However, the publishers' plight was a real one as was evident by their soaring inventory-to-sales ratios, reduced or vanished net incomes, shortage of working capital, and arrested sales development. Perhaps what had come to concern us most was the clear reluctance (of the Canadian-owned houses particularly) to continue to initiate new Canadian educational publications in the face of the market situation and their own reduced resources. One or two foreign-owned Canadian houses seemed still to be expanding their Canadian catalogues, but others in this group were as loud as any of the indigenous publishers in expressing alarm over immediate prospects in the Ontario educational market. A number of very small Canadian-owned firms, which had yet to enter seriously into Canadian educational publishing, seemed farther away from realizing the ambition than ever before.

In the end we reached the conclusions we did not so much through tabulating replies to questionnaires and detailed analysis of figures showing comparative purchases in relation to enrolment, nor through other statistical studies of this kind (although they absorbed a substantial part of our research effort), as through personal interviews with educational officials, studies of publishers' certified operating statements and lengthy discussions based on such information, and through review of the large number of truly informative briefs included in the 185 briefs which we received. Most of all, the information gathered and the leads provided through the public hearings which were held on the majority of these briefs were invaluable to us in our further researches, and greatly assisted in planning the many interviews and group discussions which were held apart from the public hearings themselves. (The evidence taken at the public hearings alone, *apart* from the briefs, occupies more than 4400 pages.)

Before outlining the conclusions we came to finally regarding the changes we think should be made in financing educational book purchasing and the reasons for our recommendations, it would be useful to look more closely at Circular 14 itself. What is its status in theory and practice, and what are the conditions and procedures for listing books on it? A particularly relevant question is: What would the condition of Canadian educational publishing be today if there had never been a Circular 14 supported by a Canadian preference policy?

CIRCULAR 14

Throughout the past century and a quarter in Ontario, the shape and condition of the educational publishing industry has been determined by the textbook policy of the Department of Education, now the Ministry of Education. The history of the authorization and prescription of textbooks in this province is reviewed by Viola E. Parvin Day in her background paper prepared for the Commission and now published. This history had previously been traced up to the year 1950 in greater detail by the same author in her book-length work *Authorization of Textbooks for the Schools of Ontario 1846-1950*.

These and other studies corroborate the conclusion that Circular 14 and its related regulations have had a profound bearing on the development of educational publishing in this country. This influence became particularly strong after a system of textbook stimulation grants was introduced in 1951. Under this system, Circular 14 became virtually a list of free books available to boards of education by virtue of direct provincial subsidy.

The advent of the new policy of direct provincial subsidy of textbooks gave Circular 14 a new dimension, and to some extent obliterated its earlier permissive purpose. Both textbooks and library books were affected, provision being made for reimbursement of school boards for expenditures on textbooks listed in Circular 14 up to $3 per pupil (or more according to grade, as already explained) and also for matching grants for the purchase of prescribed library books. (Public and separate school boards in urban municipalities of under 2500 population and in rural municipalities under 20,000 population were to receive grants equal to the amount actually expended in the same year for the purchase of prescribed books of reference up to $1 per pupil.)

As Circular 14 assumed its new role as a free textbook list, it was planned that the majority of books included on it should be written by Canadians, and published and manufactured in Canada. Compromises continued to be necessary, however. A certain number of textbooks, particularly in the high school grades, had for some while been Canadianized versions of foreign textbooks. Even in the primary grades, the American Dick and Jane Series could not be replaced until Canadian readers for these grades began to become available about 1950, as recounted in Chapter 1.

In 1950, the Royal Commission on Education (the Hope Commission) recommended a "multiple listing" approach for Circular 14. Under this policy, individual teachers would be free to choose from a number of books, possibly as many as ten, for each subject. However, in spite of this new approach it remained the practice for many years for schools and teachers to adopt a single basic textbook (from among the approved choices available) and to use this in classroom sets and to make little or no use of other books listed in the same option groups. This continued to be common practice well into the 1960s, and in some subjects the practice still persists.

We have already traced the way in which the changing philosophy of education during the past decade (especially the recent trend away from the use of classroom sets of single books) began to fragment the market for publishers. The situation was aggravated by the rise of non-book media, a logical development of the trend away from single basic textbooks, and was climaxed by the decision of the Department in 1968, also already reported, to eliminate stimulation textbook grants and to incorporate the legislative grants for such purchases in the grants for ordinary expenditure. It would thereafter be for boards of education to determine how much should be allocated to the purchase of books. Ministry of Education officials consider that these were key changes in policy from the standpoint of textbook publishers, and the Commission agrees whole heartedly.

Some of the other developments that compounded the problem of efficient inventory planning for educational publishers had to do with the geometrical expansion of the number of titles on Circular 14 in very recent years, tabulated earlier in this chapter. This compounded the fragmentation of ordering that resulted from the trend toward literal interpretation of multiple listings. It could of course be asked what would have happened to those educational publishers who had produced new Canadian materials if they had found it more difficult than they did to secure listings for their new products. At the same time, we endorse the Ministry's apparent policy to retain in the list tried and proved textbooks even when they have been on Circular 14 for a number of years, although updating of content and point of view at reasonable intervals will of course be desirable.

As we shall see, there were other problems as well for the educational publishers. Chief among these seems to have been a de facto erosion of the status of books on Circular 14, which is reviewed later. The establishment of the new county school boards had been accompanied by assumptions that there was also to be a decentralization of responsibility for curriculum. That there was to be a greater flexibility in regional administration of the curricula under provincial guidelines seems to have been a matter of general agreement and satisfaction. But some misunderstanding seems to have developed regarding the degree of autonomy to be exercised at the local level, and where this touched the purchase of textbooks other than those approved in Circular 14, whether in full classroom sets or not, the difficulties of planning were aggravated for publishers. When unapproved Canadian books were introduced, the careful central screening undertaken by the Department was circumvented. And when non-Canadian books were introduced, the incentive for further original Canadian textbook creativity was undermined.

How are books selected for inclusion on Circular 14, and what are the regulations regarding their use? The following excerpts are from the 1972 edition of Circular 14:

When a new book is published, the publisher submits copies to the Curriculum Branch for evaluation. The Department then sends a copy to each of several readers or critics for comments and criticisms. The books are examined in the light of certain established criteria, and reports are submitted to the Department. When the reports are received, they are reviewed in detail, and a recommendation is prepared. This process takes some time, but *it is necessary to ensure by thorough examination that only the best textbooks are put into the hands of students* [Italics added].

Textbooks are those books that boards are required to provide in numbers sufficient for the use of pupils . . .

In all subject areas for which books are listed in Circular 14, textbooks must be selected from those listed in Circular 14, *unless permission for another selection has been granted by the Minister* [Italics added].

In those subject areas and programs for which no textbooks are listed in Circular 14 (for example, English literature, littérature française, the "authors" in modern languages and classics, and special education), textbooks to be provided by the school board are to be selected by the principal in consultation with the teachers, and the selection approved by board resolution.

Where textbooks are to be selected locally under [the preceding provision], preference should be given to books by Canadian authors or editors, printed and bound in Canada . . .

Requests for permission to use textbooks not listed in Circular 14 or not covered under [the special provision just mentioned] must be submitted by the chief education officer for a school board to the Regional Director of Education for the attention of the provincial Director of Curriculum.

New or experimental courses not included in the rationale of existing Departmental guidelines require approval for purposes of credit towards an Ontario school graduation diploma. Permission is also required for the use of textbooks to be used in connection with new or experimental courses, exclusive of courses leading to the Secondary School Honour Graduation Diploma.

The chief education officer for a school board will send a request for approval to the Regional Director of Education, along with an outline of the nature of the studies to be undertaken, the level at which the course will be given, the textbooks and reference materials proposed for use, and the intended date of introduction of the course.

The Regional Director will enlist the assistance of the program consultants and central office curriculum personnel in examining the course. *At the same time, central office curriculum personnel will consider the proposed textbooks* [Italics added] . . .

In the case of new or experimental courses leading to the Secondary School Honour Graduation Diploma, in addition to the textbook and reference materials proposed for use, there will also be a statement that the board has approved the use of the textbook and reference materials.

The procedures envisaged in these directives have statutory authority. Among the extracts from the acts and regulations quoted in Circular 14 are the following:

The Schools Administration Act: 20(1) A teacher shall not use or permit to be used as a textbook in a prescribed subject in an elementary or secondary school any book that is not approved by the Minister or the regulations, and the Minister, upon the report of the inspector concerned, may withhold the whole or any part of the legislative grants in respect of any school in which an unapproved book is so used.

(2) Where a teacher uses as a textbook, or negligently or wilfully permits to be used as a textbook by the pupils of his school, in a prescribed subject, a book that is not approved by the Minister or the regulations, the Minister, on the report of the inspector of the school, may suspend the teacher and the board that operates the school may deduct from the teacher's salary a sum equal to so much of the legislative grants as has been withheld on account of the use of the book or any less sum at its discretion.

22(2) It is the duty of a principal, in addition to his duties as a teacher . . . to prevent the use by pupils of textbooks that are not approved under the regulations.

Regulation, Elementary and Secondary Schools – General: 7(1) Subject to the approval of the board, the principal shall select from the approved list of textbooks, the textbooks for the use of pupils in Grades 1 to 12, both inclusive.

(2) Where no textbook for a subject is included in the approved list, the principal shall select suitable textbooks where required and such textbooks that are being introduced for use in the school for the first time shall be subject to the approval of the board.

ANNUAL REVISION OF CIRCULARS 14 AND 15

The process whereby the Ontario Department of Education meets its evolving textbook needs from year to year does not seem to have been paralleled elsewhere in the country, at least not on an annual schedule. Its policy has been to incite the creation of new Canadian textbooks as part of an ongoing program, and there can be no doubt that it has been extraordinarily successful in this, although diminishing returns may have set in latterly as the range of curricular options as well as textbook choices has continued to expand more rapidly than has the school population.

What the Department (now the Ministry) has done has been first to announce to all concerned that a new course is being prepared in a particular area, and then to invite and encourage publishers to submit new Canadian books to support it or to develop new ones if necessary, all publishers being advised simultaneously. A common procedure elsewhere in North America is to build a course around an available book rather than a book around a course, although many exceptions to this pattern can be offered.

The Ministry in Ontario deals exclusively with the publisher rather than with the author whenever a new book is being developed under this procedure, and no final approval – not even a conditional approval – is ordinarily given until the work has actually been published. The public hearings indicated that this last point of policy is a particularly controversial one. The publishers generally took the position that their investments would be materially reduced if they could be advised whether or not their manuscripts were acceptable before the expense of publishing was incurred.

It is difficult to agree outright with the publishers' contention here, and we endeavoured to make our position clear in the hearings. If quality is to be maintained, competition must not be less serious than it is at present, and the commitments of all contending publishers must also continue to be earnest ones. And if the public has any stake in Canadian publishing, it is because it has a stake in Canadian authorship; no procedure which would allow authors to be exploited without a commitment from the publisher to publish would normally be desirable. Perhaps there are exceptional situations, e.g. the preparation of a multi-colour atlas or of an editorial project tied exclusively to a particular curriculum, where some kind of conditional acceptance might be essential in advance of final production. But even in these situations, and in certain respects especially in these situations, the quality of the total execution through to publication should be assured. With responsible publishers, quality standards can often be considered to be assured in advance, but not all publishers are responsible.

For the Ministry to commit itself to a new publication that is still in the production stage could create many problems that do not now exist. Public officials would have to make value judgments in advance regarding numerous technical publishing matters, which would inhibit the adoption of new textbooks rather than assist it. It is unthinkable that the Ministry should have to assume editorial and production responsibilities (even when the publisher might not wish it to do so) for the checking of facts, art work, graphs, tables, design details, and the like.

Not only might the Ministry have to take on a variety of production responsibilities on behalf of publishers (of some more than others, doubtless, but how to select?), but it could easily become as deeply involved in the outcome of the book as the author is himself. To say "yes" in advance of publication can be an awesome responsibility; to say "no" while the work is still malleable can lead to even greater complications. In the end, the Ministry might easily become enmeshed in editorial, production, and costing functions which belong to the publisher. We believe that the present procedures for official consultation demonstrate a commendable and probably an adequate degree of patience and cooperation on the part of a public administrative body.

The cooperative approach to publication whereby many new books have been included on Ontario's Circular 14 may occasionally have prejudiced the prospects for adoption of some books in other provinces. We have heard this observation even in provincial education departments. There is an understandable tendency for other administrative areas to assume that a book that has been tailored step by step for a new course in Ontario is unlikely to be more suitable for their own use than competing books in general use elsewhere, including the United States. But at least the Ontario procedure has permitted publishers to develop many Canadian books on the basis of full consultation without their ever having been subjected to the degree of censorship and control that might be invited if official approval were furnished earlier in the process than it is.

We do not think that any publishers were advocating that they should be expected to publish a new book only after it becomes a "sure thing," nor do we think that authors should be expected to prepare books in the absence of a thoroughly serious commitment to publish. It is one thing for an author to write a novel or other trade-book manuscript speculatively, hoping that he will be able to find a publisher. It is quite another for him to write it at the specific invitation of a publisher who wishes to have a particular kind of book for a particular educational market. In the latter case, we believe that the author deserves to know what his reward will be if he works closely with the publisher to produce what is wanted, but eventually sees his manuscript go unpublished because it did not secure adoption.

There may be extraordinary projects whose production costs would be too high to justify a Canadian publishing risk without some indication of likely curricular status before publication. But these should be the exceptions, limited to situations in which a new book is earnestly desired and the publishing risk is unusually high.

In such cases the author should be made fully aware of any publishing uncertainty that may exist, and the contingencies should be anticipated in his contract. Apart from occasional situations of this kind, the equitable compensation to the author and to the public would seem to be competent publication of any manuscript developed in accordance with understandings reached in advance. Otherwise there will be a tendency for some authors to be exploited by some publishers, including no doubt many would-be publishers not now in view. It is also to be remembered that there is more than one provincial market in the country, and many books that have been prepared for one course of studies in the past have achieved their first success with another. Finally, the flexibility of choice given to schools and teachers, among Canadian books at least, will increase in Ontario if the Commission's principal recommendations in this area are implemented.

In June, 1972, a meeting between representatives from almost all the educational publishers listed in Circular 14 and members of the Curriculum Development Branch of the Ministry of Education was convened under the latter's auspices. It was there explained that the basic purpose of the Curriculum Development Branch (replacing the former Curriculum Branch) was to be the development of ideas and policies necessary to education, and that the major activity of the Branch would be the production of curriculum guidelines for the development of courses. The summary of the meeting said in part:

A related function of the Curriculum Development Branch is that of identifying extant educational media and stimulating the development of new learning resources that support the Ontario school program. Special emphasis is placed on encouraging the development of a wide range of educational media that is Canadian in both authorship and manufacture . . . In addition to the recognition given in curriculum guidelines . . . the main vehicles for recognition are the annual publications *Circular 14: Textbooks* approved for use in Ontario schools and *Circular 15: Canadian Curriculum Materials*.

The last reference was to a new annotated list of Canadian books and other learning materials first issued in the spring of 1972, having been announced during the previous year. Circular 15 is essentially a consolidated catalogue of Canadian books and other media; at the least it should be a useful tool in book selection in view of the tendency to substitute wide ranges of books for the former classroom sets of one title. Some of the further information announced at the meeting mentioned assists in understanding the procedures followed in book selection for both Circulars 14 and 15:

The 1973 edition of Circular 14 is scheduled to appear in February 1973. All textbooks to be considered for this edition must be received by the Ministry by October 13, 1972. A publisher who wishes that a textbook be considered for Circular 14 listing should provide for evaluation by the Ministry nine bound copies of the textbook, together with nine sets of information sheets that indicate the applicability of the book to the Ontario school program and that give pertinent information concerning the development of the book that attests to its origin.

The announcement continued by outlining further details of submission procedures to be followed for Circular 14 as well as Circular 15:

When a Curriculum Committee is appointed to revise or develop a course outline, Mr. Best [Educational Officer in charge of Education Media Liaison] will inform all publishers about the establishment of the committee and give the name of the chairman of the committee.

If a publisher is interested in consulting the Ministry about the preparation of a textbook for the proposed curriculum guideline, the publisher should contact Mr. Best, who will arrange any discussions on that matter. A prospective author may be included in such discussions only if the publisher's representative is also present . . .

Textbook approval is a prerogative of the Minister. In any discussion with publishers, no commitments can be given in regard to textbook approval by Curriculum Development Branch staff members.

The practice whereby the textbooks listed in Circular 14 were the subject of an Ontario Regulation has been resumed in 1972 . . . Subsequent editions of Circular 14 will likewise be the subject of an Ontario Regulation . . .

All publishers will be invited to a general meeting convened by Mr. Best in June each year for an exchange of information.

There was considerable discussion with the publishers at the June 1972 meeting regarding the deadlines for submission of materials for consideration and the dates of publication of the two circulars, of Circular 14 in particular. One of the concerns of the publishers had to do with the delay they might face in securing a listing if they barely missed the deadline for an annual revision of the circular. They were reminded at this meeting that "one or more supplements to Circular 14 will be published as needed from time to time." It would seem to the Commission that the publication of a regular quarterly supplement, which could be anticipated by all concerned, might serve a useful purpose.

A CHANGING KIND OF EDUCATION

Ministry of Education officials told us that we are moving from rigidity in school administration, characterized as late as the 1940s by the single basic classroom textbook, to divergence of opinion today where there is a rebellion against anything that is inflexible and not designed to accommodate individual differences. Does this change mark a turning-point or simply a further evolutionary stage in education? Certainly, educators are finding it necessary to develop a completely new philosophy with regard to textbook selection.

The classroom is no longer the prime conveyor of information to children. Whether we welcome it or not, in this function television has long since outstripped the school. Today the teacher must help the pupil sort and classify the **vast amount** of information that is available, information which may be said at one time to have been thrust upon him, and it must show him how to set about establishing his own priorities. But it remains the responsibility of the provincial authority to endow the curricula with needed flexibility while at the same time it establishes the parameters within which this flexibility is to be exercised.

Any consideration of Circular 14 and its implications for Canadian schoolbook publishing demands some appreciation of the changes that are taking place in educational philosophy generally. The Commission decided that it was its responsibility to study what education is trying to do, although hardly to make value judgments regarding the science of curriculum planning; it was not competent to do this. The Commission recognizes that the prime concern of educators is education. Nothing else should matter, not the health nor even the survival of the book publishing industry, *except in so far as one cannot exist without the other*. But the Commission also believes that education should inculcate knowledge of one's own country and culture. It should succeed in encouraging creative talent where it exists, and in developing a point of view which, if not distinctly national, is at least unencumbered by foreign nationalism. To the extent that books – be they texts, reference books, or just plain books – play a part in this complex process, Canada's educators and publishers can logically be expected to be allies in a common cause, not indifferent observers of each other's problems. This partnership has well served the best interests of Canadians in the past and it is to be hoped that it will adjust to the changing approaches to education now taking place.

CANADIAN PREFERENCE IN CIRCULAR 14

A special feature of Circular 14 has been its intended bias in favour of Canadian books, which has meant books that are written and produced in this country. Canadian preference has characterized Ontario textbook prescription policy for many years, although as explained in Chapter 1 the acceptance of "Canadianized" editions from abroad (which were re-edited and manufactured here) became common before the last war. Following the development of new Canadian reading materials for the primary grades in the early 1950s at the suggestion of the Department of Education (and published by an American subsidiary, as described earlier), a definite preference for Canadian books became the stated policy of those responsible for the periodic revision of Circular 14.

So long as the textbook used in full classroom sets remained in fashion in fact, even if not in theory, and so long as curricular needs remained sufficiently simple and uniform throughout the province to encourage this textbook practice to continue, Canadian preference presented relatively few problems at the classroom level. It was criticized occasionally, but usually by publishers who were anxious to find a way into the market for textbooks published by their parent company

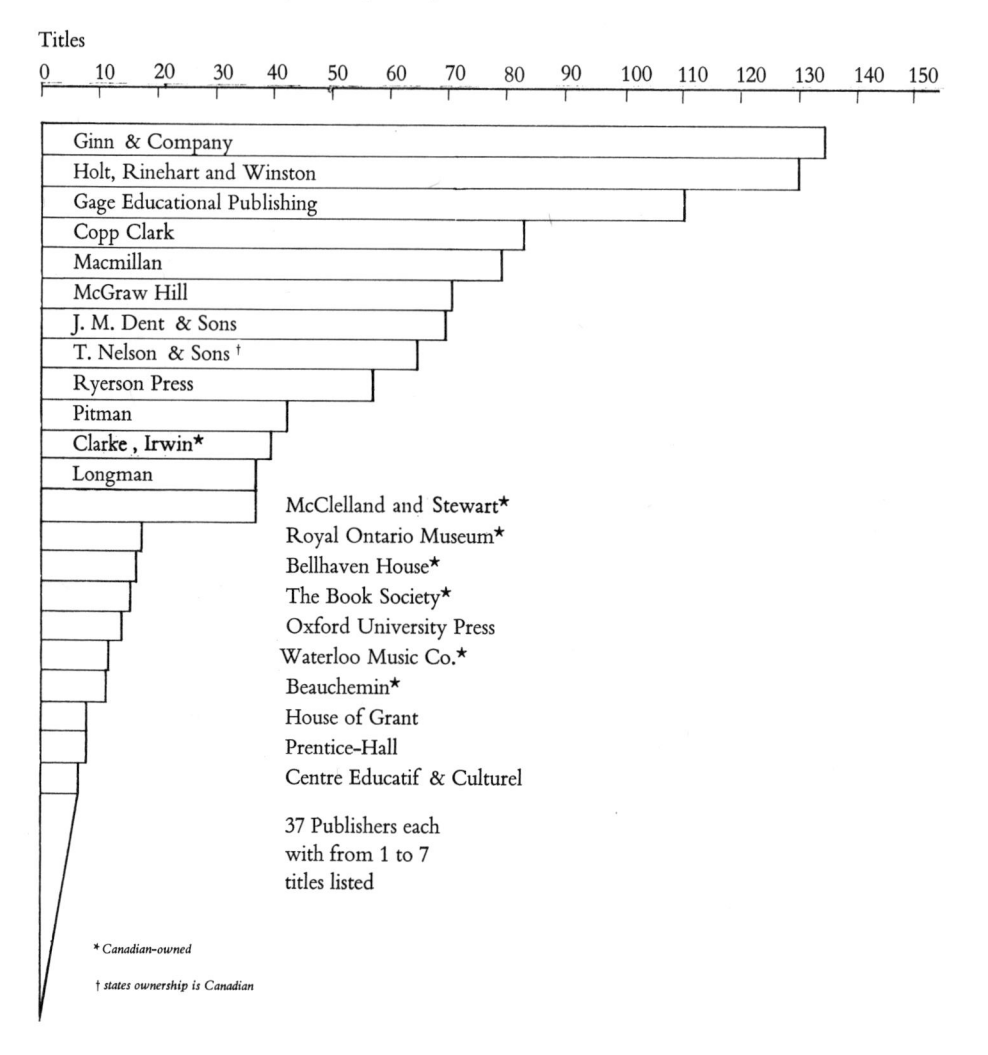

NUMBER OF TITLES PER PUBLISHER IN CIRCULAR 14 (1971)
based on Schedules A, B, C, (excluding D & E)

Publisher	Approx. Titles
Ginn & Company	~140
Holt, Rinehart and Winston	~130
Gage Educational Publishing	~115
Copp Clark	~90
Macmillan	~80
McGraw Hill	~75
J. M. Dent & Sons	~60
T. Nelson & Sons †	~55
Ryerson Press	~50
Pitman	~40
Clarke, Irwin*	~35
Longman	~30
McClelland and Stewart*	
Royal Ontario Museum*	
Bellhaven House*	
The Book Society*	
Oxford University Press	
Waterloo Music Co.*	
Beauchemin*	
House of Grant	
Prentice-Hall	
Centre Educatif & Culturel	

37 Publishers each with from 1 to 7 titles listed

* Canadian-owned
† states ownership is Canadian

abroad (or by their foreign principal in the case of Canadian publisher-agents). There is no question but that with the mounting trend toward the use of multiple classroom books in the place of class sets, with the increasingly optional character of the courses of study, and with the integration of the textbook stimulation grants with the general educational grants, pressure for relaxation of the Canadian preference policy began to increase. At the present time, however, there is no indication that the Ministry of Education has lost faith in the ability of Canadian authors and of Canadian book manufacturers, working for publishers in this country, to satisfy the textbook needs of our evolving curricula. At least, the percentage of Canadian books on Circular 14 remains high, and there has been no change in the announced

CIRCULAR 14 (1972) — NON-CANADIAN CONTENT

Schedule	I Foreign Author and Foreign Manufacture	II Canadian Author and Foreign Manufacture	III Canadian Author, Foreign Printing and Canadian Binding	IV Foreign Author and Canadian Manufacture
A—510 Books	4 (.79% Schedule A Books)	6 (1.2% Schedule A Books)	1 (.2% Schedule A Books)	
B—585 Books	35 (5.9% Schedule B Books)	4 (.7% Schedule B Books)		3 (.5% Schedule B Books)
C—355 Books	49 (13.8% Schedule C Books)			2 (.6% Schedule C Books)
D—201 Books	46 (22.9% Schedule D Books)			7 (3.5% Schedule D Books)
E—307 Books	15 (4.9% Schedule E Books)	9 (2.9% Schedule E Books)		
Total—1958	149 (7.6%)	19 (.8%)	1 (.05%)	12 (.6%)

policy of the officials to consider selections for it with respect to Canadian authorship and manufacture.

The accompanying chart shows in the five schedules in Circular 14 for 1972 (Schedules A to E inclusive) a total of 1958 titles. Of these, 149 were written by foreign authors and manufactured abroad, 19 were of Canadian authorship but foreign manufacure, 1 was by a Canadian author with manufacture partially in Canada and partially abroad, and 12 were written by foreign authors but manufactured in this country. Thus 181 books, amounting to 9.2 per cent of the total number of books listed, might be termed non-Canadian in that they were not wholly written, published, and manufactured in Canada.

Publishers who are interested in expanding this country's elhi market for foreign textbooks (in Canadianized editions if need be), and who have a commercial responsibility to do so, usually acknowledge that certain subject areas may have to be reserved for Canadian-written texts, but that others are international in nature and should therefore be freely open to foreign textbooks. Canadian history and geography, for example, are generally admitted to be appropriate areas for domestic creative authorship, as well as other subjects in the Canadian social sciences. One Canadian manager for an American publisher in this country said to us:

In some subject areas, not specifically Canadian (e.g. math and science) the onus is . . . on the educators whether or not to utilize materials developed in other countries, at great time and expense, and often funded by foundation grants of millions of dollars, or to define a specific curriculum to meet special needs, for which original material must be published. In some subject areas, however, this option is not possible because of very small enrollments in Canada. To automatically rule out anything from outside Canada would result in an intellectual ghetto in this country. However, the responsibility . . . lies with the educators to make the best decision on behalf of the education of Canadian children.

On the other hand we were told by some of those in the best position to make comparisons, including senior Ministry officials, that "once Canadian authors are encouraged to write books they tend to do well, and if not as well as others at first, at least as well or better in due course." We have noted, and we have received much authoritative confirmation, that Canadians have been successful in writing excellent textbooks, expecially in primary reading and mathematics. We were told that the first publishing attempts in some of these new fields were not uniformly as successful as competing textbooks, which is understandable, but subsequent Canadian books from competing publishers overcame the deficiencies. It early became clear to us that the amounts of money available abroad, in the United States for example, to redesign courses as well as textbooks far exceeds the funds available in this country. This seems to remain so notwithstanding the rapid expansion of research programs here recently, e.g. under the auspices of the Ontario Institute for Studies in Education. We shall comment briefly on the latter's research programs later.

CANADIAN PREFERENCE AND CANADIAN CULTURE

It became clear early in our work that the areas of alleged threat to Canada's cultural security were numerous and by no means confined to book publishing. But our terms of reference were clear and we decided that we should generally resist the temptation to pursue many well-intentioned but possibly irrelevant lines of inquiry proposed to us in briefs and correspondence. One of these concerned the ratio of foreign-educated to Canadian-educated staff members in this country's university faculties. Although we decided that books used at the college level were only an aspect of this population question, we did find ourselves in many discussions regarding the relatively low proportion of prescribed university titles that are published in Canada. We have already commented (in Chapters 2 and 4) on the causes of this apparent bias, and no recapitulation is needed here. Nor do we wish to be unduly distracted by the question of national origin of faculty members.

Suffice it to say that we found the question of foreign influence in university curriculum planning–especially in the humanities and social sciences–a lively topic wherever we travelled. The controversy described in Mathews and Steele, *The Struggle for Canadian Universities*, had not subsided. Critics of the existing situation claimed that the threat to our cultural identity was implicit in the faculty population statistics; the Canadian Association of University Teachers replied that freedom from interference and criteria of excellence were what should count. In 1971

Alberta appointed a special committee to inquire into non-Canadian influence in post-secondary education in that province under the chairmanship of Arnold F. Moir, Q.C. Our Commission had the privilege of meeting in Edmonton with this committee, which submitted its final report in the summer of 1972.

The Moir Committee's conclusions generally confirm our own thinking regarding the reasons for a non-Canadian emphasis in the imprints that appear on books prescribed for reading in universities in this country, even though that committee was more concerned with composition of faculties than book lists. It confirmed that the proportion of non-Canadian instructors in the humanities and social sciences was high, and offered compelling reasons why this temporary situation had developed. It pointed out that persons who take "extreme views either way" on the question of foreign representation in the university teaching community "add much to creating a problem and nothing to its solution." The report agreed that competence should be the principal consideration in staff recruitment, but that in fields in which there is a high Canadian course content, Canadians should be given preference. The findings of the committee were that earlier allegations that universities have ignored Canadian course content are "absolutely false." It recommended, among other measures related to staffing policy, a study of the need and economic feasibility of a new university press in Western Canada because of an apparent shortage of Canadian materials in some fields.

Our Commission believes that the need for Canadian textbooks (by which term we mean classroom books generally) that are written from a Canadian point of view becomes progressively more important as one moves downward through the secondary and elementary grade levels. College textbooks in sociology, for example, which discuss minority problems exclusively in terms of black and white and Chicano populations or which illustrate economic studies exclusively with American statistics can be an inconvenience to Canadian university students. To the extent that they are irrelevant to the Canadian experience their value may be questioned, but we find it difficult to see how they are likely to contaminate mature students. And as we noted earlier, many if not most college textbooks by Canadian authors are published in the United States by American firms. Until Canadian publishers enter the international publishing markets more aggressively than they have until now, this situation is unlikely to change. And under no circumstances would we recommend legislation or regulations that would require it to change; to do so would simply be a kind of reverse censorship.

The situation with regard to books published for college use is one thing. But pupils in the elhi grades have no experience to help them decide what is relevant and what is not, what is included and what has been left out that is important to Canadians. The textbook experiences of these younger readers are trail-blazing experiences. It is our view, therefore, that in so far as may be practicable, the trail-blazing for pupils below the university level should continue to be done by Canadian textbooks written by Canadian authors. There may be exceptional situations, but these should be proclaimed and treated as exceptions, and both teachers and pupils should be made aware of them when they arise.

It is fatuous to read into this statement of Canadian preference any restriction on reading foreign authors in English literature courses, to mention one oft-cited objection to the position we support. Nor would we discourage foreign studies of any kind in the curriculum; absolutely no such limitations are intended. But we do believe that elementary and secondary textbooks in, say, British or American history, will be better suited to Canadian curricular needs if they are written by Canadians with Canadian readers in mind. We would say equally that where Canadian studies are pursued at the elhi levels in the United States, quite probably specially devised textbooks written by American authors are indicated, although to make such a recommendation is far beyond this Commission's function. Yet in both cases, quality and suitability of content as well as presentation must be uncompromised if the pupils affected are not to be short-changed. Suggestions and recommendations on how Canadian textbook writing might be improved in quality as well as quantity in the future were made elsewhere in this report.

We would not confine Canadian preference to history books, either. There are good reasons why a Canadian society can defend a preference for Canadian teaching materials even "in some subject areas . . . not specifically Canadian," e.g. in science and mathematics, subjects which are often contrasted with the social sciences in this context. The thrilling epic of man's recent achievements in space, for example, should be recounted objectively and attributed honestly–which in this case means attributed in the main to American national commitment and enterprise, with due regard for Soviet initiative as well. But these achievements should be evaluated in a Canadian context, or we shall end up by supporting a public education system which short-changes its own citizens in training.

Not only should important Canadian contributions in science, say, be told about in our textbooks, and told about in uncoloured perspective, but consideration could also be given to why satellite communications have special significance for our country, domestically as well as internationally. New methods of meteorological forecasting that employ computer technology should use Canadian examples wherever these are appropriate, which should not be interpreted as meaning only Canadian examples. Certainly the defence implications of long-range ballistics weaponry should give clear priority to Canada's own national security–assuming that this topic is to be discussed at all, which is itself a Canadian policy question.

The study of ecology is concerned with problems and priorities which have at long last been recognized as international. But if this subject is to achieve its fullest meaning for Canadian students, it must be endowed with all the Canadian relevance possible. The kinds of precautions needed to protect the environment against, say, oil spills in the Gulf of Texas or off the coast of California are important and should be set forth. But similar problems in the Canadian arctic or off the Pacific and Atlantic coasts of our country deserve equal or greater attention, surely. Pollution in all its forms is a continent-wide and world-wide concern, but it is pollution in Canada which our own textbooks should use as a base for discussion.

Throughout the elhi grades especially, Canadian pupils will find the greatest relevance in examples that they can recognize from past experience or anticipate encountering in their future occupations. These will always be more meaningful than illustrations drawn from another country and another culture. Thus there is a choice to be made between a foreign and a domestic orientation in books chosen for normal classroom use. It is hardly necessary, it seems to us, to develop further the ways in which one point of view or the other is constantly reflected in reading materials even in such wide-ranging fields as biology, agriculture, physics, and chemistry as they find their practical applications in industry, transportation, communication, public health, safety, business practice, law, and occupational guidance.

For all these reasons the Commission rejects the view that this country's special responsibility for its textbooks is limited to such regional subjects as history and geography. We commend in principle the policy followed for many years by the Ontario Department of Education in restricting Circular 14 listings, in so far as possible, to Canadian-authored and Canadian-produced works. Moreover, we believe that the proponents of discontinuation of that policy (whoever they may be) have a progressively weaker case as Canadian authors and Canadian manufacturers continue to improve and to multiply the supply of original Canadian books. The latter process must be persuaded to go forward, and it must also be encouraged to improve its own standards.

The importance of this Canadian preference policy, which has so long been a feature of Ontario's Circular 14, is best illustrated by what has actually been accomplished over the years by Canadian authors and Canadian publishing, the latter by no means meaning only Canadian-owned publishers. We need but ask ourselves, what Canadian books would have been available if no Canadian preference policy had been pursued? How many Canadian books would have gone unwritten? How much sooner would the present crisis regarding Canadian-owned publishers have arisen? Without this policy, no doubt many good books imported from abroad, or reprinted from books first published abroad, would be available. But the Canadian perspectives of a whole generation of pupils reared on them would have had to be developed through some other media than the books of the classroom. It is difficult to guess what these alternatives might have been.

Of course the arguments against continuation of Canadian preference in Ontario classroom book selection must not be brushed aside lightly. We are reminded (most often by those who are special pleaders) that Canadian authors and publishers do not have access to the major research programs undertaken abroad, "often funded by foundation or government grants worth millions of dollars." But scholarship is international. How is it that the results of such research programs are withheld from Canadian educational authors while they remain accessible to foreign writers? We believe that this disability tends to be exaggerated in the telling. Nevertheless it would be well to stimulate international communication at the level of research. We say this even though we have seen little evidence that the programs of such bodies as the Ontario Institute for Studies in Education suffer from provincialism either in staffing or in outlook.

It is natural that much of the research reflected in our teaching materials should continue to be done abroad, in various countries, but we think that the selection and interpretation of such findings and their application to Canadian needs can best be done (for our purposes) by Canadian authors. But where there is insufficient Canadian-oriented research in progress to satisfy the need for specifically Canadian information, the solution is surely not to look abroad for writers; rather, we should support additional research in the areas of greatest concern.

We have been told by some of those who submitted briefs that existing Canadian educational research programs have limited relevance for publishing. On the other hand, too restrictive a direction of research activities can be dangerous, especially should they ever come to be measured by the popularity and usefulness of the findings rather than by the quality and objectivity of the research itself. But it does seem that the primary areas of concern to Canadian educationists, including Canadian publishers, could often be better defined and, where necessary, funded according to whatever broad order of priorities may be established.

A memorandum from the Ministry's Director of Curriculum Development in the summer of 1972 indicated that research areas of special concern were now being marked out in very much the way suggested above. The Ministry was also indicating that there would be additional grants, over and above the annual research and development budget for the Ontario Institute for Studies in Education, earmarked for specific projects in areas in which the Ministry itself was anxious to see research undertaken. Topics proposed for study included such questions as "How has the computer contributed to education?" "Has it freed or rigidified the schedule?" "What are the contemporary attendance patterns?" "What kinds of offences are considered worthy of 'notice' by the school?" etc. We think that this kind of approach to research-planning can be useful, provided that it is not permitted to take over the whole research program, thereby adversely affecting the latter's spontaneity and quality. We also see here an excellent opportunity to encourage more research of the kind that textbook editors and others have said would lend useful momentum to Canadian educational publishing.

LIMITATIONS ON CANADIAN PREFERENCE

There is a practical limit to which this province should go in seeking to have all books on Circular 14 written and produced in this country. This is largely determined by costs, although occasionally a genuine unlikelihood that Canadian materials can be prepared at all must be taken into account as well.

For example, certain kinds of school atlases containing a large proportion of international maps may have to be procured from the few publishers in the world who specialize in the production of maps, wherever such publishers are based. As a rule it would be uneconomic to try to develop specialized publishing resources of this kind in Canada, even though it has been shown that an atlas of Canadian maps produced in this country can rival or surpass the best foreign cartography.

There probably must be a compromise, too, in the case of comprehensive reference dictionaries, although Canadian printing and binding may often be reasonably demanded. Should special Canadian editions of dictionaries be accepted? And what about so-called British spellings versus American spellings? In the case of dictionaries, a completely integrated revision is certainly preferable to a mere Canadian addendum. But while we must accept the fact that there are preferred Canadian styles in spelling (as well as pronunciation), and these are neither consistently British nor consistently American, the preferences themselves change from time to time and from place to place, even within our own country. The development of new basic dictionaries (or encyclop(a)edias for that matter) calls for financial and editorial resources which sometimes may be better applied to other Canadian publishing priorities. Thus Canadian initiatives in some special areas are not always feasible (although they should be welcomed), and the Ministry of Education will no doubt have to modify its Canadian preference rules accordingly, as it has done in recent years.

Let it be clear that we would never advocate the artificial incorporation of Canadian content where this would be irrelevant to the purpose of a book. What we do call for is the presentation of subject matter from a Canadian perspective whenever the alternative is a foreign perspective. As we have already stated, there are many fields other than the social sciences in which a Canadian point of view is both possible and desirable. Word and picture illustrations can be selected to assist this Canadian orientation without requiring that foreign illustrations be excluded when to do so would distort or limit the value of the material; yet captions can be written from a Canadian viewpoint, as can the text itself, and questions and topics for discussion can often be put forward in a way that makes the subject-matter more meaningful to young citizens of Canada.

We have tried to make out position on the question of Canadian preference in prescribed books adequately clear. Indeed, the policy we advocate seems to be close to the one now being followed by the Ministry of Education. **We have outlined** one kind of exception which we think should be admitted; there are others that should be mentioned as well. These have to do with the meaning that we think should be attached to "Canadian authorship."

The reasons that make it desirable that prescribed elhi classroom books should be written by Canadians make clear that we are concerned with writing by authors who have a personal Canadian commitment, not merely Canadian nationality in the technical sense. All persons who have adopted Canada as their home, and who have lived here for a reasonable time, should qualify as Canadian authors for this purpose, whether or not they have acquired legal Canadian citizenship. Thus we think that books written by persons who are bona fide residents of this country should qualify for consideration for adoption; in this context, country of domicile is as important as citizenship. It would be a disservice to many, including the pupils, if all works by Canadian residents were not eligible for consideration on their merits. Thus the foreign wife of a Canadian national who might have retained her original citizenship, or for that matter an educationist who has made his career in this country but has not changed his nationality, should be regarded as a Canadian author. This would not normally qualify a sessional appointee from abroad or a consultant imported for a special project. It might or might not include a foreign editorial consultant to a Canadian team of authors. There will obviously be marginal situations of many kinds, and the Ministry will have to decide what exceptions should be made. What is desirable is that, in so far as possible, prescribed books should be written by Canadian citizens, or should be developed in this country, and always presented from a truly Canadian perspective. We hope this description of the kind of guidelines we recommend will not be distorted.

Canadian manufacture, which is a further condition of prescription that we recommend, is justified by cultural as well as economic considerations. It is the cultural importance of this requirement that gives it its importance in the view of this Commission. It is already a part of Ministry policy, with reasonable exceptions that parallel those for authorship. We discuss in Chapter 6 why the well-being of the Canadian graphic arts industry should not be separated from that of other segments of the Canadian book industry, including authorship, publishing, bookselling, and the public library system.

SOME IMPLICATIONS OF CANADIAN PREFERENCE

What all this requires is that Canadian writers should be prepared and must be encouraged to enter every field of elhi classroom book writing for which they are qualified. Education and educational research facilities in this country enjoy international respect and there is no reason why they cannot contribute their full share of the creative talent that must be tapped if an adequate supply of Canadian classroom materials is to be ensured. As already observed in this report, textbook writing and writing for children seem to be authorship fields which are beginning to overlap; therefore not all authors of the kinds of books now coming into use in the schools need themselves be specialists in education. Nor are they.

It also means that if adequate publishing facilities are not available for all competent work written in Canada, the public has a responsibility to encourage the development of such outlets. This will involve more than the provision of financial assistance to Canadian-owned, Ontario-based book publishers, although we earlier made recommendations regarding ways in which this should happen under careful controls designed to ensure full accountability. It will also require incentives and encouragement of other kinds; there must be improvement, for example, of facilities for professional development in every aspect of book publishing, namely editorial, design, production, accounting, and the many aspects of marketing. It will be further assisted if the establishment of new Canadian book publishing enterprises under experienced management can be brought about. Some of the recommendations in the Commission's Third Interim Report were designed to encourage this.

If the ground rules are just, and also clear, Canadian branches of foreign-owned publishing firms will no doubt continue to make a valuable contribution to the output of books written and produced in Canada, and their experience and expertise will stimulate rather than lower the editorial and production standards of indigenous houses, especially those which have entered publishing recently. We reject the view widely expressed by some ultra-nationalists (regrettably including a few publishers, who are special pleaders), that foreign-owned firms should in some way be prohibited from publishing books by Canadian authors, and even be required to discontinue their Canadian publishing operations altogether. We have discussed elsewhere the futility and the undesirability of restricting the public's access to international literature, good or bad, and have pointed out that books which Canadians want will for the most part be the books which Canadians acquire, whether or not they must be imported. No publisher in Canada should be prohibited from making a contribution to Canadian publishing merely because he is foreign-owned, provided that he is making a bona fide investment in Canadian culture as such. In saying this we recognize the conflict of commercial motives that may exist, which we discussed in Chapter 1. We also recognize the outstanding Canadian publishing records of a few firms such as Macmillan (indeed, so do the most vigorous proponents of repression of all foreign subsidiaries). What we should remember is that when foreign enterprise invests in our economy, its net contribution sometimes amounts to little more than a measure of employment, and even this may be temporary. But when it invests in Canadian cultural activity – whether for profit or for some other reason – it can confer a permanent benefit on our society and leave us all richer.

It is when foreign-owned publishers substitute foreign cultural materials for what should be the products of Canadian creativity, or when they eliminate indigenous publishers by outright purchase, or when they seek to alter the cultural ground rules for Canadian publishing, that the public may have to step in to defend its own interests. We have indicated ways in which these limits have been broken, or at least threatened, and the government action we recommend has been designed at all points to encourage a genuine Canadian cultural commitment. Moreover, everyone has a duty not to delegate to foreign interests any part of the right to decide what the nature of that commitment should be. This Canadians must decide for themselves.

CANADIAN PREFERENCE OUTSIDE ONTARIO

The preference for books of Canadian authorship and Canadian manufacture underlying Ontario's Circular 14 makes that list by far the most important stimulus to Canadianism in educational book publishing in Canada. This is so notwithstanding the various problems related to the classroom status of the books it lists, its great expansion in recent years, and possible problems of administering it, all of which are discussed elsewhere in this report.

In almost all other provinces, with the possible exception of the Northwest Territories, the official policy respecting Canadian preference in book selection is less restrictive than in Ontario. Some provincial educational officials assured us that their own systems acknowledged no policy of Canadian preference at all, although it is only fair to add that we found little evidence anywhere in English-speaking Canada of real indifference to the importance of reflecting the Canadian scene in approved textbooks wherever practicable. However, Ontario's virtual proscription of foreign textbooks which have merely been "Canadianized" is certainly not the rule in the other provinces.

Particularly in Western Canada there seems to be no reluctance to use American textbooks in such subjects as mathematics and science if they meet curricular requirements in content and method. It was pointed out to us in Alberta, and the situation there is probably not exceptional, that it is possible (from the standpoint of the Department of Education) for any school board to use textbooks that have not been recommended by the province. Such freedom of choice must in many situations place the Canadian-written textbook at a considerable disadvantage, if only because of the unit-costing problems discussed in Chapter 4.

It is true that the English-language book publishing industry in Canada remains essentially an Ontario industry, even though a significant amount of high quality regional publishing and printing is now done in British Columbia and some publishing programs have also been founded elsewhere, including Alberta and Manitoba. Although very much a minority of the total book manufacturing industry in Quebec, a few well-known English-language imprints are also based in Montreal.

INTERPROVINCIAL COORDINATION OF CURRICULUM

A suggestion that is frequently made, and that was echoed in a number of the briefs received by the Commission, is that there should be closer coordination in curriculum planning and textbook selection among the several provinces, at least for English-speaking Canadians. There are many appealing arguments in favour of such a proposal and they are usually all put forward. For example, it is urged that such a policy would lead to better national understanding, facilitate movement of students as well as teachers from one province to another, and reduce the cost and so increase the number of Canadian textbooks. But the plan is simplistic, and impinges on the most sensitive of all areas of provincial automony – education. And whose leadership would be acknowledged? After all, Ontario textbooks can be as foreign as any American or British textbook to a province like Alberta, for example, as was diplomatically pointed out to the Commission during its visit there.

But the greatest weakness in the argument for standardization in Canada is that the trend within each province is toward more decentralization of the curriculum, not less. It takes a certain naiveté to suppose that at the interprovincial level a reverse trend can be set in motion and maintained. The whole subject of coordination in curriculum among the provinces has been expertly reviewed by Charles E. Phillips and Freeman K. Stewart in their background paper on this subject, which has already been published.

The Commission was told in several other provinces that more federal involvement in programs conducted by existing Canadian publishers could lead to a greater degree of interprovincial coordination and cooperation in curriculum matters. Alberta officials, for example, pointed out that more could be published on the native peoples of Canada, although this would be only the first of a number of areas that could be named. Some mechanism, supported by the federal and possibly the provincial governments as well on a basis yet to be worked out, with reasonable permanency of financing assured, might be the best approach, we were told. It was several times suggested that because the costs of research and development are so much of the problem for Canadian publishing companies, a federally sponsored Institute of Canadian Studies might offer a feasible basis for interprovincial cooperation in curriculum. But many problems concerning the way in which the results of such research could be translated into Canadian classroom publications by established book publishers would remain to be worked out, even if the numerous policy obstacles in the way of this proposal could be overcome.

Some federally financed publishing programs of the kind just described were found already under way in the Northwest Territories by the member of the Commission who met with the Director of Curriculum at Yellowknife. Twenty-five Dog Rib Readers were being introduced in 1971, the drawings and texts of which are produced by a low-cost method of reproduction, but nevertheless printed in colour, and produced in stapled bindings for less than forty cents a copy. Unfortunately, the economies of scale often make production by commercial publishers for a small market uneconomical. A physical education textbook based on Eskimo games has been prepared by an author in Inuvik, among other projects. But we were also told that to a regrettable degree most of the Canadian texts that are submitted by publishers for consideration are geared to the white middle-class urban child; perhaps here is further evidence to support the proposal for a federally or federally-provincially sponsored Institute of Canadian Studies.

PUBLISHING FOR FRANCO-ONTARIANS

It would be appropriate to sketch briefly the publishing programs that exist for the special benefit of Franco-Ontarians. This can be done quickly, for there are almost none. Of course recreational reading needs are supplied up to a point by Quebec publishers and by books imported from France, but the market is limited in Ontario and too widely diffused to result in any organized system of retail bookselling catering especially to Franco-Ontarian needs. The situation for educational books is even more unsatisfactory, because here at least it can be said that an extensive demand exists; it is also vocal.

The Association des enseignants franco-ontariens (AEFO) summarized the educational problem for Franco-Ontarians in a brief it submitted to the Commission in Ottawa. AEFO, which is one of five branches of the Ontario Teachers' Federation, represents more than 5000 French-speaking teachers in this province. The student body they serve included more than 90,000 elementary pupils in 1969 and more than 21,000 secondary pupils, and has grown appreciably since then. Between 1962 and 1969, AEFO itself made modest grants, ranging from $200 to $400, to four authors to encourage development by them of some four French-language textbooks for Ontario schools. During the same period, the same association expended $4000 on the preparation of teaching aids for the same purpose.

As AEFO pointed out in its brief, the principal problem in French-language educational publishing stems from a diffused and insufficient market, aggravated by the need to keep textbooks up to date, thereby making it difficult for a publisher to reach necessary minimum sales even over an extended period. The trend away from the basic textbook used in complete classroom sets to a selection of different books used in small quantities exacerbates this situation. This is the same trend that we have already discussed in relation to English-language schools; if it generates publishing problems in the latter market, it is obvious that it has a crippling effect on the development of new French-language books of Canadian, to say nothing of Ontario, origin. The multiplication of curriculum options has further fragmented the small market that existed in this province. The significance of foreign competition has been substantially increased by all these developments, because of the way in which they inhibit domestic publishing. Against this background, uncertainties regarding the acceptability of new textbooks for inclusion in Circular 14 has made their development increasingly difficult, AEFO told us.

It was also pointed out that since the legislation of 1968 which provided for French-language schools at both elementary and secondary levels is so recent, a considerable slack must be taken up if the new demand for suitable classroom materials is to be met even in part. "The principal sources of supply for French-language textbooks," the brief said, "are France and Quebec. In both cases, the cost is high and very often the textbooks are not adapted to Franco-Ontarian needs ... Very often, it is necessary to make use of French- as well as English-language texts; thus there are in use in a French-language school more textbooks than in an English-language school."

The Association des enseignants franco-ontariens also recommended, among other things, that the principle of Circular 14 be maintained, but that it be divided into two sections – one for French-language textbooks and one for English-language. (The present inclusion of some French-language titles appears to be inadequate.) It was further recommended that at the provincial level approval of French-language textbooks become the responsibility of French-language superintendents within the Ministry of Education. At the local level, when there is no French-language superintendent, the school principal (directeur d'école) should be authorized to submit to the French-language superintendents in the Ministry of Education the list of textbooks for which approval is desired.

In addition to the above proposals, AEFO made a number of recommendations regarding the need for financial aid to Canadian authors and publishing houses to make possible the preparation and publication of French-language textbooks suited to Franco-Ontarian needs, including paid leaves-of-absence where necessary, the special taxation of non-Canadian publishers, and support for low-priced editions. But its principal recommendation was that the Ministry of Education establish a commission of inquiry into the whole question of French-language textbooks which would make an inventory of available materials, establish priorities of need, determine long-term requirements, make specific recommendations regarding translation or preparation of materials, suggest better lines of communication among provincial departments of education regarding French-language textbook distribution, and propose means of financing the purchase of the needed French-language texts.

The special problems surrounding book publishing for Franco-Ontarian schools set forth by AEFO were reflected in other briefs received as well. The French Language Advisory Committees of the Ottawa and Carleton Boards of Education echoed most of the AEFO recommendations, but seemed to place more stress on looking to "international publishing firms for the distribution of French textbooks and educational films, inasmuch as these textbooks and films are adapted to the needs of the Ontario French-speaking population." It also asked that the correspondence course service of the (then) Department of Education "take into account the needs of the French-speaking population . . . and prepare French texts to guide the students." The Association canadienne-française de l'Ontario (ACFO) and the Conseil des Ecoles Separées Catholiques d'Ottawa also submitted briefs touching on the same problem.

It is necessary to agree that to the extent that English-language publishing encounters growing problems in the educational field in this province, these are greatly increased for publications appropriate for use in Franco-Ontarian schools. Some of the remedial measures we are proposing to assist the former should help French-language schools as well, but we are well aware that the needs of the two groups are disproportionate, and that special programs will be required if some degree of equalization of opportunity in reading materials available is to be achieved. This is an appropriate area of concern for the Ontario Book Publishing Board, and will also be dealt with further in our Recommendations.

COMPARATIVE COST OF TEXTBOOKS

Any review of educational book sales over the years raises the question of comparability of costs during the period. The Commission was interested in developing a cost index for textbook production in Ontario that would show the behaviour of these costs during at least the last decade. Development of valid statistics presented

AN IMPLICIT COST OF PRODUCTION INDEX "PUBLISHING ONLY" (S.I.C. 288) CANADA

	Cost of Materials and Supplies $'000	Value Added $'000	Gross Value of Production $'000	Gross Value of Production	Volume of Production	Cost of Production
				Index 1961 = 100		
1961	27,225	39,005	66,230	100.0	100.0	100.0
1962	27,429	36,889	64,318	97.1	96.8	100.3
1963	27,968	39,400	67,368	101.7	96.6	105.3
1964	31,112	44,486	75,598	114.1	101.2	112.8
1965	35,030	50,479	85,509	129.1	109.5	117.9
1966	41,886	57,029	98,915	149.4	115.4	129.4
1967	48,303	64,094	112,397	169.7	125.7	135.0
1968	54,252	72,203	126,455	190.9	136.9	139.5
1969	63,704	81,540	145,244	219.3	141.4	155.1
1970	64,233	86,803	151,036	228.0	N.A.	N.A.

SELECTED COST INDICATORS – CANADA

							Commercial Printing	Industry Selling Price Indices	
		"Publishing Only" (S.I.C. 288)							
	Wages and Salaries $'000	Employees Number	Labour Income Per Employee (Index 1961 = 100)	Labour Income Per Unit of Output	Average Weekly Wages and Salaries $		Average Weekly Wages and Salaries $	Book Paper (Index 1961 = 100)	Printing Inks
1961	17,184	4,364	100.0	100.0	81.14		83.99	100.0	100.0
1962	17,406	4,332	102.0	104.7	85.75		86.93	99.9	96.5
1963	18,159	4,192	110.0	109.4	86.92		90.24	100.2	96.5
1964	19,458	4,372	113.0	111.9	92.05		94.71	102.0	96.3
1965	21,204	4,397	122.4	112.7	97.21		99.12	104.0	96.3
1966	24,301	4,565	135.2	122.6	106.98		104.40	110.6	97.6
1967	27,193	4,894	141.1	125.9	112.46		110.77	117.8	99.8
1968	30,656	5,.71	150.5	130.3	114.26		117.57	117.8	103.3
1969	35,613	5,656	159.9	146.6	121.82		126.93	118.8	107.1
1970	37,974	5,628	171.3	N.A.	131.75		136.90	121.8	109.1
1971	N.A.	N.A.	N.A.	N.A.	139.45		148.33	125.4	110.1
Average Annual Percent Increase 1961 to date	9.2	2.9	6.2	4.9	5.5		5.8	2.3	1.0

Source: Statistics Canada, Catalogue Nos. 36-203, 72-201, 62-528, and 62-002.

many problems however; the best available figures from either branch of the industry, printing or publishing, or from Statistics Canada simply did not yield the necessary breakdowns, at least not on a comparable basis. It would have been possible to initiate a rather complex historical study of such costs, but in the end the Commission decided that its problems were more qualitative than quantitative, that the expense and time involved in developing retrospective statistics in this degree of detail would be unduly great, and that the more precise data that might be produced would not affect the principles underlying its report anyway. Nevertheless, further studies may be desirable in order to implement the Commission's principal recommendations regarding future financing of approved textbook purchases. If these are undertaken, they could be made a responsibility of the Ontario Book Publishing Board, which at the same time could gather other valuable historical statistics which would be useful to it and to the industry in the future.

We were not altogether without comparative cost figures, however. On the basis of currently published information from Statistics Canada, it was possible to create a cost of production index for the "publishing only" segment of the printing, publishing, and allied industries on an all-Canada basis. However, even this group includes enterprises which publish newspapers, periodicals, and certain other miscellaneous materials in addition to books.

The cost of production index for this industry grouping recorded an average annual increase of 5.7 per cent over the 1961-1969 period. It appeared to be theoretically possible to disaggregate the annual census of manufacturers data for the "publishing only" industry (Standard Industrial Classification 288) for those enterprises primarily engaged in book publishing in Ontario. The current dollar gross production data so produced, in combination with an estimate of the volume of production, would then produce an implicit cost of production index. However, the resulting cost index would refer to books in total and not specifically to educational books. For the reasons already given, the Commission decided against

VALUE OF SHIPMENTS – 1969
PRINTING, PUBLISHING, AND ALLIED INDUSTRIES

Activity	Publishing Only $'000	% of Total	Publishing and Printing $'000	% of Total
Newspapers and Periodicals	107,744	74	512,505	89
Books — textbooks	24,923	17	9,400	2
— other	12,689	9	6,251	1
— Total	37,612	26	15,651	3
Other*	(318)		44,498	8
Total Shipments	145,038	100	572,654	100

*Includes negative adjustment for value of sales taxes, excise duties, etc. which could not be deducted from individual commodity items described above.

WAGE RATES IN PRINTING TRADES — TORONTO

	Average weekly wages paid to hourly rated workers	Average wage rate per hour					
	Commercial Printing $	Compositor, Hand $	Linotype Operator $	Pressman, Offset $	Pressman, Cylinder $	Pressman, Platen $	Bindery Girl, Hand $
1961	84.92	2.77	2.80	3.02	2.65	2.48	1.34
1962	87.07	2.98	3.00	3.12	2.72	2.59	1.41
1963	91.37	3.08	3.10	3.26	2.88	2.73	1.49
1964	96.90	3.26	3.28	3.32	2.98	2.86	1.57
1965	100.61	3.38	3.39	3.46	3.15	2.99	1.63
1966	106.50	3.41	3.51	3.58	3.31	3.07	1.74
1967	111.56	3.55	3.64	3.86	3.52	3.26	1.82
1968	118.34	3.93	4.04	4.15	3.70	3.46	1.97
1969	129.00	4.16	4.27	4.54	4.17	3.81	2.20
1970	136.41	4.57	4.62	4.87	4.50	4.11	2.57
Average Annual Increase 1961 to date	5.4%	5.7%	5.7%	5.5%	5.4%	5.8%	7.5%

Sources: Statistics Canada, Catalogue No. 72-002 and Canada Department of Labour Catalogue No. L2-557.

refining this part of their investigation so far. However, available wage rate information confirmed that this part of production costs had increased at an average rate of 5 per cent to 6 per cent per year since 1961.

Additional comparative studies of average textbook prices were undertaken for us by the (then) Curriculum Branch of the Ontario Department of Education. The

COMPARISON OF COST OF TEXTBOOKS APPROVED FOR USE IN THE INTERMEDIATE DIVISION FOR MATHEMATICS AND SOCIAL STUDIES (GEOGRAPHY AND HISTORY) 1951, 1961 AND 1971

YEAR	MATHEMATICS		SOCIAL STUDIES	
	No. of listings	Average Price	No. of listings	Average Price
1951	9	$1.28	13	$1.62
1961	21	$2.22	45	$2.64
1971	47	$3.69	(1) 208	$2.57
			(2) 94	$3.76

Note: Two sets of figures appear for social studies in the 1971 tabulations; the first set represents those textbooks which do not provide textual material for an entire course.

TEXTBOOK PRICES COMPARED TO COMPOSITE INDEX   1951 – 1961 – 1971

Textbooks approved for use in the Intermediate Division for Mathematics
----

Textbooks approved for use in the Intermediate Division in Social Studies (Geography and History)
– – – – – – – –

Composite Consumer Price Index (1961 = 100)
_____

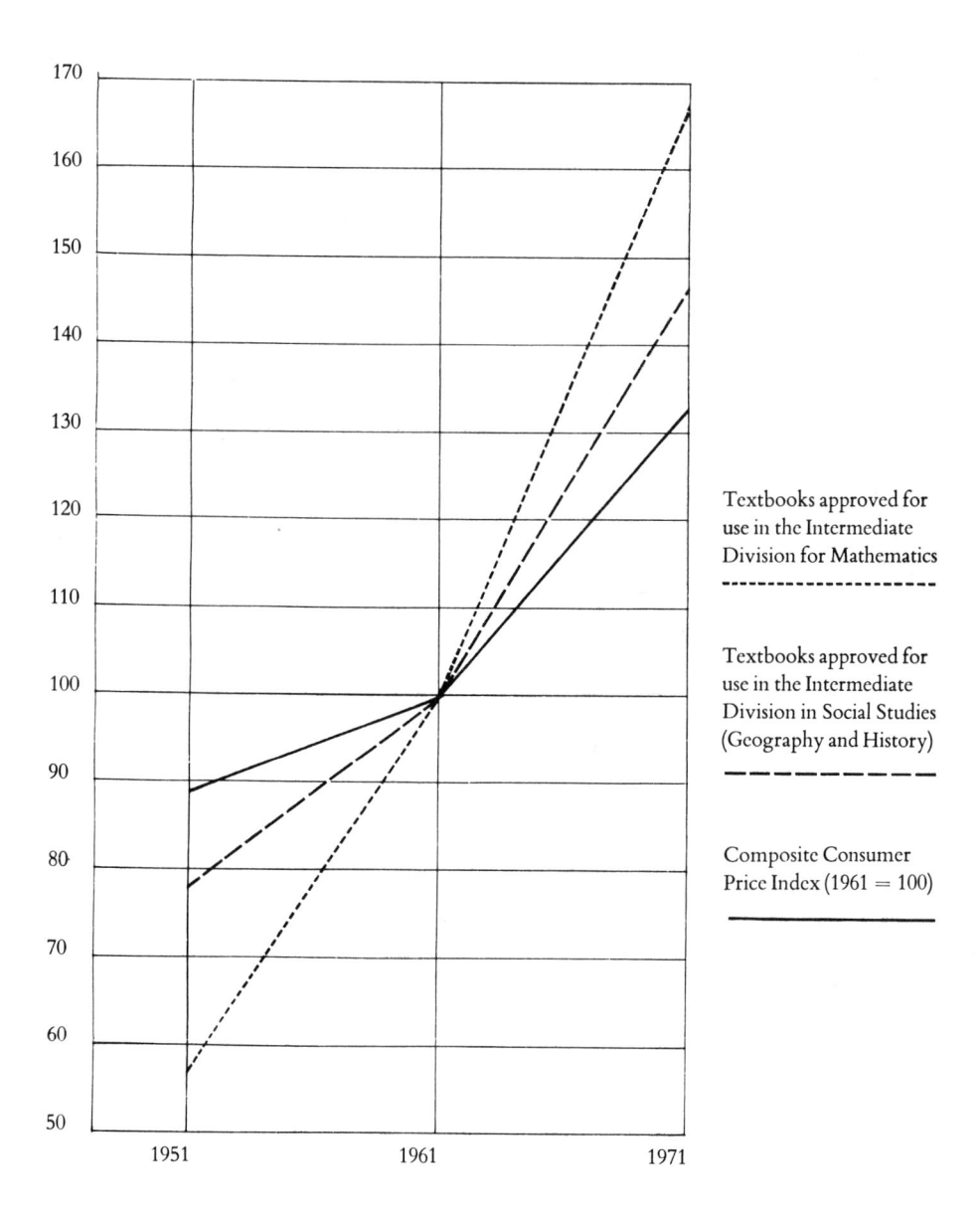

figures thus obtained related sensibly to price information also checked in back catalogues and past listings in official circulars. The accompanying table shows a comparison of average prices for textbooks in mathematics and social studies (geography and history) as they appeared in Circular 14 in the editions published for 1951, 1961, and 1971. The numbers of textbooks indicated represent those listed in Schedule B, Intermediate Division (Grades vii – x).

These price comparisons are not able to take into consideration the differences in production specifications for the books being reported upon. Although book design standards experienced further sophistication during this period, reflected in more ambitious and therefore somewhat more costly production specifications, multi-colour textbooks were already in general use in these subject areas before 1951. Thus price comparisons spread over a number of titles, as has been done here, are broadly valid. Increases shown reflect not only mounting total costs, but also increasing unit costs caused by shrinking markets for individual titles. This last factor began to exert itself on the price levels shown for 1971, and then only respecting new books first published at or shortly before that time.

It is interesting that the average price increases for both mathematics and social studies textbooks (including only those useful for a full course) show increases between 1961 and 1971 that are slightly lower than the corresponding percentage increases in manufacturing costs reported earlier. It would appear, subject to further statistical verification proposed earlier, that comparable costs and prices for comparable textbooks might be assumed to have increased approximately fifty per cent from 1961 to the present time. That is to say, costs and prices of Canadian books are now approximately fifty per cent higher than they were ten years after the inauguration of the textbook stimulation grants, which lasted from 1951 until the end of 1968.

COMPARISON OF CONSUMER PRICE INDEX IN SPECIFIC GROUPS
AND TEXTBOOK PRICES

	Composite Index	Food	Clothing	Transportation	Recreation & Reading	Math Textbooks	Social Studies Textbooks
1951*	88.0					57.66	68.94
1961	100.0	100.0	100.0	100.0	100.0	100.0	100.0
1965	107.4	109.6	107.9	104.8	105.6		
1969	125.5	127.1	124.5	120.0	126.8		
1971	133.4	131.4	128.7	129.9	135.6	166.22	146.30

*Figures not available for specific groups in 1951 as groupings changed in 1961, rendering classifications not comparable.
Source: Prices Division, Statistics Canada and Ministry of Education, Ontario.

BOOK EXPENDITURE LEVELS

We indicated earlier in this chapter that costs and prices of Canadian books are now about fifty per cent higher than they were ten years after the inauguration of textbook stimulation grants, a program which began in 1951 and lasted until 1968. Our efforts to arrive at a firm price index that would reflect the price inflation that has occurred were sufficiently thorough to satisfy us that a completely objective comparison of increasing costs for equivalent values is impracticable. Too many variables – some of them of a wholly subjective kind – are involved. But the resegregation of book grants from the general educational grants (which we earnestly recommend) would necessitate establishing some basis of comparison between current book budgets and those of a decade or so ago, i.e. about midway during the book stimulation grants program. We are satisfied that the fifty per cent factor that we have recommended is the most conservative differential that should be provided for; if it were to be less, there would be a significant discouragement to the use of books, even after allowance is made for the changing role of books in the classroom which we have discussed at some length.

We can find, of course, some bench-marks from book purchasing levels in other provinces and abroad, and we have taken these into careful account. The range of expenditures elsewhere is indeed wide, and suggests that the figures obtained from central sources are not wholly comparable, and may not adequately reflect the value of books purchased for classroom and library use in other ways, and not accounted for centrally. Indeed we found clear evidence of this in some cases, for which reason the comparative figures are most significant as floors of expenditure elsewhere, rather than as budgetary ceilings. Even so, when considered together they substantiate our own conclusion that a significant increase in the *median* per pupil expenditure in this province for classroom books of all kinds is desirable not only in the interests of the Canadian book publishing industry, but to ensure that reading opportunities and incentives for pupils in this province will compare favourably with those elsewhere in Canada and the United States.

The figures showing total combined annual library and textbook expenditures in elementary and secondary schools, respectively, in the provinces indicated were reported to us as follows:

Alberta	$9.00 (el.)	$16.50 (sec.)
Manitoba	5.52	8.73
Saskatchewan	9.45	15.01

The provinces of Prince Edward Island and New Brunswick show no separation between elementary and secondary schoolbook expenditures. But the consolidated figures for library and textbook expenditures for these provinces were:

Prince Edward Island	$15.20
New Brunswick	9.95 (established schools)
	14.45 (new schools)

Figures from the provinces not reported above were not in a form that was sufficiently comparable for tabulation. The figures shown above are for the 1971-72 school year.

Although reliable comparable figures covering both textbooks and library book expenditures were not available from the United States, data for textbook expenditures (only) is gathered annually by Stanley B. Hunt & Associates for the Association of American Publishers, Inc. Their figures for 1970 and 1971, covering textbook expenditures only, are shown in the accompanying table, reproduced here by permission.

TEXTBOOK EXPENDITURES IN THE UNITED STATES

	Expenditure per capita in elementary and high school grades	
State	1970	1971
Alabama	$ 5.67	$ 7.11
Alaska	8.30	9.34
Arizona	11.13	11.48
Arkansas	8.15	8.99
California	4.64	5.40
Colorado	8.42	9.22
Connecticut	9.67	9.73
Delaware	8.76	9.53
Florida	9.49	9.05
Georgia	8.67	9.43
Hawaii	8.64	9.13
Idaho	10.51	9.63
Illinois	10.97	11.34
Indiana	9.89	8.77
Iowa	9.64	9.90
Kansas	8.75	9.49
Kentucky	8.49	8.16
Louisiana	9.46	9.01
Maine	9.06	9.68
Maryland	7.49	7.50
Massachusetts	9.77	9.93
Michigan	8.18	8.04
Minnesota	9.17	9.61
Mississippi	12.39	11.94
Missouri	9.60	10.54

	Expenditure per capita in elementary and high school grades	
State	1970	1971
Montana	9.83	9.88
Nebraska	10.05	10.91
Nevada	9.19	10.90
New Hampshire	9.63	9.79
New Jersey	10.02	10.63
New Mexico	9.35	10.55
New York	9.38	9.23
North Carolina	8.12	11.96
North Dakota	11.20	11.62
Ohio	7.14	7.45
Oklahoma	8.01	8.99
Oregon	7.99	8.55
Pennsylvania	9.05	9.33
Rhode Island	9.45	9.26
South Carolina	10.60	13.33
South Dakota	10.59	9.56
Tennessee	7.91	7.62
Texas	10.83	10.76
Utah	8.63	8.47
Vermont	9.50	9.23
Virginia	8.85	9.66
Washington	7.99	8.55
West Virginia	10.43	7.93
Wisconsin	9.34	9.44
Wyoming	10.46	10.98
District of Columbia	11.70	14.62
Average per capita expenditure:	$ 9.21	$ 9.63

Source: *Survey by Stanley B. Hunt & Associates for The Association of American Publishers, Inc., May 1972.*

CHANGING SIGNIFICANCE OF CIRCULAR 14

Earlier in this chapter we said that the problem for educational publishers seems to have been not so much diminution in book buying following consolidation of the school boards in Ontario (although most of the publishers apparently still believe that a serious drop-off occurred) as a substantial decline in the significance attached to books because they were listed on Circular 14. As previously reported, we found our personal interviews with educationists and others, many of the briefs submitted, and our public hearings and further research suggested by them to be more illuminating than the statistics produced by questionnaires.

This was so even though the latter earned a high percentage of replies, which were spot-checked by our consultants in the way already described.

Our own follow-up interviews included personal visits to a number of directors of education and meetings with many other educational and library officials, local and provincial. We had personal interviews also with representative public librarians, as well as with library coordinators and consultants in public and separate school boards. Senior officials in the Department of Education were interviewed (including the Assistant Superintendent of Curriculum in charge of school libraries). Numerous additional interviews were arranged with representative book publishers. Both the specific requirements and the general purposes of Circular 14 were discussed, and out of these meetings emerged a reasonably clear picture of the diminishing status of Circular 14. Perhaps it is not surprising that in view of the wide-ranging changes that had taken place in school administration and in educational philosophy traced earlier in this report, a certain disparity should arise between the status of Circular 14 in theory and its status in practice. This disparity did not necessarily turn on the question of enforcement of the regulation under which it was published. School superintendents had been replaced by chief education officers, and although these are appointed by the Minister their salaries are now paid by the regional school boards. The boards in turn are subject to many pressures, and sometimes face practical problems when they endeavour to adhere strictly to the Circular 14 requirements or ask their schools to do so. And what came through most clearly is that the disappearance of the stimulation grants (notwithstanding their incorporation in the general education grants), which had formerly been earmarked chiefly for the acquisition of books listed on Circular 14, invited a completely new approach to the budgeting of schoolbook purchases.

A senior official in a city board of education discussed with us some of the implications of the termination of textbook stimulation grants. While he doubted that book purchasing had not at first been affected adversely, he concurred that it provided an obvious area for budgetary economies. "When it is necessary to economize, it is better to cut down on things than on people," he told us. "Books and equipment can be dropped more easily than teachers." We received several submissions that mentioned situations in which this choice was apparently actually being made, and in this way, in the spring of 1972.

We asked the head of one large publishing firm (not Canadian-owned) who met with us privately, just how much importance he attached to securing listings for his books on Circular 14. We were mildly surprised when he said, after reflecting: "I think I would rather have a new book listed than not listed, but that is about as far as I would now go."

A teacher in one large high school told us that he could select any textbook for classroom use "if it is on Circular 14 or if I secure approval from the board."

He assumed that no kind of provincial approval had to be secured by the latter body. He said that if a desired book were not approved in one of these two ways, he could still obtain it (even in a classroom set) by including it in his "instructional supplies" budget, normally used for consumable stationery, but he did not like to do this except when necessary because he wished to keep this budgetary option open. Or he might simply categorize it as a library reference book – perhaps the most common practice of all where only small sets or single copies were being requisitioned.

Some boards of education seemed to resent Circular 14, or at least the regulations pertaining to it. But most accepted it as a kind of bench-mark for ordering, while they remained ready to circumvent it when they thought necessary. The director of one large city board of education, who says that he abides by the letter of Circular 14 against his better judgment, said: "Does our duty to the student not outweigh our duty to the Department of Education?" In this case, an application to the (then) Department of Education for permission to use a particular series of American books in an elementary school course had recently been refused.

As just suggested, the most popular way of circumventing Circular 14 seems to be to define unauthorized books as reference materials. Sample comments we heard include the following:

"Circular 14 restricts our teachers because there is so little choice. But people mostly close their eyes to it, so it does not really limit us. It all boils down to what is the difference between a textbook and a book. If a teacher wants to use a book of his choice for reference purposes, there is no problem."

"We present a list of textbooks to the Board of Education every year and they approve it, don't even look at it. If a teacher wants to go outside Circular 14 there is no problem, if for no other reason than that there are so many ways of going outside."

"Who pays attention to Circular 14? Who looks at it?"

"We think we can live within Circular 14; we don't feel stifled or restricted." [The author of this comment, who is a director of education, did not find Circular 14 restrictive because] "no policies are laid down concerning reference books. We sure have a lot of Addison-Wesley reference books around."

"We frankly ignore Circular 14 where French books are concerned; we simply buy thirty volumes and call them reference books."

One of the most complimentary comments about Circular 14 came from the director of a county board of education:

"We don't find it a restrictive requirement at all; we find it very helpful. Circular 14 and its revisions are most satisfactory to ninety-five per cent of our teachers in mathematics, science, economics [identified in the course of our interviews as problem areas]. I have not heard of any case of rejection of a Circular 14 book because of its inappropriateness; but we find increasingly teachers can't find a book which in total would cover all aspects of a course." [The last observation may indicate that this official was a traditionalist.]

A point which came up over and over again in our interviews was that educators are willing, perhaps even anxious, to use Canadian textbooks so long as this does not mean "short-changing the kids." In the words of one teacher, "We use Canadian books assuming they are comparable in value and content to what you can get elsewhere."

Some specific areas of inadequacy were identified in a special study on Canadian content conducted by the Scarborough Board of Education. Sample quotations from the report include the following:

"At upper intermediate and senior levels, specialized instructional reading materials of Canadian content and origin are extremely rare."

"Science suffers as much as any subject at most levels from a shortage of good Canadian textbooks."

"At elementary levels, good geography textbooks and audio-visual materials are inadequate. History textbooks are wholly Canadian but tend to be obsolete in suggested instruction procedures. New textbooks are needed in geography."

"One of the main reasons for including non-Canadian authors in a junior grade reader is the dearth of well-written Canadian prose for children in the nine- to twelve-year range."

One secondary school contacted by the Commission's research staff claimed to use no textbooks at all. Perhaps more typically, an investigation conducted under the auspices of the Ontario Institute for Studies in Education revealed that fifty-one per cent of 850 teachers observed in action "still rely on a textbook approach". The author of the report described this percentage as discouragingly high; to some publishers, it may seem dismally low.

Circular 14 is being circumvented by many teachers and by many boards, and is being honoured by most with varying degrees of reluctance. Regrettable though it may be from the publishers' point of view, it would be wrong to call for its enforcement only to subsidize the publishing industry at the expense of the educational needs of school children. In order to survive and to grow in value, Circular 14 must become an acknowledged guide to excellence and usefulness. If there are areas, and there appear to be some, where first-rate Canadian texts have not yet been published (textbooks for Ontario's French-language schools are a glaring example), Circular 14 should identify such gaps, and should certainly avoid including second-rate materials only because they are Canadian. (If this is an area where too few suitable books from all sources are available, the shortage should be overcome in some other way.)

With some possible exceptions of the kind just mentioned, it would be a mistake to try to make Circular 14 more universally popular by increasing the proportion of non-Canadian titles listed in it. Single copies of individual books written and published outside this country will continue to be available as true works of reference even though implementation of what we consider to be our most important recommendation will discourage the unnecessary proliferation of non-Canadian books in our schools.

It is our considered opinion that if our original educational book publishing is left in its present vulnerable position, we must anticipate a continuing diminution in the supply of new Canadian works regardless of the growing need for new and more varied books for use with the expanding number of optional courses of study. At the same time we must expect growing pressure, and an increasing willingness to accede to such pressure, for the acceptance of works written by non-Canadian authors and published outside this country. Some of these may be offered in "Canadianized" editions, at least where and so long as markets warrant and the conditions for being listed make such special editions necessary. Others will only be available in their original editions, which will not always be blatantly foreign in content although they will certainly never be Canadian in point of view. In a few subject areas, chiefly the Canadian social sciences, the need for Canadian materials will remain keen enough to ensure the continued development of special books for this market for some years to come, although there may be a falling off in demand for them if content and viewpoint become progressively more continental and less national in character. Although there will doubtless be some schools and teachers who will welcome Canadian-prepared and Canadian-published materials for a long time to come, market uncertainties would make the production of these steadily more unattractive for foreign-owned branch publishers, while the few remaining Canadian-owned firms (who publish almost nothing apart from Canadian works) could not reasonably expect to publish them and survive.

It is an unattractive prospect, at least for anyone who believes that a Canadian capacity to serve Canada's cultural interests should be preserved. Yet we have identified few factors that would warrant a more optimistic forecast. Let us recapitulate briefly what the factors are that militate against survival of the residual Canadian educational publishing houses at the present time:

1. The trend toward the use of multiple references in lieu of classroom sets of a single textbook; as these two categories of publication have merged a change has been taking place in the kind of classroom book that is wanted, and most particularly in the average size of market for the latter. Ironically, perhaps, the new interest in using what once were called "supplementary materials" as principal sources of information has exposed Canadian publishers to heightened competition from a tempting variety of books imported from abroad. These are often useful only in small quantities and only in connection with particular aspects of a Canadian course, but they can nevertheless be published successfully (most often in the United States) because their sale is continent-wide and Canada is simply an overrun export market. Canadian publishers lack the marketing facilities to reach the same continental market efficiently with their own products.

It is for this last reason that at the college level Canadian authors often find it more profitable to publish through American firms.

2. Curricular options have continued to multiply, a trend which partly accounts for the great expansion that has taken place in the number of titles listed in Circular 14. Again the effect has been to cause average markets to shrink, which has caused unit costs to spiral upwards, i.e. developmental costs must now be written off over substantially smaller total circulations. And the incentive to authors to write has dropped correspondingly.

3. New competition has been offered by other kinds of learning materials, some of the latter being much more costly than books, but purchased from the same budgets.

4. While the average Canadian markets for many educational books have been shrinking, manufacturing costs have continued to increase steadily and substantially.

5. The discontinuation of textbook stimulation grants at the end of 1968 closely coincided with the consolidation of boards of education into county units, moves which combined to reduce the practical importance and status of Circular 14 listings.

The Commission is presenting a substantial number of recommendations aimed at alleviating these and other problems that threaten to deprive this province and this country of its own educational publishing industry, or at least to weaken the latter to the point that it ceases to be an important cultural force in our educational system. But none of our recommendations is viewed by us as being more important than the one which advises that some means be found of again segregating per-pupil book grants from the general educational grants, i.e. of re-introducing book stimulation grants or their equivalent. What we call for is a repartitioning of existing total grants, not an increase in them – although that may be warranted for quite different reasons. As will be explained in connection with this recommendation, we think that Circular 14 (and the new Circular 15) should be preserved, but that the regulation under which it is published should be changed so that the titles listed on it will acquire a status and character consistent with present trends in curriculum building and classroom book selection at the regional level. This will have to include authorizing classroom use of most books approved by school boards, but the book stimulation grant portion of educational grants would be strictly reserved for the purchase of books – in any quantity – appearing on Circulars 14 and 15. We have weighed the advisability of recommending the melding of these two lists, but in view of the distinctly different purposes of the two circulars we would leave any such decision to the Ministry itself to make, perhaps at a somewhat later point in time. They might, however, be incorporated in the same volume, for reasons of convenience.

Nothing in this key recommendation ignores the fact that many school boards are probably spending as much as or more than their predecessors did on book purchases before the stimulation grants were discontinued. But it takes into account that Circular 14, with its Canadian preference features backed by careful screening procedures, is falling into disuse and – because it is a textbook list – is losing its relevance to the motives behind the book selection done by teachers today. In no sense is this a criticism of leadership or of educational communications in the Ministry of Education itself; rather it is a recognition of the problems inherent in trying to administer a Canadian educational book policy for the province at large, in the flexible way which the Ministry itself deems desirable, by means of centralized lists issued under a regulation which no longer meets the needs of the schools. It is the regulation under which Circular 14 is issued that we think has lost its validity. We hope that it is clear by now that under no circumstances would we favour dropping Circular 14 (or Circular 15) altogether, and we hope that no such step will be contemplated.

6
Nurturing a Canadian Identity

Our Commission was directed to examine and report on the economic condition of the Canadian publishing industry, on its contributions to the cultural life and education of the people of Ontario and Canada, and on the consequences for the people of the substantial control of publishing firms by foreign interests. Our first responsibility was not to decide how the book industry might be assisted, but to decide what recommendations regarding the industry could be made in the public interest. From the beginning of our work we have sought to avoid the too-easy assumption that publishing should be supported for its own sake. We hope that this has been apparent in our report up to this point.

Government assistance, in whatever form, can be justified only to the extent that furnishing it will enrich and protect the cultural life of the people of Ontario and Canada. Just how large a stake does the public have in the well-being of Canadian book publishing? To arrive at a satisfactory answer to this question has been one of our principal concerns.

The problems of publishing in this country are economic ones, but the importance of publishing in the life of Canada is cultural before it is anything else. As we have observed at several points already, the Canadian book publishing industry simply makes too small a contribution to the gross national product for economic considerations to earn it any priority over many other fields of enterprise. But from the cultural standpoint, the fact that book publishing is the indispensable interface between Canadian authors and those who read their books places it squarely in the centre of our stage.

BOOK PUBLISHING AND THE BOOK INDUSTRY

When we say that the public interest must come first, it means that when we look at textbook publishing we should be primarily concerned with education, or if you like, not with the interests of the schoolbook publisher so much as those of the child. When we consider imaginative or informational or recreational publishing, we should do so first in relation to Canadian creative authorship of such books now and in the future, and only secondarily in relation to the prosperity of their publishers.

Nevertheless, one quickly comes to recognize a community of interests among publishers and booksellers and librarians and readers which places them all in a condition of mutual dependence on the author who creates the works in the first place. The name of the game is indeed authorship, and for Canadian publishing it is Canadian authorship. No degree of financial assistance to publishing in this country will be of the slightest avail if creative authorship itself is not stimulated and sustained. But authorship in turn will benefit more from the availability close at hand of capable and interested editors backed up by competent publishers than it will by any kind of welfare system devised especially for its members. That a strong publishing facility operating primarily on behalf of Canadian books, and possessing adequate editorial, administrative, and marketing capacity, can be the key to the further stimulation of Canadian writing of every kind is implicit in much of what has already been said in this report. Indeed, the target should be more than to ensure the future strength of publishing itself; it should be broadened to include the future strength of the whole Canadian book industry. Thus any kind of program of assistance, direct or indirect, to Canadian book publishers must also take into account the interests of the total Canadian book industry, including bookselling, book manufacturing, the library system, and (above everything) the ultimate consumer of all these services – the reader himself.

There is some danger that any program aimed at protecting and encouraging the development of Canadian-owned publishing will be interpreted as a move to misuse books by making them instruments of political indoctrination, quite possibly in the interests of extreme nationalism. No educational system could justify such an abuse of power. No one wishes to convert our school children into little Nazis, although everyone can name communities abroad where this is still being done. Let it be said once and for all that the Commission abhors every kind of indoctrination as much as it abhors censorship, and that it counts the freedom to read as important as the freedom to speak or to write or to criticize or to enjoy any of the other well understood rights and privileges of a democratic society. These ideals are indeed self-evident, we think, and need no reinforcement from us. At least we shall indulge in no such tiresome exercise here.

NEGATIVE CENSORSHIP

What does concern us greatly is a possible distortion of the mix of reading matter readily available to Canadians, whereby a subtle – and often innocent – suppression of the Canadian viewpoint takes place without any general realization of what is happening. This can happen if competitive conditions cause imported books or imported editorial content to strangle the domestic product. When this occurs, and we have been almost overwhelmed with evidence that it is occurring in many ways, then Canadians will indeed be subjected to a kind of negative censorship and indoctrination which free people everywhere should seek to avoid. This kind of censorship must be done away with, too.

Canadians ought to be allowed consciously to nurture the cultural and historical traditions that distinguish them as a people without meriting the charge of extreme nationalism. Indeed, freedom from a sense of cultural identity is not a true freedom at all, and those who idealize such a condition fail to perceive how temporary a state it can be. To have no appreciation of the historical development of one's nation or of the values and ideals it has symbolized in the past arises more often from ignorance than indifference. But either way, one positive assertion can be made whenever a country's national consciousness sags until its sense of cultural identity vanishes: the resulting vacuum will sooner or later be filled by a cultural idealism imported from somewhere else. And it will come most easily from a country which fosters its nationalism in dynamic fashion. If the ties of language with such a country are close, its influence will be even more profound. We do not have to look farther than Quebec in recent years for an illustration of this, although other international parallels can be pointed to as well.

Our history, our society, our geography, and our special problems are Canadian topics which are of considerable interest to authors and publishers outside this country. And there is no reason to say that all the books about Canada that are written and published abroad are necessarily bad books. Many of them are excellent works, of their kind. But what almost always distinguishes them from Canadian books on the same topics is that they are addressed primarily to non-Canadian readers, and often are not written from a Canadian background of experience.

A certain objectivity is sometimes supposed to endow the history of Canada written especially for, say, American readers. Even when this objectivity is founded on too little rather than too much information, it does not follow that such books should not be written. But because they are not written for Canadian readers, they should never be allowed to become the only available reference books in their subject areas in this country. In the elhi grades, it would be best if they were not used at all, because they are more likely to mislead young readers than to broaden their outlooks. More mature readers, who are not so likely to be misled if they also have access to similar works with a Canadian viewpoint, will discover that these books are apt to dwell on details which every Canadian reader already knows. Or they may be insensitive – or worse, patronizing – regarding international and social issues which are of special concern to us. Our views regarding the importance of preserving a Canadian point of view in the great majority of our textbooks used below the university level have been set forth in Chapter 5.

Where a policy of Canadian preference has not been followed, as it has not in many of the other provinces with respect to schoolbooks, or where no such policy can be practicably applied, as for almost all reading matter other than schoolbooks, the extent of the foreign cultural invasion has already been very substantial. Although the influx of trade books from the United Kingdom has been significant, an overwhelming proportion of all kinds of books that are imported comes from the United States. Ashok Kapoor and Edward H. Breisacher, both of the Graduate School of Business Administration of New York University, offered but one of countless summaries of the situation when they wrote in the *Business Quarterly* (University of Western Ontario; Summer, 1971) as follows: "In Canada, the wholly owned subsidiary is the typical arrangement with indigenous publishing programs in English and, recently, in French. But Canada is unusual in that it accounts for over one-third of the dollar volume of U.S. book exports; in fact this country [Canada] can be viewed almost as a [U.S.] domestic market."

MISCONCEPTIONS REGARDING BOOK IMPORTS

It is possible to be misled by statistics of imports into exaggerating the share of the Canadian book market assumed by foreign books. The commonest error (one which has been made by associations of Canadian printers among others) is to make a straight dollar-value comparison of books manufactured in this country and books imported. The conclusion is then drawn that a little more tariff protection would cause a substantial proportion of the imported books to be made in Canada. Such assumptions fail to take into account the fact that the sales of imported books are spread over tens of thousands of titles, of which only a small proportion sell in sufficient quantities to make manufacture, or even partial manufacture, in this country economically feasible. Titles whose total sales in Canada are twenty-five, fifty, or even a hundred copies cannot be manufactured here under any circumstances, and yet the vast majority of books imported enjoy sales within or below this turnover range. What makes such imports loom large in value is the number of titles that are involved. After all, the annual British and American output of new books is made up of approximately 91,000 titles; the number of new titles added to *Canadian Books in Print* each year is about 1700, not counting government publications or theses.

This tendency to base comparisons on dollar values rather than on average editions sold in this country clearly invites some faulty assumptions regarding the nature of the Canadian book market. It is a confusion that was graphically illustrated a few years ago by a decision of the Department of National Revenue, Customs and Excise Division, to apply special duty (dumping duty) on book imports when discounts beyond a nominal level were allowed the importer. This was done in pursuance of the principle that special duty is applicable in such cases because "books are a class or kind of commodity manufactured in Canada." It was not until importing publishers succeeded in demonstration that the criterion should be whether or not the *title* in question is or is not made in Canada that this confusion between books and titles was eliminated. Subsequently the rule was adopted that special duty is applicable only where the title is already manufactured in Canada (and where an excessive discount is made available to the importer). That is to say, special duty thereafter became applicable where true competition arose between similar goods, e.g. a title made in Canada and the same title imported from abroad.

This history is relevant, because the right to read carries with it the right to have access to literature generally, with due regard for the principle of Canadian preference which we have acknowledged in the case of certain kinds of educational books. To seek to redress the dollar imbalance in Canada's foreign trade in books would require a rigorous degree of what can only be characterized as censorship, and we can only reiterate that we do not consider that this could ever be considered a cultural accomplishment.

PUBLISHING – A CREATIVE ACT

Publishing is creative before it is competitive. This is because publishing involves the selection and sponsorship of creative works which are protected against competition in the form of duplication by virtue of copyright.

The normal consumer market for books (excluding institutional markets) is much more elastic than for most other kinds of merchandise. People who have the habit of buying and reading books, and one could wish that they were more numerous, are usually responsive customers for additional books in their fields of interest whenever they become available. "But I already own one," can account for buyer resistance with regard to many kinds of merchandise, but with reference to books the remark is ludicrous. This is only one reason why there should be no reason to fear a glut of Canadian books on the market – provided that they are good books.

It therefore does not follow that whenever one publisher fails to publish, another will do so – the book in question may never be written, and this is particularly true of non-fiction works including informational books about our own country. Indeed, publishing which is socially important tends usually to be publishing which is highly creative, not merely competitive.

Nor is it true that when two publishers issue best sellers in the same season the sales of one will interfere directly with the sales of the other. In the trade field especially, book sales tend to stack. This is even beginning to become true in the educational field, as a result of the trend toward multiple adoptions. Indeed, only limitations on book budgets prevent its being equally true for schoolbooks. At the college level, any instructor will confirm that students read far more widely than they did, say, twenty years ago.

Until recently the most competitive field in book publishing was doubtless the schoolbook market, where exclusive adoptions meant exclusive sales. Today, even though budgets do limit the school market, there is much greater flexibility of choice and whenever Canadian books are not to be had, imported books will be purchased. Admittedly, if Canadian books are available but are not as well written and not as well produced, imported books deserve to be preferred. Therefore, in addition to encouraging the use of Canadian books by again ear-marking a small part of the educational grants for their purchase, as we recommended in Chapter 5, we must also do what we can to ensure that they compare favourably with foreign books in all aspects of quality – educational, literary, design, and production.

In the end, the prosperity of Canadian book publishers – and of Canadian authors, artists, and manufacturers along with them – will depend not only on their adventuresomeness, foresightedness, and literary discernment, although all these qualities are important. It will depend as well on the book-reading habits of the Canadian public. The expansion of the market for Canadian books will no doubt also be contingent on an expanded degree of internationalism in Canadian publishing. But alongside any growth in Canadian book exports, if not as a prerequisite to such development, we must aim at the creation of the friendliest possible climate for Canadian books in our own country. This can be brought about by encouraging the writing and production of the kinds of works which are most likely to earn a place on the bookshelves of the world.

Thus an important condition for the future advancement of Canadian book publishing must be the continued advancement of Canadian authorship. The primacy of the writer over the publisher in our view has, we hope, been reflected at many points in this report, but it is examined with superb insight in the background paper which Professor George Woodcock has prepared for the Commission, "On the Resources of Canadian Writing." "Our main concern," writes Woodcock, ". . . should not be with publishers, but with writers, and with encouraging writers to develop alike their creative and their self-critical powers...by creating a favourable ambience."

PUBLISHING NEEDS OF CANADIAN NATIVE PEOPLES

Minority groups in all countries must be concerned with the quality of communications available to them if they are to preserve their cultural traditions and at the same time to understand and be understood by the larger societies in which they live. "Unity in diversity" is meaningless if there is no public willingness to give it practical support. After all, indifference and repression have a good deal in common. The Canadian social commitment therefore clearly demands a strengthening of the publishing services available to minority groups throughout the country, and not least to our Indian and Eskimo peoples.

Too little has been written in the past for and about our native peoples, and what has been written has often been patronizing, having been aimed at exploiting the quaint and romantic aspects of the subject rather than at establishing mutual understanding and communication. Public encouragement must be given to Canadian authors and publishers to become more closely and more continuously involved in interpreting the lives and thought and aspirations of Canada's native peoples and ethnic groups. This will require conscious planning, if only because there has been so little accomplished thus far without it. To the extent that this encouragement may require public financial support either at the provincial or federal levels, it should be forthcoming.

Canadian authors and publishers should not confine their efforts on behalf of our minority groups to the provision of a two-way communications link with the rest of society, although they should do that as well. They must also be encouraged to provide a richer assortment of learning materials of all kinds (this Commission is chiefly concerned with books, it must be remembered) which are relevant to our Indian and Eskimo schoolchildren. For example, there have been representations regarding the inappropriateness of school readers which are exclusively illustrated, in words as well as pictures, with so-called "child experience" material based on life in urban or semi-urban communities, whose consumer goods and values have no real meaning throughout much of this country's expanse. It is true that there have been some exploratory efforts to meet this shortcoming, including some interesting experimental publishing. Unfortunately, where this has been undertaken by commercial publishers it has been commercially unprofitable. There is a public responsibility at least to make more publishing of this kind possible without loss. What kind of cultural identity are we serving if we do less?

CANADIAN STUDIES IN CANADIAN SCHOOLS

While this Commission was at work, a project entitled "Canadian Studies in Canadian Schools" was completed by Norman B. Massey for the Council of Ministers of Education. This survey was concerned with such questions as the following: Are today's students able to gain through their school activities a knowledge of modern Canada and the complex web of Canadian events? Do they acquire a sympathetic understanding of their fellow Canadians? The survey explored such topics as whether schoolbooks and other educational materials answer current needs, and whether there should be offered courses of a new design for the study of Canada. The Massey study and its conclusions are at many points relevant to the question of nurturing a Canadian identity by encouraging indigenous writing and publishing. Among its conclusions appear the following observations based on interviews with over 450 students, teachers, administrators, and curriculum experts across Canada:

From the interviews and other discussions, it appears that there is scope for much broader study of Canadian life. Present courses could be revised so that young people could meet more of the culture of Canadians even without the introduction of new courses centred around Canada. Both students and administrators expressed concern that a further study of things Canadian might foster a nationalism incompatible with the general conviction that Canadians now live in an international world.

Students want to know more and more about what is significant in their lives, and they judge the contemporary as most relevant. So, in the revision of current programs the domain of study should be broadened to include more aspects of contemporary Canada. Students and teachers might select topics related to *Canada today*; examples might be the flowering of poetry, music, art and theatre, the struggle for social justice and personal survival, the current issues in economics and politics, and the maintenance of the kind of an environment where there can be quality of life. At present students look to the social sciences and literature as their main source for information about Canada and for gaining a sensitivity to the feelings and aspirations of Canadians.

While students quite naturally view the world from their own local contemporary viewpoint, their study necessarily will be much broader and deeper. The present has roots in the past and local events are linked to a network connected with every settlement in Canada...

Three approaches are suggested, any and each of which might contribute to improved education. First, in most present school courses there might be more references to Canadians and Canadian events. Second, specific aspects of Canadian life might be examined through short-term units... Third, interdisciplinary studies, some based on Canadian themes, might find a more prominent place in school programs...

... special efforts are needed to unlock the cultural heritage. For example, more children's books might be translated and more cultural contacts assured. Perhaps two or more Departments of Education could co-operate to ensure development of materials reflecting the language and culture of Canada's multi-cultural heritage... In brief, the report looks for the continued evolution of studies centred around Canada and Canadian life so that Canada's youth may live enriched by their full heritage.

What is wanted, it would seem, is not new courses so much as a shoring up of existing programs of study by giving them a better-rounded Canadian perspective. We would concur. We are also conscious of the way in which such conclusions underline the importance of encouraging the production of books addressed primarily to Canadian readers, which means books that are written and published in Canada.

THE CANADA STUDIES FOUNDATION

Six years before the Massey Report was completed, an even more extensive survey of Canadian studies in Canadian schools was undertaken as part of the National

History Project by a group including Mr. A. B. Hodgetts, in the course of which more than a thousand classrooms were visited across the country. The results were summarized in *What Culture? What Heritage?* published in cooperation with the Ontario Institute for Studies in Education in 1968, and included the following observations:

Let us frankly recognize that what we are teaching our young people about Canada and its problems is antiquated. The courses of study in Canadian history are based on the interests and concerns that preoccupied academic historians of the 1920s. These courses lack any contemporary meaning... We are teaching a bland, unrealistic consensus version of our past; a dry-as-dust chronological story of uninterrupted political and economic progress told without the controversy that is an inherent part of history...

They [the majority of English-speaking high school graduates] have found very little in the Canadian past which is interesting and meaningful to them and practically no source of inspiration in their cultural heritage. They are future citizens without deep roots, lacking in historical perspective and only vaguely aware of traditions that have by no means outlived their usefulness. Contrary to clearly stated national goals in education, they develop an apathy toward Canadian history which tends to influence adversely their feelings toward modern Canada...

Educators at all levels of the hierarchy in every province must share some of the responsibility for the conditions documented... Academicians, professors in faculties of education, school administrators and supervisors – through unconscious neglect, indifference or even outright antagonism – have erected a number of intellectual barriers against Canadian studies. These barriers are strengthened by the theorists who toy with teaching tactics divorced from the nature of the subject being taught; who overemphasize the changing nature of society and contend that, since all knowledge is transistory and relative, it does not matter what we teach; who have prematurely concluded that nation states have outlived their usefulness and therefore concentrate their thoughts exclusively on citizenship in the world community; who set up a dualism between domestic issues and foreign policy; and who fail to recognize the intimate relationship between individual and sociological goals in education...

Civic education in Canada... should not only consider areas of agreement but also face frankly the differences of opinion which have always been and will continue to be an essential element in our society. But a stable political community also requires a minimal ability among its citizens to resolve conflict with some understanding of opposing viewpoints... The fundamental objective in any new program of Canadian studies should not be national unity but national understanding.

The Hodgetts Report quoted from above went on to recommend the initiation of a broadly based study of possible teaching methods and programs that might carry Canadian studies to the levels it envisaged as desirable.

In February, 1970, the study bore fruit with the incorporation of the Canada Studies Foundation, whose exclusive purpose was to improve the quality of studies about Canada in the elementary and secondary schools of Canada. Under its program, several important projects have since been undertaken, and one can look forward with hope not only to the findings but to the impact of its future reports on provincial curricula and on the books used in Canadian classrooms. One hopes that instead of being required to complete its work over a period of five years, as has been proposed, the program of the Canada Studies Foundation will be expanded, and even duplicated if necessary, on an ongoing basis.

Dr. Norman Massey, summarizing the work of the Canada Studies Foundation, notes that there are at least three ways by which schools can enhance their study of things Canadian: (*a*) by achieving an emphasis on Canadian aspects of current school subjects and activities; (*b*) by including the study of discrete units, each focussed on one aspect of the total Canadian environment; and (*c*) by adding to present programs cross-disciplinary studies based on specific aspects of Canadian life. Surely it is to programs of this kind that Canadian authors and Canadian publishers can look for their commissions in years to come.

CANADIAN SCHOLARLY PUBLISHING

It has been said that the standards of true scholarship are international, or should be, but that the scholarly preoccupations of professors and others engaged in research are likely to be regional. Because this is so, a major stream of scholarly writing has flowed forth from Canadian universities in recent years. And also because this is so we can already count some eleven Canadian scholarly presses which are busy publishing it. Not that American and British researchers lack interest in this country's economic or political or ecological problems, to mention just a few areas. They do not, but their perspective is inevitably foreign, and this restricts the value that their publications relating to this country hold for Canadians. We should encourage the interest they take in us, but it would be unwise to depend upon their writings for all our information, ideas, or conclusions.

Scholarly presses at Oxford or Yale or Columbia might one day have embarked on the publication of a dictionary of Canadian biography, for example. If one of these great institutions, or another like them, had done so, no doubt a valuable international reference work would have resulted. But nothing other than the foresight of an imaginative Canadian benefactor, who established by his will a monumental project of research in Canadian biography, could have assured future scholars of access to a definitive bicultural reference work planned and edited from a Canadian historical viewpoint.

An almost endless list of examples of books written by academic authors and incorporating their research could be cited to illustrate the degree to which works of this kind have expanded Canadians' awareness of themselves. This is hardly surprising when one considers that between eleven and twelve per cent of all English-language Canadian books in print are published by this country's scholarly presses. Especially in the Canadian social sciences, the direct contribution to knowledge made by this country's academic authors has been enormous.

If the importance of scholarly research in Canada and the publication of its results were to be measured only by the number of books produced and by the critical acclaim that they have earned internationally, the publishing of academic research would justify itself. But its significance in Canadian letters is much more far-reaching than this. What textbook in Canadian history, political science, economics, geography, or sociology – to name but a few subject areas – could have been written and what courses in such fields could have been devised without the trailblazing explorations done by this country's scholarly publications, both books and journals? What historical novels, what popular studies of government and politics, indeed what new basic research works of any kind could have been undertaken without access to the scholarly publications that came before? It is this seminal quality of academic research and writing that makes it so important in the Canadian publishing scheme, and even where it is not concerned with domestic issues it can – if its standards are kept high – enrich the reputation of the country as a publishing centre throughout the world.

Not all scholarly publishing is done by university presses. Nor has all the output of scholarly works by commercial publishers in this country been done by Canadian-owned firms, Macmillan again being an outstanding example of a foreign firm which has made a substantial contribution to Canadian academic publishing. But in the end most scholarly publishing cannot be profitable, or at least it must be selected and edited and produced with the purpose of maximizing its academic service rather than its profitability. For this reason, the non-profit university press plays as critically important a role in the publishing development of Canada as it has played in the United States, where more than a hundred such presses are now active.

It is to be earnestly hoped, however, that Canadian university presses will not be called upon by their parent institutions to become more commercial in order to survive and develop. There is a real danger that the increasingly stringent financial circumstances of our universities today will encourage this kind of perversion of their publishing programs. The issue is sufficiently important to the future of Canadian publishing that it justifies brief consideration here.

The first purpose of a university press is to ensure the efficient communication among scholars of the results of their academic research (not to be confused with the publishing of theses, with which such presses are rarely concerned). This is a wholly uncommercial goal, but it should be pursued with the highest degree of commercial efficiency that can be mustered – provided that this does not involve altering the goal itself. Not that a scholarly press should be defined as one which loses money and a commercial publisher as one which makes a profit; occasionally even the most academic kind of publication will repay its costs to a scholarly publisher, and no one will deny that commercial publishers frequently subsidize the books they issue, and not always inadvertently, either.

There are inconsistencies, nonetheless, in the ways in which universities support the publishing and para-publishing activities for which they are responsible. Some institutions, not necessarily in Canada, have spent millions in less than successful attempts to introduce closed circuit television, computerized information retrieval systems (to say nothing of computerized accounting systems), and audio-visual installations of every description. Some of these may even include cumbersome and uneconomical schemes to publish and disseminate the related program material. Occasionally such universities already possess their own presses, but these are more likely to be excluded than included in the administration of the needed new publishing facilities. There is something incongruous when such scholarly publishing departments (which could be called into being where they do not exist) do not participate fully in the application of new technologies to the process of disseminating knowledge. The fact that they do not participate, and are often not even consulted in such matters, must be attributed to the fact that the operating structure of a university press partakes of that of a commercial organization, even though its purposes may be different. Because commercial publishing is expected to be profitable (whether it is or not), it is sometimes allowed to cast a reflection on university publishing operations which are not profitable and which could become so only if they were transformed into something other than what they were designed to be.

There is of course *no way* whereby the scholarly publishing arm of a university could fund from its normal operations even the down payment on the capital installation costs of most of the non-print media, much less the salaries of the staffs of technicians needed to operate them. The latter can multiply equivalent book production costs by factors of 10 to 100 times per unit. The difficulty must lie in the fact that the university press has an organization and terms of reference which make it accountable; the research library, the academic research project, even the university accounting department do not. By accountability in this sense we mean the responsible budgeting of costs against anticipated net benefits in advance, the careful scrutiny of actual operating results in relation to budget, and the subsequent review of performance on a profit and loss basis. Because this is precisely what most university presses do, their closer involvement in university programs involving the new non-print media would seem to be overdue.

It is sometimes pointed out that university presses are non-taxable, and so long as they serve the scholarly purposes of their parent institutions this is accepted. Of course the corollary of their becoming taxable would be for them to become fully competitive. Presumably this would mean that they would then specialize in the publishing of textbooks at all levels in the curriculum, and other things as well, possibly even including children's books. But if university presses are ever forced to become competitive they will contradict the function and purpose of their parent universities. For a university press to be businesslike in the discharge of its function is one thing; for it to go into business is a different matter altogether.

Thus it is to be hoped that the purely commercial criteria of success in academic publishing will be scorned more and more generally in the future by Canadian university presses and by Canadian university administrations alike. The business acumen of these specialized departments, which can make so rich a contribution to Canadian publishing, should be tested by the precision of their advance budgeting, and not by the size of their net incomes. Their editorial competence will be measured by the scholarly worth of what they publish, and this judgment will continue to be rendered by academic reviewers around the world.

REVIEWS AND CRITICISM

Canadians, particularly authors and publishers, often say that there is insufficient information about books written and published in this country, and that the quality of reviewing is generally poor anyway. No research will yield precise answers to the qualitative question, although bookmen of all kinds are in general agreement regarding which critics usually write most soundly, just as they also agree that in this country there are too few who do.

If this opinion is shared by publishers and booksellers, among others, it does not seem to stem from a desire for chauvinistic praise of Canadian books because they are Canadian. There have been times when awareness of the limits of Canada's writing resources has been the principal factor in discouraging the launching of a popular national literary journal whose object would have been to present literary criticism and other serious writing of the first rank.

It might be argued that if Canada has been deprived of such opportunities, it must be because marketing and financial considerations alone have stood in the way. Not so. If an even level of editorial content could have been assured *in a steady flow*, there would have been a serious effort to establish a Canadian version of a magazine like *Encounter* before this time. Good, and even excellent, writing of the kind that was wanted has been and is being produced in this country, but Canadian literary creativity of high quality must be greatly expanded if its outpouring is to become sufficient to persuade a responsible publisher (with or without foundation assistance) to support a regular literary periodical aimed at achieving real international acceptance. This is what the Canada Council had to say about such a possibility in its annual report for 1961-62:

It has been suggested to us that the Council might call into existence an English language review of the highest quality, thoughtful and stimulating, which would provide the best of comment on literature and the arts, and indeed on the whole social and intellectual substance of Canada. Such a review need not be chauvinistic but could deal with international topics and draw from time to time on foreign writers. But Canada has not yet been able to produce and maintain a magazine of Canadian origin and point of view that could perform for English Canadians the services of an *Encounter*, an *Atlantic Monthly* or a *Harper's*. There seems to be an increasing body of opinion that such a publication is sorely needed, and we have, in fact, entertained wistful thoughts on the subject. One thing is quite clear: it will not be produced until the Canada Council or some other philanthropic organization or person can find scores of thousands of dollars annually for its support over a period of years.

But, quite apart from the cost involved, it is no simple matter to create a review of quality. Much depends on finding the right editor. In all honesty, too, we must say that Canada, with its smaller population and consequently less established intellectual traditions and resources, will have difficulty in finding writers with the attainments of those who grace the pages of *Encounter* or *Harper's* or the *Atlantic Monthly*. Milton Watson, whose experience as editor of *The Canadian Forum* entitles him to speak with authority on the subject, wrote this to the editor of *Exchange*:

"Forgetting readers for the moment, what community are you going to draw on for your writers? The odd intellectual reporter or journalistic academic isn't the answer. They're a pair of intellectual hybrids in this country anyway, and between them lies the under-populated desert in which any aspiring Canadian journal of opinion is going to dry up. The first-rate intellectual commentators whom you will need are an under-developed class; since there's no real Canadian market for them, you'll have to create them as you go along, and most of the time you will have to do with a poor makeshift."

The Canada Council adds the following comments on Milton Wilson's pungent remarks:

We are not going to let Mr. Wilson's wise words of warning discourage us completely about the future of Canadian periodicals, and critical reviews in particular; we notice that the difficulties have not led him to overthrow *The Canadian Forum*. We would rather take note of his remarks about the need for a market to develop such talent. This is not the least service which existing periodicals provide, and they have already given us writing of distinction.

We think these remarks remain almost as pertinent as when they were written. It is a fact that the writing expertise required to float a journal of the kind we have been discussing is still limited in quantity and might therefore not be continuously available.

Notwithstanding the fact that sources of good Canadian critical writing continue to expand, that there remains a shortage is not disproved by the commendable, but in some respects inbred, review, *Books in Canada*, with its limited and consequently repetitive cast of contributors. This country needs such a review medium and needs it badly. But it also needs a supply of reviewers who write authoritatively and interestingly; most of all it needs a larger supply. Negative criticism is not a literary accomplishment in itself, and we think – and have found agreement among many people in the book industry – that *Books in Canada* has indulged too often in what almost appears to be author assassination for its own sake. But all this is a vicious circle: good criticism encourages good writing; and great writing indubitably stimulates worthwhile criticism. But to achieve either, one must first expand Canadian opportunities for publication. It should by now be clear that to do this has become a principal concern of this Commission.

The suggestion that Canadian books do not receive their proportionate share of what book reviewing is done in our own country does not stand up to scrutiny, we find. True, there are some who say that all Canadiana should be reported upon before any foreign books, or who propose some variation of this notion. But unless one subscribes to such extreme views, and we do not, one has to admit that a quantitative comparison of domestic versus foreign book reporting indicates that Canadian books receive their fair share of what reviewing is done. Apart from the several academic journals which carry literary reviews (some of which are chiefly concerned with Canadian writing) we found the lineage accorded books by Canadian authors (however published) to be respectable in proportionate if not in absolute terms. Indeed, during the past couple of years at least, Canadian books seem to have been deemed as newsworthy (by book review editors) as most books other than international best sellers. And this in spite of the fact that almost all review copies reach Canadian reviewers from Canadian companies which act as agents for publishers abroad and are sometimes but not always foreign-owned themselves.

Although a national literary journal like *Encounter* does not exist, we did make an extensive study of the review media that are available in Canada. The only firm conclusions to which we have been able to come, however, are that the review media are uneven in quality, somewhat random in their selection of books, and (perhaps as a consequence) less effectual than those concerned with the welfare of books might wish. This is opinion only, but it is supported by the views of many individuals in the book industry, including publishers, as well as by the editorial priority given book reviewing by the media themselves. We shall comment further on this last point shortly.

A quantitative analysis of book reviewing in three of the most sought-after book review media (at the time, at least) confirmed our impression that Canadian books are not overlooked. For one year beginning in October, 1970, column inches devoted to book reviews of all kinds were measured in the *Globe Magazine*, the *Toronto Star*, and *Saturday Night* and the reviews categorized as Canadian or non-Canadian in subject matter. As the accompanying table indicates, Canadian books commanded a share of reviewing attention which far exceeded their proportion on the basis of titles published or dollar value sold. The *Globe Magazine* and the *Toronto Star* allocated 43 per cent and 33 per cent of their reviews, by number, to Canadian books, and interestingly the space devoted to the same books was 47 per cent and 43 per cent, respectively. *Saturday Night*, which in earlier years had come closest to being a national literary periodical, showed an overwhelming Canadian preference both in selection and in space allocated; it is regrettable that it has encountered economic difficulties of its own almost in direct proportion to the nationalism of its interests.

What is disconcerting is the seeming lack of priorities or promptness in Canadian book reviewing. On the one hand, perhaps it is fortunate that it is hard to guess what Canadian book will be reported upon next; if there were more unanimity

BOOK REVIEWING IN THE CANADIAN PRESS FROM OCTOBER 1970 TO SEPTEMBER 1971
A STATISTICAL SURVEY

		1970			*1971*								
	Total	*Oct.*	*Nov.*	*Dec.*	*Jan.*	*Feb.*	*Mar.*	*Apr.*	*May*	*June*	*July*	*Aug.*	*Sept.*
THE GLOBE MAGAZINE													
No. of Titles													
Canadian	225	27	34	23	16	18	11	16	19	19	12	14	16
Non-Canadian	302	23	56	25	30	17	20	24	22	20	29	18	18
No. of Column Inches													
Canadian	2571½	266	279¾	293¾	221¼	196¾	182½	171½	272¾	157½	160¾	144¼	224¾
Non-Canadian	2881½	224¼	236½	208¼	348¼	207	193¼	206½	264½	232½	356¾	209¾	194
THE TORONTO STAR													
No. of Titles													
Canadian	251	31	64	27	25	15	16	9	11	14	14	13	12
Non-Canadian	497	27	40	37	42	35	26	37	45	48	71	53	36
No. of Column Inches													
Canadian	2453¾	397¾	312¼	250¾	288¼	154¼	245¾	113¼	130	130½	157	106½	167½
Non-Canadian	3201¾	161	158¾	170¼	308¾	274¼	143½	305¾	328¼	306	420¼	369¾	255¼
SATURDAY NIGHT													
No. of Titles													
Canadian	38	3	6	4	2	2	2	3	7	2	3	1	3
Non-Canadian	3	0	1	0	0	0	0	1	0	0	0	1	0
No. of Column Inches													
Canadian	715¾	71¾	87¾	71¾	38¼	32¾	37¾	67	136¼	50	46¾	26¼	49½
Non-Canadian	51¼	0	5½	0	0	0	0	22¾	0	0	0	23	0

among reviewers the lack of space available would probably ensure that many domestic books might be reviewed hardly anywhere. On the other hand, both publishers and authors are exasperated when weeks pass after carefully scheduled publication dates without acknowledgment, good or bad, in some of the principal review media.

Of course, publishers have only themselves to blame when they do not allow sufficient lead time before publication date to permit reviews to be commissioned and written. Even when they do allow enough time, they probably should attribute the delays that still occur to the space restrictions within which the best book reviewers are forced to work. Newspaper publishers have economic problems, too. Space costs have risen so steeply in recent years that book publishers are less and less frequently able to justify advertising in the mass media. When they do buy space, it is more likely to be in connection with a highly specialized marketing project, or simply in a continuing spirit of obligation. From the standpoint of the news media, book review pages may be justifiable editorially, but not for the dollar value of the advertising they attract from publishers. If they are to develop as editorial features, it will more likely have to be in response to reader demand than to advertising pressure. Because news feeds on news, it will be necessary to make book publishing much more newsworthy than it is if reader interest is to be stimulated. Something can be done through intelligent public relations programs on behalf of Canadian books, perhaps, but we are again drawing a vicious circle.

CANADIAN BOOK REVIEWS ABROAD

Canadian authors and publishers have to be concerned about the future of Canadian book reviewing, but they have a more immediate problem in getting their books reviewed abroad. Their need to broaden their market base through expanded exports has already been discussed, but American review columns have an understandably limited interest in Canadian publications, and some of the most important media in the United States have a policy of refusing to consider for review any books not published in that country. (The University of Toronto Press has resolved this problem to a limited extent by formally publishing its books simultaneously in Toronto and Buffalo, where it operates a branch.) Major Canadian reference works often go unreported in such media as the *New York Times* and *Saturday Review* for months and even longer, while the prospect for serious critical coverage in New York and Chicago of new Canadian fiction, poetry, and plays is even more disheartening.

Canadian scholarly books have generally fared best in securing reviews abroad, especially in the international learned journals. Important popular media such as the *Times Literary Supplement* in Great Britain or even *Scientific American* in the United States not infrequently devote lead reviews to such Canadian publications.

It is to be hoped that with the development of Canadian book centres abroad (now planned by the federal government for London, Paris, and New York) and with the mounting of adequate public relations and publicity campaigns through these centres, there will be some easing of the review restrictions that do exist. After all, it is not entirely reasonable for Canadians to expect their books to be reviewed abroad until their sale is also being vigorously promoted and supported outside the country.

THE ANALOGY WITH BROADCASTING

In the field of broadcasting, the question of Canadian versus foreign content has been the subject of parliamentary debate, royal commissions, and government committees ever since radio was recognized as a powerful medium for mass communication in the 1920s. This Commission has carefully reviewed the history of domestic content regulations in Canadian broadcasting because of the inviting analogy it may seem to offer to book publishing. But the analogy is more apparent than real, and most of our discussions with persons informed in the field of communications have confirmed this conclusion. Consequently we see no purpose in taking space here for more than the barest summary of the history of Canadian broadcasting policy, even though the story is an interesting one in its own right and was carefully researched by the Commission's staff early during our work.

The Broadcasting Act of 1958, which created the Board of Broadcast Governors, did enjoin the latter to "regulate the establishment and operation" of public and private broadcasting in order to ensure "the continued existence and efficient operation of a national broadcasting system and the provision of a varied and comprehensive broadcasting service of a high standard that is basically Canadian in content and character." The Board was specifically empowered to make regulations "for promoting and ensuring the greater use of Canadian talent by broadcasting stations." The Act included a stipulation that the Board deny permission to broadcast to any applicant who was not a Canadian citizen or a Canadian corporation, i.e. one in which the presiding officer and at least two-thirds of the directors were Canadians and in which three-quarters of the shares were Canadian-owned.

In 1959 the BBG announced regulations which called for the raising of Canadian content, duly defined in two stages, first to 45 per cent and subsequently to 55 per cent. For the purposes of the regulations, partial degrees of Canadianism were conferred on programs produced in other Commonwealth countries and in French-language countries, details which concern us here only because of the way in which they emphasize some of the practical administrative difficulties that have to be faced in any such kind of regulation. In 1964, further restrictions on the percentage of non-Canadian content were imposed, and additional interpretations of what might qualify as Canadian content were introduced. It is interesting that the latter were modified in response to a protest from the Independent Television Authority in Great Britain (where Canadian programs were considered fully British) although no change was made regarding French programs as no comparable understandings were in force in France and other French-speaking countries.

The second Fowler commission, reporting in 1965, observed that

> ... an adequate Canadian content in television programs is unlikely to be achieved by a laissez-faire policy of minimum regulations governing advertising volume, morality and the like. Economic forces in North America are such that any substantial amount of Canadian programs will not appear on television schedules unless room is reserved for them by regulation.

This Report led to the enactment of a fourth Broadcasting Act in 1968 designed, among other goals, to "contribute to the development of national unity and provide for a continuing expression of Canadian identity." The new body established to fulfil the directives of the Act, which called for the use of "predominantly Canadian creative and other resources among other things," was the Canadian Radio-Television Commission. This Commission was empowered to make regulations and to issue and revoke licences where necessary. The CRTC continued and developed the policy of Canadian ownership of broadcasting stations, and further restricted the proportion of non-Canadian content permitted. Considerable further definition of terms and conditions was associated with the new regulations, which also had to be adjusted to cope with new technological developments such as Community Antenna Television (CATV).

The Commission's reasons for distinguishing book publishing from radio and television broadcasting are not that it rejects the CRTC's end purposes in seeking to stimulate Canadian creativity by furnishing a continuing expression of Canadian identity. Rather, we think that the analogy between publishing and broadcasting is a poor one, given the differing nature of the media involved. Consider what some of these differences are.

There are inescapable technological restrictions on the number of outlets for broadcasting in this country, and in any area within it. Anyone can publish a book next month if he chooses to invest his money in such a venture, and we have had no difficulty in agreeing that anyone should be allowed and encouraged to do so. In book publishing, Canadian authorship and Canadian publishing can expand laterally as far as creativity and finances permit; in broadcasting there is a sharp limitation on the number of frequencies or channels that can be allocated in any area, and this alone necessitates control through common consent, i.e. by government. But any kind of supervision of how much Canadian authors should be permitted to write, or which publishers should be permitted to publish, would strike at freedom of expression. (We see no contradiction of this freedom when a Ministry of Education, responsible to the people and elected for the purpose, assumes the responsibility for deciding which educational materials it will approve for use in the schools and which it will not.)

For a very substantial proportion of the population at least, Canadian radio and television audiences can receive broadcasts directly from American stations and networks, and in the absence of regulation by Canada of its own stations, their temptation to compete by rebroadcasting foreign program material would leave little or no outlet possible for a "continuing expression of Canadian identity." To regulate the origin of what is broadcast in this country, therefore, achieves the positive end of ensuring that Canadian content will be available to those who wish to receive it. To regulate what books may be purchased in Canada, or imported from abroad, would be to regulate what adult citizens are allowed to read. We will have no part of any such censorship, nor would Canadians at large. The Commission wishes to emphasize again that it is much less concerned with denying access by mature readers to whatever books they wish to read than it is with improving the climate for Canadian authors and Canadian publishers. We are interested in achieving and maintaining a happier balance between domestic and imported books of all kinds, yes, but we believe that this must be done by stimulating domestic productivity, not by suppressing foreign publishing.

There is one area where some of the principles of broadcasting control can be applied to publishing, but it is an extremely specialized one. This is in the distribution of mass periodicals. Here the Commission has already recognized the possible advantage to the public of supporting natural monopolies, selectively and only where necessary, in order to ensure efficient distribution of magazines and similar literature throughout regional markets. Consequently we have favoured a policy of licensing such regional distributors in Ontario, sometimes on an exclusive basis. As explained in our *Final Report on the Distribution of Paperbacks and Periodicals in Ontario*, we believe that a licensing system under public control, with provision for public hearings of applications for licences, may be justified in this case, but in this case only. These last procedures might have something in common with those of the CRTC, even though only some of the purposes are the same. But this is as far as we think one can go to find a solution by equating Canadian publishing with Canadian broadcasting.

SOME NATIONAL AND REGIONAL CULTURAL POLICIES ELSEWHERE

Although the United States is nominally opposed to the establishment of a federal cultural program, it has sought to assist cultural projects through a National Foundation on the Arts and the Humanities since the establishment of this body in 1965. This Foundation participates only in collateral funding of approved projects, and avoids involvement in their direction. The purpose of this policy is to ensure local support, both in money and interest. In addition to the Foundation, there exists a Federal Council on the Arts and the Humanities, which coordinates the activities of the Foundation with programs of other federal agencies. A special function of the Council is the coordination of international cultural exchanges.

There are two branches of the Foundation, the National Endowment for the Arts and the National Endowment for the Humanities. The Foundation receives support from Congressional appropriations, although most of its operating moneys come from contributions by individuals, corporations, and other foundations, in descending order of importance. Foundation givings have recently amounted to $60 million annually; there is a ceiling of $9 million on Congressional appropriations. The existence of the Foundation, and of the National Endowment for the Arts in particular, has encouraged the development of parallel agencies in the various states, all but two of which now possess their own arts councils.

In Japan, an Agency for Cultural Affairs was established within the Ministry of Education in 1968. Its responsibilities include the promotion and dissemination of culture, the preservation and use of cultural property, as well as the management of religious affairs. In many cultural fields, however, its jurisdiction is shared with other government bodies, including other divisions of the Ministry of Education. There is within the Agency itself a Cultural Affairs Division, which has a wide assortment of responsibilities ranging from improvement of the Japanese language to copyright registration and religious affairs. Another Arts Promotion Section assists artists by administering an annual awards program (amounting to over 3 million yen, or $10,000 annually), and also subsidizes a country-wide arts festival during two months each autumn.

Cultural affairs in Great Britain are administered by the Arts Council of Great Britain, which in turn funds a Scottish Arts Council and a Welsh Arts Council. The parent arts council in this program comes under the Department of Education and Science for purposes of its own grant moneys, but is otherwise substantially autonomous and free of direct government supervision. The principal concern of the Arts Council has been in the field of the performing arts; its purpose has been to work as closely as possible with local groups, with the result that a number of regional arts groups have been formed in recent years. Its literary projects have included the sponsoring of a national survey of writers in Great Britain ("The Book Writers–Who are They?"). Legal developments of concern to writers are held under study by the Literature Panel of the Council, including such issues as the Protocol to the Stockholm Convention and the principle of the public lending right. The 1970-71 budget of the Arts Council of Great Britain was approximately $9\frac{1}{2}$ million pounds, of which 11 per cent was used to support the Scottish Arts and 6 per cent the Welsh Arts Council.

France established a Ministry of Culture in 1959 on the principle that "it is the business of the State to combine what private enterprise has to offer with the action of a genuine public cultural service." The responsibilities of the Ministry are set forth as (*a*) the dissemination of the arts through the removal of social and psychological barriers; (*b*) overview of the cultural impact of the environment on the individual; and (*c*) the relation between knowledge and culture. Its special areas of action are defined as the conservation of the national artistic heritage, training, creation, and dissemination. Within the Ministry of Culture is the Cultural Development Commission comprising one hundred permanent members including senior government officials, representatives of various cultural areas, sociologists, and others. This Commission's function is to study public needs in the cultural field and to assess the efficacy of various programs for dissemination of cultural information.

Cultural policy in the USSR is regulated by the Supreme Soviet through the Ministry of Culture. Administration is characterised by centralized control of each branch of cultural activity. The application of central government policy occurs through the supreme soviets of the republics to whom local organizations are responsible. The state budget for cultural affairs is directed toward the support of libraries, museums, broadcasting, art exhibitions, and the printing and publishing industry. The USSR's Council of Ministers' State Committee for the Press controls the entire book trade throughout the nation. Most publishing and printing houses are budgeted to be self-supporting, but where the nature of the publishing programs makes this impossible, deficits are met by the state.

It is frequently not realized in the West how far the book publishing industry has advanced in the USSR, whether measured by the range of subjects covered, by circulation, or by number of titles published annually. Although that country's own claim that between one-quarter and one-third of all books being produced in the world today are published in the Soviet Union is to be discounted (some titles are issued simultaneously in multiple languages, and some titles are leaflets only, to mention two difficulties in making such comparisons), the annual output is nevertheless formidable. Moreover, the high interest shown in books by the average citizen can be attested to by any observant visitor. Indeed, the importance attached to books in Russia perhaps justifies a few further comments on the cultural importance of publishing in the Soviet Union today.

Manuscripts in Russia are measured in units known as authors' "signatures," each of which comprises 40,000 characters, or a little less than twenty double-spaced typewritten pages. The number of an author's signatures is an important factor in the calculation of his fee. There is an increasing effort to include quality along with length as a factor in determining compensation and therefore incentive in creative writing. But the Soviet system of author payments has some redeeming features. Compare it, for example, with one which overpays for formula fiction and pot-boiler biographies but would pauperize most of the poets and playwrights that our society can produce.

Widespread supposition to the contrary, the Soviet author enjoys a high degree of copyright protection under state legislation for his literary creation. Nor does he have to comply with any formalities in order to procure the benefits of copyright. Each of the Union republics is free to establish its own limits on the duration of copyright, which normally lasts for the author's lifetime and for varying periods of from ten to fifteen years thereafter. However, in the absence of international agreements, the benefits of Russian copyright protection are confined strictly to Soviet authors, and such royalty payments as have been made to western writers whose works have been republished there have been made de gratia and in no case, according to Soviet interpretation, because of legal obligation. It is interesting to add, however, that in very recent times there has been much speculation as to the direction in which the balance of royalty payments between Russia and the United States would run if completely reciprocal copyright were established even between those two countries. The volume of Soviet writing, especially in the technical and scientific fields, being republished in translation now in the United States, has attained major dimensions, and some authorities believe that it now exceeds the distribution of unauthorized editions in the other direction.

In Sweden, the Ministry of Education and Culture includes a Department of Cultural Affairs, which was established in 1963. Its areas of concern include art, literature, music, theatre, cinema, non-military archives, public libraries, museums, education in the cultural sector, and radio and television. In 1969, a National Council for Cultural Affairs was appointed to undertake a three-year study and to make recommendations regarding the long-term structure of state cultural policies, with particular reference to the role of cultural policy in promoting social equality.

At the present time there are four "producer cooperatives," or centres for dissemination of cultural products, operating with state grants, one to represent each of writing, film-making, art, and the theatre. The Writers' Centre, which has the largest budget ($40,000 in 1970-71) comprises 400 writers. It has two principal functions: It serves as an employment-information centre, and it coordinates lectures, debates, and "culture weeks" in the community at large. In one recent year, the Swedish Writers' Centre handled no fewer than 1300 commissions to authors.

This summary of how cultural affairs are administered and the national importance attached to such activities in various countries could of course be continued almost indefinitely. It would be appropriate to include here a review of the programs of support to literature by the Canada Council over the years since its establishment in 1957, but that has been adequately done by Robin Farr in his background paper, already published by the Commission. The structure and program of the Ontario Arts Council is discussed elsewhere in connection with one of our principal recommendations. The high priority which Quebec has given through its Department of Cultural Affairs to matters concerning book publishing needs no reiteration here. Among its wide-ranging programs in this area, the most relevant has already been reviewed by Georges Laberge and André Vachon in their background paper on Quebec's new *politique du livre;* nothing could more clearly indicate the significance which that province attaches to the book industry in relation to the cultural identity and development of its people.

Perhaps the point has been made, and it would be tiresome to pursue it further. As much as any of the countries and regions just discussed, Ontario clearly has as much justification, and perhaps an even more urgent responsibility, to establish its own policy respecting the Canadian book industry, an industry which is so largely concentrated within its own borders. By doing this in unequivocal terms now, it will serve not only all the people of the province, but the present and future citizens of the whole Canadian confederation.

PARALLEL BETWEEN MAGAZINES AND BOOKS

It is now eleven years since another body similar to our own, the federally appointed Royal Commission on Publications, submitted a report which dealt with the impact of imported periodicals on the Canadian magazine publishing industry, including the social role of publishing. Although it was primarily concerned with the cultural implications of a domestic periodicals industry which was rapidly diminishing in the face of competition from abroad, we find more parallels between the situation in book publishing today and the one with which that earlier Commission was seeking to cope than between book publishing and radio and television broadcasting. A very few quotations from the Report of the Royal Commission on Publications will illustrate what we mean. Moreover, some of the comments of that previous Commission's report on split-run "Canadian" editions have a special relevance to book publishing, and particularly to the reissue in this country of so-called "Canadianized" editions of foreign textbooks:

> The role of the periodical press in building . . . Canadian unity cannot be ignored. But it cannot contribute its share if it is beset by overwhelming competitive conditions that threaten its existence...

> "Canadian" editions are the ultimate refinement in the re-use of second-hand editorial material to provide a vehicle for a new set of advertising messages . . . The main complaint of "inequitable competition" made against "Canadian" editions by the Canadian magazine publishers concerned the re-use, in whole or substantial part, of the editorial content of parent editions . . . The unfairness of this competition may be measured in two ways: The actual cost of obtaining and preparing the editorial material made available to these "Canadian" editions is far beyond what they or Canadian magazines could possibly afford, bearing in mind the size of the Canadian magazine-reading population . . . Clearly, these publications have the advantage of being able to use high-cost editorial to obtain large circulations.

We have pointed out elsewhere that our concern regarding the prescription of Canadianized editions of foreign textbooks in Ontario schools goes beyond this problem of unfair economic competition. We think that curricular content should be prepared and presented throughout from a Canadian point of view, and that Canadian authors and artists should be encouraged to bring this about. But there can be no denying that a question of unfair competition does also present itself. Provided, however, that in the course of being republished in Canadianized editions the foreign copyright matter is not made available at what would be bargain prices at home – and we have had no evidence that this is what happens – it would be unfair to characterize the practice as editorial dumping. But in its glossy packaging, it can sometimes appear to be an abnormally cheap buy in our relatively minuscule provincial market, and if this leads us to compromise the goal of securing material written from a Canadian perspective, such competition from abroad will stifle, not stimulate, new domestic writing and publishing.

BOOKS FOR THE BLIND IN CANADA

When even the most enterprising of Canadian publishers must struggle to find a national popular market sufficient to sustain their industry, it is hardly surprising that there are a few special readership groups in our society whose needs tend to be overlooked in so far as domestic authorship is concerned. We are not referring for the moment to such obvious examples as specialized technical publishing or the dissemination of scholarly research. Even when the markets for such publications are restricted, they are at least international, and the commerce in them will also be international. What we have in mind here is an apparent shortage of Canadian books published in Braille or on audio-tapes for the use of the blind and partially blind. We received a useful brief on this subject from the Canadian National Institute for the Blind, and the discussion at the hearing on this submission exposed some unexpected impediments in the way of Canadian publications in special editions of this kind.

There seems to be no shortage of reading material for the blind available through the CNIB (and through other channels) in the form of Talking Books and Braille editions, as well as in a less used type of embossed edition known as Moon Type. What struck us was that the representation of Canadian books in these formats, all considered together, seems to be disproportionately low, and we were concerned to discover the nature of the disability that must exist for them.

In December, 1970, 4060 readers in Canada received the Talking Book library service, 712 readers used Braille, and 17 readers used Moon Type. We were told that the use of Talking Books is increasing rapidly, and that it was anticipated that within three years one-quarter of Canada's total blind population of 28,000 will be using them.

We were also informed that periodicals and books are actually published by the library of the CNIB in Braille editions, and that an additional and significant quantity of Braille materials are made available to the library by 170 volunteers who have learned the system and transcribe single copies of books. These copies are held in the library and become masters for making duplicates on plastic through a thermal vacuum forming process. Books supplied by volunteers were said to consist mainly of textbooks used by blind high school and university students.

It seems that "English language Talking Books are acquired almost exclusively from the United States. There the Library of Congress has books recorded for its Books for the Blind and Physically Handicapped program." These Talking Books are chiefly distributed in disc form abroad; the CNIB library acquires one copy and duplicates it (presumably with permission) in tape. The evidence they gave us is relevant:

Since the cost of preparation of a book is spread over copies issued, we are able to purchase the material for 50c per recorded hour. The cost of preparing a book for recording [e.g. for recording a Canadian book for the first time] varies with its length. A book of nine hours reading time costs in the neighbourhood of $ 1,500 ...

Since books acquired for general circulation come primarily from sources abroad, the Canadian content of our holdings tends to be low. Books by Canadian authors are at times issued in Braille and in Talking Book form in Great Britain and the United States. These are, however, usually taken from editions published by firms in those countries ... One per cent of our holdings in Talking Books are by Canadian authors. Three per cent of our holdings in Braille are by Canadian authors ... Throughout the years we have always experienced the utmost courtesy and consideration from publishers in Canada in granting us the use of copyright free of charge ...

At present, there is a need for more Canadian content in all forms of publishing for the blind so that blind people may become more conversant with Canada's problems and potential. The cost of producing a full length book ranges from $1,500. to $2,000. to transcribe it into either Braille or as a Talking Book ... We would recommend that the Province of Ontario lend financial support for the provision of a modern library service for blind readers.

Some of the Canadian Talking Books are prepared by volunteer readers but we were told that the voices of professional readers are preferred. Original Canadian Talking Books are normally "read by our professional reader; the rate is very high ..." The reason for the high rates for reading, it was explained, is that this professional service is furnished by members of the Association of Canadian Television and Radio Artists (ACTRA), which has on one special occasion cited waived the full union rate. In short, the reading to tape of original Canadian books is an extremely expensive procedure and a definite impediment to republication of Canadiana in this form, but authors and copyright owners make the material itself available free of charge! We consider this situation incongruous, if not reprehensible, and we are of the opinion that the proposed Ontario Book Publishing Board should review it in all its aspects and make such recommendations as may be necessary to increase the availability of Canadiana to blind readers in Ontario in a form and quality that meets their requirements.

CANADIAN MANUFACTURE AND FOREIGN MANUFACTURE

One of the dilemmas of Canadian book publishing, and it should be evident now that there is no shortage of these, is that it is possible to manufacture most books somewhere abroad at lower cost than in Canada. In spite of the economic imperatives which govern Canadian book publishing policy, domestic manufacture is often preferred nonetheless. Indeed, while available statistics confuse importations of Canadian books manufactured abroad with foreign books imported in the normal course of marketing, we are satisfied that the great bulk of books written by Canadians, by dollar value, are produced in this country. In saying this we take account of certain well-known best sellers which have, regrettably we think, been manufactured outside Canada. Nevertheless, the threat to the Canadian graphic arts industry of foreign competition is serious and according to most reports it continues to grow. More than one avowedly purely Canadian publishing house is now sending most of its books abroad for manufacture in Britain, Holland, Hong Kong, or Japan. Surprisingly, perhaps, there are classes of book manufacturing – even including very limited editions – which can be produced in the United States at lower cost for equivalent quality than they can be produced here. At what point, if any, does the economic threat to the printing industry become a cultural threat to the Canadian book industry as a whole? And if there is no connection between the two interests, is there a common public interest which needs protection from the present condition of laissez-faire?

Well not quite laissez-faire, perhaps. We have already dealt at some length with the conditions regarding manufacture as well as authorship which are prerequisites for listing on Ontario's Circular 14, and we have commended the Canadian preference policy involved there. But is it really of any cultural consequence where Canadian books are made? Should we pay heed to the argument, advanced by one of the smallest as well as by one of the largest commercial trade publishers in Canada, that to have to pay the costs of domestic manufacture would render many Canadian books not viable? On the face of it, our publishers would seem to have a duty to make their available finances stretch as far as possible, and we ourselves have counselled them in this report, and elsewhere, to be more business-like than they have been in the past.

The Commission's view is that the book industry in this country cannot afford to allow its various parts to be indifferent to one another's welfare. We have already indicated that we are impatient with the amount of recrimination we have read and heard between librarians and publishers, between authors and reviewers, and between booksellers and publishers; we believe that they should all recognize a common Canadian commitment, and certainly no rationalization of the total industry in this country dare omit the Canadian book manufacturer. Considering the disabilities under which the latter works, disabilities that range from international competition of the kind just described to overt foreign discrimination such as the manufacturing provisions in the United States copyright legislation, it is remarkable that he is able to maintain the high quality of work that he does. It was only in 1970 that a commercial printer in Toronto produced for a Canadian publisher the book which won the international competition at Leipzig as the Most Beautiful Book in the World, an honour which has yet to be won by the great majority of competing countries.

Not that the Canadian book manufacturer has any right to be complacent regarding the quality or cost of his products or the service he offers. The distressing fact is that there has been a steady diminution in the number of comprehensive book manufacturers in this country, by which we mean firms that provide a total book manufacturing service – type composition, printing by letterpress or offset, and edition binding – as tabulated in Chapter 1 of this report. This deterioration in the competitive strength of the book manufacturing industry has not necessarily been offset by the establishment of a new Canadian Book Manufacturing Association within the Graphic Arts Industries Association, although this group is still in its teething stages. We do however note the greatly reduced responsibility which the latter body has assumed in the field of copyright, for example. Yet copyright should be as much the concern of the Canadian book manufacturer as of the book publisher in this country, and considering the fact that a major proportion of the latter is not Canadian-owned, we should judge that the Canadian book manufacturing industry may have the greater stake of the two. Certainly the American book manufacturers came to this conclusion long ago.

With these cautions to guide a future Ontario Book Publishing Board in its dealings with the industry, however, we wish to reiterate our belief that if the Canadian book industry is to develop in healthy fashion over the years it is absolutely essential that it do so as a whole. In particular, we do not believe that the Canadian book publishing industry can ever achieve international viability if it is not based solidly on a healthy Canadian book manufacturing industry. This is a provincial Commission, and to a substantial extent both book publishing and book manufacturing, in English at least, are Ontario industries, although there are admirable exceptions. Book design is a creative art, and is as dependent on those who execute it as on those who commission it, i.e. it can only flourish as a Canadian art if manufacturer and publisher coordinate their services to Canadian authorship. Our publishers must stop cherishing the notion that in the long term their industry will flourish if it has to depend on transoceanic communications or the vagaries of international exchange or local employment conditions throughout the world.

We have noted the proportion of quality printing produced for New Zealand publishers by Japan, to cite one example that might be considered a parallel, and we do not think that Canadian publishing should endeavour to build its reputation on such a tenuous model. We believe there is much to be said for Australia's Bounty

Act, discussed by George Ferguson in his background paper, even if the legislation mentioned has not fully succeeded in its purpose. The expertise required to produce good Canadian publications should be developed as completely as possible in this country in editing, in marketing, and in manufacturing. We cannot delegate half the capacity we need to produce good books and then expect to achieve more than short-term success as publishers in our own country, much less in the book markets of the world.

Although we believe these to be compelling considerations, we realize that they do not set aside the assertion that fewer books can be published with the same money if they must be manufactured in Canada. What we would question is the relevance of that assertion, however, to a publishing industry that has already had to turn to government for help in order to survive. If such assistance is justified – and our earlier and present recommendations surely make our views on this question clear – it will have to be provided from public funds. We think that Canadian publishers have a duty to share such government assistance with Canadian book manufacturers, whose survival and expertise is also important to the Canadian book industry. We would stop short of recommending that the provincial government urge Ottawa to adopt non-tariff barriers *at this time* similar to the manufacturing provisions in the as yet unamended United States Copyright Law, but we have no hesitancy in saying that we do not believe that any further government-subsidized printing contracts from Canadian publishers should be executed outside this country except in extraordinary circumstances, and we are entering a strong recommendation to this effect. Nor should they be produced with non-Canadian materials if materials of equivalent quality can be procured in Canada. We believe further that the export of printing for publication that is subsidized with federal grants (e.g. by the Canada Council and the Research Councils which it supports) is undesirable, and we recommend that the provincial government request, through appropriate channels, that it be actively discouraged, at least in so far as English-language publishing is concerned.

In making these recommendations, we recognize that occasional exceptions may have to be permitted in the interests of encouraging greater Canadian participation in international publishing. We refer specifically to situations in which a Canadian publisher has a bona fide opportunity to co-publish with a foreign publisher by purchasing his own edition in unbound form from such a co-publisher's printing manufactured abroad. It would be unfortunate if Canadian firms were discouraged from entering into arrangements of this kind, lest it become more difficult than it already is for them to sell overruns of their Canadian-manufactured editions to foreign publishers in parallel situations. Another possible exception would be the need to procure, for bona fide design reasons duly approved in advance, art-type reproductions of a kind not commercially available in this country, e.g. colour gravure or collotype. Similarly, the use of imported paper and binding materials might be justified in particular situations for design reasons when equivalent Canadian materials cannot be obtained, but not otherwise.

The exceptions just mentioned should only be admitted after the closest scrutiny in each case. We consider that in practice they should apply only to a small proportion of books appearing over Canadian publishing imprints (of whatever ownership) where any kind of public assistance to publication is being provided specifically to the titles in question. In the case of books receiving title grants from Ontario public funds, presumably the Ontario Book Publishing Board should be satisfied that the recommended conditions are being met and should authorize any exceptions that may be permitted for reasons such as those which have just been discussed. With regard to books receiving assistance in the form of title grants or the equivalent from federal public funds, we can only recommend that the Ontario government urge through appropriate channels that similar conditions be attached, at least to English-language publications. We expect that similar considerations should also apply to French-language works, but because so small a proportion of the latter are produced in Ontario we feel reluctant to recommend that similar restrictions be suggested regarding them without further study by the governments concerned.

If these recommendations regarding Canadian manufacture of Canadian books which receive title grants from public funds are considered to be protectionist in nature, we can only say that they are designed to preserve the Canadian graphic arts industry as a national cultural asset. No copyright impairment as a consequence of foreign manufacture of books by Canadian authors is being recommended at this time, for example, although parallel provisions continue to exist in the United States Copyright Law respecting works of American authorship, thereby working a severe unilateral disability on the corresponding Canadian industry. The latter problem has been reviewed for the Commission by W. E. Curry in his background paper, "The Impact of the U.S. Manufacturing Provisions."

If the policies recommended here with regard to foreign manufacture of Canadian books which receive title grants from public funds are implemented, and if they continue to be closely reviewed by the Ontario Book Publishing Board, there is every reason to expect that Canadian book manufacturing will acquire its own competitive momentum alongside Canadian book publishing. The Canadian book industry as a whole will then benefit, and the interests of the public will be much better served.

7
Summary of Recommendations

INTRODUCTION

The Commission anticipates that this will be the first chapter which most readers will scrutinize, and that it may be the only one that some will ever read at all. If these expectations are fulfilled, it will be unfortunate, for what follows is the conclusion to a study, not the study itself. Moreover, it is only a summary of the principal recommendations contained in the text of the report, where these and other proposals are developed in more detail. It sets forth what we think are the most effective lines of action open, for the public particularly, to deal with a complex series of issues. The issues themselves have been defined and discussed in the course of the preceding six chapters, throughout one hundred and eighty-five briefs received (most having been reviewed in public hearings), and in the series of research studies that constitute the *Background Papers*. All this material, occupying almost 8000 pages, has now been published. In addition, there have been countless interviews, letters, and informal submissions of various kinds concerning the work of the Commission over a period of a little less than two years.

It is our hope, therefore, that those who may possibly be charged with implementing our recommendations, as well as those who may find themselves in disagreement with some of them, will not overlook entirely the considerations which the Commission has endeavoured to weigh in reaching them. We say this not in defence of what follows, but to remind all concerned readers that the recommendations are the outcome of a long process of analysis and advice, to a considerable extent furnished by others. The recommendations should therefore not be reviewed and appraised in any final way, favourably or unfavourably, except in relation to the background material just mentioned. We are confident that responsible readers will not do so.

After much consideration, we decided that the main thrust of our report had to be directed toward book publishing as such, in keeping with our interpretation of our terms of reference. Nevertheless, we at times found the invitation to broaden these terms to include multi-media generally almost irresistible, and some special pleaders repeatedly urged us to expand our study in this way. We concluded that if we did so, we would obscure the issues that called the Commission into being; these had to do almost exclusively with the future of Canadian books. In some places in the text of our report as well as in the recommendations that follow, account is indeed taken of other types of media; our decision not to give them more prominence than we have does not mean that we refuse to acknowledge the importance of many of the new tools of learning. But we are satisfied that at this stage in the evolution of publishing, public concern should lie first with conserving a Canadian book publishing capacity, and that the new media may safely be allowed to fend for themselves. They have been doing this very successfully during the past four or five years, and indeed their success has contributed to the problems of book publishers.

We should add a word about the nature of the recommendations. Most of them are intentionally couched in the most general terms possible, although they are put forward no less seriously for this. What we have tried to create is maximum flexibility for the implementation which we hope they will receive. Accordingly, we have not stipulated the budgetary dimensions of every program that is recommended, because this will be done by the policy makers who we hope will set them in motion. On the other hand, we have looked closely at potential new tax revenues in related areas and have made a specific recommendation in this regard. If this is implemented, we calculate that the added costs of the new programs we now propose could be funded without the need to encroach on existing tax revenues. That is to say, the financial recommendation would provide the funds needed to meet new costs of new programs, although not the cost of restructuring existing programs such as educational grants to school boards. We also assume that funds required to support programs already accepted by the government will continue to be available at approximately their present budgeted levels. Again, we have usually refrained from stipulating the number of participants who should be included in each program from year to year, where the programs should be conducted, the detailed mechanism whereby they should be implemented, and the precise form of certain recommended projects or even under whose immediate supervision they should fall. We think that most questions of this kind can best be resolved in the light of precise knowledge regarding the amount of support actually approved, the policy priorities of the responsible ministry, and information gleaned from continuing evaluation of results achieved.

On the other hand, the whole body of recommendations is intended to outline with some precision the strategy which we think is required in order to cope with a serious cultural threat. We leave the tactics to be framed and adjusted as time goes on by a new body, one which we hope will be able to devote itself undistractedly to the wise conservation of Canada's writing and publishing capacity as it is represented in this province. If this valuable cultural resource is not made the object of a carefully planned public conservation program – which is what our recommendations really call for – it will become further depleted and soon must disappear. Although no body whose principal concern is the conservation of our writing and publishing resources now exists, we anticipated the need for one in our Third Interim Report and we are convinced that the time has come to call it into being. We speak of course of the establishment of an Ontario Book Publishing Board, a body which is implicit in many of the proposals discussed in this report and in the recommendations that follow. We have usually referred to it simply as the Board, although, as we shall now explain, its name and location in government are less important than that it should have the services of one or more competent experts on publishing, the ear of the industry, and the clearest possible terms of reference.

If the conservation of Ontario book publishing, and thereby the conservation of a large part of Canadian authorship in the future, could be brought about by a one-shot program there might be no need for a Board of the kind which this report envisages. The Commission could instead prescribe a single recipe aimed at ensuring the survival of an indigenous publishing industry and the creative productivity which it serves and stimulates. But we cannot do this. It should be clear by now that all the evidence which we have examined leads, directly or indirectly, to the conclusion that the Canadian book publishing industry in this province – and elsewhere in Canada, too, for that matter – is facing almost insuperable economic pressures. These threaten either to force it under, or so to attenuate it that it could only survive as an enfeebled regional cultural activity; in the latter event, the ground rules that bring foreign-owned subsidiaries into full competition for Canadian authors will change. Thus, if there is no public intervention, the market trend will favour more and more run-on editions of foreign-published books, and the proportion of these which would be Canadian-written, much less written for Canadian readers, would be small indeed, and have no reason to increase. This is the danger which we have identified in our study. We are convinced that whatever corrective programs are introduced, they must be supervised closely and wisely, and modified to suit changing requirements, and that these responsibilities call for continued scrutiny by a competent public agency.

What is needed, then, is a single, permanent interface between the book industry and government in Ontario, that is between authors, publishers, manufacturers, booksellers, and librarians on the one hand and the public on the other. The agency that provides this interface would concern itself with all matters of policy that relate to books and the public interest, and would supervise programs such as we have proposed in this report as well as others developed ad hoc as the need arises. It would also make regular reports and necessary recommendations regarding the economic health of the book industry in the province to the responsible minister. In addition, it would furnish the mechanism whereby a working liaison, directed through appropriate official channels, could be established with federal as well as with other provincial book publishing programs. In the course of this, it would furnish the necessary coordination of Ontario programs with cooperative plans for Canadian book development at home and abroad. It would have nothing to do with censorship, and it would be fatuous to suggest that any of the duties we have prescribed for it should be construed as inviting censorship.

The role of the proposed Board in the development and administration of many of the corrective measures recommended in this report is thus apparent; indeed, we do not think that most of our proposals can be effectively implemented except through such a specialized agency. Nevertheless, we realize that in recommending the establishment of a special Board we beg a question regarding how it can be established without adding to the government's existing substantial financial burdens. The Commission has been deeply conscious of its responsibility to minimize additions to the tax load, and believes that it has been successful in this regard, provided that its related proposals regarding financing of the Board and the programs it would supervise are implemented.

Any consideration of a new Board that would be charged with establishing and supervising a variety of programs affecting the cultural activity of book publishing and with coordinating functions of the kind just described calls for serious examination of the services available or that might be made available from the Ontario Arts Council, established in 1962-63 as the Province of Ontario Council for the Arts, and responsible to the Minister of Colleges and Universities. It would seem logical, and it did at first seem so to us, that the Council is a ready-made mechanism to plan and develop the remedial measures we are recommending. But in the end we concluded that nothing in the history of its policies to this time nor in its present procedures or expertise qualifies the Ontario Arts Council to assume the responsibilities which we think should be accepted by government in the highly specialized field of book publishing. This conclusion should not be interpreted as a reflection on the policies and programs of the Council in the other cultural areas in which it has been active up to this time; these have been effective, according to all reports we have. But book publishing and its immediately related fields, including authorship and the graphic arts, have certainly not figured prominently in the planning of the Council until now, and a fundamental policy change in that planning would seem to be necessary if the present perspective of its activities is to be adjusted to meet the needs of book publishing and the literary and graphic arts that depend on it.

It is true that the Ontario Arts Council has developed an interest in Canadian writing and publishing since the appointment of this Commission, but although we applaud this we remain skeptical regarding the probable adequacy and effectiveness of these new programs in the long term. We are not without our reasons for this concern. As recently as this past spring we received from the Ontario Arts Council the latest available information regarding its policies and programs respecting our field of interest, in answer to a series of questions which we had put to it. What follows are excerpts from a number of the questions and answers:

Question: Would you ... advise us (*a*) whether or not the expansion of your program [to include our field of interest] is still considered to depend on the availability of ... 'new' grant funds, and (*b*) what additional funds have you actually received for such extended activities?

Answer: (*a*) It is still Council's conviction that the expansion of any Council granting program, or, indeed, the introduction of any new granting program, is dependent on the availability of additional funds for granting through our annual appropriation from the Ontario Government, "since," to quote our earlier submission, "grant money (can) not be diverted away from other art forms, where Council (has) committed its support on a continuing basis..." ... It might interest the Commission to know that in 1968 Council in a five-year forecast to the Ontario Government projected a need of some $11,000,000 in 1972 to fund adequately the arts of the province. This year, Council requested an appropriation of $4,718,000. The appropriation is, in fact, $3,400,000.

Answer: (*b*) The Council's 1972-73 appropriation of $3,400,000 represents an apparent increase of $900,000 over our 1971-72 appropriation of $2,500,000. But from this increase must be subtracted an amount of $373,000 to accommodate the extra responsibility of granting to four new institutions (the National Theatre School, the National Ballet School, the Theatre Hour Company and the Stratford Festival Student Performances), previously supported through direct grants from the Department of Education. In the face of a literal explosion of activity and concurrent demand for assistance in all the arts, Council has allocated the actual increase with certain priorities across the full range of arts activities. So, with this year's budgeted allocations, the literary arts will receive a 25-per-cent increase in grants. The allocated increases in other disciplines are: drama and dance 10%, music 9.5%, visual arts 12%, film and photography 30%, Franco-Ontarian and ethnic arts 43%, regional arts 30% and special projects (for youth, the aged, prisons, hospitals, native peoples, etc.) 11%.

Question: Might we ask you to bring us up to date regarding the allocation of grant funds at your disposal indicating in particular the proportion of all grants being devoted to the performing arts and the proportion being devoted to the literary arts, and to other fields if any.

Answer: Here is a percentage breakdown of granting for this year and last:

	1971-72	1972-73
Drama and dance	32.2%	32.9%
Music	33.3	33.4
Visual Arts	12.3	11.3
Literary	4.8	5.4
Film	4.4	4.9
Franco-Ontarian & ethnic	5.6	6.3
Special projects	3.8	3.8
Regional	3.3	4.5

In addition, we have prepared the following record of percentage growth of literary granting over the last eight years:

	Number of all grants	Value of all grants	Literary grants	Literary total	Literary percentage
1964	30	$ 152,174	0	$ 0	0.0
1965	50	452,850	1	750	0.17
1966	55	585,520	2	7,750	1.32
1967	70	595,559	2	2,420	0.41
1968	90	884,507	5	5,700	0.64
1969	92	1,355,205	6	5,782	0.43
1970	171*	1,963,552	15*	25,719*	1.31
1971	240*	2,213,444	43*	107,966*	4.87
1972	?	2,477,106 budgeted	?	134,666* budgeted	5.44

* Figures include grants to individuals . . .

Question: Finally, we would welcome a re-statement of policy by the Council with respect to the literary arts in general and to original Canadian book publishing in particular. It would be appreciated if the plans of the Council in these areas could be placed in the perspective of its policy with regard to support of other art fields and of the performing arts in particular.

Answer: Council's policy with respect to the literary arts is perhaps best indicated in its granting record of the last few years, most notably as represented by the abrupt increase in literary granting from 1969 to 1970. Between 1969 and 1970 the level of literary granting jumped by almost 350% from $5,782 to $25,719. Obviously, by this action, Council indicated its concern both for the needs of the literary arts and its own responsibility to respond to those needs. Last year, Council redoubled its response with a further 336% increase, from $25,719 to $107,966. Unfortunately, this level of increase cannot be maintained year by year, because the level of literary granting, for so many years virtually negligible, is now reaching a more realistic level. But Council's concern continues to be evidenced in the 25% increase in budget allocated to the literary arts. The literary arts are a priority concern to Council but they are not the sole priority. Equal, if not superior priority has been expressed by Council, both in its representations to Government and in its own budget allocations, for: (a) more equitable access to the arts for Ontario citizens living outside the metropolis of Toronto; (b) more encouragement to creative, as opposed to performing, artists; (c) the need to respond to new pressures as expressed through new art forms and new organizations to explore them.

Happily, at least one of these competing priorities – that of encouraging creative artists – coincides with Council's concern with the literary arts and one third of Council's new grants to individuals are going to those in the literary arts.

In the matter of original Canadian book publishing, Council last year launched itself into this 'new' area with first-time grants totalling $23,000 to five Canadian publishing houses – Anansi, New Press, Oberon, Peter Martin Associates and Coach House Press. Council determined to make its assistance in this new area as freely and flexibly available as possible with simple, operating grants based on past publishing performance, rather than title-subsidies of the type used by Canada Council. This year Council will double its assistance in this area, with a budget allocation of some

$45,000 for operating grants to an anticipated 10 to 12 Canadian houses. (The Commission might note some priority concern here in the fact that the extra $22,000 earmarked for publishing grants represents the total increase allocated to literary granting this year.)

One more evidence of Council concern with original Canadian publishing may be indicated in a new plan for the handling of literary grants to individuals. Next month Council hopes to announce a scheme by which a number of Canadian publishing houses (probably 10) will be invited to recommend to Council worthy, emerging writers as candidates for assistance. Each house will be allotted a reserve of some $4,000 to draw on for these recommendations. The Council's only conditions upon these publisher-recommended grants to writers will be: (*a*) that the candidate is not already receiving similar assistance from another source (e.g. Canada Council); (*b*) that no single candidate receive more than $1,000; (*c*) that the publisher's recommendation be matched by some commitment in the form of a contract to publish; (*d*) that the Council grant must not be designated as an advance on royalties, publishers will recognize their responsibility to pay full royalties above the Council grant.

It will be clear from the above interchange (there were others) that the Ontario Arts Council does not consider itself to be in a position at present to meet the problems of Canadian book publishing on the scale which we are convinced is necessary if this particular cultural capacity of the country and the province is to be conserved. The programs we advocate are set forth in the recommendations that follow, and the reasons for them have already been developed in the text of this report. We respect the judgment of the Arts Council when it says, in effect, that it would like to do more in our area but that its difficulties are budgetary ones, surely not a new situation for any government agency. But even if the funds were available, we do not consider that the Ontario Arts Council could, under its present policies and with its present expertise (which is considerable, but not in the right field) successfully administer the kind of programs we are about to propose.

As we shall explain, we think that the Council might restructure its policies and staff in a way that could accommodate the duties which we have assigned to a hypothetical Ontario Book Publishing Board, provided that it were given the required budgetary scope. As anticipated already, we are including in our recommendations a specific proposal whereby the necessary additional funding could be achieved by means of withdrawing a tax exemption in an area which, as much as any, should contribute to the development of Canadian publishing. Let us consider briefly, however, the particular kind of expertise which the proposed Ontario Book Publishing Board should possess, whether its functions were carried out within or without the Ontario Arts Council.

The Board itself need meet perhaps only quarterly, and could represent the government as well as provide a link with the constituencies being served. The day-to-day administration of the programs which this Commission is recommending will need the services of a relatively small staff only, but at the head of the responsible unit there should be a full-time administrator who possesses an adequate practical experience in Canadian book publishing, and who has earned the respect of the industry on the basis of his record. This experience should be broad enough to include at least several of the main departments of publishing discussed in Chapter 1 of this report. Ideally, the person thus charged with the executive responsibilities of the Board (as we shall continue to describe it) should combine editorial, design, and marketing experience. He should be personally acquainted with trade practices in all fields of book publishing, including standard discounts and terms, channels of distribution, contracts with authors, normal promotion procedures, book reviewing and reporting, and policies of existing cultural foundations, as well as the main principles of cost accounting and pricing as applied to book publishing. We have no doubt that it will be difficult to find such an individual, but we do not think it will be impossible; after all, Canadian subsidiaries of foreign-owned publishers have made many excellent appointments of this kind, and of Canadian citizens at that. Especially if consideration is given to possible candidates nearing normal business retirement age, candidates might be found who would be willing to sever completely their commercial ties to accept a term appointment.

We have sketched the profile of the administrative head of the proposed Board in this much detail because we believe that no lesser degree of expertise would be acceptable, whether the duties of the Board were absorbed by the Ontario Arts Council or assigned to a new body. Provided that an administrator were found who could speak with publishers about publishing on at least equal terms, however, there are many reasons why the Ontario Arts Council would be a desirable umbrella for such a body. It is a fact that the duties and purpose of the Board are consistent with the function of the Council as set forth in the Act under which it operates, viz. "to promote the study and enjoyment of and the production of works in the arts." Moreover, the Ontario Arts Council reports to the Minister of Colleges and Universities. Having regard for the significance of educational publishing to the welfare of Canadian book publishing in this province, we cannot think of a more appropriate ministry to administer the programs to be outlined.

ONTARIO BOOK PUBLISHING BOARD

1. Our first recommendation, therefore, is that a specialized agency, referred to by us elsewhere as the Ontario Book Publishing Board, be appointed to act as an interface between the Canadian book industry and the public in the manner indicated throughout the text of this report and in the recommendations set forth herewith.

NURTURING A CANADIAN IDENTITY

2. We recommend that the Board develop and administer a program of title grants to Ontario-based, Canadian-owned publishers to assist the publication of completed book manuscripts by Canadian authors. This program would include every category of manuscript the Board considered appropriate, with the exception of those intended primarily for educational use, for which see Recommendation 40. To implement this program would require the use of sophisticated and objective evaluation and selection procedures, for which there are well-established models. Areas of interest eligible for consideration should be reviewed and, if deemed advisable, re-defined from time to time in guidelines issued by the Board. Such title grants should in no case exceed budgeted deficits, and should take full account of collateral grants available. It would be a responsibility of the Board to verify such budgets. A program of this kind could provide valuable stimulation to creative literary and publishing activity within the limits of the support possible; it should be noted that it would complement similar programs of the Canada Council already in existence, which should be considered when establishing the guidelines. Although these title grants would be directed to publishers, it is assumed that the cost of commissioning special work by Canadian illustrators and book designers would be provided for in the cost budgets where creative contributions of this kind are required.

3. We recommend that the Board develop a program of assistance to bring about the re-issue of out-of-print Canadian works, aimed at making available both library and paperback editions (where the latter are appropriate) of important titles that have been out of print for not less than five years. This program should be open to all Ontario-based, Canadian-owned publishers, who should be required to submit detailed budgets with applications, including full information regarding collateral grants available, if any. The Board should issue detailed guidelines, and would be responsible for screening all reprint proposals, including the procurement of confidential editorial reports from qualified independent critics. One of the secondary purposes of this program would be to permit Canadian publishers to distribute their fixed costs over a slightly broader sales basis, although subsidies for such reprints should in no case exceed budgeted net deficits, as verified by the Board.

4. We recommend that the Board devise and introduce a program of annual Ontario Literary awards, giving special attention to areas of book publishing in which existing incentives of this kind are few or are less adequate than they should be, e.g. children's books, classroom books as such at all levels,

dramatic works, translations from any language, and other selected areas including academic non-fiction. In addition to the literary awards program (which should be restricted to Canadian authors but not to Canadian-owned publishers) there should also be awards for the best examples of Canadian book design and Canadian book illustration, respectively, given to the creative person chiefly responsible in each case. Each of the awards in these two programs should take the form of medals or other kinds of trophies appropriate to the honour intended, and identical awards should go to the publishers. In addition, uniform cash prizes (to be shared in case of multiple authors only) of substantial value should go to the winning authors, illustrators, and designers. However no cash prices to the publishers would be useful, and none are recommended. Judging should be by an independent panel of qualified critics, appointed by the Board and given broad guidelines and necessary facilities, but otherwise permitted to operate with complete independence. It is suggested that its members might be appointed for three-year terms with provision for annual rotation. This awards program should be related to, if not the focus of, an intensive public relations program, of the kind assigned to the proposed Canadian Book Centre in Ontario as discussed in Chapter 4.

5. We recommend that all books that may receive title subsidies from agencies of the Ontario Government should in the future be manufactured wholly in Canada, making use of Canadian-produced materials in so far as this may be practicable without appreciable sacrifice in quality or production standards, subject to rare exceptions authorized in advance by the Board for reasons set forth. As explained in the text of the report, we endorse the policy of Canadian preference in manufacture (as well as authorship) already established by the Ministry of Education for books listed on Circulars 14 and 15. We believe further that the export of printing for publication that is subsidized with federal grants (e.g. the Canada Council) is undesirable, and we recommend that the provincial government request, through appropriate channels, that it be actively discouraged, at least in so far as English-language publishing is concerned. We have indicated in Chapter 6 certain exceptions that may have to be admitted.

6. We recommend that a system of insurance should be devised whereby payment to authors of their earned royalties would be guaranteed, applicable to all books published under royalty contracts by Ontario-based, Canadian-owned book publishers. Premiums covering such insurance costs, which are likely to be nominal, should be funded by compulsory payments by the publishers concerned as well as by the province, and should apply to future book contracts only; there should be no cost to the author. In making this

recommendation, the Commission takes full note of the protection already afforded authors involved in publisher bankruptcies under the provisions of Section 61 of the federal Bankruptcy Act. The purpose of the insurance program here recommended would be to provide relief to an author whose earned royalties are due but unpaid, rather than to involve the province in bankruptcy legislation as such.

7. We recommend that the Board, acting only in a coordinating role, encourage the establishment of and serious support from the industry for more numerous and more intensive training courses in such fields as bookselling, book designing, book production, and book editing, as well as authorship. Such courses might be conducted independently, by correspondence, at Colleges of Applied Arts and Technology, or in some cases in Ontario universities; it is to be hoped that they would involve apprenticeship training on the job as well. One of their principal purposes would be to improve and standardize qualifications in as many departments of the book industry as possible. The extremely high degree of professionalization achieved by librarianship (which is an integral part of the industry and depends on it) may be cited at least to indicate the direction in which such training should be aimed, if not the levels to which it need carry.

8. In addition to encouraging the development of specific courses related to the book industry, the Board should support programs which would furnish independent professional consultative services to the Canadian publishing industry. These services might relate to such areas as finance, accounting, management, editorial, production, design, and marketing. Consideration should be given to extending these consultative services into other related fields in the Canadian book industry, including book manufacturing, bookselling, and possibly even selected areas of authorship.

9. We recommend that the Board plan a program of assistance, which should be reviewed from year to year, to one or possibly more than one Canadian literary journal whose principal editorial purpose would be to provide adequate book review service of high standard regarding publications written and/or edited and published in Canada.

10. The opening of additional Ontario-based book publishing enterprises owned or controlled by non-residents (as defined in *The Paperback and Periodical Distributors Act, 1971*) should no longer be permitted without prior approval obtained from or through the Board, for reasons discussed in Chapter 2 of this report. The same comments apply regarding implementation of this recommendation as are made in the accompanying recommendation regarding possible transfers of existing firms to foreign ownership.

11. We reiterate the proposal contained in our Third Interim Report that the sale of book publishing firms or branches in Ontario should not in the future be permitted to non-residents (as defined in *The Paperback and Periodical Distributor Act, 1971*), without prior approval of the Ontario Book Publishing Board. Should implementation of this recommendation encounter constitutional difficulties, careful attention ought to be given to the feasibility of exercising control over such transfers by restricting the use of provincial funds to purchase from such suppliers.

12. As explained in the text of the report, we believe that it is essential that the market base of the Canadian book publishing industry be broadened as rapidly as possible through the development of export sales. For obvious reasons, much of the initiative in this area can be taken more effectively by the federal government. We therefore recommend that the provincial government recommend to the appropriate federal authorities that, in addition to the latter's announced plans for Canadian book centres abroad, consideration should be given to the following possible programs of assistance and cooperation: (*a*) placing selected Canadian books in school and public libraries as well as in classrooms abroad; (*b*) encouraging Canadian publishers to produce low-priced editions, based on run-on manufacturing costs, of selected titles for export and in some cases for special distribution abroad; (*c*) placing selected Canadian books in Canadian embassies, consulates, and other government agencies abroad, in so far as practicable with the advice and counsel of such offices; (*d*) mounting literary contests abroad regarding the Canadian scene and way of life, these to be supported by the provision of Canadian books; (*e*) support of a continuing public relations program abroad on behalf of Canadian books, based on the planned Canadian book centres; (*f*) careful examination of other special incentive programs aimed at increasing book exports, including possibly export bonuses, doubling costs for tax purposes in case of exports, etc. (cf. Australian Bounty Act). Although, as observed above, the principal opportunities and responsibilities for assisting Canadian book export development belong to the federal authority, the Board should not fail to note the many areas in which the Canadian book export interests of Ontario-based publishers can also be assisted, without mounting expensive special programs, through the activities of such bodies as the proposed Canadian Book Centre in Ontario, discussed in Chapter 4.

13. We recommend that the Board furnish Ontario House in London with a representative library of appropriate new Canadian-written and Ontario-published books as these are issued, and that such books be kept on perma-

nent display for examination by visitors to this important overseas Ontario centre.

14. Although we have discussed the importance of scholarly publishing in the text of our report, we recommend that the development of special programs of assistance in this area – except to the extent that our other recommendations may impinge on it – be left for separate study and action by the Board.

MARKETING CANADIAN BOOKS

15. We recommend that the Board coordinate and, on an experimental basis, help to finance consultation services provided by professional librarians to booksellers in the same community, especially in smaller centres. In any such program of cooperation, the advisory role of the librarian respecting book selection should be clearly understood, and precautions taken to preserve in every way the autonomy of the bookseller in all commercial decisions. The purpose of this program would be to bring the professional librarian and the regional bookseller into a closer liaison involving practical objectives, which might well include mutual cooperation in each other's showrooms in the form of public talks, displays of posters announcing books or giving advice regarding new Canadian publications, and similar projects.

16. We recommend that the Board coordinate a program whereby public libraries located at a greater distance than ten miles from the nearest comprehensive bookseller, may be encouraged by means of special financial assistance to carry Canadian books for sale to the public until such time as a comprehensive bookselling facility is established in the area. A comprehensive bookseller for the purposes of this recommendation would be one who normally carries a representative selection of books, including Canadian books, for display and sale to the public as defined by guidelines which the Board should issue from time to time. The purpose of this recommendation is to encourage the development of bookselling facilities, not to compete with them, a principle which the Board should consider first in its coordinating role. In certain cases, the interim program of assistance to a library might be transferred, after reasonable notice, to a new bookseller in the area for a further temporary period, subject to conditions of performance which the Board would establish and supervise.

17. We recommend that every public encouragement be given, through the Board and in other ways, to persuade retail booksellers to cultivate educational authorities as potential customers. At the same time, schools and school boards should be encouraged to order books for classroom and li-

brary (resource centre) use – which it should be noted are more and more often likely to be children's trade books – from local booksellers where the latter exist, and to press for the establishment of such facilities where they do not exist.

18. We recommend that the provincial government request the federal government to establish a comprehensive regular statistical survey of the Canadian book industry, developing and broadening the kind of information collected for the first time in *The Canadian Book Industry* (Ernst & Ernst; Ottawa, 1970). Such a survey should in our view be undertaken annually, or at least biennially, and its findings should be published as promptly as possible – an important consideration. It should further be requested that the planning and review of such a survey should involve regular consultation with representatives of the various segments of the industry, French and English, including publishing, manufacturing, and retailing. An effort should be made to give such a survey a creative dimension as well, by including representative authors in some of the planning consultations. Although it is desirable that such a regular survey be structured along lines that take into account the needs of the industry, it is important that the filing of returns be nation-wide and that it be mandatory, as would be possible if the administrative responsibility were vested in Statistics Canada. The Ontario Book Publishing Board, as well as representative bodies from other provinces, might itself play a consultative role.

19. The Board should be specifically charged with the duty of monitoring developments in relation to the new *politique du livre* in Quebec, and with reporting on this subject to the responsible ministry in Ontario after that program has been in existence for at least two years but not more than three years.

20. We recommend that Ontario-based, Canadian-owned book publishers be encouraged by the Board to continue to explore and develop all possible avenues for consolidation of non-competitive functions, including in particular fulfilment and marketing operations that are subsequent to editorial planning and selection. A program of financial assistance, possibly budgeted over five years, with conditions set and administered by the Board, would be appropriate to this end.

21. We recommend that a Canadian Book Centre for Ontario be established, partly with public support, with functions and organization generally as outlined in Chapter 4. The effectiveness of such a multi-faceted Centre should be the subject of continuing review and report to the responsible ministry by the Board.

22. We recommend that the Board mount and finance, in whole or in part, travelling displays of Canadian books to be shown in schools, libraries, public buildings, etc. throughout the province. Supervision of this program would be a function of the proposed Canadian Book Centre in Ontario. Some of these travelling displays should be planned in close consultation with the appropriate officials in the Ministry of Education, and should feature books included on Circulars 14 and 15, or on their successor list or lists.

23. We recommend that excessive exhibits fees charged by some regional educational conventions should be discouraged, at least in so far as these added expenses militate against the adequate display of Canadian books at meetings attended by educationists who wish to examine such books.

24. We recommend that the Board encourage, and possibly sponsor to some degree, a series of market research programs, e.g. to identify book purchasers' buying motives in the province and then to delineate areas and types of promotion that would serve such interests and at the same time maximize sales. This activity could best be delegated by the Board to the proposed Canadian Book Centre in Ontario. The planning of such market surveys should involve the fullest possible participation by the different branches of the book industry, and the surveys themselves should be made part of a program which would uncover market trends much more promptly than has happened hitherto.

25. We recommend that the government seek to obtain as much prominence as possible for news and information regarding Canadian-published books through all appropriate media which it supports, including educational TV and official publications of all kinds, as well as provincial displays. What is recommended here is the adoption of a broad policy pattern, rather than a specific program which by being obtrusive could become counter-productive; nor do we favour title advertising as such, which might require the making of selective value judgments at the official level, although major award winners could be a reasonable exception. The purpose would be to upgrade important book news to the level of being newsworthy in a broader context.

26. We recommend that the Board examine ways and means whereby Boards of Education in Ontario might be enabled to pay accounts with Ontario-based publishers not later than sixty days from date of invoice, and that it make recommendations to the responsible ministry accordingly.

27. The Commission considers that one of the major priorities for Canadian publishing is the development of book export markets with a view to

broadening the market base for Canadian publications and to reducing unit production costs. Only in this way can research and development be maintained adequately without increasing costs to uncompetitive levels. The Commission believes that the principal initiative in providing public assistance to Canadian book exports must come from the federal government, and notes the program for Canadian book centres abroad already announced by the federal Department of Industry, Trade and Commerce. The Commission recommends that the latter program, and all other coordinated export development activities, be complemented by the programs of the Canadian Book Centre in Ontario, recommended separately.

28. As indicated in Chapter 4 of this report, the gradual merging of trade and educational publishing, at the more junior levels especially, opens various opportunities for the retail bookselling trade as well as for the public to give increased support to the Canadian bookseller. If this tendency continues, there is likely to be a melding of trade and educational discount percentages as well. As this happens, and the Board should scrutinize developments in this area closely, it may become possible to differentiate wholesale discounts as applied to books according to the function of the purchaser, and to extend so-called trade bookselling discounts only to the trade, in return for displaying and selling books. If institutional purchasers (including educational authorities and libraries) were then supplied either at list price, or more probably at a limited discount for quantity orders, a substantial incentive for the development of regional book retailing, as well as of Canadian book wholesaling, could result. Federal legislation would have to be taken into consideration in any such development, but as indicated in Recommendation 19 above, a precedent in this area has been set in Quebec, which deserves to be monitored; if necessary, appropriate representations should be made to the federal government if special exemptions to permit desired legislation or regulation become necessary. In recommending that the possible advantages of encouraging such differentiation in discount percentages be closely studied, as we now do, it should be noted that the purpose would not be to make books cost more to institutions, but to cover some of the fixed overheads of booksellers by helping them to sell more books. If this were done, Canadian publishers would also be able to publish more books.

29. We recommend that every effort should continue to be made to coordinate the interests of active publishers of Canadiana who also act as exclusive agents for foreign publishers and the interests of librarians, including university librarians, in such important matters of common concern as ordering procedures, stock supply, net prices, quality of service, and channels of supply, in the context of our comments in Chapter 4 on this subject. The dia-

logue that has been begun between these groups under the auspices of the Commission should continue, either bilaterally or under the auspices of the Board. Interests of secondary concern in such discussions would be those of agents who call themselves publishers but rarely publish, as well as those of wholesalers whose operations weaken rather than strengthen original Canadian publishing.

EDUCATIONAL PUBLISHING

30. We recommend that the present policy whereby neither head office personnel in the Ministry of Education, nor regional office program consultants are permitted to enter into publishing contracts for the preparation of textbooks be reviewed in the light of changing competitive circumstances. The listing of books in Circular 14 (or its successor circulars) has long since lost the prescriptive force of earlier years, and indeed is often now interpreted, however incorrectly, as meaning that such works are approved, and little more. At the same time, the prohibition mentioned effectively bars some of the province's greatest expertise from contributing to Canadian publishing, while the pressure from foreign-written books continues, even against some resistance. We think that curriculum officials whose function it is to recommend or approve books for listing or for use must continue to be barred from considering or reporting on their own publications because of the conflict of interests which obviously would occur, but beyond this we would favour a revision in the policy in order to remove a disability now imposed not only on many highly qualified authors, but on original Canadian book publishing.

31. We recommend that the Ontario Institute for Studies in Education adopt as one of its important program objectives the development and evaluation of Canadian learning materials, and that in so far as may be practicable (without compromising the quality of the research responsibilities involved) it accomplish this in close cooperation with the Ministry of Education and in liaison with the publishers concerned. Nothing in this recommendation is intended to comment adversely on the quality or importance of recent programs of the Institute. Rather, we wish to stress how important we believe it is that Canadian publishing should be relieved of the oft-cited disabilities pertaining to research and testing of new works under development in comparison with the extensive public and private research and testing facilities to which foreign educational publications have access, especially in the United States. It is because we believe that no finer facilities for this purpose are available anywhere in North America than in the Ontario Institute for

Studies in Education that we advocate the judicious encouragement of a more relevant relationship between the Institute and Canadian book publishing programs, coordinated if necessary by the appropriate ministry. In advancing this recommendation, we believe we are sufficiently cognizant of the dangers of directing research, especially in areas where results may depend upon critical evaluation and where creativity among research scholars can be as important as it is in the field which concerns this Commission – Canadian writing and publishing.

32. We recommend that teacher-training institutions provide special training in the evaluation of learning materials, and particularly in the selection of books for educational resource centres (school libraries), giving special attention to such skills as assessing the adequacy of presentation of Canadian points of view as explained in Chapter 5. We further recommend that this special training aim at providing insights into the writing and publishing processes as well as into the principles of selection, with a view to encouraging wider participation, including experimental participation, in the creative development of new Canadian learning materials. The value of visits to and from editors and manufacturers engaged in educational publishing should not be overlooked.

33. We recommend that the Board develop guidelines and procedures whereby applications for partial defrayal of research and development costs of selected book projects (only) proposed by Ontario-based, Canadian-owned educational book publishers may be considered, within budgetary limits, in advance of their being undertaken. This should be done with careful regard for priorities of educational publishing requirements as the latter may be established from time to time by the Curriculum Development Branch of the Ministry of Education, as well as for the demonstrated competence of the authors and publishers concerned. (See also Recommendations 2, 40 and 45.) It is assumed that where such programs may require the commissioning of special illustrations or book design services these would be assigned to Canadian illustrators and designers. Apart from the encouragement that would thus be given to original Canadian publishing, reductions in development costs achieved in this way should be reflected in appropriate reductions in the prices of books so assisted – at least in Ontario.

34. We recommend that a proposal be made by the Minister of Education to the Council of Ministers of Education that a national survey of Canadian educational research and development programs in progress and planned be undertaken to determine whether and how these relate to future needs for new Canadian learning materials. We further recommend that the Board should coordinate continuing review of this kind in Ontario.

35. The Commission recognizes that Franco-Ontarian pupils are doubly disadvantaged in the matter of Canadian classroom books, and therefore makes the following recommendations:

(a) The greatest possible variety of separate sections should be incorporated in Circular 14 (or its successor) designed to meet, and to encourage publishers to meet, the needs of Franco-Ontarian schools at all levels.

(b) The Correspondence Courses Branch of the Ministry of Education should offer courses in French, supported by French-language textbooks, in so far as and as soon as practicable, it being recognized that this recommendation is not the kind that can be fully implemented immediately.

(c) Special attention should be given in the paid leaves-of-absence proposal (recommended separately) to selecting some teachers and officials who may be competent and willing to prepare French-language teaching materials, preference to be given to areas where these are needed most.

(d) The resegregation of stimulation grants for the purchase of approved books for classroom and resource centre use, as recommended elsewhere, should contain an appropriate upgrading in the measure of support in the case of Franco-Ontarian pupils, at least for a period of time. This would be in recognition of the special market limitations on original publishing in this area.

(e) Special research and development grants of the kind referred to in Recommendation 33 should be made available to all Ontario-based publishers in this field, within approved budgetary limits.

(f) There should be a wider recognition that English-French translation may not in itself always result in the ideal classroom book.

(g) Consideration should be given, especially by the Board, to the export possibilities of future Franco-Ontarian publishing, even to other provinces.

(h) Although the Commission does not consider most proposals to bring about interprovincial standardization of curricula to be realistic, for reasons discussed in the text, there are particular areas where continued efforts to achieve closer cooperation of this kind might be amply justified. Included might be closer cooperation with other provinces where a substantial minority group is French-speaking, respecting Canadian books for francophone pupils.

36. The Commission reiterates its view that it is not the proper body to make judgments on purely professional questions concerning the philosphy of curriculum development. Nevertheless, it wishes to express some apprehension regarding the possible adverse effects of unnecessary and avoidable proliferation of courses, expecially where these presuppose the availability of multiple choices of as yet unwritten Canadian materials. For reasons related only to markets, such assumptions by curriculum planners

may not always be realistic. Consequently, we recommend that where the introduction of new courses (e.g. under H.S.1) anticipates that new Canadian books will be produced, there should be advance investigation to ensure that they will indeed be written and can be published, and we recommend that the Ministry of Education plan and encourage such investigation.

37. With further reference to the introduction of new courses, we recommend that the Ministry of Education seek to permit more lead time for the preparation of text materials for new courses, in so far as this may be practicable. The Commission recognizes that in some respects all courses must be regarded as experimental, and that there may often be advantages in announcing new courses somewhat in advance of the time that they can be widely adopted. But to the extent that available materials still tend to structure courses, to some degree at least, it is desirable that both the Curriculum Development Branch and interested Canadian publishers appraise in advance the markets that will possibly be created, and that there always be adequate consultation between them before unnecessary commitments or assumptions are made. Nothing in this recommendation is intended to abridge the right of the Curriculum Development Branch to defer approval of new books until they have been published; rather, it is intended to encourage more liaison between this Branch and publishers at an earlier stage than at present, i.e. during the curriculum planning stage rather than the manuscript preparation stage. In the main, the Commission commends the degree of cooperation which the Curriculm Development Branch already extends to publishers who have new books in preparation, which it considers compares favourably with that extended by provincial and state educational authorities anywhere else in the world.

38. We recommend that educational institutions seek ways and means whereby Canadian authors, artists, book designers, editors, and other creative people closely connected with book publishing may be brought into contact with school pupils at every level. The Board should be expected to play a coordinating role in this process, possibly working through the Canadian Book Centre in Ontario after the latter has been established. This program should, where practicable, be extended to include representatives of other branches of the Canadian book industry, e.g. booksellers, book manufacturers, and certainly professional librarians possessing special training or experience in connection with children's books.

39. Because of the greater economies of scale which can be realized by publishers operating from bases abroad, and for other reasons discussed in Chapters 1, 2, and 4, the Commission recommends that educational institu-

tions and boards of education in this province recognize that a certain premium in price may have to be paid for some Canadian learning materials in the future, especially where the content of these precludes their being sold extensively in other markets. The Commission finds that for many years Canadian-written and Canadian-published materials have been made available at prices that compare favourably with prices of equivalent foreign materials, but as explained in the text of the report, book selection trends are affecting the domestic market in a way that makes it likely that this situation will change. Many of the Commission's other recommendations are aimed at minimizing unfavourable price differentials between domestic and foreign books in the future as well as with making Canadian publication possible, and we recommend that the Board be concerned with seeing that both these purposes are realized to the greatest possible degree.

40. We recommend a program of title grants, to be available to Ontario-based, Canadian-owned publishers, to encourage the production of needed Canadian books of serious non-fiction, especially but not exclusively in non-profitable publishing areas, to be administered by the Board in consultation with (and quite possibly within) the Ministry of Education. This program should be aimed primarily at encouraging the publication of books intended for educational use, and should not embrace works of popular non-fiction. (See also Recommendations 33 and 45.) It is distinct from the program of title grants intended to encourage publications not primarily intended for use in schools (see Recommendation 2).

41. We recommend that the Ministry of Education, in collaboration with boards of education, establish and coordinate professional observation courses related to teaching situations, in addition to discussion seminars, for textbook writers and textbook publishers. These should be designed with sufficient flexibility that publishers interested in particular fields might arrange for their editors and/or authors to pursue a series of observation classes and to discuss principles and methods with teachers and appropriate officials of teachers' colleges and colleges of education. Obviously great care would have to be exercised to guard against disrupting normal teaching routines, and to keep observers to a minimum. This should be done by planning such programs well in advance, and by carefully selecting applicants for enrolment; guidelines would have to be established governing such matters, and they should be adhered to. Such a program should be rigorously restricted to professional development and editorial research, and avoid any kind of direct commercialization. But carefully conceived, we believe that an official program of this kind could yield dividends to

Canadian education and to Canadian publishing of a kind that would be unique in the western world.

42. We recommend that the policy of Canadian preference regarding authorship and manufacture in relation to Circulars 14, 15, or new central lists of approved books, should be extended to require Canadian book illustration, art, and design as well, in so far as this may be practicable. As we have tried to make clear with regard to authors, nothing in this recommendation is intended to restrict study of the work of foreign illustrators, artists, or designers in any way.

43. We recommend that the Board include in its budget a program of title grants designed to encourage the publication of books dealing with or written by Canada's native peoples, including classroom books which serve desired curricular objectives from the perspective of Indians and Eskimos.

44. We recommend that the Minister of Education, acting possibly through the Council of Ministers, endeavour to enlist the cooperation of other provinces in seeking the establishment of a national office of educational research which would furnish, through named provincial bodies, special funds for the research and development of Canadian classroom books which would adequately reflect the regional as well as the national interests of this country. The terms under which such an office might be established should of course be drawn with full regard for constitutional considerations.

45. We recommend that the Board, acting in consultation with or under the jurisdiction of the Ministry of Education, be empowered to entertain three-way joint applications from boards of eduction, author-educationists, and publishers, requesting grants of at least one-quarter salary for periods up to one year for completion of educational book manuscripts, subject to guidelines to be established from time to time. Such grants should neither preclude royalty arrangements nor make publication mandatory, although the Board should count worthwhile publications as a measure of the success of this program. Book plan outlines, authorship experience, and budgetary limitations would be important factors in judging such applications. It would be the expectation that the board of education concerned might make an equal grant as part of the leave-of-absence arrangement, and that a similar additional allowance – perhaps as an advance on future royalties – might be made by the publisher. In this way, up to three-quarters of normal income could be assured the author, who would be in

a position to speculate on other possible professional and economic benefits in the future. A similar program should be developed to serve the textbook needs of Colleges of Applied Arts and Technology, but we do not recommend this kind of program of support for authors of textbooks at the university level. (See also Recommendations 2, 33 and 40.)

46. We recommend that Circulars 14 and 15, or their successor list of approved classroom books, be published in seasonal instalments, preferably four times a year (although not necessarily quarterly), one of which would be the consolidated cumulative edition.

47. One of our most important recommendations is aimed at enhancing the status of educational books listed in Circular 14 (as well as in Circular 15), the overwhelming majority of which are of Canadian origin. At the same time we recognize the desirability of admitting more flexibility in book selection in special situations, e.g. where no satisfactory Canadian books have yet been developed. We think this flexibility need not be greater than it is already assumed to be in many quarters (however incorrectly). We therefore favour amending the regulations so that they may relate reasonably to all situations, and then be complied with fully, in spirit as well as fact. The following recommendation takes into account that many boards claim, with seeming justification, that they are now purchasing books to the same or to a greater dollar value than before the book stimulation grants were terminated and consolidated with the general educational grants at the end of 1968. However, this is not the situation for all boards. The recommendation also takes into account the serious overall impact which the termination of the stimulation grants program had on original Canadian publishing, for reasons discussed in detail in the text of our report. In the reconstituted program we are recommending, we also propose that an appropriate allowance be made for the substantial inflation that has occurred in book production costs since the former stimulation grants program was first introduced in 1951. Perhaps the most important feature of what we now bring forward as a central recommendation is the continued publication and full use of Circulars 14 and 15, albeit in a revised form and with an important new function. Moreover, we believe that the changes here proposed would best articulate the advantages, educational and cultural, of a provincial list of approved classroom books with the ever-expanding range of differing regional requirements that mark the recent evolution of curriculum everywhere, and in Ontario particularly.

We therefore recommend as follows:
(*a*) That the principle underlying the former book stimulation grants be re-introduced, in an appropriately modified form, to apply exclusively to

purchases of any books listed on the equivalent of either the present Circular 14 or Circular 15;

(b) That these stimulation grants be wholly funded by segregating their value, whether or not they are claimed and used as above indicated, from the general education grants which may be in force from time to time;

(c) That the value of the reconstituted book stimulation grants be based on an allowance per pupil of average daily enrolment, the amount to be determined from time to time by the Minister of Education in the light of the textbook and library book grant formulas in use from 1951 to 1968, but suitably corrected to take into account increased manufacturing costs as well as minimum Canadian book requirements throughout the province. On the basis of the costs reviewed in the text of this report, we are inclined to believe that the basic book stimulation grants formerly in use should be increased by approximately one hundred per cent;

(d) That the Minister of Education have the widest possible discretion in deciding whether or not the reconstituted book stimulation grants should include a provision for equalization grants as well; we are inclined to question whether the necessity for the latter is as compelling as it was before the establishment of larger units of administration;

(e) That Circulars 14 and 15 continue to be published, subject to the policy suggestions and observations contained elsewhere in the text of this report and in the adjoining recommendations (see Recommendations 35, 42, and 46), but that consideration be given to the advisability of consolidating these two Ministry publications within the covers of a single circular. (The other recommendations mentioned relate to desirable frequency of publication and the need for special regional emphases.) This would bring classroom books and library (resource centre) books together for the purposes of establishing grant eligibility only;

(f) That, subject to implementation of the preceding sections of this recommendation, the conditions restricting the use of unapproved textbooks set forth in the Schools Administration Act and in the related Regulation cited in Circular 14, as well as in the separate directives contained in Circular 14, be rescinded. The effect of this should be to translate Circulars 14 and 15 (possibly in a consolidated form) into a reference list of approved classroom and library books (preponderantly of Canadian origin), although the Circular 14 section would still serve its curricular function. All books listed in the consolidated circular would be eligible for book stimulation grants. It is not intended that implementation of this recommendation should require new funding; rather, it is designed to discourage Canadian classroom and library book purchases from becoming inadequate because of short-term economies at the regional level. At the same time, it is our purpose to eliminate a degree of blurring that has occurred between the definitions of textbooks and library or reference books, and to make possible the use of some books of foreign origin where suitable Canadian publications are not yet available; book stimulation grants would not be available for such purposes, however. It should be noted that we are not making a specific recommendation regarding how claims for reimbursement under the reconstituted stimulation grants program should be audited; this is a routine responsibility, which can be discharged today much more easily than was possible before the establishment of the larger units of administration.

GOVERNMENT PUBLISHING

48. With regard to government publishing in this province, we would generally endorse the recommendations contained in Interim Report Number Seven of the Committee on Government Productivity. This report, submitted in June, 1972, is discussed in Chapter 1, and calls for the discontinuation of a central publishing function (not to be confused with the printing function). However, to the extent that publishing programs will continue to be mounted in the individual ministries ("where publishing initiative, planning, decisions and accountability actually reside") we think that the existing Canadian-owned book publishing industry should be called on to provide such services wherever the market available and the facilities they offer are the most suitable. Especially when sales promotion is required, their services are likely to be superior to those available from government agencies, which necessarily must be concerned more often with the kinds of publications which require a distribution service rather than sales development.

49. We recommend that the Government of Ontario confirm to the federal government that it would be helpful to the Canadian book industry if the future publishing policies of Information Canada, or any publishing structure that may replace it (discussed in Chapter 1), could be soon clarified. In so far as practicable, we would like to see government publishing programs (including provincial programs) cooperate with existing Canadian-owned book publishing facilities by making maximum use of the latter. Areas in which clarification of future policies would be particularly helpful include pricing, discounts, advertising, retail credit, marketing plans, contractual relations with authors, selection and sources of manuscripts, the decision to publish, and relations generally with the Canadian book publishing industry.

50. We recommend that the Government of Ontario make representations to the federal government that the latter should review and in so far as possible

arrange to limit unfair competition with the Canadian book publishing industry posed by the book publishing (only) programs of the Canadian Broadcasting Corporation and the National Film Board, by urging that new efforts be made to integrate such activities with the book publishing industry along lines discussed in Chapter 1. There should also be representations that the copyrights of the CBC and the NFB, in so far as these bodies are able to administer the copyrights of works they produce, should be made more easily available to book publishers, it being understood that the interests of the creators should be fully protected under appropriate contracts for royalties or other payments.

COPYRIGHT AND PUBLISHING

Our reasons for offering recommendations in an area that is clearly in federal jurisdiction were set forth at the beginning of Chapter 3, and hardly require recapitulation here. Suffice it to say that the principal purpose of all copyright legislation must be to furnish continuing creative incentive, and in this we believe we are in accord with the Economic Council of Canada. However, when legislation regarding copyright, or regarding another field to which copyright is artificially joined, is enacted without regard for its impact on the incentive to create, the publishing industry loses coherence, and therefore its creative momentum. What is worse, the shortcomings of such ambiguous legislation will bear most heavily on that segment of publishing which is indigenous, and which lacks financial and editorial support of corporations located outside the country. For the reasons explained in Chapter 3, the Commission views with apprehension certain of the proposals and points of view expressed in the *Report on Intellectual and Industrial Property* issued by the Economic Council of Canada, as well as the implications of the inclusion of copyright in Bill C-256 (The Competition Act) and possibly, therefore, in its successor Bill in the future. In addition, changing circumstances have understandably necessitated many changes in the existing Copyright Act, and we feel obligated to deal specifically with some of these that have important implications for creative writing and publishing in Canada. Finally, it should be stressed that the recommendations respecting copyright which follow are addressed to the Government of Ontario for transmittal, at its discretion, to the appropriate authority representing the Government of Canada.

51. We reaffirm our belief that the quality of copyright protection carries social, cultural, and economic consequences for all Canada, and that it directly affects the books that will be written as well as the books that will be read in every province. We recommend therefore that any revision of the Copyright Act should take full account of the interests of Canadian authorship

and Canadian-owned book publishing, as well as of the Canadian consumer, noting that the long-term cultural interests of the latter will best be served by the survival and strengthening of the former. It is especially important, in the view of this Commission, that publication in Canada should carry with it no disabilities for the author, regardless of his country of citizenship or domicile, that would not be attached to publication in the other principal publishing countries of the western world.

52. If Canadian publishing is to find an international market, it must become involved in co-publishing on an ever-expanding scale. This will involve the buying and selling of territorial rights, which are the life-blood of international publishing. For the reasons set forth in Chapter 3, we recommend that no revision be made in the Copyright Act which would further restrict the ability of Canadian publishers to buy, sell, and license territorial rights, and to protect the copyright in the regional editions which such international publishing arrangements thus make possible. Specifically, no revision of the Copyright Act should have the effect of making lawful the importation into Canada of copies of copyright works where copies of an edition specially printed or bound for sale in Canada with the permission of the copyright owner are available in this country.

53. The procedure under Section 27 of the Copyright Act whereby the owner of the copyright may give notice "that he is desirous that such copies should not be ... imported" and whereby they are thereupon included in Schedule C to the Customs Tariff has been applied in a way that makes it unworkable in practice, and we think this should be reviewed and clarified. It is particularly important that co-publishing arrangements respecting individual titles be adequately protected against the kind of competition by importation which could limit the ability of Canadian publishers to participate in the publication of regional editions either abroad or in this country, for the reasons we have outlined in Chapter 3.

54. We commend the proposal of the Economic Council of Canada to recognize format copyright, but we think it would be desirable to extend the lifetime of such copyright sufficiently to permit recovery of costs in average situations, including those involving large and expensive original works. For these and for other reasons outlined in Chapter 3 we would recommend that format copyright endure for a term of twenty-five years.

55. Although the doctrine of fair dealing should not be limited in any way, Canadian copyright protection should not be qualified merely because the unauthorized use may be in such non-profit fields as research and education. As explained in Chapter 3, this recommendation is not intended to limit the

right of access, which indeed might well be facilitated by statute in various ways, with provision for fair compensation where the long-established limits of fair dealing must be exceeded. What must be ensured is that no disability comes to be placed on large areas of original writing and publishing in Canada.

56. We would favour a wide-ranging, federally sponsored program of research studies into photocopying practices in which specialists representing all the fields affected could be directly involved and adequately represented – specialists, that is, in the art of writing, publishing, manufacturing, bookselling, librarianship, as well as law and economics.

57. Over and beyond copying that involves fair dealing, which we believe can be and has been generously interpreted from the standpoint of copyists, a very large amount of unauthorized copying of a kind which should not be characterized as fair dealing is being done, probably reaching many millions of copies per year. We believe that this should be paid for, without adding to public inconvenience, and that the Copyright Act should be amended to ensure that it is. Nor would it be in the interests of Canadian authors if publishers were not entitled to receive such payments where the publishing contracts provide that they should; under the latter, they normally share subsidiary income with their authors. We are speaking here of revenues lost from the *Canadian book market* (not including copying done in the course of fair dealing, as already noted), and this is an area of joint concern for Canadian publishers and Canadian authors, as well as for the Canadian public itself.

58. We recommend that the federal government be earnestly requested by the provincial government to keep under continuing review the advisability of following any clear leads given by such countries as Great Britain and the United States with regard to embedding a public lending right in the copyright law, although for the reasons outlined in Chapter 3 we consider that unilateral action in this direction by Canada would be premature at the present time.

59. We consider that the manufacturing provisions contained in the United States Copyright Law impose wholly unjustifiable disabilities on the book manufacturing and publishing industries of this province and this country. This imbalance must not continue indefinitely to be shielded by international copyright agreements which contain exceptions and conditions that are not mutual. If present hopes for relief are not realized, public opinion can be expected to demand it, provided that it is adequately and accurately informed. We believe that it would be in the interests of all segments of book publishing and book manufacturing in this country, as well as of the Canadian

public, if the federal government could ensure that the public is adequately and accurately informed on this subject, if the hoped-for relief is much longer delayed.

60. We recommend that the provincial government urge the federal government to adhere to its present policy of deferring ratification of the Florence Agreement until an exemption for Canada from all manufacturing provisions in the United States Copyright Law has actually been achieved. This recommendation is made in the context of the Agreement of Toronto, reviewed at page 151 ff. in the *Background Papers* of this Commission (Queen's Printer and Publisher, Ontario, 1972).

61. We think that it would be in the interest of all concerned with Canadian writing and publishing if the Copyright Act were revised to extend the statutory definition of publication to include the authorized exposure to the public of even one copy of a manuscript continuously over a period of time. Some of the advantages of such a re-definition of publication are set forth in Chapter 3.

62. We concur with the view of the Economic Council of Canada that a system of statutory registration of copyright, presumably relating only to works by Canadian authors and domiciliaries, be incorporated in the Copyright Act. We believe that assignments of such copyrights should be registered in the same way. In so far as may be practicable, such registration might include identification of the work by International Standard Book Number (ISBN). It is assumed that deposit of copies for this purpose would not be required, and that the statutory deposit copies already furnished to the National Library would be sufficient.

63. We recommend that the International Standard Book Number (ISBN) system be given statutory recognition, that its use on all works first published or co-published in Canada be made mandatory, and that the administration of the system be assumed by the federal government at the earliest possible date, e.g. by the National Library or by the Copyright Office. In so far as possible, however, such an adoption by government should be planned to interfere with the existing register and accessibility of ISBNs to the least extent possible.

64. We believe that Section 2 of the Copyright Act should be amended to broaden the definition of a "work" to include speeches, lectures, and interviews whether or not these exist in manuscript form, so long as their form is tangible, e.g. a sound recording made by anyone. Section 3(2) of the Act should also be revised to extend the meaning of "publication" to include creative works of the kind just mentioned.

65. We would recommend that Section 14 of the Copyright Act not be rescinded, for the reasons set forth in Chapter 3.

66. We recommend that Sections 7 and 12(5) of the Copyright Act be rescinded, for the reasons given in Chapter 3.

67. We reiterate our belief that it is in the interests of Canadian authorship and Canadian publishing for this country to participate in and to support the principal international agreements on copyright, viz. the Universal Copyright Convention and the Berne Union. In the latter regard it is noted that Canada has remained a member of the Berne Union at the Rome level of 1928. We recommend that Canada favourably consider ratifying the Berne Union at the level of the Paris Act of 1971.

68. For the reasons set forth in Chapter 3, we are strongly of the opinion that neither federal Bill C-256 (now withdrawn for re-introduction later) nor any successor Bill respecting monopolies should contain any reference to copyright as such, and that the rights and privileges of copyright should be defined in the Copyright Act, amended as may be necessary, and nowhere else.

69. This Commission would favour the establishment of a government-sponsored copyright research organization (necessarily federally sponsored) on whose council all interested bodies could be represented alongside government, but which would not answer to any special interests in the conduct of its research or in the publication of its findings. We do not believe that such a program of research can adequately consider all aspects of copyright unless the practical problems and advice of those who create, publish, deal in, and lend books can be fully taken into account. We believe that such a research organization should be as sensitive to the long-term cultural implications of copyright as to the economic ones, and its terms of reference should be explicit on this point.

COSTS AND FUNDING

As explained at the beginning of this chapter, we have couched most of our recommendations up to this point in general terms in order to permit flexibility in their implementation, and have refrained from proposing either budgetary dimensions for each program or detailed guidelines concerning how they should be administered. But it has of course been necessary for us to rationalize our recommendations from a budgetary standpoint, both with respect to the cost of implementing them and the ways in which this cost might be funded most logically and most easily. To do this, we must set forth suggested ranges of financial support which we think should be given to the programs themselves, i.e. to those whose implementation would represent *added* costs to the province. (For example, resegregation of book stimulation grants from other educational grant funds does not.)

In presenting these budgetary figures, we wish to reiterate that they represent only what we think should be minimal programs under the headings indicated. If additional funds can be generated, either in the manner we shall propose or in some other way, it would be desirable for some of these programs to be substantially enlarged, on a selective basis, with the advice of the Board (which would itself be the first fruit of the recommendations made in this chapter). In the course of devising and developing the recommendations that are presented here, the Commission has already rejected many interesting programs simply on the ground that they would be unduly expensive, or do not stand up well to an analysis of their probable costs and possible benefits. For this reason, and because we do not believe that any of the programs we are recommending could yield meaningful results if they were conducted on more limited scales than we are proposing, we consider that the budget of support now being put forward is minimal, and that any important changes should be in the direction of increasing it rather than reducing it. Apart from the fact that we shall also suggest special sources for the necessary funding, we think that the total annual investment we recommend is a modest price to pay to conserve so fundamental a cultural capacity as that of being able to ensure a continuing flow of Canadian-written, Canadian-produced books to our schools and homes. In short, the programs we propose are intended to ensure the continued health of Canada's indigenous publishing industry, as it is represented in this province. We are satisfied that if this support is not given, then for the reasons discussed in the preceding chapters, book publishing as a purely Canadian enterprise will continue to become weaker and less important, both relatively and absolutely. That part of it which might survive would chiefly be concerned with issuing regional books, on a limited scale, to regional markets, and any thought of this country developing a national book publishing industry by which it would be known throughout the world could well be forgotten.

Subject then to the considerations just outlined, as well as to those set forth throughout the earlier chapters of this report, we think that a minimum annual budget for new costs resulting from the programs now being recommended would break down as follows:

RECOMMENDATION NUMBER	RE	BUDGET
1	Administrative overhead of Board	$ 150,000
2	Title grants re manuscripts not primarily intended for use in schools	150,000
3	Canadiana reprint program	25,000
4	Ontario literary awards	20,000

6	Royalties insurance program	20,000
8	Professional consultative services to industry	20,000
9	Support of literary review media	25,000
13	Ontario House library project	10,000
15	Librarian-bookstore consultation services in smaller centres	30,000
16	Library retailing pending establishment of bookstore in community	30,000
20	Assistance to consolidate non-competitive marketing functions	15,000
21	Canadian Book Centre for Ontario	100,000
22	Travelling displays project	50,000
24	Market surveys assistance	35,000
33	Partial defrayal of R & D costs on selected book projects	125,000
40	Title grants for educational manuscripts	100,000
43	Title grants for books by and about Canada's native peoples	25,000
45	Leaves-of-absence assistance program	70,000
	TOTAL	$1,000,000

Although this Commission's concern has been primarily with book publishing, its terms of reference were broad and have already carried it into the field of periodical publishing, particularly in connection with the distribution of magazines in Ontario; two of our interim reports were devoted to this subject. Although we do not wish to retread the ground of either the O'Leary Commission or the Davey Committee, there are aspects of the mix of periodical literature that circulates in Canada which have far-reaching cultural implications for our community, and for the Canadian book publishing industry in particular.

As every Canadian realizes, and as the statistics of magazine distribution included in the Appendix corroborate, the overwhelming majority of periodicals circulating in this country and in this province are imported. Most of these are both edited and manufactured abroad; however, in two special cases their contents are principally written outside Canada but manufacture occurs here. The imbalance continues, notwithstanding attempts to redress it through federal legislation respecting the claiming of advertising expenses and the right to import, although there can be no doubt that these measures helped to alleviate a deteriorating situation. In all its investigations of the sources and methods of distribution of magazines in Ontario, this Commission was constantly confronted by the fact that it was dealing in the main with imported material, and only to a limited degree with the editorial products of Canadian-owned publishers. We were naturally concerned with the cultural consequences of this, a point we emphasized in our interim reports regarding the distribution of paperbacks through the same channels. It was adequately demonstrated long before this Commission was appointed that, in magazine publishing, imported reading material has tended to stifle the development and publishing of Canadian writing. Much of this report has been concerned with the interaction between imported and indigenous books in the domestic market, and what we have concluded is that the effect is much the same.

We do not propose to offer new solutions to the cultural threat posed by imported periodical literature, but we do take the position that its continued expansion should not be sheltered in this province by special tax concessions of any kind. Yet Section 5 of *The Retail Sales Tax Act* (Ontario), exempts from tax most kinds of books, all newspapers, and all magazines and periodicals. Excluded from the exemption regarding books are those which contain advertising, directories, price lists, time tables, rate books, catalogues, reports, fashion books, albums and other similar works. It would probably be unconstitutional, and certainly it would be undesirable in our opinion, for the province to revise the exemptions for any of these classes on the basis of country of origin of the goods themselves, as this would be tantamount to imposing an import tariff; it would also discriminate between im-

COMPARATIVE CIRCULATIONS AND COSTS OF MAGAZINES, 1962-1971

		1962			1971	
		Circulation	Circulation		Circulation	Circulation
	Cover	per issue	per issue	Cover	per issue	per issue
Magazine	price	in Canada	in Ontario	price	in Canada	in Ontario
Better Homes and Gardens	35¢	174,715	100,222	50¢	114,011	59,658
Chatelaine	15¢	810,709	370,923	50¢	967,958	443,866
Cosmopolitan	35¢	60,312	26,507	75¢	87,881	41,071
Good Housekeeping	35¢ }	185,804	89,784	60¢	186,845	96,144
(Oct.)	50¢					
Ladies' Home Journal	35¢	244,755	108,940	50¢	166,488	81,581
Maclean's	15¢	522,409	216,421	50¢	747,934	349,514
McCall's	35¢ }	257,038	124,335	60¢	168,270	81,651
(Aug.)	50¢					
Popular Mechanics	35¢	67,817	30,660	50¢	77,252	35,302
Reader's Digest	35¢	918,746	404,917	60¢	1,213,080	564,259
Redbook	35¢	239,643	110,162	75¢	134,076	60,359
Saturday Night	20¢	78,837	44,596	50¢	96,286	43,098
Time	25¢	255,834	103,159	50¢	510,406	215,616
TV Guide	15¢	477,294	373,333	25¢	913,475	604,448

Sources: Magazine Association of Canada and Audit Bureau of Circulation. 1962 figures for Better Homes and Gardens, Cosmopolitan, Good Housekeeping, Ladies' Home Journal, McCall's, Popular Mechanics, Redbook and TV Guide were supplied on request by those companies.

ported and domestic reading matter on a basis other than quality or educational suitability. As we said earlier, we believe that Canadian publishing should be assisted, but not by putting foreign publishing down, and least of all by placing any kind of trading restrictions on it.

However, the withdrawal of the sales tax exemption on all magazines (but not on books or newspapers) would be a different matter, and this is a step which the Commission strongly favours in principle, subject only to practical considerations related to administration and collecting the substantial additional revenues that would thereby be provided. To begin with, we do not believe that circulations would be adversely impaired if retail sales tax were collected; in so far as cost of collection is concerned, most magazine sales other than those made in response to mail-order subscription are made by retailers who are accustomed to collecting retail sales tax on a large proportion of the merchandise they sell, and from the same customers as buy magazines. The accompanying table showing comparative sales of a random selection of magazines over a ten-year period indicates that the price increases during that time have not impeded circulation development. Nor, in our view, would the withdrawal of the existing sales tax exemption for such merchandise, which for the most part has a recreational purpose.

On the other hand, the question of collecting sales tax on sales of magazines to subscribers by mail raises administrative questions which warrant careful study before policy is determined. It should be noted, however, that the sales tax revenue from retail sales only would be substantial – between $800,000 and $900,000 annually according to the most precise estimates we have been able to make. If both subscription and single copy sales of magazines were made subject to sales tax, the tax would be based on an estimated retail sales value of approximately $35,035,000 annually, which at the present tax rate of five per cent (and disregarding separate sales of magazines priced at 20 cents each or less) would yield a theoretical tax revenue of over $1,750,000. We recognize, of course, that there could be practical problems of enforcement with respect to subscriptions ordered by mail from suppliers outside the province, and that this would account for a substantial proportion of this kind of magazine sale. (See "Analysis of Magazine Sales in Ontario" in Appendix.)

It might be useful at this point to consider the practice elsewhere in Canada with respect to the imposition of sales tax on magazines. General sales tax rates in other provinces range from five per cent to eight per cent, with the exception of Alberta where no sales tax has yet been put into effect. (The Ontario rate is five per cent except for admissions to amusement shows, for meals costing over $2.50, and for liquor, which carry a rate of ten per cent.) Newspapers are exempt from tax in every province except Newfoundland (which does not, however, impose a sales tax on newspapers published within the province; at the same time the minimum sale subject to Newfoundland sales tax is 8 cents.) Books are non-taxable in all provinces except Prince Edward Island, Newfoundland and Saskatchewan, where most approved textbooks are tax exempt, notwithstanding. However, magazines and periodicals, apart from newspapers, are taxable in New Brunswick, Nova Scotia, Saskatchewan, Prince Edward Island, and Newfoundland (the exception re newspapers in the last province has already been noted). They are exempt from tax in Manitoba, British Columbia, and Quebec. Interestingly, Nova Scotia, New Brunswick and Saskatchewan specify that magazines and periodicals purchased by subscription for delivery by mail are exempt from tax, but are taxable when purchased from a newsstand. It is significant, perhaps, that some provinces have found such a provision desirable, while others have not.

An additional source of funds available to implement the programs recommended in this report has already been budgeted by the province for assistance to book publishing. We refer to the interchange of correspondence between this Commission and the Ontario Arts Council, reported in the introduction to this chapter. Although the segment of the Council's budget set aside for assistance to the literary arts was only 5.44 per cent of the value of all its grants budgeted for 1972, it nevertheless amounted to $134,666. Together with the additional revenue that might reasonably be expected from a removal of the exemption from sales tax for magazines, the financial resources available would be adequate to meet the costs of implementing the programs proposed in this report at the minimal levels recommended. Depending on the extent of the exemption that might continue to be extended to magazine sales, e.g. subscription sales, it might be possible to extend these programs significantly. We believe that if this could be done, the cultural dividends would make it a sound public investment.

There are, of course, alternative sources of revenue that could be turned to in order to help fund the recommended programs. We shall mention two that we have studied at some length; although we do not ourselves give them equal priority with those already proposed, we refer to them here because it is possible that the government might wish to explore them further. First, it would be possible to establish a substantial fee for geographical wholesalers licensed under *The Paperback and Periodical Distributors Act, 1971*. But there would be a very real likelihood that this would merely be converted into the equivalent of a sales tax by an increase in wholesale and therefore in retail prices of both magazines and, unfortunately, paperbacks as well. It is our view that under no circumstances should a tax be added, either directly or indirectly, to the cost of books to the consumer, wherever they may originate – and we are anxious that wholesalers should have increased rather than decreased incentive to handle Canadian paperbacks.

Thought has also been given to the advisability of licensing the manufacturers and distributors of photocopying equipment and supplies, having regard for the fact that such processes necessarily affect the market for books adversely, although the degree of interference thus caused has yet to be accurately measured. There is a prima facie case to be made, perhaps, for funding needed programs of assistance to book publishing from the profits of such operations, even if the charges for the latter increased slightly as a result. The difficulty, however, of course lies in the fact that copyright is inextricably involved, that this is a federal jurisdiction, and that any system of licensing might be interpreted by users as a licence to infringe copyright without restriction. We have mentioned these alternative possible sources of revenue for the purposes described in this report not to recommend them, but to indicate that they have been explored.

We have one final concern regarding the removal of the sales tax exemption from magazines, which we have recommended, but it can easily be satisfied. In the event that both subscription sales of magazines as well as retail single copy sales were made subject to normal retail sales tax, a small proportion of the added cost would have to be borne by Canadian magazines and periodicals, other than newspapers (and other than magazines priced at 20 cents or less). The most reliable figures we have been able to procure indicate that of a total dollar value of magazine subscriptions and single copy sales in Ontario in 1971 of $45,932,235, only $3,609,277 (7.85 per cent) represented sales of Canadian magazines. (*Time*, *Reader's Digest* and *Sélection du Reader's Digest* are not included as Canadian magazines in this context.)

Even so, the interests of some important Canadian "little" magazines with a high cultural value could be adversely affected, however slightly. These would include literary, art, and academic journals, sometimes highly specialized, whose financing is already marginal; it would be counter-productive to force any of these to cut back further, much less to discontinue altogether. Therefore we suggest (we do not offer it as a formal recommendation, because of the contingent nature of the problem) that the Ontario Book Publishing Board be authorized to develop a special program of support for such journals if their interests were shown to be adversely affected by the removal of any sales tax exemptions under Recommendation 70, which we now are making:

70. We recommend that the exemption from retail sales tax extended to magazines and periodicals by Item 46 of Section 5(1) of *The Retail Sales Tax Act* (Ontario) be rescinded for the reasons and subject to the considerations set forth in the immediately preceding paragraphs of this report.

Appendix

FIRST INTERIM REPORT · MARCH 23, 1971

LETTER OF TRANSMITTAL

To His Honour,
The Lieutenant Governor of Ontario.

May It Please Your Honour,

We, the undersigned, Richard Heath Rohmer, Q.C., Dalton Kingsley Camp, and Marsh Jeanneret appointed Commissioners by Order-in-Council OC-3991/70 pursuant to the provisions of The Public Inquiries Act, R.S.O. 1960, c. 323, and approved by Your Honour on the 23rd day of December, 1970 to inquire into and report upon:

(*a*) the publishing industry in Ontario and throughout Canada with respect to its position within the business community;

(*b*) the functions of the publishing industry in terms of its contributions to the cultural life and education of the people of the Province of Ontario and Canada;

(*c*) the economic, cultural, social or other consequences for the people of Ontario and of Canada of the substantial ownership or control of publishing firms by foreign or foreign-owned or foreign-controlled corporations or by non-Canadians

beg to submit to Your Honour the following Interim Report.

RICHARD ROHMER	DALTON CAMP	MARSH JEANNERET
Commissioner	*Commissioner*	*Commissioner*

23rd March, 1971

FIRST INTERIM REPORT

It has been apparent from the outset of the Commission's inquiry at the beginning of January that Canadian book publishing is an industry which is of major importance in creating that sense of identity, political, historical, and cultural, which is Canadianism. Moreover, English-language book publishing in this country is preponderantly an Ontario industry, and this Province therefore has a special responsibility to nurture and encourage it.

A striking consequence follows from the fact that on the one hand the contribution to the gross national product made by book publishing is relatively unimportant while on the other its cultural importance to the nation is substantial. Not only does every fluctuation in the economic health of publishing thus bear on the Canadian public interest, but even minimal degrees of help or hindrance to the industry can have an important impact on our national well-being. For the same reason, adverse business factors can be offset by public assistance at much less expense in the book industry than in other depressed areas of the economy. That the development of the book publishing industry can be stimulated, effectively and properly, by carefully planned economic assistance has long been recognized elsewhere, and we are of the opinion that situations may arise in our own book industry which justify similar assistance from the Province of Ontario, acting alone or in concert with federal agencies. We further believe that such a situation has arisen recently and that it is of such importance and urgency that it requires special consideration at this early stage in the work of the Commission.

The situation to which we refer is that of the proposed sale of McClelland and Stewart Limited, one of Ontario's and Canada's major Canadian owned book publishing firms.

The president and principal shareholder of McClelland and Stewart Limited, Mr. Jack McClelland, recently announced his intention to sell his shares in that Company because of its and his inability to raise sufficient capital to continue in business. In his announcement Mr. Clelland also indicated that he might sell to foreign interests. He has recently notified the Commission that he has opened negotiations with American sources.

Immediately after Mr. McClelland made the public announcement of his intention to sell, the Commission met with him at which time Mr. McClelland agreed to provide to the Commission information concerning the current financial status of his Company. Financial statements of McClelland and Stewart Limited and its associated companies were provided to the Commission on the 12th day of March, 1971.

By this time the Commission had retained as consultants Messrs. Clarkson, Gordon and Company, the Canadian firm of chartered accountants. They were asked to analyze these documents, to meet with officials of McClelland and Stewart

Limited, and to report to the Commission on the financial condition of McClelland and Stewart Limited and its associated companies.

The consultants reported their findings to the Commission on March 15 at which time the principles set out in this interim report were formulated by the Commission. A copy of the report of Clarkson, Gordon and Company, which the Commission requests be kept confidential, is enclosed with this interim report.

There are two brief but significant statements in the Clarkson, Gordon report to which reference should be made.

The first is on page eleven:

It can be seen from a comparison of the current assets and the current liabilities ... that the Company is vulnerable to a petition in bankruptcy.

The second is on page twelve:

The Company is seriously undercapitalized and must obtain additional funds through the issue of capital stock in order to overcome its financial difficulties.

The Commission concurs with these statements and is of the view that such additional funds could not be obtained in Canada without the assistance of Government. Messrs. Clarkson, Gordon and Company have advised us that the requirement is approximately $1,000,000.

McClelland and Stewart represents an accumulated creative momentum in original Canadian publishing which could not quickly be replaced by other Canadian publishing enterprises should its program terminate or be sharply curtailed. We recognize the fact that part of the firm's present difficulties must be explained by the very scope of the program it has mounted, but that program is itself a national asset worthy of all reasonable public encouragement and support. The Commission is of the opinion that such encouragement and support, subject to prudent safeguards, should be offered at this time. In short, we believe it to be in the public interest that McClelland and Stewart should be preserved from bankruptcy if at all possible, and furthermore that it should not be permitted to be transferred to foreign ownership.

Therefore without prejudice to and without prejudging the final recommendations of the Commission at the conclusion of its deliberations some months from now the Commission deems it appropriate to make interim recommendations to the Government of Ontario concerning actions which it might initiate in order to ensure that McClelland and Stewart Limited remains in business and under Canadian control.

The Commission recommends to the Government of Ontario that the following steps be taken.

The Government of Ontario through the Ontario Development Corporation (o.d.c.) as its agent should offer to acquire from McClelland and Stewart Limited (the Company) ten year term convertible debentures issued by the Company in an amount not to exceed $961,645. which is the rounded equivalent of one third of its reported current assets ($2,884,930.) as at December 31st, 1970. The o.d.c. should satisfy itself as to the validity of the aforesaid current assets figure and in the event that it should be reduced then the amount of debentures to be acquired should be reduced proportionately.

The debentures so acquired would bear no interest during the first five years and low interest thereafter. They would be convertible at the option of the o.d.c. into treasury common shares in sufficient number to provide at the minimum control of the Company (i.e. more than 50%). The option to convert would be exerciseable at any time during the ten year term.

The security for the debentures would be negotiated to the satisfaction of the o.d.c. However, the debentures should rank ahead of all other security provided to present creditors.

The proceeds of the convertible debentures should not be used to retire the Company's indebtedness to the secured creditors or to relieve any guarantor of the Company's indebtedness from his or its obligations.

The membership of the Board of Directors of the Company should be reorganized so that one of the following alternatives might be achieved.

(*a*) There should be an odd number of directors and the o.d.c. and Mr. McClelland (with his associates) would each be entitled to appoint an equal number of directors; the directors so appointed would then select a chairman but not from among themselves; the chairman and all directors who are nominees of the o.d.c. should be provided with appropriate indemnities or,

(*b*) o.d.c. would have the right to elect an equal number of directors at any time but until the time of such election Mr. McClelland and his associates would be left in control of the Board.

It would be one of the more important duties of the Board to require that strict budgetary and financial controls be instituted and adhered to. Furthermore it is our opinion that the Board of Directors, however constituted, would be prudent if they were to engage a comptroller who would be directly responsible to the Board.

A further condition of the offer of the Government should be that Mr. McClelland would enter into a five year exclusive employment contract with the Company upon such terms and conditions as might be negotiated between the parties.

It follows that there should be no sale of common shares of the Company or rights thereto sufficient to dispose of control of the Company to a third party without prior agreement and consent of the o.d.c.

The proposals which we place before you should not be deemed to be inflexible and should not operate to prevent the sale of the shares of that Company to any other Canadian or Canadian controlled corporation, nor should it operate to prevent a Canadian public underwriting of the Company.

The Commission's recommendations should be considered to be an emergency measure and because the implications of our recommendations relate not only to Ontario but to the national interest as well we recommend that the Government of Canada be invited to participate to a substantial extent in the acquisition of the proposed debentures. In this connection it is appropriate to inform you that the Honorable Gérard Pelletier in a speech to a conference on publishing in Ottawa on Tuesday, March 2nd made the following observations in commenting on the problems of the Canadian book publishing industry:

Much will have to be done in cooperation with the provinces who, I am aware, are greatly concerned with the problem. The Government of Ontario has appointed a Royal Commission on Publishing problems... In order to find solutions, the efforts of all government bodies must be coordinated.

Although we are informed that the Federal Government as of the 23rd day of March, 1971 has advised McClelland and Stewart Limited that an Industrial Development Bank loan would not be available to the firm we believe that the Government of Canada is prepared to participate in working out a solution to the difficulties of McClelland and Stewart Limited.

The Commission recognizes that its function is merely advisory to the Government. Accordingly these recommendations are made in general terms with the details to be negotiated by the Government and the o.d.c. should the Government find that this interim report is acceptable.

In any event if circumstances require, the Commission is prepared to make a further interim report to the Government which would recommend legislation designed to prevent, among other things, the sale to foreign interests of any Canadian book publishing company operating in Ontario to foreign interests during the course of the Commission's deliberations and before its final report.

All of which is respectfully submitted.

SECOND INTERIM REPORT · JUNE 8, 1971

LETTER OF TRANSMITTAL

To His Honour,
The Lieutenant Governor of Ontario.

May It Please Your Honour,

We, the undersigned, Richard Heath Rohmer, Q.C., Dalton Kingsley Camp, and Marsh Jeanneret appointed Commissioners by Order-in-Council OC-3991/70 pursuant to the provisions of The Public Inquiries Act, R.S.O. 1960, c. 323, and approved by Your Honour on the 23rd day of December, 1970 to inquire into and report upon:

(*a*) the publishing industry in Ontario and throughout Canada with respect to its position within the business community;

(*b*) the functions of the publishing industry in terms of its contributions to the cultural life and education of the people of the Province of Ontario and Canada;

(*c*) the economic, cultural, social or other consequences for the people of Ontario and of Canada of the substantial ownership or control of publishing firms by foreign or foreign-owned or foreign-controlled corporations or by non-Canadians

beg to submit to Your Honour the enclosed Second Interim Report of the Commission.

RICHARD ROHMER   **DALTON CAMP**   **MARSH JEANNERET**
Commissioner   *Commissioner*   *Commissioner*

8th June, 1971

SECOND INTERIM REPORT

This Interim Report recommends, among other things, restrictions on the sale to non-residents of Canada of firms or corporations whose principal business in Ontario is the distribution or wholesaling of periodical publications. It is noted that the distribution of mass market paperback books is commonly associated with operations of this kind. It is obvious that periodical publications include magazines and may include newspapers.

Although book publishing has been the central concern of the Commission up to this time, it has been apparent since early in our inquiry that the writing, publication, and distribution of books must be considered in relation to the same activities with regard to other kinds of printed matter. It has been helpful therefore that our terms of reference have not restricted our investigation to book publishing only, but have required us, among other things, to

... conduct an examination of and report upon:

(a) the publishing industry in Ontario and throughout Canada with respect to its position within the business community; ...

(c) the economic, cultural, social or other consequences for the people of Ontario and of Canada of the substantial ownership or control of publishing firms by foreign or foreign-owned or foreign-controlled corporations or by non-Canadians.

As to the specific question of distribution of published printed matter, we have noted that those editions of books that are popularly known as "mass market paperbacks" normally reach Canadian customers from their original publishers through the identical supply channels used for most periodicals, including magazines and similar publications. It is not surprising that mass market paperbacks moving in this way tend in their selection to be no more representative of original Canadian authorship and publishing than are the magazines and other periodicals with which they travel. Indeed, the Canadian aspects of book publishing would appear to be poorly served by the news distribution channels just referred to.

Our preliminary investigation of this subject indicates that developments are taking place with respect to the ownership and control of the above channels of supply which fully warrant our submitting this second Interim Report to Your Honour. And for reasons which are referred to below, we attach considerable urgency to the recommendations it embodies.

The service of distributing periodical literature to consumer outlets in this Province is furnished almost exclusively by regional wholesalers, or news companies, each normally operating within a clearly defined geographical area. The retail outlets within each area are heavily dependent upon the regional news companies that supply their stock-in-trade, and in general they do not have access to alternative channels of supply. To the extent that they sell mass market paperbacks in addition to periodicals, they usually secure these books from the same sources. Even the selection of titles and authors to be displayed for sale is normally made by the news company as part of its service; moreover, the selection of titles which the latter may have to draw upon may be determined at an earlier stage in the distribution network, and determined not necessarily even in Canada.

It is obvious not only that the regional news companies thus exercise a substantial control over what publications, of all kinds, are or are not offered for sale by most Ontario retail outlets, but that any degree of common ownership of the news companies themselves could have a profound influence on the selection and sources of reading materials offered to the public in the future through newsstands, cigar stores, supermarkets, and similar retail outlets. A possible exception from such control would be bookstores (i.e. stores the principal business of which is the selling of books), the total number of which is regrettably small in any event. Clearly, any trend toward monopoly conditions of ownership or control of the regional news companies would be contrary to the public interest, inviting as it would attempts to influence terms of supply, including conditions of price, discount, source, and conceivably even content. And if such monopoly power should ever come to be vested in non-Canadian hands, the threat to the public interest would clearly be rendered correspondingly more grave.

The Commission has been informed that there is in process of development at this moment just such a threat of monopoly, one which appears to have as its objective unified ownership or control of most of, if not all, the regional news companies in Ontario, and moreover, ownership or control by a foreign interest. Specifically, we have evidence that a concerted effort is under way on the part of one or more non-Canadian individuals or corporations engaged in the wholesaling and distribution of periodicals and mass market paperback books to gain control of the principal distributors or wholesalers of similar merchandise in Ontario and possibly elsewhere in Canada.

If such an effort is successful, any cultural intention this country may have to further the interests of its own authors and of its book and periodical publishing industries will be largely thwarted. At best it will be dependent on such token support as the foreign monopoly interest may give Canadian publications from time to time, and on whatever terms it wishes to impose. We speak here not of a situation in which ownership is foreign while management remains fully Canadian and largely independent in matters of day to day policy. Rather we are speaking of a situation in which practical control and management will be exercised by non-resident foreign owners, almost necessarily without knowledge of or regard for Canadian cultural interests. We believe that such a situation should not be permitted to develop.

The matters on which we are now reporting have come to our attention very recently as a result of investigations which we have conducted, and there has not yet been an opportunity to pursue them in special public hearings. However, even though some difficulty may be encountered in bringing about the attendance of all relevant witnesses for the purpose, we do at this time intend to proceed in this way.

Your Commission understands that some Canadian publishers and retailers of periodicals may in fact be reluctant to give information to it concerning this growing and powerful intrusion. They fear that the foreign-owned distributors and wholesalers may refuse to carry their publications, or may impose unacceptable terms when they do so. Such decisions would of course be made outside this country. They would affect not only Canadian publishers, but Canadian retailers and their customers as well.

It is the hope of the Commission that retailers, newsstand operators, and all others engaged in the wholesaling, distribution, and retailing of paperback books and periodicals in Canada, will feel free to provide and will indeed provide the Commission with information and evidence bearing on the matters raised in this Interim Report. All such communications will be treated in whatever degree of confidence is requested.

Even though special hearings are planned, your Commission is of the opinion that reported acquisitions of wholesalers already completed in this Province and reports of other negotiations under way at this moment are sufficient reason for us to recommend to Your Honour that precautionary steps in the public interest be taken by your Government at the earliest possible moment. It is our unanimous and firm opinion that further acquisitions by non-Canadians of firms engaged in the wholesaling and distribution of periodicals and mass market paperback books can only be prevented if action is taken by your Government forthwith to give notice to prospective foreign purchasers that such acquisitions may well be subject to reversal, and indeed that your Government is prepared to enact legislation that would effectively prohibit further takeovers of these important links in the communications industry in Ontario.

The legislation envisaged in our recommendations would be similar in nature to that embodied in the Loan and Trust Corporations Amendment Act, 1970. However, as such legislation would in this case be aimed at preventing further reduction in Canadian ownership and control of Ontario wholesalers and distributors of periodical literature (with which distribution mass market paperbacks may be associated), care should be taken not to extend the restrictions to cover other kinds of wholesale publishing organizations. We believe this intention could most easily be realized by having the proposed restrictions apply only to individuals and organizations "engaged principally in the wholesaling and/or distribution of periodical publications".

To sum up, your Commission respectfully recommends that your Government forthwith submit to the Legislature of Ontario legislation which will:

(*a*) using the Loan and Trust Corporations Amendment Act, 1970 as a model, limit the ownership a foreign person or corporation may acquire in any undertaking whose principal business in Ontario is the distribution or wholesaling of periodical publications (we note that the Act referred to prohibits the transfer of shares in a loan or trust corporation to a non-resident where the total foreign ownership would exceed 25 per cent of the capital stock or where any one foreign owner would be registered in respect of more than 10 per cent of the capital stock); and

(*b*) provide for full disclosure to the Department concerned of all corporate information necessary for the administration of the proposed legislation.

In addition to the above recommendations, your Commission respectfully suggests that this second Interim Report be specially communicated to the Minister of Consumer and Corporate Affairs of The Government of Canada and to the Director of Investigation and Research, Combines Investigation Act, Ottawa, in anticipation of their co-operation with the Commission in its investigation of this vital sector of the Canadian publishing industry.

THIRD INTERIM REPORT · AUGUST 20, 1971

LETTER OF TRANSMITTAL

To His Honour,
The Lieutenant Governor of Ontario.

May It Please Your Honour,

We, the undersigned, Richard Heath Rohmer, Q.C., Dalton Kingsley Camp, and Marsh Jeanneret appointed Commissioners by Order-in-Council OC-3991/70 pursuant to the provisions of The Public Inquiries Act, R.S.O. 1960, c. 323, and approved by Your Honour on the 23rd day of December, 1970 to inquire into and report upon:

(a) the publishing industry in Ontario and throughout Canada with respect to its position within the business community;

(b) the functions of the publishing industry in terms of its contributions to the cultural life and education of the people of the Province of Ontario and Canada;

(c) the economic, cultural, social or other consequences for the people of Ontario and of Canada of the substantial ownership or control of publishing firms by foreign or foreign-owned or foreign-controlled corporations or by non-Canadians

beg to submit to Your Honour the following Third Interim Report of the Commission.

RICHARD ROHMER DALTON CAMP MARSH JEANNERET
Commissioner *Commissioner* *Commissioner*

20th August, 1971

THIRD INTERIM REPORT

The Commission is satisfied that it is virtually impossible for Canadian book publishers to obtain access to lines of credit with chartered banks on a competitive basis with foreign subsidiaries. For example, banks do not generally attach collateral value to inventories under Section 88 of the Canadian Bank Act. On the other hand, foreign subsidiaries are commonly able to secure guarantees of their loans from their parent companies, even when such loans are furnished in this country. Alternatively, such subsidiaries may have access to substantial amounts of working capital in other ways and from other sources. Canadian publishers enjoy much more limited credit privileges, being normally unable to find acceptable guarantors in order to expand their working capital within similar lines of credit.

Book publishing is a capital-intensive business, and Canadian firms thus find themselves at a double disadvantage. Not only do they quickly reach the point when their total available capital is tied up in inventories, often with relatively slow turnover prospects, but as a consequence new Canadian publishing opportunities are lost by them to the Canadian branches of foreign publishing firms which are naturally interested in expanding their share of the Canadian market.

For reasons already mentioned, such foreign subsidiaries ordinarily do have access to the necessary capital, subject of course to the continued efficiency of their operations. Such efficiency is normally assured in their cases by expert financial supervision both locally and by the parent corporations. Indeed, recent history has supplied strong evidence that any continued growth of competition beyond the ability of the market to sustain it must result in the demise of Canadian-owned publishing enterprises first.

It is sometimes asked whether or not the disappearance of the residual Canadian-owned book publishers would be a real loss to Ontario and Canada. We acknowledge that an important proportion of what original Canadian publishing is produced is done by subsidiaries of foreign firms operating here, and that they thereby contribute in an important way to the cultural development of our country. But to what extent are the latter's Canadian publishing programs stimulated by the relatively more favourable market conditions that now exist for books written by indigenous authors?

Canadian-owned firms do tend to publish Canadian authors exclusively and to sell their books chiefly in Canada. No doubt this lack of internationalism on their part has contributed to their economic difficulties. But so long as they concentrate on serving indigenous authorship in this way, Canadian creative writing is likely to enjoy a certain priority in school curricula, libraries, and bookstores from coast to coast. It is when these domestic (possibly overly introverted) publishing facilities disappear, that the ground rules which now favour Canadian materials would probably also have to change. At least there is every business reason to suppose that concerted pressure for their modification would be exerted.

The arguments against a curricular preference for Canadian-authored textbooks which the Commission has already heard carry some teaching logic, in certain subject areas at least, it must be admitted. But the most powerful consideration weighing with foreign subsidiary publishers who advance these arguments must surely be that the profits from overflow marketing of the home product outweigh any profits available from regional publishing, or even from regional editions. That is to say, the one-time publishing costs related to editorial, art, typesetting, plate-making, and production expenses can then be distributed over a continental or world market. When this happens, unit costs are reduced to a level of competitiveness that eliminates the publisher who publishes for the limited market only. And together with the latter disappear the last reasons for supporting regional authorship as such – in this case, Canadian authorship.

The problems that beset all book publishing firms in Canada – Canadian-owned as well as foreign-owned – are as numerous as they are complex. Some of these can be substantially alleviated by cooperative planning involving the industry and, in some cases, the provincial and federal governments. Some are reflections of market trends, including reading habits as well as educational philosophies and administrative organization. In so far as may be possible, all of these will be carefully reviewed in the final report of this Commission in due course. It is sufficient to say here that where corrective measures can be proposed at that time, they will be proposed.

But by no means all of the recommendations which will be made will call for public financial support. Indeed, a striking aspect of the book publishing industry in Canada is one to which we alluded in our First Interim Report. While on the one hand its contribution to the Gross National Product is relatively small, its cultural importance to the nation is substantial. Thus adverse business factors can be offset, by public assistance where need be, at much less expense in the book industry than in almost any other area of the economy that may be in difficulty from time to time. And as we also pointed out in our First Interim Report, the fact that the development of an indigenous book publishing industry can be stimulated, effectively and properly, by carefully planned economic assistance has long been recognized and acted upon in other parts of the world.

The problems related to a severe shortage of operating capital which created the emergency for McClelland and Stewart are now being felt with full force elsewhere in the Canadian-owned sector of the book publishing industry. We therefore believe it desirable that a general formula rendering capital assistance available to Canadian-owned book publishing firms, while at the same time protecting the public interest, be established now as government policy in this province. Such a policy has been recommended in some fifty of the briefs received by the Commission up to this time. Moreover, the financial information we have procured through auditors acting for us has led us to conclude that recommendation of such a formula to the Lieutenant Governor in Council should not be postponed until our final report is submitted. While we by no means suggest that the general program of capital assistance to Canadian-owned publishers which we now put forward will be the only kind of assistance we shall be recommending for Canadian book publishing as such in our final report, we do recommend to Your Honour that immediate government action be taken along the lines described below.

The program of capital assistance we propose at this time would be limited to Canadian-owned book publishing firms based in Ontario, and would be directly related to the operating capital requirements connected only with the original Canadian publishing activities of such firms.

A further word of explanation is necessary with regard to the specific recommendations to follow. At an early stage, although not immediately, administration of any new financial assistance program – whatever its scope or nature – is going to require the services of a now non-existent government supervisory body. This might tentatively be described as the Ontario Book Publishing Board. Such a board will have many other supervisory functions in the context of the Commission's final report, and its creation should therefore be deferred until after the latter has been submitted to and tabled by the government. In the meantime a temporary supervisory authority would be required, but only to discharge the advisory functions which this Third Interim Report envisages. We do not believe that a government agency now exists with the necessary information regarding the book publishing industry to assume these duties, even on an interim basis, except at the cost of redundant and time-consuming study. Whatever kind of interim supervising body might be established, references to it in the recommendations that follow will be to the Board, meaning an Ontario Book Publishing Board or an interim supervisory board.

We recommend that the Government of Ontario, acting on the advice of a Board as just explained, offer to guarantee loans made by commercial lending institutions to Canadian-owned book publishers with head offices in the Province of Ontario, and to subsidize a portion of approved interest costs of such loans subject to the following guidelines:

(*a*) Loans to be guaranteed and/or interest costs assisted only within credit lines to be approved from time to time as outlined below, and only after the Board has fully studied applications received and reached a favourable business judgment on all aspects of the loan in question.

(*b*) Line of credit in no case to exceed 75% of inventories of Canadian books (taken at lower of cost or market) plus 75% of accounts receivable relating to sales of Canadian books only, the latter to be valued after full provision for doubtful accounts and bad debts. For the purpose of these recommendations a Canadian book might be defined as a book written by a person or persons whose permanent domicile is in Canada, or whose nationality is Canadian.

(*c*) The Ontario Government, when it becomes a loan guarantor, to become a preferred and secured creditor through the assignment or transfer of any previous assignments of accounts receivable and inventories.

(*d*) Approval within such credit lines to be subject to ongoing review by the Board of all relevant information and policies of applicant firms, including financial statements and operating budgets.

(*e*) Implementation of a standard format for financial statements to accompany applications by publishers in order to facilitate review by the Board on a uniform basis. These statements would provide essential background information on such factors as value of accounts receivable and inventories against which loans might be guaranteed, including such essential data as cost of inventories, provision for write-down of inventories, inventory write-down policy, aging of inventories and accounts receivable, provision for bad debts, etc.

(*f*) Loans to be procured from Canadian-owned commercial lending institutions on conditions of repayment and interest to be approved in advance, although existing loans may be considered for guarantee and/or assistance under this program within the credit lines approved. The total amount of approved interest subsidies would be a specific charge against a fund to be provided by the Government of Ontario and administered by the Board. The degree to which interest costs may thus be subsidized should be the subject of annual policy review and budgeting. In the opinion of the Commission the level of subsidy might be expected to achieve its purpose best if it were initially set at fifty per cent of the approved interest rate negotiated for a particular loan under this program.

(*g*) Where a guarantor, other than the Ontario Government, is available, and is acceptable to the lending institution, the provisions for subsidy of the approved interest rate outlined above would apply, although the Ontario Government would not act as guarantor.

(*h*) Where the Ontario Government acts as guarantor incorporation under the laws of Ontario or the laws of Canada would be required, but only in the case of firms whose loans were guaranteed by the Government of Ontario.

(*i*) For the purposes of this program, a book publisher should be deemed to be Canadian-owned, if, in the case of a corporation, not more than 25 per cent of the total number of equity shares of the corporation are beneficially owned, directly or indirectly, by non-residents or are subject to the control or direction of non-residents, provided that not more than 10 per cent of the total shares are owned or controlled by a single non-resident.

(j) No application to participate in this program would be considered from McClelland and Stewart Limited unless a condition of such application were redemption of any of its outstanding debentures held by the Government of Ontario.

(k) Nothing in these guidelines is intended to preclude a future application for a guaranteed loan and/or for assistance in the payment of interest by new publishers or by publishers who may at this time be ineligible to apply, whether for reasons of ownership or otherwise. Similarly, firms may apply for additional guaranteed loans and assistance under these guidelines if their operating positions change to permit them to do so. However, the Board should in all cases have the right to approve, refuse, or defer action on such applications in the light of the information available to it from time to time and the budgetary limitations on the funds it administers.

There is an important corollary to the capital loans assistance program recommended above. The program is obviously one which can benefit Ontario book publishers generally, even though eligibility to participate in it must remain subject to the business judgment of an Ontario Book Publishing Board. We turn now to consider what this corollary is.

The Commission has not needed to be reminded, although it has been reminded on various occasions, that any restriction on the right of a Canadian book publishing firm to sell to a non-resident could significantly reduce its sales value in the more limited domestic market that would remain. There are some reasons, including changes in tax laws as well as a widespread concern that control of this country's residual cultural assets should remain Canadian, why the likelihood of foreign purchases of important Canadian book publishers is less probable in the immediate future. But such a possibility cannot be eradicated unless the Government is prepared to take the position that sales of book publishing firms to non-residents will not be permitted.

On the other hand, our present recommendations regarding capital loans assistance will, if they are adopted, confer a substantial benefit on Ontario-based Canadian book publishers. In view of this, and in view of the pressing importance that book publishing in this province not become less Canadian than it is at present, the Commission is prepared to enter a further recommendation at this time. It is our opinion that, coincident with implementation of the capital loans program recommended in this report, the Government of Ontario should announce that any further sales of Canadian-owned book publishers to non-residents will be considered contrary to the public interest. Whether or not specific prohibitory legislation may also be necessary is a decision which can be taken later. It seems likely that a policy statement alone would serve the purpose of deterring further sales to non-residents. After all, most book buying in Ontario, whether for schools or libraries, is in the end paid for chiefly by public funds – a fact that the publishers themselves have been tireless in pointing out to us in another important context. As they have told us, the right to determine where public funds should be spent for the purchase of books is a prerogative of the public, and we think it might rightly be so considered here.

FINAL REPORT ON THE DISTRIBUTION OF PAPERBACKS AND PERIODICALS IN ONTARIO · MARCH 27, 1972

LETTER OF TRANSMITTAL

To His Honour,
The Lieutenant Governor of Ontario.

May It Please Your Honour,

We, the undersigned, Richard Heath Rohmer, Q.C., Dalton Kingsley Camp, and Marsh Jeanneret appointed Commissioners by Order-in-Council OC-3991/70 pursuant to the provisions of The Public Inquiries Act, R.S.O. 1960, c. 323, and approved by Your Honour on the 23rd day of December, 1970 to inquire into and report upon:

(*a*) the publishing industry in Ontario and throughout Canada with respect to its position within the business community;

(*b*) the functions of the publishing industry in terms of its contributions to the cultural life and education of the people of the Province of Ontario and Canada;

(*c*) the economic, cultural, social or other consequences for the people of Ontario and of Canada of the substantial ownership or control of publishing firms by foreign or foreign-owned or foreign-controlled corporations or by non-Canadians;

(*d*) the contracts or proposed contracts between any geographical wholesaler of mass market paperback books and periodicals and any retailer of such goods that creates or tends to create an obligation on the retailer to purchase all merchandise supplied by the wholesaler from that wholesaler to the exclusion of other sources of supply and, without limiting the generality of the foregoing, to inquire into the merchandising of paperback books, periodicals, and other merchandise normally carried by geographical wholesalers and sold by their retailers

beg to submit to Your Honour our Final Report on the Distribution of Paperbacks and Periodicals in Ontario.

RICHARD ROHMER	DALTON CAMP	MARSH JEANNERET
Commissioner	*Commissioner*	*Commissioner*

27th March, 1972

FOURTH INTERIM REPORT

The Second Interim Report of this Commission, submitted on June 8, 1971, questioned whether the system whereby paperbacks and periodicals were being distributed in Ontario served the public interest, and made certain recommendations regarding legislation it considered desirable in order to prevent "further reduction in Canadian ownership and control of Ontario wholesalers and distributors of periodical literature (with which distribution mass-market paperbacks may be associated)." The Government introduced Bill 64 almost immediately thereafter, which was later enacted as *The Paperback and Periodical Distributors Act, 1971*. The provisions contained in this legislation became effective on the 14th day of June of the same year. The complete text of the Commission's Second Interim Report is included herewith as Appendix A.

The Act introduced a system for registration of businesses engaged in the distribution of paperback and periodical publications, with some important exceptions, and made Canadian ownership a condition both for the registration of any new enterprises of this kind and for the geographical expansion of existing businesses. During the month of July, 1971, the Commission held a series of public hearings in relation to its Second Interim Report, in the course of which a wide range of evidence was heard regarding the system whereby periodicals and so-called mass-market paperbacks are distributed in Ontario. The testimony also dealt with the method whereby exclusive rights to market in specific territories are exchanged from time to time under agreements for sale, and sometimes acquired and lost where no such agreements have been entered into at all.

A principal concern of the Commission in its Second Interim Report had to do with evidence accumulated in the course of its research which indicated that ownership of the channels of distribution for periodicals and mass-market paperbacks was rapidly passing from Canadian to foreign control. The Commission stated that it had reason to believe that a threat of monopoly was developing which had as its objective unified ownership or control of most, if not all, regional news companies in Ontario, otherwise referred to as geographical wholesalers. That a major foreign takeover in this field had been imminent was amply supported by the evidence received at the July hearings, as will be pointed out shortly. However, because *The Paperback and Periodical Distributors Act, 1971* effectively prevented the further erosion of Canadian ownership in this area of publishing, it seemed at the time that any long-term recommendations regarding organization, control, or ownership of periodical and paperback wholesaling in Ontario could be dealt with by the Commission in its final report. Consequently, no further recommendations for withdrawal or modification of the legislation already passed have yet been made, although the Commission has always envisaged the possibility that amendments in the Act may be called for in the light of experience.

The situation, however, has undergone some change. Certain new developments in periodical wholesaling practices have been reported. There has been a further evolution of public policy regarding the cultural consequences of foreign ownership in certain areas, and this is summarized in the *Preliminary Report of the Select Committee of the Legislature on Economic and Cultural Nationalism* (March 1, 1972). Finally, the Commission itself has now had an opportunity to consider fully, in the light of hearings that have been held, the implications of the present situation to the people of Ontario and Canada. The Commission has decided therefore that additional recommendations ought to be made concerning the distribution of paperbacks and periodicals at this time, including suggestions for certain amendments to *The Paperback and Periodical Distributors Act, 1971*. These recommendations, and the reasons for them, are dealt with in this report. By presenting its conclusions on this rather special phase of its work now, the Commission in its final report on book publishing, which is being written, will be free to concern itself more exclusively with the problems of Canadian book publishing as such, and the ways in which they relate to the public interest. The latter problems differ from those discussed in this report, and so must their solutions.

An additional reason why the Commission is submitting its report on the distribution of paperbacks and periodicals in Ontario at this time is the extension of its terms of reference under an Order-in-Council dated the 18th of November, 1971. The Order-in-Council directed the Commission to examine any contract or proposed contract between any geographical wholesaler and retailer in the mass-market and paperback field "that creates or tends to create an obligation on the retailer to purchase all merchandise supplied by the wholesaler from that wholesaler to the exclusion of other sources of supply..." A special hearing was held on 10th December, 1971 following a subpoena issued by the Commission under these added terms of reference to Mr. John Romanez, a representative of Metro Toronto News Company, asking for the production of certain information. Mr. Romanez, accompanied by counsel, attended this hearing and gave evidence. The Commission feels that its findings pursuant to these added terms of reference should also be reported at this time.

Mass-Market Paperbacks

The July (1971) hearings following the Commission's Second Interim Report were held on six days between July 13 and July 23, during which time a considerable number of witnesses were heard and a great deal of evidence was taken concerning the channels through which mass-market paperbacks and periodicals normally move from their publishers, wherever these may be located, to their readers in Ontario.

The phrase "mass-market paperbacks" normally refers to special paperback editions issued by specialist mass-market paperback houses. As a general rule, these comprise only reprints of fast selling, if not best selling, books originally issued by other publishers in traditional formats. The rights to republish mass-market editions in this way are ordinarily leased from the original publishers, even when those publishers may have issued the same works in paperback editions of their own – often known as "quality paperbacks." However, mass-market paperback editions are produced in much larger printings, frequently of several hundred thousand copies at a time, and are consequently capable of being published at much lower and somewhat standardized list prices.

The marketing of mass-market paperbacks in large quantities requires a specialized system of distribution leading to as many points of retail display and sale as possible. Access to these must be had even if the exhibit of individual titles can continue only so long as sales turnover remains rapid, competition for the display space being great. It is not surprising therefore that the marketing system best suited to the needs of mass-market paperback publishers in North America is the one which has developed for the marketing of most periodicals (apart from newspapers and apart from magazines that are distributed by mail directly to subscribers).

To the extent that they can do so efficiently, mass-market paperback publishers do distribute their products through bookstores as well. Many American publishers of mass-market paperbacks appoint publishers or establish distribution centres in Canada in order to warehouse their publications in this country. These mass-market paperback agencies supply both bookstores and news wholesaling companies; the latter were defined in the hearings as geographical wholesalers, and are so referred to in this report. Unfortunately, some of the Canadian agencies established by American mass-market paperback publishers are unwilling to supply all booksellers in Canada. The exclusive right to do this is sometimes claimed by an intervening geographical wholesaler, who relays paperbacks from the agency to such booksellers at a reduced wholesale discount. In such cases, the mass-market paperbacks move from American publisher to Canadian agent to Ontario geographical wholesaler to Ontario bookstore to Ontario reader – a circuitous route which involves the stacking of many separate overheads and limits the service possible to a reader wishing to procure a particular title.

Mass-market paperback publishers selling their products through the periodical marketing system have to accept some disadvantages along with the undoubted advantages of increased turnover. For example, the geographical wholesalers who distribute magazines are accustomed to dealing with merchandise which carries a built-in expiry date. Unsold copies of periodicals are therefore not normally returned to their suppliers except as torn covers (which may be returned for accounting purposes). Similarly, mass-market paperback books are not normally returned to their publishers for resale, even though books are not dated as are periodicals. We have been told of exceptions to this practice, but geographical wholesalers, or the news dealers whom they service, ordinarily do destroy unsold paperbacks and claim credit for them from their suppliers. The reason why they prefer to handle them in the same way that they handle ephemeral magazines is clear.

What determines the time that a mass-market paperback title stays on a display rack is its rate of turnover, just as the quantities and points of distribution for periodicals will be determined exclusively by their profitability. The whole system of distribution is geared to monitor profitability of turnover through many different outlets with maximum speed and minimum expense, and it is not surprising that we were told that computerized procedures are being substituted for human decision-making wherever possible.

It will be seen from the preceding brief description of how mass paperbacks are distributed that the Canadian segment of the market tends to be too small to support separate Canadian publication of mass-market paperback editions, especially of original Canadian books. Publishing experience to date has confirmed this, although a few exceptions could be given. Nor does it follow that mass-market paperback editions of best-selling Canadian books (best-selling internationally, that is) are never published. A number of Canadian authors appear regularly in series issued by American mass-market publishing houses, often, it must be admitted, without having been published by a Canadian publisher in the first place. There are a number of quality paperback series of Canadian books, however. What is difficult, if not almost impossible, is to secure display space for these Canadian quality paperbacks at the news dealers, whose stands are serviced by geographical wholesalers or, in the case of small accounts, by "rack jobbers" who buy from the geographical wholesalers. Because the competition for space is too keen, and the turnover and profitability of original Canadian publications generally too low, the latter rarely appeal as merchandise to the geographical wholesaler. It is only fair to add that the retail news dealer as well is inclined to be indifferent to such publications, although under present circumstances he finds it difficult to procure Canadian items for sale even when he wishes to. Certainly no geographical wholesaler endeavours to carry a really wide range of Canadian quality paperbacks as such. Although the Commission recognizes that to enforce any system of quotas, for example, respecting Canadian content in paperback displays, would be counter-productive (it would put marginal retail outlets out of business, if nothing else) we believe that geographical wholesalers have a responsibility to supply Canadian publications to those of their accounts willing to display them. This conclusion is reflected in a proposed amendment to the Act which appears as *Recommendation 1* at the end of this report.

Distribution of Periodicals

Mass-market paperbacks, then, ride on the backs of periodicals in the distribution system. It is a system to which original Canadian books normally have poor access, when they have any at all. But what should be even more discomforting to Canadians, in the opinion of the Commission, is that geographical wholesalers of periodicals in Ontario are completely dominated by the national distributors who supply them, and that with few exceptions these national distributors are located outside Canada.

It is necessary to trace briefly the channels through which periodicals move from publisher to reader in order to explain the degree to which our domestic distribution of magazines is thus controlled from beyond our borders. It is also important to understand how this fact militates against the operation of any kind of free market economy in the buying and selling of those Ontario businesses concerned with geographical wholesaling of periodicals, whether such businesses are owned in Canada or not.

It should be noted that we are not concerned here with the distribution of magazines by mail to subscribers. But for the vast quantities of magazines which reach readers via newsstands, a rather remarkable chain of successive custodians is involved. It is true that many of these stages in distribution never see the periodicals themselves; obviously there would be no time for them to do so; accordingly, magazines are frequently shipped from printers abroad directly to geographical wholesalers in this country. Nevertheless, the complete list of stages of control in the distribution system is as follows:

PRINTER
↓
PUBLISHER
↓
NATIONAL DISTRIBUTOR
↓
GEOGRAPHICAL WHOLESALER
↓
RACK JOBBER (for small accounts)
↓
RETAIL NEWS DEALER
↓
READER

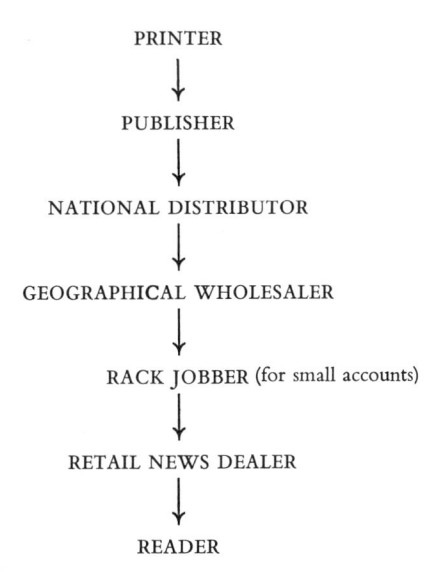

For foreign magazines – and most magazines sold in Canada are foreign – the national distributor in the above chain is located abroad, normally in the United

States. The geographical wholesalers whom he supplies, however, and whose exclusive rights to distribute his periodicals he claims can be determined by him alone are located in Ontario, at least in so far as they concern us. Substantial sums have been paid in the past to purchase such geographical wholesalerships, and although these sales have ordinarily resulted in the purchaser acquiring the exclusive right to sell the periodicals controlled by the national distributors concerned, we were told during the course of the July hearings that there is no guarantee that these vitally important rights are included automatically in such sales. Certainly this was the position taken by the representatives of two national distributors whom we heard from, namely Triangle Publications Inc. and MacFadden-Bartell Corporation. In this position they had the support, and in the opinion of the Commission, the active co-operation as well, of Metro Toronto News Company.

Metro Toronto News Company is a limited partnership, representing the interests of the Molasky family of St. Louis, Missouri, and the Rottman family of Bridgeport, Connecticut. The Molasky family owns Pierce News Company of St. Louis, Missouri, which carries on business as a geographical wholesaler in several important regions in the United States. Metro Toronto News Company Limited is owned by Pierce News Company of St. Louis. Metro Toronto News Company Limited owns 50% of the limited partnership known as Metro Toronto News Company. The other 50% of Metro Toronto News Company is owned by the Rottman family. Management of Metro Toronto News Company is by Pierce News Company of St. Louis through its wholly owned Canadian subsidiary Metro Toronto News Company Limited. Mr. Mark Molasky is the President of Metro Toronto News Company Limited and President of Pierce News Company of St. Louis. The senior officer of Metro Toronto News Company on the other hand is Mr. John Romanez, who holds the title of General Manager.

If the rights of a particular geographical wholesaler in Ontario to distribute the publications of a given national distributor are subject at all times to the latter's approval, it is a little difficult to understand exactly what the vendor contracts to deliver when such businesses in Ontario are sold, even though such sales have in the past involved very substantial sums, as the evidence in the hearings indicated. While physical assets have normally been included, we noted that the value of these is usually only a minuscule part of the prices that have been asked and offered. One national distributor protested the use of the word "franchise" to describe the exclusive territorial rights he gives a geographical wholesaler. Yet by whatever name one describes such rights one thing became completely clear to the Commission in the course of the hearings. This was that geographical wholesalers of periodicals in Ontario do indeed exercise substantial monopolies in the areas in which they operate, and that these monopolies can be made and broken at will by the national distributors who grant them.

Because almost all the national distributors are located outside Canada, and regulation of neither their terms of sale nor whom they supply is therefore possible under *The Paperback and Periodical Distributors Act, 1971* in its present form, the interests of the public cannot be guaranteed under the existing system. In order to remedy this situation the Commission is recommending a further amendment to the Act at this time. The purpose of this amendment is to transfer monopoly control of geographical wholesalers of periodical literature in Ontario from the national distributors located abroad to the province itself. The proposed amendment is set forth as *Recommendation 2* at the end of this report.

Some national distributors may claim that without the right to transfer and cancel franchises among geographical wholesalers their ability to ensure good service and to achieve maximum profitability will be impaired. The Commission believes that the public interest would be less well served, however, if national distributors retained the right to manipulate the ownership of geographical wholesalerships as they can do now. The business interests of national distributors can be given full consideration by the Registrar in the public hearings at which applications for changes of registration among geographical wholesalers should be reviewed in the future.

Extension of Terms of Reference

The extension of the terms of reference of this Commission under an Order-in-Council dated the 18th of November, 1971, was referred to early in this report. Because this extension directed the Commission to examine possible contracts between geographical wholesalers and retailers which might restrict the rights of the latter to purchase from other suppliers, affidavits were requested by the Commission from all geographical wholesalers in Ontario describing the details of any such possible contracts to which they might be party. All such requests were complied with, the affidavits indicating that with one exception no contracts of this kind had been either entered into or proposed. A review of the exceptional case follows.

A contract reportedly circulated earlier by Metro Toronto News Company, which had been the subject of complaints received by the Commission, led to a subpoena dated the 29th day of November, 1971, being served upon Mr. John Romanez, General Manager of Metro Toronto News Company, requiring him to appear at a special hearing. This hearing was convened on the 10th day of December following. The proceedings were recorded as part of the regular transcript of the Commission's hearings, the testimony given appearing on pages 4346 through 4408. (The previous hearings on the subject of geographical wholesaling, referred to elsewhere in this report as the "July hearings," are recorded on pages 2791 through 3676.)

It appears that during the autumn of 1970 someone in the Metro Toronto News

Company organization decided to have a contract dealing with credit terms and terms of return of merchandise drawn up for submission to its retail accounts. To this end, Metro Toronto News Company apparently consulted informally the firm then known as Enfield, Kimberley & Hemmerick, who drafted a "proposed consignment contract" which they forwarded to Metro Toronto News Company with a letter dated the 8th day of September, 1970. That letter, together with the draft referred to, is Appendix B to this report. It is to be noted that this draft made no reference to any exclusivity with regard to the purchase of books, periodicals or merchandise from Metro Toronto News Company.

A second draft "dealer agreement" was prepared by the same legal firm and submitted to Metro Toronto News Company on 21st April, 1971. This draft contained substantial alterations from the text of the previous draft, in that it made provision for an exclusivity which is of concern to this Commission. Correspondence has been received by the Commission from Mr. Frank A. Enfield of the above firm since the December hearing in which he submits that this dealer agreement was intended only as a draft for discussion and analysis. At all events, the draft dealer agreement in question read as follows:

METRO TORONTO NEWS COMPANY

DEALER AGREEMENT

The undersigned dealer hereby agrees to and with Metro Toronto News Company to purchase merchandise and publications under the following terms:

1. The dealer agrees that he will deal exclusively with Metro Toronto News Company in regard to any merchandise or publications supplied by Metro Toronto News Company, and that he will not purchase the same publications or merchandise from any other supplier or source. Metro Toronto News Company agrees to make available to the dealer on request details of all of the publications or merchandise that are available from time to time.

2. The dealer and Metro Toronto News Company agree that any merchandise and publications supplied by Metro Toronto News Company remain the property of the dealer until sold or returned for credit, with the proviso that Metro Toronto News Company shall have the right to take possession of and remove merchandise or publications from the dealer's possession at any time or times and credit the dealer's account for the value of the merchandise or publications repossessed.

3. Procedure for shipments to dealer and payments for merchandise by dealer:

   (i) Merchandise and publications will be delivered by Metro Toronto News Company at regular intervals to dealer's place of business;

   (ii) The invoices will be delivered with the merchandise and publications;

   (iii) All returns of merchandise and publications are to be made up by the dealer and picked up at regular intervals by Metro Toronto News Company;

   (iv) Payment for merchandise and publications sold by the dealer, being the invoice price less credit for returns, shall be paid for weekly/monthly by the dealer. There will be a service charge of $1.00 payable by the dealer to Metro Toronto News Company for each week that any payment remains overdue and unpaid.

4. Either party may terminate this dealer agreement at any time, either by oral notice or otherwise.

On such termination, dealer is liable for immediate payment of all outstanding accounts less credit for returns.

5. In the event of the sale or transfer by the dealer of the assets or shares of his business, Metro Toronto News Company to be informed prior to the effective date of sale so that proper arrangements can be made regarding the rendering of a final account to the dealer and payment by the dealer of any accounts outstanding subject to credit for returns. In the event the dealer does not inform Metro Toronto News Company of the change in ownership, the dealer herein will be liable for all accounts incurred by the new dealer. The dealer agrees to pay Metro Toronto News Company in full on or before the effective date of transfer of ownership of the business. The dealer acknowledges and agrees that any equipment supplied by Metro Toronto News Company to the dealer for display purposes or otherwise is on loan to the dealer and is the property at all times of Metro Toronto News Company and that it will not be removed from the dealer's premises unless with the consent of Metro Toronto News Company.

Dated this _____ day of _____, 19____.

METRO TORONTO NEWS COMPANY

by:.............................

....

Dealer's signature

(DEALER PLEASE NOTE: When signing please designate whether you are a sole owner or a limited company and show the official position of the person signing, for example, "owner", "partner", "president", or "secretary" or other officer of a limited company.)

Mr. Romanez testified that it was he who instructed Enfield, Kimberley & Hemmerick to insert paragraphs 1 and 2 of the above "dealer agreement", which dealt specifically with exclusivity.

On or about the 29th day of September, 1971, this agreement in substantially the form quoted, but omitting the sentence referring to a service charge on overdue accounts, was sent by Metro Toronto News Company to 787 of its retail accounts for signature. A copy of the letter of transmittal is Appendix C to this report. Mr. Romanez further testified that Mr. Mark Molasky, president of his parent company (Metro Toronto News Company Limited), knew nothing about this agreement, but that although he himself had approved it in principle it was actually sent out by his Credit Manager on 29th September, the same day that he (Romanez) departed to attend a convention in California. Although Mr. Romanez testified that he was not aware until later that the agreement in question had been despatched, it is the opinion of the Commission that he ought to have been told about the mailing of a document embodying so important a policy departure. Moreover, the Commission considers that only one interpretation would have been placed upon it by the average recipient, and this was that by signing it a retailer would obligate himself to deal exclusively with Metro Toronto News Company "in regard to any merchandise or publications supplied by Metro Toronto

News Company, and that he will not purchase the same publications or merchandise from any other supplier or source." A different interpretation of the agreement was offered at the hearing by Metro Toronto News Company and is reviewed later below.

Evidence was received that 143 of the above dealer agreements were actually returned. There was further testimony to the effect that some dealers requested rewording of the agreement and that in such cases it was amended. These amendments, we were told, were intended to "make it clear that [what was referred to by the agreement was] returnable publications and merchandise." Mr. Romanez also testified that there was no intention on the part of his company to discriminate in any way against dealers who failed or refused to sign the agreement. When asked whether or not this meant that the agreement was meaningless, he replied that it was "psychological." Later in the testimony it was submitted that the original purpose of the agreement was to make it possible for the company to seize and recover in the event of bankruptcy of an account. Still later, Mr. Romanez interpreted the agreement to mean that if a dealer bought paperbacks from his firm, then he would expect them under the agreement to buy them exclusively from his firm. In the course of the hearing, the counsel for Metro Toronto News Company, Mr. Sedgwick, Q.C., was asked if he would provide the Commission in writing with his argument concerning the meaning of the dealer agreement set forth above, and particularly with regard to paragraphs 1 and 2 of that document. Mr. Sedgwick responded with a letter dated December 14, 1971, which reads in part as follows:

During the proceedings before your Commission on Friday last, you asked that I make a submission as to my interpretation of the Metro Toronto News Company "Dealer Agreement". I have read and re-read the document, and have done so in the light of Mr. Romanez' evidence as to what the Company intended.

I take the words in paragraph 1 "he will deal exclusively with Metro Toronto News Company in regard to any merchandise or publications supplied by Metro Toronto News Company, and that he will not purchase the same publications or merchandise from any other supplier or source" to be referable only to such precise merchandise or publications as the dealer chooses to purchase from Metro *on a returnable basis*, and this I think is supported both by the evidence and by paragraph 3 (iii) and (iv) of the agreement. This interpretation is further inferentially supported by paragraph 2, which speaks of merchandise and publications remaining the property of the dealer "until sold *or returned for credit*", it being clear as I see it that all purchases by the dealer are returnable for credit. The contract does *not* say that the dealer may not purchase *similar* publications or merchandise from any other supplier, but only "*the same*" publications, etc.

Thus, if a dealer has purchased from Metro (and of course, on a returnable basis) a quantity of, for example, "Logix Enterprises, 'Decals' " (Item 1 on the list supplied, Exhibit 5), he is at liberty to purchase from any other supplier any other "Decals". Metro merely wants to be able to identify the returns made *to it* as being returns of articles purchased *from it*.

The concluding words of paragraph 1 "Metro Toronto News Company agrees to make available to the dealer on request, details of all the publications or merchandise that are available, from time to time", **have in** my opinion, no reference to the earlier language, but are merely a statement that

Metro will, at the dealers request, supply him with a list of the publications and merchandise which they handle, and from which list he may choose, or not choose, as he sees fit.

For myself, I do not consider the language of the agreement ambiguous, but if it is thought to be so one may properly refer to the evidence of Mr. Romanez as to what was intended. There was, so far as I know, no contrary evidence, and certainly no evidence of any attempt on the part of Metro News to enforce, as against their dealers, a broader exclusivity.

As Mr. Sedgwick observes, if the agreement is considered to be ambiguous one may "refer to the evidence of Mr. Romanez as to what was intended." The difficulty for retailers who received this agreement, however, is that it would have been impossible for them to be privy to the intent of the agreement as interpreted by Mr. Romanez at the December 10th hearing.

In other words, the dealer agreement must speak for itself, and it does so eloquently. In the opinion of the Commission, it required exactly what it said it required, which was that the dealer signing it obligated himself to deal exclusively with Metro Toronto News Company in relation to any merchandise or publications supplied by that company, and not to purchase such merchandise or publications from any other supplier or source. As was made clear during the earlier July hearings, some 6,000 Ontario retailers have in the past had no choice but to buy their mass-market paperback books and periodicals from Metro Toronto News Company. In our opinion, paragraphs 1 and 2 of the dealer agreement reviewed above effectively placed the retailers who received it in a similar "no choice" position with regard to all merchandise that might be carried by Metro Toronto News Company from time to time. A dealer who declined to sign might, regardless of the testimony received as to the real intentions of the agreement, have some reason to fear that his supply of periodicals would be cut off, there being no other source of supply for the latter available to him. This in no way implies that Metro Toronto News Company at any time threatened such action, but it would be reasonable for a dealer to infer that it might occur.

Since the conclusion of the December hearing and the exchange of subsequent correspondence with Mr. Sedgwick, Q.C. mentioned above, the Commission has been advised that the Metro Toronto News Company has in fact returned the completed copies of the dealer agreement form which it had received to those dealers who had mailed them in following its original request of last September. In view of the events summarized above, the Commission is of the opinion that no other course of action by Metro Toronto News Company would have been proper under the circumstances.

Limitations on Geographical Wholesaling Areas

As observed earlier it was forcefully demonstrated during the July hearings that the trading value of geographical wholesalerships in Ontario has until now been dependent on the pleasure of national distributors based outside Canada. *Recommendation 2*, previously referred to, will therefore do more than simply serve the public interest by transferring control of the geographical wholesalers from the national distributors to the Province of Ontario itself. It will also substantially guarantee the values of the geographical wholesalerships themselves, at least to the extent of protecting them against manipulation of their resale values by national distributors in the future. That an attempt at such manipulation did occur in the case of Kitchener News Company Limited subsequent to Mr. Molasky's unsuccessful efforts to purchase it there can be no doubt whatsoever, unless the transfer of the right to supply certain key publications by their distributors, Triangle Publications Inc. and MacFadden-Bartell Corporation, from Kitchener News Company Limited to Metro Toronto News Company was a sheer coincidence. The Commission is unprepared to accept such an explanation. If this kind of manipulation has been possible in the past, it would again be possible in the future, except for the protection which implementation of *Recommendation 2* will afford. But with that protection, the sale of geographical wholesalerships in Ontario to Canadian residents, subject only to registration of the purchaser under the Act, will be possible on a competitive basis.

With respect to interference by some national distributors in the rights exercised by geographical wholesalers as described above, the Commission has very recently received evidence of renewed activities of this kind in an area outside its jurisdiction. Specifically, we have been told that Pierce News Company of St. Louis, Missouri, sought unsuccessfully to purchase Benjamin-Montreal News Reg'd. in Montreal, Thereafter, Benjamin-Montreal News Reg'd. was informed by Triangle Publications that the latter intended to discontinue supplying the former with copies of its magazines for resale, including *TV Guide*. At the same time, Benjamin-Montreal News Reg'd. was informed by Colonial Distributors of Scarborough, Ontario, that it also was appointing another geographical wholesaler in the Montreal area. The latter communication is reported to have been conveyed on behalf of Colonial Distributors by Mr. John Romanez, an officer of that company and also General Manager of Metro Toronto News Company. Although these reported activities have not been reviewed in hearings at which all interested parties could be represented and give evidence under oath, the pattern is familiar. The present report of the Commission is not, however, based on the evidence reported here concerning Benjamin-Montreal News Reg'd.

This raises a concern which has weighed heavily with the Commission since it prepared its Second Interim Report, a concern which has been in no way allayed by the evidence taken at either the July or the December hearings. A geographical wholesaler may – in the future at least – enjoy exclusive distributing rights in the area for which he has been registered, except when the Registrar deems it to be in the public interest to grant one or more competing registrations in the same area. The evidence taken in the hearings seems to indicate that overlapping wholesalerships would be likely to create chaotic conditions in the matter of returns of unsold copies, and possibly inefficiencies in servicing as well. Nevertheless, there may well be situations where such overlapping might be considered by the Registrar to be in the public interest, e.g. where investigations of complaints indicate that inadequate service is being provided. But apart from such special situations, it seems probable that the Registrar will be concerned with ensuring that areas are assigned to registrants in a way that ensures optimum servicing of all parts of the Province, and we anticipate that to this end exclusivity in territories assigned will be the rule rather than the exception. If, then, most such geographical wholesaling areas are to be exclusive, and if they can be bought and sold relatively freely, subject only to the approval of the Registrar, what is the largest exclusive wholesaling area that would be consistent with the public interest?

The Commission has studied this question, which it recognizes is a critical one, at great length. Consideration has been given to establishing permanent statutory areas based on existing population quotients, but these tend to lack the flexibility which changing conditions of transportation and urban development might make desirable over the years. Having regard for the public hearings that would be available, the Commission has come to favour leaving maximum discretion with the Registrar regarding boundaries of areas accepted by him for registration from time to time, provided that a reasonable limitation on the total area assigned to any one registrant is prescribed in the Act itself. The Commission is of the opinion that the most equitable basis for determining the maximum size of any geographical wholesaler's territory will be for the Registrar to limit the area assigned to any one registrant under the Act to an approximate population ceiling. Imposing a statutory limitation in this way would recognize the fact that geographical wholesalerships tend by their nature to preclude competition, practically if not absolutely. Thus it is in the public interest that they should never be acquired by too small an ownership group whether through the disproportionate expansion of one or two of their number, or through independent purchase.

It is assumed that the Registrar, in reviewing possible registrations, will give as much importance as the Commission gives to existing geographical wholesaling areas and to the firms which now serve them – both with a view to minimizing disruptions in present distribution patterns and to recognizing vested interests. However, the Commission has also concluded that the statutory population limit which should be established for all geographical wholesaling areas should be set at a sufficiently high level to accommodate and permit reasonable growth of as many existing wholesalers as possible. The one firm which cannot be accommodated by any useful population ceiling is Metro Toronto News Company itself. The following tabulation illustrates the approximate populations of geographical wholesaling areas as they existed at June 14, 1971, and as they might possibly be registered to-day subject to the discretion of the Registrar and to the limitation now being recommended:

ONTARIO PAPERBACK AND PERIODICAL WHOLESALERS

Company	Owner	Address	Estimated Annual Gross Sales	Approximate Population Served
Central News Company Limited	Can.	Thunder Bay	$ 800,000	185,949
Churchill News Limited	Can.	Kingston	450,000	100,000
Cornwall News Distributors Limited	Can.	Cornwall	660,000	113,000
General News & Novelty Company Limited	Can.	Brantford	650,000	180,000
Kent News Service	Can.	Chatham	290,000	100,000
Kitchener News Company Limited	Can.	Kitchener	1,340,000	260,000
Lambton News Service (Somerset Specialties Limited as of June 11, 1971)	U.S.	Sarnia	430,000	80,000
Metro Toronto News Company	U.S.	Toronto	10,500,000	3,323,522
Mountain City News Co. Limited	Can.	Hamilton	1,680,000	400,000
National News Company Limited	Can.	Ottawa	2,280,000	447,000
Ottawa Valley News Company Limited	Can.	Arnprior	550,000	60,000
Sault News Service	U.S.	Sault St. Marie	290,000	74,594
Seaway News Company Limited	Can.	St. Catharines	1,210,000	337,642
Sudbury News Service Limited	U.S.	Sudbury	1,100,000	169,346
Teck News Agency Limited	Can.	Kirkland Lake	1,000,000	41,969
Timmins News Service	Can.	Timmins	170,000	78,542
Upper Canada News Limited (assets sold to Metro Toronto News Company Limited June, 1971)	U.S.	Belleville	1,410,000	280,000
Western News Distributors Limited (shares sold to Somerset Specialties Limited June, 1971)	U.S.	London	1,500,000	340,000
Windsor News Company Limited	U.S.	Windsor	1,300,000	293,000
Wentworth News Agency Limited (sold to Mountain City News Co. Limited January 3, 1972)	Can.	Hamilton	418,000	(part of Hamilton only)

The Commission considers that a population of approximately $1\frac{1}{4}$ millions is the maximum size which any geographical wholesaling area should be allowed to attain at this time if there is to be assurance that all operations of this kind in Ontario will continue to be held by a reasonable number of separate owners. Such a ceiling would leave substantial room for growth by the largest existing geographical wholesaler, with the sole exception of Metro Toronto News Company as just noted. The latter firm together with other firms having common ownership now claim exclusive wholesaling rights in areas with a total population of approximately 4 millions, including all of Metropolitan Toronto. The other firms just referred to include the geographical wholesalers based in Sarnia, London, and Belleville. Much of the territory in Ontario in which this overlapping ownership group now claim exclusive wholesaling rights was acquired quite recently, indeed during the period immediately preceding the effective date of *The Paperback and Periodical Distributors Act, 1971*. However the Commission considers that the date of acquisition of such selling areas is less relevant to the public interest than the possibility that relatively large total areas should be controlled by a common interest.

Specifically, if an appropriate ceiling for geographical wholesaling areas were being established without regard for the present interests of Metro Toronto News Company, the Commission would be inclined to favour a limit that would cause the largest urban region (Metropolitan Toronto) to be shared among three or four independent enterprises. That is to say, it would favour a limit of between a half and three-quarters of a million population to be serviced by any one geographical wholesaler. Under the circumstances, it is the Commission's considered opinion that the Metropolitan Toronto area should be divided so that it may be served by a minimum of two geographical wholesalers, each presumably with an exclusive territory. One of these might well be Metro Toronto News Company. This objective would be attained if the ceiling for all areas is established at $1\frac{1}{4}$ million population as already proposed; any larger population base in the Toronto area must lead to inequitable situations in the province at large, or else to future amalgamation of other areas into undesirably large units.

A statutory limitation of $1\frac{1}{4}$ million population in all geographical wholesaling areas would make it necessary for the owners of Metro Toronto News Company to divest themselves of a substantial part of their present Ontario interests. We think that adequate time should be permitted for this divestment, and suggest that a full year be allowed from the date of this report for it to take place. As has already been pointed out, the legislative amendments now being recommended will ensure a maximum and free market value for those areas of which Metro Toronto News Company may elect to dispose, by encouraging optimum competition – among potential Canadian purchasers – for their acquisition. The Commission also expects that the Registrar will give fair consideration to the interests of Metro Toronto News Company in establishing the boundaries of new geographical wholesaling areas to be registered under the Act as a result of the legislation being proposed, which is outlined in *Recommendation 3* at the end of this report.

Ownership of Retail Outlets

If there are cogent reasons why only Canadians should be allowed to acquire regional wholesalerships in the future, there are even stronger reasons why new ownership and control of retail outlets by non-residents should no longer be permitted. The testimony heard by the Commission has amply demonstrated the degree to which foreign control of the wholesale channels of distribution of periodicals and paperbacks invites monopolistic practices that show little regard for the private or public interests of the people of this province.

From the standpoint of Canadian cultural needs, a somewhat more serious situation would arise if retail outlets whose principal business is the display and sale of publications should also largely pass into foreign control. There would be little merit in assuring that geographical wholesalers stocked Canadian periodicals and paperbacks, for example, if the retail selecting of reading materials ceased to be done by Canadian owners. The situation could also be serious for publishers of original Canadian books in other than paperback editions. If, for example, new chains of foreign-owned bookshops were to spring up in shopping centres and elsewhere in this province, it is possible and reasonable that their inventories might be largely selected, and largely acquired, outside this country.

The Commission believes that the retail bookseller must play a critically important role in the literary development of Canada, as its final report will make clear. If one or more foreign-owned chains of news dealers in Ontario were set up, and possibly even supplied, from abroad, the purpose of encouraging Canadian participation in the wholesaling of periodicals and paperbacks could largely be thwarted. Similarly, vertical control of retailers through ownership by geographical wholesalers, whether Canadian or not, would tend to defeat the purposes of *The Paperback and Periodical Distributors Act, 1971*.

For these reasons the Commission has recommended that new ownership of retail news dealers and booksellers be permitted neither to non-residents, nor to geographical wholesalers registered under the Act.

RECOMMENDATIONS

In view of the cultural importance to the public of periodicals and mass-market paperbacks distributed by geographical wholesalers in this province, as well as the importance of many publications which may not be so distributed, and with careful regard for the evidence reviewed in the preceding pages, the Commission is of the opinion that certain amendments to *The Paperback and Periodical Distributors Act, 1971* should now be enacted in order to give effect to the following recommendations:

Recommendation 1. All Ontario geographical wholesalers registered under the Act should be required to carry reasonable inventories of all Canadian-edited and Canadian-published periodicals as defined in the Act, which are issued in English four or more times annually and which are for sale to the public. Geographical wholesalers registered to do business in areas which have substantial French-speaking populations should be required to carry equivalent Canadian periodicals issued in French.

All such geographical wholesalers should be required to furnish complete information at frequent intervals to all their retail accounts regarding the periodicals so carried, and should satisfy the Registrar that such information is being furnished regularly and in a useful form. However, the Registrar should be empowered to authorize any geographical wholesaler from time to time not to list and/or not to carry particular periodicals which may not be easily available, or which cannot be procured on reasonable terms with respect to discount and return privileges, or which the Registrar may concur are not intended for public distribution. Similarly all geographical wholesalers registered under the Act should be required to carry reasonable inventories of all Canadian-published paperback books where these are written by Canadians and have been published during the preceding twelve months, subject to the same conditions as are attached above to Canadian periodicals.

Necessary discretion should be vested in the Registrar to determine what quantities might constitute reasonable inventories in each situation and for each periodical or paperback carried as proposed, to determine the way in which unsold copies should be reported or returned, as well as to authorize in writing particular exemptions from any of these responsibilities where he deems such exemptions to be warranted. If this recommendation is implemented, the Amended Act should make clear that nothing in its provisions is intended to establish quotas of Canadian and non-Canadian publications which shall be displayed by dealers; they are intended only to ensure continuous availability, on terms published in advance and approved by the Registrar, of current Canadian periodicals and paperback books.

Recommendation 2. Every national distributor of periodicals and mass-market paperbacks as defined under the Act as amended should be required to supply all geographical wholesalers (who are registered under the Act and whose registrations are in force) on an equal-terms equal-service basis at all times, provided that if the Registrar shall have circulated a notice in writing to the effect that any national distributor or other supplier of periodicals and paperbacks to geographical wholesalers has failed to discharge the responsibility just described, then no registered geographical wholesaler in Ontario may sell any periodical or mass-market paperback procured from such a national distributor or supplier until the Registrar has indicated in writing that such sales may be resumed. The legislation should note that this recommendation is intended to ensure equal terms and equal service to all geographical wholesalers, and does not prohibit the sale or purchase of particular titles or periodicals as such.

Recommendation 3. The area or areas in which a geographical wholesaler is registered to carry on business by the Registrar should not exceed a total population of $1\frac{1}{4}$ millions according to the latest population statistics available. The boundaries of such areas may be reviewed from time to time with regard to population fluctuation.

Any geographical wholesaler currently operating in an area or areas whose total population exceeds $1\frac{1}{4}$ millions should be given one year from the date of this report to comply with this legislation and during that time, but not beyond that date, should be considered eligible for registration as a geographical wholesaler in the areas in which it actively operated on June 14, 1971, the effective date of the present Act.

Failure to comply with this geographical restriction should result in the cancellation of the offending geographical wholesaler's registration to carry on business, in addition to the other penalties prescribed in the Act. In order to be re-eligible for registration the geographical wholesaler must give proof of his compliance with the Amended Act.

For the purposes of this provision "geographical wholesaler" includes any corporation or partnership which the geographical wholesaler owns, controls, or manages, or with which it is associated in any way.

Recommendation 4. The definitions in section 1 of the present Act should be amended to include definitions of "national distributor" and "geographical wholesaler," based on the respective functions of each in the distribution system and on their functions as referred to throughout this report. Except as further recommended below, any firm whose principal business in Ontario is the distribution of periodicals or paperbacks directly to retailers should be considered to be a "geographical wholesaler" for the purposes of the Act.

Further, the exemptions from the responsibility to register set forth in section 1(2) of the Act should be amended to embrace those publishers and publishers' agents in Canada whose principal business is not the distribution of periodicals or paperbacks directly to retailers.

The Act should also make clear that only geographical wholesalers of periodicals and/or paperbacks are required to register under the Act, and that there is no provision for the registration of national distributors and publishers as such. One of the purposes of this Recommendation is to restrict registration to geographical wholesalers, as defined in the Act as amended.

Recommendation 5. Provision should be made in the Act for public hearings of applications for changes in ownership of registered geographical wholesalers as well as of applications for additional registrations as geographical wholesalers whenever the Registrar considers that the consideration of additional applications for registrations may be in the public interest.

In referring to the "Registrar" in this report, the Commission recognizes that it may be appropriate for the Government to constitute a board or tribunal to assume the enlarged responsibilities which it recommends should be given to the Registrar. Such a board or tribunal would make recommendations to the appropriate Minister of the Crown for implementation.

Recommendation 6. Provision should be made that after the date of this report new ownership of retail news dealers and/or retail booksellers in Ontario, including branches of same, not be permitted to non-residents as defined in the Act. Also, after the date of this report, no registered geographical wholesaler should be permitted to acquire, establish, or obtain an ownership or management interest in any retail news outlet or retail bookstore in Ontario.

APPENDICES

APPENDIX A

Second Interim Report (*See above*) (*See page 289*)

APPENDIX B

APPENDIX "B"

ENFIELD, KIMBERLEY & HEMMERICK
BARRISTERS and SOLICITORS
Frank A. Enfield, Q.C.
Harold E. Kimberley
William J. Hemmerick, Q.C.
Frederick H. Vanston
Gordon E. Wood

Telephone 366-4655
(Area code 416)
80 King Street West
Toronto 110, Ontario

September 8th, 1970

Metro Toronto News Company
120 Sinnott Road
SCARBOROUGH 705, Ontario

Attention: Mr. J. B. Wilcock, C.A.

Dear Sirs:

Re: Proposed Consignment Contracts

Pursuant to your instructions, we reviewed the possibilities of the Company shipping merchandise on consignment to the various retail outlets and we would like to comment on this situation as follows:

One of the best writers on commercial law comments on sale on consignment as follows:

"The practice of selling goods on consignment to distributors or dealers would appear to be far less prevalent in Canada than it has been in the past, and except in certain specific trades the consignment agreement is no longer a standard commercial transaction. This development is directly related to the greatly increased emphasis on credit. If the distributor or dealer is a satisfactory "credit risk" the title to the goods will generally be passed to him and normal credit terms granted. If his credit rating is not satisfactory the manufacturer or supplier either will not deal with him at all or will deal on a wholesale conditional sale basis."

I included the above in this letter as a matter of interest. The consignment situation is a special one, therefore, and this is not to say that it would not be available for your particular situation.

In order to create a proper consignment arrangement, the consignment contract must contain the following:

1. A clear statement that the goods belong to the Consignor.
2. An acknowledgment by the Consignee that he holds the goods in trust for the Consignor as bailee.
3. That the goods will be kept separate and apart from any other goods.
4. That the Consignee will account for the money for the sale of the goods as they are sold and that the sale moneys are trust moneys for the Consignor apart from the portion of the sale moneys that belong to the Consignee as his commission.
5. That the Consignee will account for all moneys and all goods.
6. That the Consignor has the right to pick up the goods at any time.

There has been a case on the question of where the Conditional Sales Act is applicable to a contract where goods are delivered on consignment. In this case, R, a merchant, shipped goods to A, the wholesaler, "on consignment". A went into bankruptcy and R claimed the goods from the trustee. HELD, R was entitled to them. A was merely R's agent for the purpose of reselling the goods, and the title never passed to A. The Conditional Sales Act did not apply because it was never intended that A should become the purchaser.

In regard to The Bankruptcy Act, it has been held that if goods are delivered on consignment the relationship between the parties is not that of a vendor and purchaser, but of Consignor and Consignee, and the property in the goods continues in the Consignor. On the bankruptcy of the Consignee the goods in question are not available to his creditors but belong to the Consignor.

In the bankruptcy, the claimant (Consignor) and not the trustee, has to prove that there was a consignment arrangement and not a sale. In order to establish that certain goods were sold on consignment there must be more than merely the words "on consignment" on the invoice. An agreement should be established to the effect that the Consignee should keep the goods and proceeds separate, is required to account after the sale and is obligated to pay for the goods only if sold by him.

If it turns out that the arrangement between the parties was in effect one of purchase and sale, the goods in the hands of the purchaser vest on his bankruptcy in the trustee and constitute property divisible among his creditors.

Taking into account all of the above, it is therefore necessary to show a proper consignment agreement. To this end we have drafted a proposed consignment contract, a copy of which you will find enclosed. It covers, I believe, all of the points raised.

I know it is a matter of practical politics whether you are able to work such an arrangement with your customers. You will notice, for example, in the contract I have left blank all of the methods that are to be applied regarding payment by the customer. I am not sure whether they make a daily cash payment or how this is handled, but whatever method is used, it will have to be set out in the agreement.

I am not sure if it is true that the customer only pays for merchandise that he has sold. It may be that some merchandise he can return, some unsold material, and obtain full credit and that on others he has to purchase outright.

In any event, after you have reviewed the above, I would be pleased to assist in any way I can in drawing up a final form of consignment agreement.

Yours very truly,

ENFIELD, KIMBERLEY & HEMMERICK

FAE:SC
*encl.

Frank A. Enfield

Exhibit No. 10

APPENDIX "B" cont.

CONSIGNMENT AGREEMENT BETWEEN METRO TORONTO NEWS COMPANY, Consignor, and (CUSTOMER'S NAME), Consignee,

IN CONSIDERATION of the mutual agreements set out below the Consignor and the Consignee agree as follows:

1. The Consignor, a distributor of all manner of publications and printed matter, agrees to ship to the Consignee and Consignee agrees to receive upon consignment for sale in the Consignee's business, such publications and printed matter (herein called the merchandise) belonging to the Consignor as the Consignor may from time to time place in the custody of the Consignee;

2. The said consigned merchandise always remains the property of the Consignor, and the Consignee holds the merchandise as bailee in trust for the Consignor, until the merchandise is either removed by the Consignor or sold by the Consignee;

3. The Consignee will display and store the said merchandise in a suitable place and separate from all other goods and merchandise that the Consignee may have in his premises;

4. The Consignor shall have the right to take possession of and remove the consigned merchandise at any time and shall have the right to enter the Consignee's premises to inspect the merchandise and so remove it;

5. The Consignor will, at the time of each consignment send an invoice to the Consignee indicating the price of the goods shipped and the Consignee is to receive, as his commission on the sale of the said merchandise, the amount realized from such sale over and above the price at which the said merchandise is so invoiced;

6. All moneys received from the sale of the consigned merchandise shall be held by the Consignee

in trust for the Consignor and be kept separate and apart from all other moneys the Consignee may have, and the Consignee shall be entitled to deduct from such trust funds daily the amount of his commission aforesaid, and shall pay the balance to the Consignor as follows:

(method of payment to be inserted)

7. Consignee must be in a position at all times to account to the Consignor for all sales of the said merchandise and to pay the Consignor for such merchandise in the manner aforesaid, and all sales of the consigned merchandise shall be accounted for in cash;

8. This consignment contract remains in full force and effect until terminated by notice in writing from the Consignee to the Consignor, or until terminated by the Consignor so terminating without notice to the Consignee, and termination shall not effect the rights of the Consignor to forthwith take possession of and remove the consigned merchandise from the Consignee's premises or anywhere else nor shall it release the Consignee from the duty to account to the Consignor or from any other obligation to the Consignor that may then remain unfulfilled.

DATED at the Municipality of Metropolitan Toronto this _____ day of _____ 1970.

_____
(consignor)

_____
(consignee)

APPENDIX "B" cont

Dear Sir –

We are enclosing herewith a consignment agreement which sets out the method of doing business between you and our company. It has been our unfortunate experience in the last few years to find that numerous variety stores & drugstores have failed in business. In certain of these cases it has proven difficult in obtaining our consigned goods from the bailiff or trustee not having a formal agreement available to them.

We also wish to have our records as complete as possible as to trade name, proprietor, address, etc. and we have set out the area at the end of the agreement for the required information.

If there are any questions concerning this agreement, we invite you to contact either J. B. Wilcock or D. Robinson in our office (755-1166). We are enclosing a stamped addressed envelope to be used in returning the agreement to us. If you desire a copy of the agreement we will be glad to supply it to you.

Insurance

Item 6 re submission of monies (and be kept separate?) & 7 –

APP. 12

Received in handwritten form.

APPENDIX C

Toronto News Company
120 Sinnott Road
Scarborough, Ontario
Phone (416) 755-1166

Dear Dealer:

It has been our feeling for some time that there should be a clearly defined working arrangement between ourselves and our dealers.

Therefore, we would ask that you sign and return one copy of the attached dealer agreement as soon as possible.

Should there be any questions, please contact me at 755-1166.

Sincerely,

LM/s
Encl.

Larry Macfarlane,
Credit Manager.

APP. 13

Exhibit No. 9

GUIDELINES RE APPLICATIONS FOR GUARANTEED LOANS

PROVINCE OF ONTARIO

ROYAL COMMISSION ON BOOK PUBLISHING

FINANCIAL ASSISTANCE TO
CANADIAN BOOK PUBLISHERS

INFORMATION AND GUIDELINES
FOR
COMPLETION OF APPLICATION FORMS

November 1971

FIRMS ELIGIBLE FOR ASSISTANCE

Canadian-owned book publishers which have their head office in the Province of Ontario and also employ over 50% of their full-time employees in Ontario may be eligible for assistance from the Province of Ontario in the form of (a) a guarantee of a loan made by a commercial lending institution and/or (b) a rebate of interest.

The loans to be guaranteed and/or interest cost assistance will only be within credit lines to be approved annually and only after the Province (Commission) has fully studied applications received and reached a favourable business judgment on all aspects of the loan in question.

The line of credit in no case is to exceed 75% of eligible bound Canadian books valued at the lower of cost or market plus 75% of accounts receivable relating to sales of eligible books only, the latter to be valued after full provision for doubtful accounts.

The Ontario Government, when it becomes a loan guarantor, is to become a preferred and secured creditor through the assignment or transfer of any previous assignments of accounts receivable and inventories.

The degree to which interest costs are to be subsidized is to be the subject of annual policy review and budgeting, and the application for the interest subsidy must be reviewed annually.

Where the Ontario Government acts as guarantor the applicant must be incorporated under either the laws of Ontario or the laws of Canada. This restriction only applies in the case of firms whose loans will be guaranteed by the Ontario Government.

It is suggested that prior to completing the application form for financial assistance the applicant read the "Third Interim Report of the Royal Commission on Book Publishing" which outlines the financial assistance plan. A copy of the report is attached.

DEFINITIONS

– "eligible books" are bound (cloth or paper) Canadian books written by either a permanent resident of Canada or a Canadian citizen, and originally published by the applicant.
– "a Canadian-owned book publisher" which is a corporation shall not have more than 25 per cent of the total voting shares beneficially owned, directly or indirectly, by non-residents nor subject to the control or direction of non-residents, and not more than 10 per cent of the total shares shall be owned or controlled by a single non-resident.

GUIDELINES FOR COMPLETING APPLICATION AND SUBMITTING INFORMATION

1. The financial information included in the application form should not be more than 90 days old and where applicable should be as of the same date as the unaudited monthly financial statements submitted with the application (see item 7 below). If the application is submitted within 90 days of the fiscal year end only audited financial statements will be accepted and the financial information included in the application should agree with the audited financial statements, where applicable.
2. The list of parent, affiliated, associated and subsidiary companies must include all companies on which a majority of the Board of Directors of the applicant are common to the Board of Directors of any other company. An affiliated company includes any company which is effectively controlled or managed by another company and includes situations where a company is effectively controlled even when the owner holds less than 50% of the voting shares.
3. The applicant is to provide a list of all collateral pledged as security to any loan from any commercial lender. The Commission intends to have a representative of the Ontario Government discuss the application for assistance with a representative of the applicants bank and/or commercial lender, and filing of the attached application is to be interpreted as authorizing such discussions.
4. A schedule of debt of the applicant which is outstanding for a period of more than one year is to be provided. This schedule should show for each loan (a) interest rate (b) repayment terms (c) collateral pledged and (d) details of arrears, if any.
5. The following information is to be provided in connection with the eligible book inventory which is to be pledged as collateral to the guarantee–
(a) a list of eligible books showing for each book (as of the date on the balance sheet submitted with the application).
  (i) title and ISBN (International Standard Book Number), if ISBN assigned
  (ii) name and address of author
  (iii) where author is a non-resident but a Canadian citizen
  (iv) date of first publication of the edition listed
  (v) quantity on hand
  (vi) list price and normal trade discount
  (vii) cost per unit (or inventory valuation where lower than cost)
  (viii) unit sales during preceding twelve months
  (ix) accumulated unit sales (Information compiled for royalty payments should be a source which can be used to help prepare this information)
  (x) if the author is not a resident of Canada or a Canadian citizen state that the book is the first edition, if such is the case
  (xi) any obsolescence provision
(b) the list of eligible books should include as a separate category the same details for books out on consignment and a statement that unsold inventory on consignment has not been included in sales.
(c) the basis of valuing the inventory should be described. If inventory is valued at cost, the com-

ponents of costs should be described e.g. printing costs, art work, editorial costs (if any), overhead (if any). If inventory is valued at market, define market value. If there has been a change in the basis of valuing the inventory within the last two years, the details should be provided.
(d) the basis of providing for obsolescence by the applicant should be described. If there has been any change in applying this principle within the last two years, the details should be supplied.

The Commission recognizes that a substantial amount of detailed information has been requested and regrets the inconvenience to each applicant. Since it is often a policy of banks, etc. not to accept bound books as collateral, and since it is incumbent upon the Commission to make a sound business judgment on any loan it guarantees, it is necessary to obtain the above information.

If the applicant wishes to submit the analysis of the eligible inventory in a format different to that outlined above permission must be obtained from the offices of the Commission prior to submitting the application.

6. As has been stated above the line of credit is not to exceed the total of 75% of the eligible book inventory plus 75% of accounts receivable relating to sales of eligible books. The Commission recognizes the practical difficulties in ascertaining which accounts receivable are in respect of eligible books and which accounts receivable are in respect of other sales. Accordingly, the Commission intends to assume that the accounts receivable mix is the same as the sales mix for the last twelve months. The Commission will adjust for any significant inequities caused by this policy.

7. The unaudited monthly financial statements which are to be submitted must include the period ending not less than 90 days from the date of the application. These financial statements should be in comparative form showing year-to-date figures for the preceding fiscal period.

Thus it is anticipated that an application dated November 30, 1971 will be accompanied by financial statements which report on the period ending August 31, 1971. If later monthly statements are available these would be preferred.

8. The general description of the company should include (a) a brief description of the corporate structure, (b) the number of employees, (c) the names and addresses of book publishers for which the applicant acts as agent, (d) details of any planned capital expenditures in excess of 10% of the credit line sought, (e) details of any operations carried on in addition to book publishing such as book clubs, printing, etc. In addition the most recent catalogue of the books available for sale must accompany the application.

9. The summary of the publishing programme for the next twelve months should be brief and only include those projects which will be worked on during the next twelve-month period.

10. The budgeted profit and loss statement should be prepared for the twelve-month period commencing on the day following the end of the period covered by the unaudited financial statements. The statement should show by month (a) estimated sales by major category, (b) estimated cost of sales and (c) the budgeted operating expenses. Cash flow projections for the next twelve months would be appreciated.

11. Trade accounts receivable –
(a) this listing must age the accounts receivable where the amount receivable from any one customer is in excess of $25,
(b) the list should be prepared in columnar form and each customer's account should be analyzed to disclose the total amount receivable, the current portion, the portion more than 30 days in arrears and the portion more than 90 days in arrears,
(c) each column should be added so that a total is shown separately for current accounts, accounts 30 days in arrears, accounts 60 days in arrears, etc.,
(d) the total of the accounts receivable should agree with the amount shown on the balance sheet of the monthly statement required (see point 9). For this purpose it will be necessary to include in the accounts receivable listing as one figure all accounts under $25.

(e) the total of all accounts under $25 more than 90 days in arrears must be disclosed as a separate figure,
(f) the total allowance for doubtful accounts provided against the accounts receivable must be shown. If the allowance has been provided on an account by account basis, please provide the details.

If the applicant wishes to submit the accounts receivable aging list in a format which is different to that described above permission must be obtained from the offices of the Commission prior to submitting the application.

Accounts receivable from subsidiaries, associated, or affiliated companies probably will not be eligible as collateral.

Any queries on the above instructions or on the information to be included in the application should be directed to the offices of the Royal Commission on Book Publishing, Suite S-750, 252 Bloor Street West, Toronto – telephone 365-7801. On completion, please forward your application to the above address.

BRIEFS RECEIVED

Addison Wesley (Canada) Limited
Thomas Allen & Son Limited
Alphatext Systems Limited (Ottawa)
Antiquarian Booksellers Association of Canada
Professor B. J. Arnold
Association of Canadian Television & Radio Artists
L'Association Canadienne-Française de l'Ontario
L'Association des Enseignants Franco-Ontariens
Association of Universities and Colleges of Canada
Dr. D. C. Baird
Mr. W. H. E. Belt
Berandol Music Limited
Professor Vincent Bladen
Book & Periodical Acquisitions Limited
Book Promotion and Editorial Club
Books in Canada
The Book Society of Canada Limited
Mr. Michael Bradley
Mr. Max Braithwaite
The Albert Britnell Book Shop Limited
Burns & MacEachern Limited
Business Supply Company (Lakehead) Limited
Mr. R. A. Calladine
Canadian Association of College and University Libraries
Canadian Association of Principals of Independent Schools for Girls
Canadian Association of Professors of Education

Canadian Association of School Administrators
Canadian Association of University Teachers
Canadian Authors Association
Canadian Book Manufacturers' Institute
Canadian Book Publishers' Council
Canadian Booksellers Association
Canadian Books in Print
Canadian Copyright Institute
Canadian Federation of University Women (Ontario)
Canadian Historical Review
Canadian Institute of International Affairs
Canadian Library Association
Canadian Library Association Publishers
Canadian National Institute for the Blind
Canadian Society of Book Illustrators
Canadian Teachers' Federation
Canadian Writers' Guild
Canterbury House (Anglican Book Society)
Carleton University Library Editorial Board
Carswell Company Limited
Clarke, Irwin & Company Limited
Professor Stephen Clarkson
Community Resource Centre
Compkey Limited
Mr. William E. Corfield
Council of Ontario Universities
John Coutts Library Services Limited
J. M. Dent & Sons (Canada) Limited
Mr. Lovat Dickson
Dorann Publishing Company Limited
Doubleday Canada Limited
Douglas Publishing & Printing Company
Mr. George F. Doyle
Dutch Magazine and Book Import Co.
East York Board of Education
Educational Media Association of Canada
Miss Marian Engel
Festival Editions of Canada Limited
Mr. John Fisher
Fitzhenry & Whiteside Limited

French Language Advisory Committees of the
　Ottawa and Carleton Boards of Education
Gage Educational Publishing Limited
Gateway Press Limited
General Publishing Co. Limited
Mr. Jack O. Gibbons
GLC Educational Materials and Services Ltd.
Gray's Publishing Ltd. (Sidney, B.C.)
Mr. W. L. C. Greer
Griffin Press Limited
Grolier Limited
Mr. Tass T. Gundel
Dr. Francess G. Halpenny
Harlequin Enterprises Limited
Miss Eleanor T. Harman
Harvest House Limited Publishers
D. C. Heath Canada Limited
Mr. William C. Heine
Mr. Alan Heisey
Holt, Rinehart and Winston of Canada Limited
House of Anansi Press Limited
Mrs. Bettye Hyde (Algonquin College)
Independent Publishers' Association
Interested Librarians and a Bookseller from Thunder Bay
　(Separate Brief from Mr. F. Brent Scollie)
James Lewis & Samuel/Publishers
Professor J. R. Kidd (OISE)
Lake Erie Regional Library System
Lakehead Board of Education
Lakehead District R.C.S.S. Board
Mr. Dennis Lee
Lincoln County Board of Education
Lincoln County Separate School Board
London Board of Education
Professor J. P. Lovekin
Mr. J. G. I. Mackay
Mr. B. Allan Mackie
Maclean-Hunter Learning Materials Company
Maclean-Hunter Limited and Co-operative Book Centre of Canada Limited
The Macmillan Company of Canada Ltd.
Mr. John F. Marriott

Peter Martin Associates Limited
McClelland and Stewart Limited
McGill-Queen's University Press
McGraw-Hill Company of Canada Limited
Mr. William E. McLeod
Mr. D. McNeil
Mr. James H. McNeill
Middlesex County Board of Education
Middlesex County R.C.S.S. Board
Mr. James Miller
Mr. Douglas C. Moore
Moreland-Latchford Productions Ltd.
NDP Club of University of Windsor
Thomas Nelson & Sons (Canada) Limited
New Press
Northmount Junior High School
Oberon Press
Ontario Council for the Arts, Province of
Ontario Confederation of University Faculty Associations
Ontario Council of University Librarians
Ontario Institute for Studies in Education (Editorial Board)
Ontario Institute for Studies in Education (Field Development)
Ontario Library Association
Ontario Secondary School Teachers' Federation
Ontario Teachers' Federation
Orchard Park Public School (Grade 8 Students)
Ottawa – Le Conseil des Ecoles Séparées Catholiques d'Ottawa
Oxford University Press (Canadian Branch)
Professor R. J. D. Page
Palm Publishers Limited
Pendragon House Limited
Pitt Publishing Company Limited
Poseidon Press
Prentice-Hall of Canada Ltd.
Progress Books
Provincial Council of Women of Ontario
Quill & Quire
Radicals for Capitalism
Mr. Wallace H. Robb
Mr. John Rodriguez
Rev. H. R. Rokeby-Thomas

Mr. John W. Routh
Saanes Computer Publications Limited
W. B. Saunders Company Canada Limited
Scholastic-Tab Publications Ltd.
Science Research Associates (Canada) Limited
S.C.M. Book Room
Serasia Limited
68 Publishers Toronto
Mr. R. A. Smith
W. H. Smith and Son (Canada) Ltd.
Smithers & Bonellie Limited
Mr. Richard H. Steacy
Mr. R. R. Steele
Mr. James Stevens
Sudbury Public Library
Professor J. Terasmae
Toronto Graphic Arts Labour Council
Toronto Public Library Board
Mrs. Margaret I. Tyson
United Church of Canada (Division of Communication)
University of British Columbia Press
University & College Publishers' Group
University of Toronto Library
University of Toronto, School of Library Science
University of Waterloo, Department of English
University of Western Ontario,
    History of Education Department
University of Western Ontario,
    School of Business Administration
University of Windsor Press
Upstairs Gallery
Van Nostrand Reinhold Ltd.
Mr. John Velanoff
Waterloo County Board of Education
Welland County R.C.S.S. Board
John Wiley & Sons Canada, Limited
Windsor Board of Education
Wolfe's Book Store (Sudbury)
York Board of Education
York County School Librarians Association

COPYRIGHT ACT – EXCERPTS

2. In this Act

"architectural work of art" means any building or structure having an artistic character or design, in respect of such character or design, or any model for such building or structure, but the protection afforded by this Act is confined to the artistic character and design, and does not extend to processes or methods of construction;

"artistic work" includes works of painting, drawing, sculpture and artistic craftsmanship, and architectural works of art and engravings and photographs;

"book" includes every volume, part or division of a volume, pamphlet, sheet of letterpress, sheet of music, map, chart, or plan separately published;

"cinematograph" includes any work produced by any process analogous to cinematography;

"collective work" means

(a) an encyclopaedia, dictionary, year book, or similar work,

(b) a newspaper, review, magazine, or similar periodical, and

(c) any work written in distinct parts by different authors, or in which works or parts of works of different authors are incorporated;

"delivery," in relation to a lecture, includes delivery by means of any mechanical instrument;

"dramatic work" includes any piece for recitation, choreographic work or entertainment in dumb show, the scenic arrangement or acting form of which is fixed in writing or otherwise, and any cinematograph production where the arrangement or acting form or the combination of incidents represented give the work an original character;

"engravings" includes etchings, lithographs, woodcuts, prints, and other similar works, not being photographs;

"every original literary, dramatic, musical and artistic work" includes every original production in the literary, scientific or artistic domain, whatever may be the mode or form of its expression, such as books, pamphlets, and other writings, lectures, dramatic or dramatico-musical works, musical works or compositions with or without words, illustrations, sketches, and plastic works relative to geography, topography, architecture or science;

"Her Majesty's Realms and Territories" includes any territories under Her Majesty's protection to which an order in council made under the provisions of section 28 of the *Copyright Act, 1911*, passed by the Parliament of the United Kingdom, relates;

"infringing", when applied to a copy of a work in which copyright subsists, means any copy, including any colourable imitation, made, or imported in contravention of this Act;

"lecture" includes address, speech, and sermon;

"legal representatives" includes heirs, executors, administrators, successors and assigns, or agents or attorneys who are thereunto duly authorized in writing;

"literary work" includes maps, charts, plans, tables, and compilations;

"Minister" means the Minister of Consumer and Corporate Affairs;

"musical work" means any combination of melody and harmony, or either of them, printed, reduced to writing, or otherwise graphically produced or reproduced;

"performance" means any acoustic representation of a work or any visual representation of any dramatic action in a work, including a representation made by means of any mechanical instrument or by radio communication;

"photograph" includes photo-lithograph and any work produced by any process analogous to photography;

"plate" includes any stereotype or other plate, stone, block, mould, matrix, transfer, or negative used or intended to be used for printing or reproducing copies of any work, and any matrix or other appliance by which records, perforated rolls, or other contrivances for the acoustic representation of the work, are or are intended to be made;

"work" includes the title thereof when such title is original and distinctive;

"work of joint authorship" means a work produced by the collaboration of two or more authors in which the contribution of one author is not distinct from the contribution of the other author or authors;

"work of sculpture" includes casts and models. R.S., c. 55, s. 2; 1966-67, c. 25, s. 38; 1967-68, c. 16, s. 10.

3. (2) For the purposes of this Act, "publication", in relation to any work, means the issue of copies of the work to the public, and does not include the performance in public of a dramatic or musical work, the delivery in public of a lecture, the exhibition in public of an artistic work, or the construction of an architectural work of art, but for the purpose of this provision, the issue of photographs and engravings of works of sculpture and architectural works of art shall not be deemed to be publication of such works.

7. (1) After the expiration of twenty-five years, or in the case of a work in which copyright subsisted on the 4th day of June 1921, thirty years, from the death of the author of a published work, copyright in the work shall not be deemed to be infringed by the reproduction of the work for sale if the person reproducing the work proves that he has given the prescribed notice in writing of his intention to reproduce the work, and that he has paid in the prescribed manner to, or for the benefit of, the owner of the copyright, royalties in respect of all copies of the work sold by him, calculated at the rate of ten per cent on the price at which he publishes the work.

(2) For the purposes of this section, the Governor in Council may make regulations prescribing the mode in which notices are to be given, and the particulars to be given in such notices, and the mode, time, and frequency of the payment of royalties, including, if he thinks fit, regulations requiring payment in advance or otherwise securing the payment of royalties. R.S., c. 55, s. 7.

12. (5) Where the author of a work is the first owner of the copyright therein, no assignment of the copyright, and no grant of any interest therein, made by him, otherwise than by will, after the 4th day of June 1921, is operative to vest in the assignee or grantee any rights with respect to the copyright in the work beyond the expiration of twenty-five years from the death of the author, and the reversionary interests in the copyright expectant on the termination of that period shall, on the death of the author, notwithstanding any agreement to the contrary, devolve on his legal representatives as part of his estate, and any agreement entered into by him as to the disposition of such

reversionary interest is void; but nothing in this subsection shall be construed as applying to the assignment of the copyright in a collective work or a licence to publish a work or part of a work as part of a collective work.

13. Where, at any time after the death of the author of a literary, dramatic, or musical work that has been published or performed in public, a complaint is made to the Governor in Council that the owner of the copyright in the work has refused to republish or to allow the republication of the work or has refused to allow the performance in public of the work, and that by reason of such refusal the work is withheld from the public, the owner of the copyright may be ordered to grant a licence to reproduce the work or perform the work in public, as the case may be, on such terms and subject to such conditions as the Governor in Council may think fit. R.S., c. 55, s. 13.

14. (1) Any person may apply to the Minister for a licence to print and publish in Canada any book wherein copyrights subsists, if at any time after publication and within the duration of the copyright the owner of the copyright fails

(a) to print the book or cause it to be printed in Canada, or

(b) to supply by means of copies so printed the reasonable demands of the Canadian market for the book.

(2) An application under subsection (1) may be in such form as may be prescribed by the regulations and shall state the proposed retail price of the edition of the book proposed to be printed.

(3) Every applicant for a licence under this section shall with his application deposit with the Minister an amount not less than ten per cent of the retail selling price of one thousand copies of the book and not less than one hundred dollars and such amount shall, if the application is unsuccessful, be returned to the applicant less such deductions for fees as may be authorized by the regulations.

(4) Notice of the application shall forthwith be communicated by the Minister to the owner of the copyright in such manner as may be prescribed by the regulations.

(5) Where the owner of the copyright does not within a delay to be fixed by the regulations after communication of the notice give an undertaking, with such security as may be prescribed by the regulations, to procure within two months after the date of such communication the printing in Canada of an edition of not less than one thousand copies of such book, the Minister in his discretion may grant to the applicant a licence to print and publish the book upon terms to be determined by the Minister after hearing the parties or affording them such opportunity to be heard as may be fixed by the regulations.

(6) Where two or more persons have applied for a licence under this section, the Minister shall award the licence to the applicant proposing the terms, in the opinion of the Minister, most advantageous to the author, and if there are two proposing terms equally advantageous to the author, to the applicant whose application was first received.

(7) Such licence when issued entitles the licensee to the sole right to print and publish such book in Canada during such term, not exceeding five years or for such edition or editions as may be fixed by the licence.

(8) Such licensee shall pay a royalty on the retail selling price of every copy of such book printed under such licence, at a rate to be determined by the Minister.

(9) The acceptance of a licence for a book shall imply an undertaking by the licensee

(a) to print and publish in Canada an edition of the book of not less than one thousand copies, at the price specified in the licence, and within two months from the issue of the licence, and

(b) to print the same from the last authorized edition of the book in such manner as may be prescribed by the Minister, in full, without abbreviation or alteration of the letterpress, and, without varying, adding to, or diminishing the main design of such of the prints, engravings, maps, charts, musical compositions, or photographs contained in the book as the licensee reproduces.

(10) Every book published under a licence under this section shall have printed or otherwise impressed upon it the words "Printed under Canadian licence", the calendar year of such licence and the retail selling price of such book.

(11) Where the Minister on complaint is satisfied that the licensee does not print and keep on sale in Canada a number of copies of the book sufficient to supply the reasonable demands, he shall, after giving the licensee an opportunity of being heard to show cause against the cancellation, cancel the licence.

(12) Where a book for which a licence has been issued is suppressed by the owner of the copyright, the licensee shall not print the book or any further copies thereof, but may sell any copies already printed, and may complete and sell any copies in process of being printed under his licence, but the owner of the copyright is entitled to buy all such copies at the cost of printing them.

(13) Nothing in this section authorizes the granting, without the consent of the author, of a licence to publish a second or succeeding edition of any work whereof such author has published one or more editions in Canada. R.S., c. 55, s. 14.

17. (1) Copyright in a work shall be deemed to be infringed by any person who, without the consent of the owner of the copyright, does anything that, by this Act, only the owner of the copyright has the right to do.

(2) The following acts do not constitute an infringement of copyright:

(*a*) any fair dealing with any work for the purposes of private study, research, criticism, review, or newspaper summary;

(*b*) where the author of an artistic work is not the owner of the copyright therein, the use by the author of any mould, cast, sketch, plan, model, or study made by him for the purpose of the work, if he does not thereby repeat or imitate the main design of that work;

(*c*) the making or publishing of paintings, drawings, engravings, or photographs of a work of sculpture or artistic craftsmanship, if permanently situated in a public place or building, or the making or publishing of paintings, drawings, engravings, or photographs that are not in the nature of architectural drawings or plans, of any architectural work of art;

(*d*) the publication in a collection, mainly composed of non-copyright mater, *bona fide* intended for the use of schools, and so described in the title and in any advertisements issued by the publisher, of short passages from published literary works not themselves published for the use of schools in which copyright subsists, if not more than two of such passages from works by the same author are published by the same publisher within five years, and the source from which such passages are taken is acknowledged;

(*e*) the publication in a newspaper of a report of a lecture delivered in public, unless the report is prohibited by conspicuous written or printed notice affixed before and maintained during the lecture at or about the main entrance of the building in which the lecture is given, and, except while the building is being used for public worship, in a position near the lecturer; but nothing in this paragraph affects the provisions in paragraph (*a*) as to newspaper summaries;

(*f*) the reading or recitation in public by one person of any reasonable extract from any published work;

(*g*) the performance without motive of gain of any musical work at any agricultural, agricultural- industrial exhibition or fair which receives a grant from or is held under federal, provincial or municipal authority, by the directors thereof.

18. Notwithstanding anything in this Act, it shall not be an infringement of copyright in an address of a political nature delivered at a public meeting to publish a report thereof in a newspaper. R.S., c. 55, s. 18.

19. (2) Nothing in subsection (1) authorizes any alterations in, or omissions from, the work reproduced, unless contrivances reproducing the work subject to similar alterations and omissions

have been previously made by, or with the consent or acquiescence of, the owner of the copyright, or unless such alterations or omissions are reasonably necessary for the adaptation of the work to the contrivances in question.

(3) For the purposes of subsection (1), a musical, literary or dramatic work shall not be deemed to include a contrivance by means of which sounds may be mechanically reproduced.

27. Copies made out of Canada of any work in which copyright subsists that if made in Canada would infringe copyright and as to which the owner of the copyright gives notice in writing to the Department of National Revenue that he is desirous that such copies should not be so imported into Canada, shall not be so imported, and shall be deemed to be included in Schedule C to the *Customs Tariff*, and that Schedule applies accordingly. R.S., c. 55, s. 27.

28. (1) Where the owner of the copyright has by licence or otherwise granted the right to reproduce any book in Canada, or where a licence to reproduce such book has been granted under this Act, it shall not be lawful except as provided in subsection (3) to import into Canada copies of such book, and such copies shall be deemed to be included in Schedule C to the *Customs Tariff*, and that Schedule applies accordingly.

(2) Except as provided in subsection (3), it shall be unlawful to import into Canada copies of any book in which copyright subsists until fourteen days after publication thereof and during such period or any extension thereof such copies shall be deemed to be included in Schedule C to the *Customs Tariff*, and that Schedule applies accordingly, but if within that period of fourteen days an application for a licence has been made in accordance with the provisions of this Act relating thereto, the Minister may in his discretion extend the period, and shall forthwith notify the Department of National Revenue of such extension; and the prohibition against importation shall be continued accordingly.

(3) Notwithstanding anything in this Act it shall be lawful for any person

(*a*) to import for his own use not more than two copies of any work published in any country adhering to the Convention;

(*b*) to import for use by any department of the Government of Canada or any province, copies of any work, wherever published;

(*c*) at any time before a work is printed or made in Canada to import any copies required for the use of any public library or institution of learning;

(*d*) to import any book lawfully printed in Great Britain or in a foreign country that has adhered to the Convention and the Additional Protocol thereto set out in Schedule II and published for circulation among, and sale to the public within either; but any officer of customs, may in his discretion, require any person seeking to import any work under this section to produce satisfactory evidence of the facts necessary to establish his right so to import.

(4) This section does not apply to any work the author of which is a British subject, other than a Canadian citizen, or the subject or citizen of a country that has adhered to the Convention and the Additional Protocol thereto set out in Schedule II. R.S., c. 55, s. 28.

29. The Copyright Office shall be attached to the Patent Office. R.S., c. 55, s. 29.

PHOTOCOPYING IN THE ONTARIO EDUCATIONAL MARKET

The following excerpts are from the pilot survey of photocopying in the Ontario educational market prepared by Kates, Peat, Marwick & Co., as explained in Chapter 3 of the report. Omitted are samples of forms used, and portions of the introduction only.

KATES, PEAT, MARWICK & CO. REPORT

I – STUDY OBJECTIVES AND APPROACH

The following objectives were specified in our letter of January 7, 1972. They are to determine for the educational market in Ontario (as previously defined):
1. The total number of photocopying machines.
2. The names of the principal manufacturers of these machines.
3. The commercial terms governing the supply of machines and machine supplies, including paper.
4. An estimate of the amount of photocopying of printed material (which may be subject to copyright).

With specific reference to the manufacturers, we were to estimate from data made available:
1. The significance of the Ontario educational market to the manufacturers of photocopying equipment and supplies.
2. The rate of growth of photocopying with special reference to the Ontario educational market.
3. The impact of any changes in technology that are anticipated by the manufacturers on the nature and extent of photocopying.
4. The philosophy of manufacturers regarding commercial terms and any anticipated changes in this philosophy.

Finally, we were to provide an assessment of the value of the photocopying of printed material (which may be subject to copyright) from the results of a sampling of equipment in the educational market.

Approach to the Study

Following a brief review of data available on some educational institutions, we designed two sets of questionnaires with guidelines for their completion. One set was designed for a survey of educational institutions, while the other focused on the manufacturers of photocopying equipment and supplies.

We then interviewed selected institutions and manufacturers. As a result we modified the questionnaires and guidelines. Copies of the final forms were attached to our progress letter to the Royal Commission dated February 24, 1972.

To obtain a reasonably representative sampling, we selected educational institutions according to the following criteria:

– *size*, for example including the University of Toronto and Lakehead University
– *geographical environment*, for example including the Metropolitan Toronto Library Board and the South Central Library System which includes several rural libraries
– *types of service organization*, for example including the Toronto School Board Education Centre and high school libraries.

In large institutions such as the University of Toronto, faculties and library systems were chosen where photocopying utilization was high and the numbers of machines would provide a significant proportion of the total amount of photocopying currently carried out. Examples of those selected include the Faculty of Arts and Science and the Sigmund Samuel Library System at the University of Toronto, Osgoode Hall at York University and the Education Centre Library of the Toronto Board of Education.

Each institution, faculty or other sub-component was visited to review the questionnaire in detail for a correct and uniform interpretation of the data required. In addition, we explained to the coordinators of the individual machine monitoring surveys what standards were required and how each survey was to be conducted.

Appendix A contains the documentation used for data collection from institutions, including the letter, survey instructions, monitoring and tabulation sheets, and a list of data sources.

We also visited key manufacturers, to review in detail the information required, and discuss the industry and its future with senior executives.

Appendix B contains the documentation used for data collection from manufacturers, including letters, survey instructions, and lists of data sources.

The collection and tabulation of data carried out in the institutions and by manufacturers was supervised by our professional staff through interviews and by telephone. We obtained a reasonable degree of co-operation from the institutions and manufacturers throughout the project.

A feature of our approach to each organization from whom data was requested was in offering to reimburse any additional administrative costs incurred in the collection and tabulation procedures. A number of the organizations were reimbursed for such costs in this manner after review of the expenses claimed.

II – THE ONTARIO EDUCATIONAL MARKET

The Ontario educational market was defined for the purpose of the study as universities, colleges, schools and library systems including both public and educational library systems. This market is characterized by a number of customers far in excess of the number of institutions or systems since departments or faculties within universities, and constituent units of other institutions tend to work independently in obtaining photocopying equipment and supplies.

The Machine Population and the Suppliers

From manufacturers' data we estimate that the number of photocopying machines in the Ontario education market was nearly 7,000 as of December 31, 1971. We have ascertained that:
– between 60% and 70% of this total are manual machines.
– All of this portion of the photocopying machine population has been sold to the customer at between $150 and $400. Although manufacturers continue to sell these machines, the trend is towards supplying automatic machines on the basis of a leasing arrangement.
– Approximately one half of the manual machines use a thermographic process and although manufacturers continue to sell this type of machine there is a strong trend towards the use of machines using more recently discovered processes such as xerography.
– The manual machines require individual feeding while automatic machines do not. Thus, the speed of these manual machines is approximately five copies per minute, compared to automatic machines which can run at speeds near one copy per second.

Twelve manufacturers supply the market. Their names appear in Exhibit 1 *opposite*. Of these, one manufacturer has installed the largest proportion, with another manufacturer having a significant, and increasing share. Other manufacturers together have supplied a small proportion of these machines.

EXHIBIT 1

MANUFACTURERS SUPPLYING THE EDUCATIONAL
MARKET IN ONTARIO – 1971

A. B. Dick Co. of Canada Ltd.	Olivetti Canada Ltd.
Addressograph-Multigraph of Canada Ltd.	Pitney Bowes of Canada Ltd.
Apeco of Canada Ltd.	Smith-Corona Marchant Division of
Bell & Howell Canada Ltd.	SCM (Canada) Ltd.
Block & Anderson (Canada) Ltd.	The Minnesota Mining & Manufacturing
Dennison Manufacturing Co. of Canada Ltd.	Co. of Canada Ltd.
Murritt Photofax Limited	Xerox of Canada Ltd.

EXHIBIT 2

SIZE AND SIGNIFICANCE OF THE ONTARIO EDUCATION MARKET TO MANUFACTURERS 1969-1971

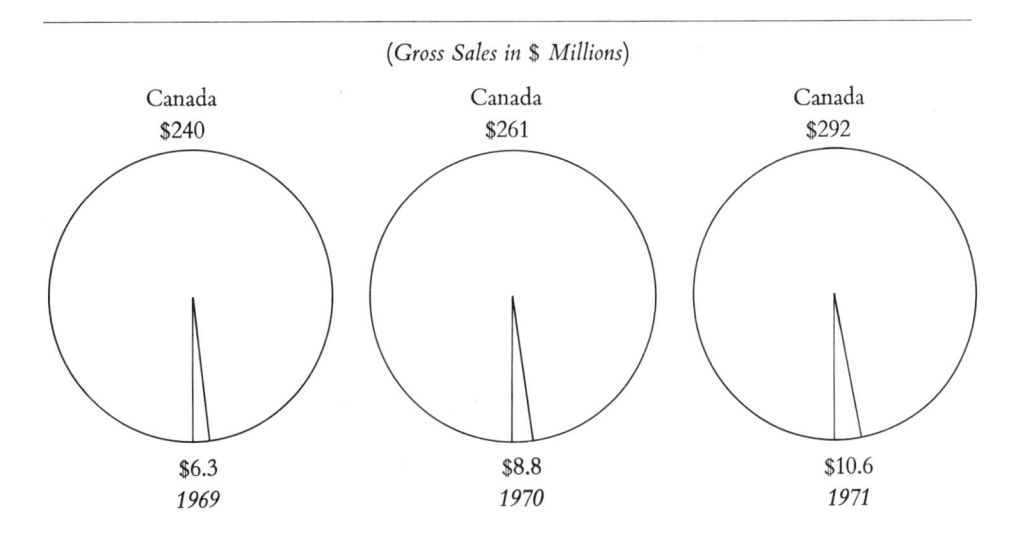

(Gross Sales in $ Millions)

Canada $240	Canada $261	Canada $292
$6.3	$8.8	$10.6
1969	1970	1971

Significance of Photocopying to Manufacturers

The manufacturers supplied data on their gross sales for photocopying equipment and supplies in Canada for the three years 1969 to 1971 and the percentage of that figure represented by their sales to the Ontario educational market. The dollar value of sales in the Ontario educational market was calculated from this data. Exhibit 2 *opposite* illustrates the size and relative significance of the Ontario education market over the period 1969 to 1971.

The Ontario education market in 1971 at $10 million comprised 3% of the total sales of photocopying equipment and supplies in Canada. However, the growth rate for Ontario differed sharply from that for all of Canada, with the Ontario market registering a 40% and then 20% increase compared to 8% and 12% respectively for the Canadian market. Thus these are indications that the Ontario educational market is becoming an increasingly significant source of revenue for the manufacturers.

Examination of individual company data indicated that most companies are experiencing minimal growth in the Ontario educational market while a few are registering significant percentage increases.

Future Trends

Representatives of each of the manufacturers were asked to comment on trends and technological changes which might affect the photocopying market.

One participant mentioned a trend in the industry toward the introduction of plain paper copiers as opposed to copiers producing copies on sensitized paper. He concluded that the trend would have little impact on costs and certainly none on volumes. In the same vein, another manufacturer observed that one factor which could impact on their sales volumes was the increasing popularity of equipment using bond paper. Diffusion transfer copiers and dry copiers are gradually being replaced by electrostatic and xerographic copying processes with a resultant decrease in sales of less technologically advanced equipment.

Another manufacturer commented that electrostatic copying can be really looked on as a form of printing, its only limitation at this time being the state of the art. He drew an analogy between Guttenberg's printing press and modern rotogravure, indicating that as the technologies evolve, quality and speed will improve, and that time has a way of increasing usage and reducing real costs. He concluded that this will encourage utilization of the process, cutting into traditional printing operations.

Coin-operated copiers are particularly susceptible to increases in utilization with reduced costs. Other factors which could impact on volume and cost figures for coin-operated machines include:

1. Colour Reproduction

The ability to reproduce colour accurately and rapidly will affect volume utilization, particularly in areas such as history, medicine, or oceanography. Initially costs per copy for colour will be high but volume usage is expected to reduce costs appreciably.

2. Multiple Copy Vending Equipment

Coin equipment which provides multiple copies from the same original is expected to have a significant effect on both volumes and costs.

Current and Future Commercial Terms

Our collection of data from institutions and manufacturers reveals that although 65% to 70% of the total number of machines are owned by the customer, a trend towards leasing seems to be emerging. Most machines installed in the last six to twelve months are operating on a lease or rental basis.

Most supplier-owned machines in the education market are leased either on a flat monthly or annual charge plus cost per copy or on an all-inclusive cost per copy plan (including equipment rental and supplies). There are numerous variations within these two categories and the actual flat charge or cost per copy differs from machine to machine or from model to model.

Our survey of manufacturers revealed a number of viewpoints on commercial terms. Two manufacturers, one currently having the largest share of the market, prefer to sell copying equipment to the education market. However, since competition is intense they will, under certain circumstances, give the customer whatever plan he requests. A third manufacturer echoed this last statement but felt that installation on a cost-per-copy basis is the most popular commercial system at present.

Two other participants indicated a willingness to establish any program of installation requested by the customer providing the installation is profitable.

The philosophy of one manufacturer is that a cost-per-copy agreement is better for the customer in that it does not conceal "true cost". Customers too are increasingly reluctant to invest in high-cost machinery which is subject to constant and rapid technological change. Many of the manufacturers therefore lean to some type of cost-per-copy or lease arrangement, with one specifically indicating that the majority of pricing in the industry will continue to be on a cent-per-copy basis.

Costs to Institutions

Photocopying in institutions is the responsibility of individual divisions, departments, libraries, faculties, schools etc. who administer their own operating budgets and assume individual responsibility for photocopying service and costs. Each selects a purchase or lease plan which seems to offer them the best value. There is seldom any administrative coordination or any central record of photocopying equipment, terms and costs. Of the institutions surveyed, none had any accurate knowledge of total photocopying resources or costs. Records maintained varied from one institution where administrators did not know how many photocopying machines were in use or where they were located, to others where data was maintained on numbers of copies made but not on dollar costs.

Two primary reasons exist for this lack of coordination. Firstly, the type of data required depends on the type of pricing plan which applies and a variety of terms may exist, and secondly, in the case of owned machines, the original purchase cost is often not available having been charged against expenses years ago.

We have obtained some examples of costs as follows:

– Faculty of Science, York University; uses two Xerox 7000 machines and estimates rental costs in 1971 at about $17,900 for these two machines; it has no record of total costs

– Faculty of Medicine, University of Toronto; uses four Xerox machines of various models, three Smith-Corona machines, and one Bell and Howell machine; total costs in 1971 are estimated at about $40,000 but no breakdown between rental costs or supplies costs is available
– Lakehead University; estimates total costs in 1971 for the University at $69,000 ($64,000 in 1970; zero dollars in 1969); a breakdown of total machines, model numbers etc. was not available.

Conclusions

We conclude from our survey that:
– although most machines are owned by the customer at present, the fastest growing and most popular commercial system is based on a leasing arrangement, with the accent on the cost-per-copy formula
– a large number of combinations of terms is available to the customer, and manufacturers will, under competitive pressure, create a sales plan that is especially tailored to the needs of his customer
– Ontario educational institutions have little uniformity of commercial terms
– to obtain comprehensive data on photocopying costs in Ontario educational institutions would require an extensive and separate study.

Exhibit 3

SAMPLING APPROACH

Types of Institutions in Ontario	No. of Each Type in Ontario	No. Included in Sample	% Sampled
Universities	16	4	25 %
Boards of Education	159	3	1.9%
Library Systems	14	4	28.5%
		Average percentage of sampling	4.8%

III – SIGNIFICANCE OF PHOTOCOPYING OF PRINTED MATERIALS

Our pilot survey, while not a statistically valid sample, clearly indicates that the volume of printed materials photocopied in the Ontario educational market is significant.

The Sampling Approach

Our sampling comprised 125 machines in a selection of educational institutions and libraries in the educational market in Ontario. In terms of the total machine population this comprised a 2% sample. However, the sample coverage of the various institutions in Ontario is nearly 5% as illustrated in Exhibit 3 *opposite*.

Our approach to the survey did not contemplate a statistically valid sample; rather during the survey organization work, we tended to select for monitoring those machines that in the opinion of the institution's staff copied large volumes of printed material.

The monitoring of photocopying was carried out over a period of a week. In most cases, survey documents were completed by employees designated by the institutions. Where no suitable staff were available, they were hired from outside sources, and our consulting team reviewed the quality of these staff with the person responsible in each organization.

Exhibit 4

SIGNIFICANCE OF THE PHOTOCOPYING OF PRINTED MATERIALS – SURVEY RESULTS

Basis of Calculation	Average Percentage of Copyright Material		
	Library Machines	Non-Library Machines	All Machines
1. Adjusted Average Percentages	52.5%	26.5%	42.6%
2. Percentages Based on Volumes	50.9%	33.8%	42.4%

Results of The Survey

The results of the survey described above are shown in Exhibit 4 *opposite*.

For comparative purposes two different bases of calculation were devised. The first basis of calculation involves tabulating the percentages of printed material photocopied for each monitored machine, removing averages which distorted the range of results and taking the average percentage of the range. This is done separately for machines in libraries, monitored machines outside of libraries, and for all monitored machines regardless of their location.

The second method of calculation is based on tabulating the total number of photocopies made by monitored machines and the total number of printed material photocopies made by monitored machines to give an average printed material percentage based on volume only. As with the first basis of the calculation, we have given three different percentages, one for libraries, one for non-library machines and one for all machines.

The first method of calculation indicates a span of 26 percentage points between library and non-library machines while the span using the method based on volume alone is 18 points. However, there is a good correlation between the high percentages on different bases and the low percentages on different bases. This indicates a satisfactory sample for our purpose.

We therefore conclude that a conservative estimate of the percentage of photocopying of printed material to total photocopying lies in a range between 30–40%.

Extrapolation of Survey Data

In order to obtain an indication of the significance of the photocopying of printed materials (which may be subject to copyright) in the Ontario educational market, we applied this range to the dollar size of the Ontario education market calculated as discussed in Section II.

In the following table we show the results using the years 1969 to 1971 and the 30 to 40% range.

Year	Ontario Educational Market ($ millions)	Estimated Range of Photocopying Printed Material ($ millions)
1969	6.3	1.9 – 2.5
1970	8.8	2.6 – 3.5
1971	10.6	3.2 – 4.2

We can conclude from this table that photocopying of printed material (which may be subject to copyright) in the Ontario educational market is significant in size and has grown substantially over the period. Indications are that growth in photocopying will continue for this market and that technological changes will facilitate an increased proportion of photocopying of printed materials.

READERS' CLUB OF CANADA QUESTIONNAIRE

ROYAL COMMISSION ON BOOK PUBLISHING

QUESTIONNAIRE (NOT TO BE SIGNED)

THE READERS' CLUB OF CANADA

PLEASE NOTE: Replies to this questionnaire are being solicited by the Commission from all members of The Readers' Club of Canada. Although your assistance in providing as much as possible of the data indicated is earnestly requested, please note that all returns should be submitted anonymously; please do not sign this form, therefore. Where a family membership is involved, it would be appreciated if the questionnaire were completed by the member of the family who most frequently uses the Readers' Club membership:

1. *Sex of respondent*   ( ) male   ( ) female

2. *Age of respondent*   ( ) 15 - 25   ( ) 35 - 45
                                         ( ) 25 - 35   ( ) over 45

3. *Highest level of formal education attained by respondent*
   - ( ) elementary school
   - ( ) some high school
   - ( ) high school graduation
   - ( ) some college or other post-secondary
   - ( ) B.A. or equivalent
   - ( ) some graduate work
   - ( ) graduate degree

4. Family income (Note: please indicate your estimate of total gross income of all members of immediate family)

( ) under $5,000   ( ) $10,000 - $15,000
( ) $5,000 - $7,500   ( ) $15,000 - $20,000
( ) $7,500 - $10,000   ( ) over $20,000

5. Occupation of respondent

( ) student   ( ) professional
( ) labourer or semi-skilled   ( ) executive
( ) skilled   ( ) housewife
( ) clerical   ( ) retired
( ) sales   ( ) other (please specify)
( ) semi-professional

6. How many miles do you live from the nearest bookstore?

Approximately ( ) miles.

7. If there is a bookstore in your community, is there one whose selection of books you consider to be

( ) poor?   ( ) good?
( ) fair?   ( ) excellent?
or ( ) no bookstore in my community.

8. Do you visit a bookstore

( ) at least once a week?   ( ) every month or so?
( ) once or twice a month?   ( ) very rarely?

9. How many books a year do you order from The Readers' Club?

( ) fewer than one a month
( ) about one a month
( ) more than one a month

10. In addition to purchases through The Readers' Club, please estimate the number of books you buy each year, including

a. hard-cover books   ( ) fewer than one a month
                                ( ) about one a month
                                ( ) more than one a month

b. paperbacks   ( ) fewer than one a month
                                ( ) about one a month
                                ( ) more than one a month

11. Please indicate any other book clubs of which you have been a member during the past two years:

( ) Book-of-the-Month Club   ( ) Readers' Subscription
( ) Literary Guild   ( ) History Book Club
( ) Doubleday Dollar Book Club ( ) other (please list)
( ) Book Find Club

12. On the average, about how many newspapers do you examine daily?

        ( ) none   ( ) one   ( ) two

13. Please indicate, as best you can recall, which general-interest periodicals you read regularly:

    ( ) Maclean's   ( ) Life
    ( ) Chatelaine   ( ) Newsweek
    ( ) Saturday Night   ( ) Time
    ( ) Atlantic Monthly   ( ) Harper's
    ( ) Reader's Digest
    ( ) Weekend Magazine (newspaper supplement)
    ( ) Canadian Magazine (newspaper supplement)
    ( ) other (please list)

    _____
    _____

14. Please indicate which of the following departments interest you most in the newspapers and magazines you read (list first two choices as 1 and 2):

    ( ) book reviews   ( ) business news
    ( ) editorials   ( ) "women's news"
    ( ) comics   ( ) international news
    ( ) sports news   ( ) feature articles

15. Do you watch television

        ( ) less than one hour daily?
        ( ) one to two hours daily?
        ( ) more than two hours daily?
        ( ) never watch television.

16. Please indicate which programming source you view most frequently:

    ( ) CBC-TV   ( ) American channels
    ( ) CTV   ( ) ETV

17. Do you listen to the radio

        ( ) less than one hour daily?
        ( ) one to two hours daily?
        ( ) more than two hours daily?

18. Please indicate which radio programming source you listen to most frequently:

        ( ) CBC radio network
        ( ) CBC-FM
        ( ) private Canadian AM stations
        ( ) private Canadian FM stations
        ( ) U.S. stations

19. Please indicate opposite each of the sources of information listed below how frequently it helps you to decide which books to read:

	OFTEN	SOMETIMES	NEVER
newspaper reviews	( )	( )	( )
general magazine reviews	( )	( )	( )
professional & specialized magazine reviews	( )	( )	( )
news stories	( )	( )	( )
recommendations of friends	( )	( )	( )
radio reviews & interviews	( )	( )	( )
TV reviews & interviews	( )	( )	( )

20. Which is your *"mother tongue"*?

    ( ) English   ( ) other (please specify)
    ( ) French   _____

21. What languages do you speak in addition to your *"mother tongue"*?

    ( ) English   ( ) other (please specify)
    ( ) French   _____
                        _____
                        _____

22. Do you belong to a public library?

    ( ) yes   ( ) no

23. If your answer to the question above was "yes", how frequently do you visit your public library?

    ( ) every week   ( ) a few times a year
    ( ) once or twice a month   ( ) very infrequently

24. How many books do you read?

    ( ) more than one a week   ( ) about one a month
    ( ) about one a week   ( ) fewer than one a month
    ( ) more than one a month

25. In your general reading, which do you prefer:

    ( ) fiction?   ( ) non-fiction?

26. Do you read

    ( ) more books by Canadian authors than by foreign authors?
    ( ) more books by foreign authors than by Canadian authors?

27. Rank the following regular features of The Canadian Reader as 1 to 6 in order of their interest and value to you (*most valuable and interesting* – 1; *least valuable and interesting* – 6):

    ( ) review of the Monthly Selection
    ( ) review of one or more Alternate Selections
    ( ) the "Views" pages (news and comment)
    ( ) the "And Reviews" pages (short reviews of Canadian books)
    ( ) "Listings" (new books received by the Club)
    ( ) "Current Choice" (past Club offerings still available to members)

28. *Are you generally satisfied with the variety and quality of Readers' Club Selections and Alternates?*

    ( ) yes   ( ) no

    Comments, if any_____

29. *Are you satisfied with the present assortment of books offered by the Club? Please indicate your preference in each category shown below:*

	WOULD LIKE MORE	WOULD LIKE FEWER	NOW SATISFACTORY
fiction	( )	( )	( )
general non-fiction	( )	( )	( )
history	( )	( )	( )
biography	( )	( )	( )
humour	( )	( )	( )
poetry	( )	( )	( )
current affairs and politics	( )	( )	( )

30. *What do you like best about The Readers' Club?*

31. *What do you like least about The Readers' Club?*

32. *Have you any comments regarding the regularity of notices and service received from The Readers' Club?*

NET BOOK AGREEMENT, UNITED KINGDOM

―――――――――――――――――――――――――――――――――――――――M―――

THE PUBLISHERS ASSOCIATION

19 BEDFORD SQUARE, W.C.1

NET BOOK AGREEMENT, 1957

We the undersigned several firms of publishers, being desirous that in so far as we publish books at net prices (as to which each publisher is free to make his own decisions), those net prices shall normally be the prices at which such books are sold to the public as hereinafter defined, and in order to avoid disorganisation in the book trade and to ensure that the public may be informed of and able uniformly to take advantage of the conditions under which net books may be sold at less than the net prices, hereby agree to adopt and each of us does hereby adopt the following standard sale conditions for the net books published by us within the United Kingdom:

STANDARD CONDITIONS OF SALE OF NET BOOKS

(i) Except as provided in clauses (ii) to (iv) hereof and except as we may otherwise direct net books shall not be sold or offered for sale or caused or permitted to be sold or offered for sale to the public at less than the net published prices.

(ii) A net book may be sold or offered for sale to the public at less than the net published price if
  (a) it has been held in stock by the bookseller for a period of more than twelve months from the date of the latest purchase by him of any copy thereof and
  (b) it has been offered to the publisher at cost price or at the proposed reduced price whichever shall be the lower and such offer has been refused by the publisher.

(iii) A net book may be sold or offered for sale to the public at less than the net published price if it is second-hand and six months have elapsed since its date of publication.

(iv) A net book may be sold at a discount to such libraries, book agents (including Service Unit libraries), quantity buyers and institutions as are from time to time authorised by the Council of The Publishers Association of such amount and on such conditions as are laid down in the instrument of authorisation. Such amount and conditions shall not initially be less or less favourable than those prevailing at the date of this Agreement.

(v) For the purposes of clause (i) hereof a book shall be considered as sold at less than the net published price if the bookseller
 (a) offers or gives any consideration in cash to any purchaser except under licence from the Council of The Publishers Association or
 (b) offers or gives any consideration in kind (e.g. card indexing, stamping, reinforced bindings, etc., at less than the actual cost thereof to the bookseller).

(vi) For the purposes of this Agreement and of these Standard Conditions:
 Net book shall mean a book, pamphlet, map or other similar printed matter published at a net price. *Net price* and *net published price* shall mean the price fixed from time to time by the publisher below which the net book shall not be sold to the public.
 Public shall be deemed to include schools, libraries, institutions and other non-trading bodies.
 Person shall include any company, firm, corporation, club, institution, organisation, association or other body.

(vii) The above conditions shall apply to all sales executed in the United Kingdom and the Republic of Ireland whether effected by wholesaler or retailer when the publisher's immediate trade customer, whether wholesaler or retailer, or the wholesaler's immediate trade customer, is in the United Kingdom or the Republic of Ireland.

We the undersigned several firms of publishers further agree to appoint and each of us does hereby appoint the Council of The Publishers Association to act as our agent in the collection of information concerning breaches of contract by persons selling or offering for sale net books, and in keeping each individual publisher informed of breaches in respect of such net books as are published by him and we further hereby undertake and agree that we will each enforce our contractual rights and our rights under the Restrictive Trade Practices Act 1956 if called upon to do so by the Council of The Publishers Association, and provided that we shall be indemnified by The Publishers Association if so requested by us in respect of any costs of such action incurred by us or by the Council of The Publishers Association on our behalf.

FORM OF ACCEPTANCE

I or WE agree to the within terms and conditions

(Signed)_____

Address_____

Date_____

BANKRUPTCY ACT – EXCERPTS

6 1.(1) Notwithstanding anything in this Act or in any other statute, the author's manuscripts and any copyright or any interest in a copyright in whole or in part assigned to a publisher, printer, firm or person becoming bankrupt shall,

(a) if the work covered by such copyright has not been published and put on the market at the time of the bankruptcy and no expense has been incurred in connection therewith, thereupon revert and be delivered to the author or his heirs, and any contract or agreement between the author or his heirs and such bankrupt shall then terminate and be void;

(b) if the work covered by such copyright has in whole or in part been put into type and expenses have been incurred by the bankrupt, revert and be delivered to the author on payment of the expenses so incurred and the product of such expenses shall also be delivered to the author or his heirs and any contract or agreement between the author or his heirs and the bankrupt shall then terminate and be void; but if the author does not exercise his rights under this paragraph within six months of the date of the bankruptcy, the trustee may carry out the original contract;

(c) if the trustee at the expiration of six months from the date of the bankruptcy decides not to carry out the contract, revert without expense to the author and any contract or agreement between the author or his heirs and such bankrupt shall then terminate and be void.

(2) Where, at the time of the bankruptcy, the work was published and put on the market, the trustee is entitled to sell, or authorize the sale or reproduction of, any copies of the published work, or to perform or authorize the performance of the said work, but there shall be paid to the author or his heirs such sums by way of royalties or share of the profits as would have been payable by the bankrupt; and the trustee is not, without the written consent of the author or his heirs, entitled to assign the copyright or transfer the interest or to grant any interest therein by licence or otherwise, except upon terms that will guarantee to the author or his heirs payment by way of royalties or share of the profits at a rate not less than that which such bankrupt was liable to pay, and any contract or agreement between the author or his heirs and such bankrupt shall then terminate and be void, except as to the disposal, under this subsection, of copies of the said work published and put on the market before the bankruptcy.

(3) The trustee shall offer in writing to the author or his heirs the right to purchase the manufactured or marketable copies of the copyright work comprised in the estate of the bankrupt at such price and upon such terms and conditions as the trustee may deem fair and proper before disposing of such manufactured and marketable copies in the manner prescribed in this section. R.S., c. 14, s. 52.

ANALYSIS OF MAGAZINE SALES IN ONTARIO

Circulation (per issue) in 1971 of Canadian-produced magazines whose circulation is audited by the Audit Bureau of Circulation

	Circulation in Ontario				
Magazine	Subscription	Newsstand	Subscription sales/year in Ontario	Newsstand sales/year in Ontario	Total
Actualité	634	50	$ 1,268.00	$ 300.00	$ 1,568.00
Au Grand Air	1,349	—	2,023.50	—	2,023.50
B.C. Outdoors	345	4	1,207.50	36.00	1,243.50
Can. Geographical Journal	10,865	61	86,920.00	549.00	87,469.00
Can. Jewish Chronicle Review	2,089	—	4,178.00	—	4,178.00
Chatelaine	408,895	34,971	817,790.00	209,826.00	1,027,616.00
Châtelaine	13,132	150	26,264.00	900.00	27,164.00
Echoes	11,021	—	16,531.50	—	16,531.50
Electron	5,409	967	27,045.00	5,802.00	32,847.00
The Freemason	5,199	—	10,398.00	—	10,398.00
Legion	104,419	—	208,838.00	—	208,838.00
Le Maclean	11,124	264	22,248.00	1,584.00	23,832.00
Maclean's	331,935	17,579	663,870.00	105,474.00	769,344.00
Midnight	293	30,045	N/A	72,108.00	72,108.00
Miss Chatelaine	50,548	23,613	75,822.00	99,174.60	174,996.60
Orah	5,928	—	N/A	N/A	N/A
Reader's Digest	517,952	46,307	2,574,221.44	333,410.40	2,907,631.84
Relations	439	—	3,073.00	—	3,073.00
Rod & Gun in Canada	17,439	—	52,317.00	—	52,317.00
Saturday Night	38,989	4,109	138,800.84	24,654.00	163,454.84
Science Forum	1,041	35	N/A	N/A	N/A
Sélection du Reader's Digest	8,086	173	40,187.42	1,245.60	41,433.02
Time	203,386	12,230	2,440,632.00	317,980.00	2,758,612.00
Toronto Life	19,619	7,484	137,324.00	67,344.00	204,668.00
TV Hebdo	90	3,165	1,080.00	41,145.00	42,225.00
Western Fish & Game	95	—	332.50	—	332.50
Calvinist Contact	6,479	—	38,874.00	—	38,874.00
United Church Observer	161,044	—	644,176.00	—	644,176.00
				Total	$ 9,316,954.30

Source: Audit Bureau of Circulation Statement, December 31, 1971

ANALYSIS OF MAGAZINE SALES IN ONTARIO

Circulation (per issue) in 1971 of U.S. magazines with Canadian circulation of more than 40,000

Magazine	Subscription	Newsstand	Subscription sales/year in Ontario	Newsstand sales/year in Ontario	Total
American Home	24,355	3,510	$ 144,668.70	$ 21,060.00	$ 165,728.70
Argosy	35,343	8,345	247,401.00	75,105.00	322,506.00
Better Homes and Gardens	38,479	21,179	153,916.00	127,074.00	280,990.00
Cosmopolitan	599	40,472	5,990.00	364,248.00	370,238.00
Family Circle	—	191,679	—	575,037.00	575,037.00
Field & Stream	18,814	8,917	94,070.00	53,502.00	147,572.00
Glamour	11,571	14,525	75,211.50	104,580.00	179,791.50
Good Housekeeping	37,254	58,890	223,524.00	324,008.00	547,532.00
Ladies' Home Journal	52,596	28,985	312,420.24	173,910.00	486,330.24
Life	74,849	5,942	898,188.00	154,492.00	1,052,680.00
McCall's	60,249	21,402	298,232.55	154,094.40	452,326.95
Mechanix Illustrated	27,201	12,750	115,604.25	53,550.00	169,154.25
Modern Romances	13,307	3,378	73,188.50	32,268.00	105,456.50
Modern Screen	10,141	13,599	55,775.50	81,594.00	137,369.50
National Enquirer	476	31,300	4,212.60	75,120.00	79,332.60
National Geographic	219,738	—	2,262,314.50	—	2,262,314.50
Newsweek	16,282	5,388	227,948.00	140,118.00	368,066.00
Outdoor Life	12,082	9,202	72,492.00	66,254.40	138,746.40
Parents' Magazine	27,602	40	178,032.40	288.00	178,320.40
Photoplay	9,010	31,616	59,565.00	189,696.00	249,261.00
Playboy	25,783	124,877	257,833.00	1,498,424.00	1,756,257.00
Popular Mechanics	12,809	22,493	73,651.75	134,958.00	208,609.75
Popular Science Monthly	17,295	13,091	103,770.00	92,895.20	196,665.20
Redbook Magazine	28,600	31,759	161,170.00	285,831.00	447,001.00
Seventeen	7,193	28,731	48,552.75	172,386.00	220,938.75
Sports Illustrated	21,264	1,616	255,168.00	11,635.20	266,803.20
True	31,060	5,411	217,420.00	38,959.20	256,379.00
True Story	27,044	36,454	162,264.00	218,724.00	380,988.00
TV Guide	55,444	549,004	554,440.00	7,137,052.00	7,691,492.00
Woman's Day	—	226,308	—	678,924.00	678,924.00
				Total	$20,372,811.44

Source: Audit Bureau of Circulation Statement, June 30, 1971

TOTAL SINGLE COPY SALES OF MAGAZINES IN ONTARIO IN 1971

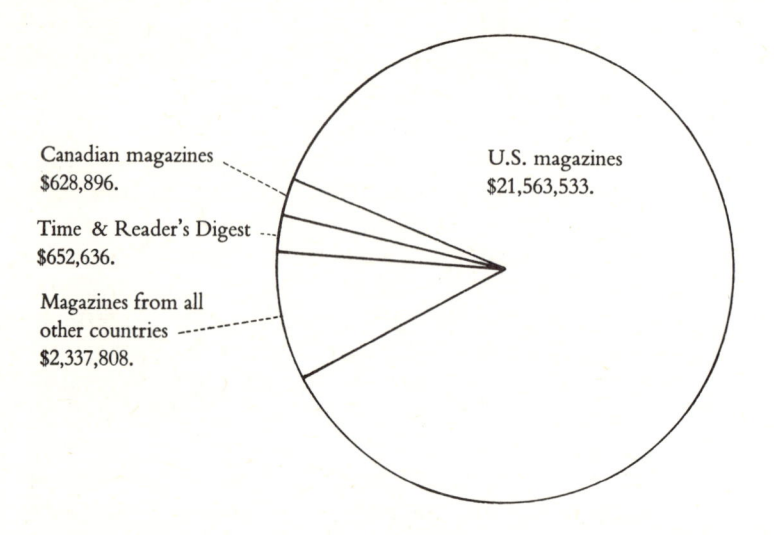

Canadian magazines
$628,896.

Time & Reader's Digest
$652,636.

Magazines from all other countries
$2,337,808.

U.S. magazines
$21,563,533.

TOTAL MAGAZINE SUBSCRIPTIONS AND SINGLE COPY SALES IN ONTARIO IN 1971

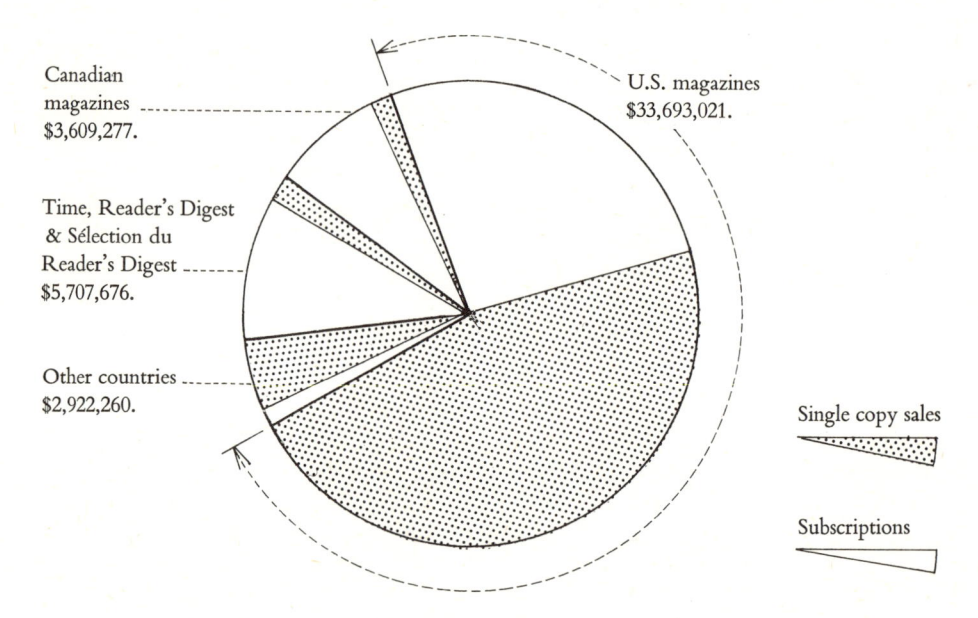

Canadian magazines
$3,609,277.

Time, Reader's Digest & Sélection du Reader's Digest
$5,707,676.

Other countries
$2,922,260.

U.S. magazines
$33,693,021.

Single copy sales

Subscriptions

BIBLIOGRAPHY

Adler-Karlsson, Gunnar. *Reclaiming the Canadian Economy: A Swedish Approach through Functional Socialism.* Toronto: House of Anansi, 1970.

Alberta, Department of Education. *Report of the Committee of Inquiry into Non-Canadian Influence in all Post-Secondary Education.* Edmonton, 1972.

American Library Association. *Standards for School Media Programs.* Chicago, 1969.

American Textbook Publishers Institute and American Book Publishers Council. *An Economic-Media Study of Book Publishing.* New York, 1966.

Arts Council of Great Britain. *Twenty Sixth Annual Report and Accounts 1970-71.* London, 1971.

Ashley, Paul P. *Say It Safely: Legal Limits in Publishing, Radio, and Television.* 3rd ed. Seattle: University of Washington Press, 1966.

Association of American Publishers. *1971 Industry Statistics.* New York, 1972.

Barker, Ronald E. *Canada – The Expanding Book Market.* London: Publishers Association, 1963.

Barker, Ronald E. *Photocopying Practices in the United Kingdom.* London: Faber and Faber, 1970.

Barker, R. E., and Davies, G. R., eds. *Books Are Different: An Account of the Defence of the Net Book Agreement before the Restrictive Practices Court in 1962.* London: Macmillan, 1966.

Barnes, James J. *Free Trade in Books: A Study of the London Book Trade since 1800.* London: Oxford University Press, 1964.

Berne Convention for the Protection of Literary and Artistic Works, Paris Act of July 24, 1971. Geneva: World Intellectual Property Organization, 1971.

Bingley, Clive. *The Business of Book Publishing.* Toronto: Pergamon, 1972.

Bladen, Vincent. *The Financing of the Performing Arts in Canada: An Essay in Persuasion.* Toronto: Massey College, 1971.

Bohne, Harald, ed. *Canadian Books in Print / Catalogue des livres canadiens en librairie.* Toronto: University of Toronto Press, published annually.

Bohne, Harald, and Van Ierssel, Harry. *Publishing: The Creative Business.* Toronto: University of Toronto Press, *in press.*

Book Publishing in the USSR: Reports of the Delegations of U.S. Book Publishers Visiting the USSR. Cambridge: Harvard University Press, 1971.

Bugbee, Bruce W. *The Genesis of American Patent and Copyright Law.* Washington: Public Affairs Press, 1967.

Bush, George P., and Hattery, Lowell H., eds. *Reprography and Copyright Law.* Washington: American Institute of Biological Sciences, 1964.

Cameron, David M. *Schools for Ontario: Policy-making, Administration, and Finance in the 1960s.* Toronto: University of Toronto Press, 1972.

Campbell, H. C. *Canadian Libraries.* Toronto: Pendragon, 1971.

Campbell, H. C. *Information Science in Canada.* Toronto: Pendragon, 1971.

Canada Council Annual Report. Ottawa, published annually.

Canada, House of Commons. Bill C-256: An Act to promote competition, to provide for the general regulation of trade and commerce, to promote honest and fair dealing, to establish a Competitive Practices Tribunal and the Office of Commissioner, to repeal the Combines Investigation Act and to make consequential amendments to the Bank Act. 3rd session, 28th Parliament, 19-20 Eliz. II 1970-71. Ottawa: Queen's Printer, 1971.

Canada, House of Commons. *Broadcasting Act.* Ottawa: Queen's Printer, 1968.

Canada, Revised Statutes. *Bankruptcy Act.* C. 14. Ottawa: Queen's Printer, 1952.

Canada, Revised Statutes. *Combines Investigation Act.* C. 314. Ottawa: Queen's Printer, 1970.

Canada, Revised Statutes. *Copyright Act.* C. 55. Ottawa: Queen's Printer, 1970.

Canada. *Report of the Royal Commission on National Development in the Arts, Letters and Sciences.* Ottawa: Queen's Printer, 1951.

Canada, Royal Commission on Patents, Copyright, Trade Marks and Industrial Designs. *Report on Copyright.* Ottawa, 1957.

Canada, *Report, Royal Commission on Publications.* Ottawa: Queen's Printer, 1961.

Canada. *Report of the Committee on Broadcasting.* Ottawa: Queen's Printer, 1965.

Canada, Special Senate Committee on Mass Media. Volume 1, *The Uncertain Mirror.* Volume 2, *Words, Music, and Dollars.* Volume 3, *Good, Bad, or Simply Inevitable?* Ottawa: Queen's Printer, 1971.

Canada, Task Force on Government Information. *To Know and Be Known* (2 vols.). Ottawa: Queen's Printer, 1969.

Canadian Publishers Directory. Toronto: Quill & Quire, published annually.

Charvat, William. *Literary Publishing in America, 1790-1850.* Philadelphia: University of Pennsylvania Press, 1959.

Chittick, V. L. O. *Haliburton: A Study in Provincial Toryism.* New York: Columbia University Press, 1924.

Clarkson, Stephen. *An Independent Foreign Policy for Canada?* Toronto: McClelland and Stewart, 1968.

Clarkson, Stephen, ed. *Visions 2020: Fifty Canadians in Search of a Future.* Edmonton: M. G. Hurtig, 1970.

Clery, Val. *Promotion and Response: Report on the Media Response Survey of Trade Book Publishing.* Toronto: Canadian Book Publishers' Council, 1970.

Cohen, Saul, and Hogan, John C. *An Author's Guide to Scholarly Publishing and the Law.* Englewood Cliffs, N.J.: Prentice-Hall, Inc., 1965.

"Daedalus: The American Reading Public." *Journal of the American Academy of Arts and Science.* Richmond, Va., 1962.

Deutsch, J., Keirstead, B. S., Levitt, K., and Will, R. M., eds. *The Canadian Economy: Selected Readings.* Toronto: Macmillan, 1965.

Directory of Directors: Toronto: Financial Post, published annually.

Ditchley Foundation. *Conference of American and British Book Publishers.* London: Publishers Association, 1969.

Dominion Bureau of Statistics. *Inter-Corporate Ownership / Liens de parenté entre firmes 1967.* Ottawa: Queen's Printer, 1969.

Downs, Robert B. *Resources of Canadian Academic and Research Libraries*. Ottawa: Association of Universities and Colleges of Canada, 1967.

Economic Council of Canada. *Report on Intellectual and Industrial Property*. Ottawa: Information Canada, 1971.

Egoff, Sheila. *The Republic of Childhood*. Toronto: Oxford University Press, 1967.

Ernst & Ernst Management Consulting Services. *The Book Publishing and Manufacturing industry in Canada*. Ottawa: Department of Industry, Trade and Commerce, 1970.

Escarpit, Robert. *Sociology of Literature*. Painesville, Ohio: Lake Erie College Press, 1965.

Escarpit, Robert. *The Book Revolution*. London: George G. Harrap & Co. Ltd.; Paris: Unesco, 1966.

Findlater, Richard, ed. *Public Lending Right*. London: André Deutsch Limited and Penguin Books Limited, 1971.

Foreign Investment Division, Department of Industry, Trade and Commerce. *Selected Readings in Laws and Regulations Affecting Foreign Investment in Canada, April 1971*. Ottawa, 1971.

Fox, Harold G. *The Canadian Law of Copyright and Industrial Designs*. 2nd ed. Toronto: The Carswell Company Limited, 1967.

Fulford, R., Godfrey, D., and Rotstein, A., eds. *Read Canadian: A Book about Canadian Books*. Toronto: James Lewis & Samuel, 1972.

Gipe, George A. *Nearer to the Dust: Copyright and the Machine*. Baltimore: William & Wilkins, 1967.

Gitlin, Paul, and Ringer, Barbara A. *Copyrights*. New York: Practising Law Institute, [1963?].

Godfrey, Dave, and Watkins, M. H., eds. *Gordon to Watkins to You: A Documentary of the Battle for Control of Our Economy*. Toronto: New Press, 1970.

Graham, Mae, ed. "The Changing Nature of the School Library." *Library Trends* 17: 343-433. Urbana: University of Illinois Graduate School of Library Science, 1969.

Grannis, Chandler B. *What Happens in Book Publishing*. 2nd ed. New York: Columbia University Press, 1967.

Gross, Gerald, ed. *Editors on Editing*. New York: Grosset & Dunlap, 1962.

Gross, Gerald, ed. *Publishers on Publishing*. New York: Bowker, 1961.

Gundy, H. P., ed. *A History of the Canadian Book Trade*. Toronto: Canadian Book Publishers' Council, microfilm of unpublished manuscript, 1963.

Harman, Eleanor, ed. "Territorial Rights." *Scholarly Publishing* vol. 3:4. Toronto: University of Toronto Press, 1972.

Harman, Eleanor, ed. *The University as Publisher*. Toronto: University of Toronto Press, 1961.

Hawes, Gene R. *To Advance Knowledge*. New York: American University Press Services, Inc., 1967.

Hiebert, Ray Eldon, ed. *Books in Human Development*. Washington: Department of Journalism, The American University, 1964.

Hodgetts, A. B. *What Culture? What Heritage?: A Study of Civic Education in Canada*. Toronto: Ontario Institute for Studies in Education, 1968.

Howard, Wm. J., ed. *Editor, Author, and Publisher*. Toronto: University of Toronto Press, 1969.

Hubbard, R. H., ed. *Scholarship in Canada*. Toronto: University of Toronto Press, 1968.

Hutchison, Bruce, ed. *Canada, A Year of the Land*. Ottawa: National Film Board, 1967.

Instant World: Report on Telecommunications in Canada. Ottawa: Queen's Printer, 1971.

Janzen, Henry. *Curriculum Change in a Canadian Context*. Toronto: Gage, 1970.

Kaplan, Benjamin. *An Unhurried View of Copyright*. New York: Columbia University Press, 1967.

Kent, Allen, and Lancou, Harold, eds. *Copyright: Current Viewpoints on History, Laws, Legislation*. New York: R. R. Bowker Company, 1972.

Kilbourn, William, ed. *Canada: A Guide to the Peaceable Kingdom*. Toronto: Macmillan, 1970.

Klinck, Carl F., ed. *Literary History of Canada: Canadian Literature in English*. Toronto: University of Toronto Press, 1965.

Klinck, Carl F., ed. *Histoire littéraire du Canada: littérature canadienne de langue anglaise*. Translated by Maurice Lebel. Québec: Les Presses de l'université Laval, 1970.

Lambert, John. *Travels through Canada and the United States in the Years 1806, 1807 and 1808* . . . 2nd ed. London: Cradock & Jay, 1814.

Levitsky, Serge L. *Introduction to Soviet Copyright Law.* Law in Eastern Europe, edited by Z. Szirmai, No. 8 Leyden: A. W. Sythoff, 1964.

Linden, Allen M., ed. *Living in the Seventies.* Toronto: Peter Martin, 1970.

Literary Market Place. New York: R. R. Bowker Co., 1972.

Lloyd, Trevor, and McLeod, J. T., eds. *Agenda 1970: Proposals for a Creative Politics.* Toronto: University of Toronto Press, 1968.

Lumsden, Ian, ed. *Close the 49th Parallel etc.: The Americanization of Canada.* Toronto: University of Toronto Press, 1970.

Mansion, J. E., ed. *Harrap's Standard French and English Dictionary.* London: George G. Harrap & Company, 1970.

Massey, Norman. *Canadian Studies in Canadian Schools.* Toronto: Curriculum Committee, Council of Ministers of Education, 1971.

Mathews, Robin, and Steele, James, eds. *The Struggle for Canadian Universities.* Toronto: New Press, 1969.

Mathias, Philip. *Forced Growth: 5 Studies of Government Involvement in the Development of Canada.* Toronto: James Lewis & Samuel, 1971.

McDiarmid, Garnet, and Pratt, David. *Teaching Prejudice.* Toronto: Ontario Institute for Studies in Education, 1972.

Mesbur, A. *Photocopying, Information Retrieval and Copyright: A Survey of the Issues.* Toronto: Canadian Copyright Institute (unpublished), 1967.

Morrison, Helen, ed. *Nunnybag* (no. 1 to 5). Toronto: Gage, 1962-67.

Morrison, Helen, ed. *Rubaboo* (no. 1 to 5). Toronto: Gage, 1962-67.

Morton, William L. *The Canadian Identity.* Toronto: University of Toronto Press, 1961.

Nemeyer, Carol. *Scholarly Reprint Publishing in the United States.* New York: Bowker, 1972.

Newsome, Harry E. *Standards of Library Service for Canadian Schools.* Toronto: Ryerson Press, 1967.

Nimmer, Melville B. *Nimmer on Copyright: A Treatise on the Law of Literary, Musical and Artistic Property, and the Protection of Ideas* (2 vols.). New York: Matthew Bender, 1972.

Ontario, Committee on Government Productivity. *Interim Report Number Seven: Report to the Executive Council of the Government of Ontario on Communications and Information Services.* Toronto: Queen's Printer, 1972.

Ontario, Department of Education. *Circular 14, 1972: Textbooks.* Toronto, 1972.

Ontario, Department of Education. *Circular 15, 1972: Canadian Curriculum Materials / Matériel Didatique Canadien.* Toronto, 1972.

Ontario, Department of Education. Regulation, *General Legislative Grants, 1967, Elementary and Secondary Schools.* Ontario Regulation 24/67. Made under the Department of Education Act. Toronto, 1967.

Ontario, Department of Education. Regulation, *General Legislative Grants, 1971, Elementary and Secondary School Boards.* Ontario Regulation 59/71 as amended. Made under the Department of Education Act. Toronto, 1971.

Ontario, Department of Education. Regulation, *General Legislative Grants, 1972, Elementary and Secondary School Boards.* Ontario Regulation 98/72. Made under the Department of Education Act. Toronto, 1972.

Ontario, Department of Education. *Report of the Minister of Education.* Toronto, published annually.

Ontario, Department of Treasury and Economics, Department of Trade and Development, Department of Financial and Commercial Affairs. *Report of the Interdepartmental Task Force on Foreign Investment.* Toronto: Economic Planning Branch, Department of Treasury and Economics, 1971.

Ontario, *Preliminary Report of the Select Committee on Economic and Cultural Nationalism.* Toronto, 1972.

Ontario. *Report of the Royal Commission on Education in Ontario.* Toronto: King's Printer, 1950.

Ontario, Revised Statutes. *The Department of Education Act.* C. 94. Toronto: Queen's Printer, 1969.

Ontario, Revised Statutes. *The Schools Administration Act.* C. 361. Toronto: Queen's Printer, 1969.

Ontario, Royal Commission on Book Publishing. *Background Papers.* Toronto: Queen's Printer, 1972.

O'Toole, Simon. *Confessions of an American Scholar.* Minneapolis: University of Minnesota Press, 1970.

Parvin, Viola. *Authorization of Textbooks for the Schools of Ontario, 1846-1950*. Toronto: University of Toronto Press, 1965.

Peers, Frank W. *The Politics of Canadian Broadcasting 1920-51*. Toronto: University of Toronto Press, 1969.

Pierce, Lorne. *An Editor's Creed*. Toronto: Ryerson, 1960.

Pierce, Lorne. *The House of Ryerson, 1829-1954*. Toronto: Ryerson, 1954.

Pink, Margaret, ed. *Canada Year Book, 1970-71*. Ottawa: Dominion Bureau of Statistics, 1971.

Porter, John. *The Vertical Mosaic: An Analysis of Social Class and Power in Canada*. Toronto: University of Toronto Press, 1965.

Priestley, F. E. L. *The Humanities in Canada*. Toronto: University of Toronto Press, 1964.

Pross, Paul, and Pross, C. A. *Government Publishing in the Canadian Provinces*. Toronto: University of Toronto Press, 1972.

Province of Ontario Council for the Arts Report. Toronto, published annually.

Publishers Association, Agreements Committee. *A Guide to Royalty Agreements*. London, 1959.

Publishers Association, Export Research Committee. *Canada – The Market for British Books*. London, 1954.

Purdy, Al, ed. *The New Romans: Candid Canadian Opinions of the U.S.* Edmonton: Hurtig, 1968.

Québec. *Rapport de la Commission d'enquête sur le commerce du livre dans la province de Québec*. Montréal. 1963.

Rose, George Maclean, ed. *A Cyclopaedia of Canadian Biography*. Toronto: Rose Publishing Company, 1886.

Rothenberg, Stanley. *Legal Protection of Literature, Art and Music*. New York: Clark Boardman Co. Ltd., 1960.

Safarian, A. E. *The Performance of Foreign-Owned Firms in Canada*. Washington and Montreal: Canadian-American Committee, 1969.

Skone James, E. P. and F. E. *Copinger and Skone James on Copyright*. 11th ed. London: Sweet & Maxwell, 1971.

Sophar, G. J., and Heilprin, L. B. *The Determination of Legal Facts and Economic Guideposts with Respect to the Dissemination of Scientific and Educational Information as It is Affected by Copyright – A Status Report*. Washington: U.S. Dept. of Health, Education, and Welfare, 1967.

Stewart, Bev. C. *Supervision in Local School Districts – Canada*. Toronto: Canadian Education Association, 1972.

Stuart-Stubbs, B. *Purchasing and Copying Practices at Canadian University Libraries*. Ottawa: Canadian Association of College and University Libraries, 1971.

Sylvestre, Guy, ed. *Canadian Writers / Ecrivains canadiens*. Toronto: McGraw-Hill, 1967.

Walters, Susan, ed. *Canadian Almanac and Directory*. Toronto: The Copp Clark Publishing Company, published annually.

Warde, Beatrice. *The Crystal Goblet: Sixteen Essays on Typography*. Edited by Henry Jacob. London: The Sylvan Press, 1955.

Watters, R. E. *A Checklist of Canadian Literature and Background Materials, 1628-1960*. Toronto: University of Toronto Press, 1972.

Watters, R. E., and Bell, Inglis F. *On Canadian Literature, 1806-1960: A Checklist of Articles, Books, and Theses on English-Canadian Literature, its Authors, and Language*. Toronto: University of Toronto Press, 1966.

Wells, F. A. *Productivity in a Printing Firm*. London: Gerald Duckworth & Co. Ltd., 1958.

Wiles, Roy, McK. *Humanities in Canada: supplement to December 31, 1964*. Toronto: University of Toronto Press, 1966.

Williams, Penelope M. *A Guide to Scholarly Publishing in Canada*. Ottawa: Humanities Research Council of Canada and the Social Science Research Council of Canada, 1971.

Woodcock, George, et al. "Publishing in Canada." *Canadian Literature / Littérature canadienne 33:3-62*. Vancouver: University of British Columbia, 1967.

Acknowledgments

The Commission has received a great deal of assistance from many sources during the course of its work and wishes to take this opportunity to thank all who participated in any way. In particular we would like to thank those people who submitted, or were associated with, briefs presented to the Commission. A list of all formal briefs received may be found in the Appendix.

In order to gain a first-hand knowledge of the problems which confront the book publishing industry the Commissioners and the research staff travelled not only throughout Ontario but also to a number of other provinces. A large number of private meetings took place with representatives of Ontario-based book publishing firms and others associated with the industry, and extensive correspondence was carried on both in Canada and abroad. The Commission met informally on a number of occasions with representatives of federal government departments and with the Conseil Supérieur du Livre of Quebec. A complete acknowledgment of its indebtedness to all those who assisted would be impossible. However, the Commission would like to express special appreciation to the following, whose contributions are not acknowledged elsewhere.

Ian Adams
H. E. Alexander
Ronald Atkey, Q.C.
F. T. Atkinson
Margaret Atwood
D. Bagshaw
Hans Badewitz
John Banks
Ronald Barker

B. Scott Bateman
E. Stanley Beacock
Hon. G. L. Bennett
L. H. Bergstrom
Norman A. Best
A. Blicq
Fred Bodsworth
Harald Bohne
Paul H. Bolton

Victor Bonham-Carter
Guy Boulizon
Albert Bowron
Max Braithwaite
Geoffrey H. Briggs
Harald Brinchmann
Barry Brooks
Hon. D. L. Brothers, Q.C.
Erhard Bungeroth
June Callwood
Donald J. Campbell
William Clare
Gavin Clark
Val Clery
François Cloutier, Député
His Excellency D. M. Cornett
Council of Ministers of Education of Canada
Ralph T. Cowan
His Excellency G. C. Crean
E. E. Creeper
John S. Crosbie
J. K. Crossley
May Cutler
Olive Delaney
George Duncan
J. Davidson Dunton
André Dussault
David Esplin
Alan Etchen
Doris Fennell
George Forrester
G. Forsstrom
André Fortier
Robert W. Frase
Guy Frégault
Hugh Garner
Judge J. Gehlim
Graeme Gibson
Dave Godfrey
His Excellency G. K. Grande

Else Granheim
Jack Gray
Graham Greene
P. J. Groulx
Roy Gurney
Peter P. Hallsworth
J. Halstead
Eleanor Harman
Gaston Harvey
George M. Harwood
Ebba Haslund
E. K. Hawkesworth
Jacques Hébert
Alv Heltne
David Helwig
Mal Henderson
Morton Hein
Ralph Hodgson
Arthur Holmesland
G. N. Houle
Campbell Hughes
Mel G. Hurtig
Erik A. Jensen
Karl F. Kaltenborn
J. F. Kinlin
William Kinmond
C. J. Kleberg
Ole Kock
A. Kuska
Goran Lannegren
Helmer Larsson
Christian Latortue
Deiter Lattmann
André Lavigne
Lloyd Leeming
Ralph Lewis
J. B. Lind
Göran Löfdahl
W. C. Lorimer
Ingeborg Lyche
David Maclellan

Hon. Gordon MacMurchy
Bruce MacNeil
John D. P. Martin
Victor Martin
Yves Martin
Bryan Mason
Norman Massey
E. C. Matheson
F. J. McAllister
Irma McDonough
Hon. J. L. McGuigan
Maurice Mercier
James R. Midwinter
Hon. Saul A. Miller
Lorne R. Moase
Ross B. Monk
E. Monkman
Richard Morin
Farley Mowat
P. K. Mutchler
Douglas Myers
H. M. Nason
W. B. Naylor
Vincent A. Needham
F. J. Nethercut
E. J. Neville
William Newton
Hon. Peter Nicholson
Thomas O'Connell
Gordon Pallant
Roland Palsson
E. Paquet
Claude Passey
J. Z. Léon Patenaude
Hon. Gérard Pelletier
Michael de Pencier
Peter Phelan
R. A. J. Phillips
Johann Phillipson

E. K. Pukacz
Al Purdy
Donald A. Redmond
R. E. Rees
Toivo Roht
R. H. N. Roberts
James K. Robertson
Paul Robinson
Karl-Heinz Rouette
Allan Rowan-Legge
Gordon Rumgay
Maureen J. Sabia
Clément Saint-Germain
Armand Saintonge
Alan E. Samuel
Torsten Matte Schmidt
Kurt Schober, M.D.B.
Barbara Smith
R. A. Smith
G. A. Snider
Douglas Spry
Malcolm Stanley
Elisabeth Steup
E. E. Stewart
B. Stuart-Stubbs
Dosent Birger Stuevold-Lassen
A. W. Sullivan
George Svensson
William Tamblyn
E. Thrane
Pierre Tisseyre
E. A. Torgunrud
J. A. Turner
H. H. Walker
W. Watson
Leif J. Wilhelmsen
Rex Williams
Ken Williamson
F. S. Wilson

Financial Consultants: Clarkson, Gordon & Co.
Legal Counsel: Bassel, Sullivan, Holland & Lawson
Special Consultant: Dr. J. R. McCarthy
Design Consultant: Keith Scott

Contributors of Background Papers:

F. L. Barrett
W. E. Curry
Sheila A. Egoff
C. J. Eustace
Robin M. Farr
G. A. Ferguson
H. Pearson Gundy
Georges Laberge
Hilary S. Marshall
David McGill
John V. Mills, Q.C.
Ian Montagnes
F. Beverley Moore
Viola E. Parvin Day
Charles E. Phillips
Roy C. Sharp, Q.C.
Sonja Sinclair
Freeman K. Stewart
S. J. Totton
André Vachon
June Whitteker
George Woodcock

Staff of Commission:

Robert J. Fleming, *Executive Secretary*
Mollie Armstrong, *Secretary*
Susan Boot, *Secretary*
Marc Couse, *Assistant to Executive Secretary*
Margaret Derry, *Proofreader*
Sharon Dyson, *Secretary*
Nancy Hawkins, *Receptionist-Typist*
Nora Jackman, *Secretary*
Susan Keene, *Research Officer*
Paul MacKeown, *Proofreader*
Gail McKinnon, *Research Officer*
Katharine Miller, *Secretary*
Jenifer Rigby, *Secretary*
Sonja Sinclair, *Senior Research Officer*

ROYAL COMMISSION ON BOOK PUBLISHING

Background Papers

Nineteen background papers studying many phases of the Canadian book industry, specially written for the Royal Commission by experts in their fields.

KILDARE DOBBS, *Toronto Star*: ". . . the best literary buy of the year at $5 from the Queen's Printer, province of Ontario . . . The quality and substance of these studies raise the Royal Commission above the provincial level. It is serving the whole country."

REG VICKERS, *Calgary Herald*: "Even a brief inspection of these papers should convince anyone that what we have here is a series of penetrating analyses of the book business, from writing to selling, as well as a very comprehensive historical documentation . . . For anyone interested in the future of book publishing in Canada, they're what you might call must reading."

Published 1972. 395 + xi pages. Paper, $3.75. Cloth, $5.00.